Marie Antoinette at Petit Trianon

Marie Antoinette at Petit Trianon challenges common perceptions of the last Queen of France, appraising the role she played in relation to the events of the French Revolution through an original analysis of contemporary heritage practices and visitor perceptions at her former home, the Petit Trianon.

Controversy and martyrdom have placed Marie Antoinette's image within a spectrum of cultural caricatures that range from taboo to iconic. With a foundation in critical heritage studies, this book examines the diverse range of contemporary images portraying Marie Antoinette's historical character, showing how they affect the interpretation and perception of the Petit Trianon.

By considering both producers and receivers of these cultural heritage exponents – Marie Antoinette's historical figure and the historic house museum of the Petit Trianon – the book expands current understandings of twenty-first century cultural heritage perceptions in relation to tourism and popular culture. A useful case study for academics, researchers and postgraduate students of cultural heritage, it will also be of interest to historians, keepers of house museums and those working in the field of tourism studies.

Denise Maior-Barron is a Visiting Research Fellow at the School of Tourism, Plymouth University, UK, and a Reader at the Huntington Library, California, USA. She obtained her PhD from Plymouth University in collaboration with the Château de Versailles, France, following two consecutive research internships at this UNESCO heritage site. Her research focuses on critical cultural heritage and tourist consumption, with an emphasis on rehabilitative history and popular-culture representations in the social imaginary.

Praise for this book:

'Marie-Antoinette has become a "commodity" for audiences the world over, and the restored Petit Trianon floods with visitors. This fine book by Denise Maior-Barron brings a completely new, multidisciplinary perspective, omitting none of the historical or socio-political aspects of the Queen's mythology. The confrontation set out by the author between the work of historians and visitor perceptions will undoubtedly provoke passionate debate, just as it will reveal the deep gap between myth and objective research.'
Jérémie Benoît, Chief Curator, Petit Trianon, France

'Denise Maior-Barron cleverly unveils the many ways Marie Antoinette was and is perceived. Her well-researched book provides new insights about interactions within the heritage process and industry, between politics, popular culture and tourism, which reveal how history, with help from artificial memories, is often manipulated, misinterpreted and misunderstood. In so doing, she challenges the orthodoxy of much historical analysis that seeks only one truth in the past.'
John Barnes, *Chief Executive, Historic Royal Palaces, UK*

'Not just a monograph on two topics of apparently perennial public interest, Marie Antoinette and the Petit Trianon, but a fascinating bran tub of related themes: historical revision, art and architectural history, political manipulation, the falsifications of mass media promotion and so it goes on.'
Martin Foley, *Director, El Porvenir, Casa Museo Feliciano Béjar, Mexico*

Routledge Studies in Heritage

International Heritage and Historic Building Conservation
Saving the World's Past
Zeynep Aygen

Corporate Responsibility for Cultural Heritage
Conservation, Sustainable Development, and Corporate Reputation
Fiona Starr

Counterheritage
Critical Perspectives on Heritage Conservation in Asia
Denis Byrne

Industrial Heritage Sites in Transformation
Clash of Discourses
Edited by Heike Oevermann and Harald A. Mieg

Conserving Cultural Heritage
Challenges and New Directions
Edited by Ken Taylor, Archer St Clair, and Nora Mitchell

The Making of Heritage
Seduction and Disenchantment
Edited by Camila del Mármol, Marc Morell and Jasper Chalcraft

Heritage and Memory of War
Responses from Small Islands
Edited by Gilly Carr and Keir Reeves

Marie Antoinette at Petit Trianon
Heritage Interpretation and Visitor Perceptions
Denise Maior-Barron

www.routledge.com/Routledge-Studies-in-Heritage/book-series/RSIHER

Marie Antoinette at Petit Trianon

Heritage Interpretation and Visitor Perceptions

Denise Maior-Barron

LONDON AND NEW YORK

First published 2019
by Routledge
2 Park Square, Milton Park, Abingdon, Oxon OX14 4RN

and by Routledge
711 Third Avenue, New York, NY 10017

Routledge is an imprint of the Taylor & Francis Group, an informa business

© 2019 Denise Maior-Barron

The right of Denise Maior-Barron to be identified as author of this work has been asserted by her in accordance with sections 77 and 78 of the Copyright, Designs and Patents Act 1988.

All rights reserved. No part of this book may be reprinted or reproduced or utilised in any form or by any electronic, mechanical, or other means, now known or hereafter invented, including photocopying and recording, or in any information storage or retrieval system, without permission in writing from the publishers.

Trademark notice: Product or corporate names may be trademarks or registered trademarks, and are used only for identification and explanation without intent to infringe.

British Library Cataloguing-in-Publication Data
A catalogue record for this book is available from the British Library

Library of Congress Cataloging-in-Publication Data
A catalog record for this book has been requested

ISBN: 978-1-138-56556-2 (hbk)
ISBN: 978-1-315-12308-0 (ebk)

Typeset in Sabon
by Apex CoVantage, LLC

Some of the figures in this book can be seen in colour on the book's product page: www.routledge.com/9781138565562

To my grandparents, Maria and Nicolae Maior, whose lives were shattered by the Romanian Communist regime, and to those others who inspired me since an early age to believe in Art and its power to bring refuge and reconciliation at all levels: the timeless painter Madame Paiu, together with artist and architect – mother and son – Nina and Boris Stuparu.

Contents

Illustrations   xi
Preface   xvi
Acknowledgements   xviii

   Introduction   1

1 'Places of memory' in the nationalist era of the French Third Republic   10

2 'Places of memory' anchored in postmodernity   29

3 Methodology and fieldwork research at the Petit Trianon   49

4 Historical and cinematic narratives encoding Marie Antoinette's contemporary perception   82

5 Eighteenth-century architectural and heritage narratives of the Petit Trianon   128

6 'Memories' of Marie Antoinette: Field research evidence at the Petit Trianon   163

7 'Ange ou Démon?': Contemporary images of the last Queen of France at the Petit Trianon   201

   Conclusion   250

Appendices: Questionnaires   259
A.1 Semi-structured questionnaire for French nationals completed by the interviewer – French-language version also applied to other nationals   261

x   Contents

 A.2 Semi-structured questionnaire for American nationals completed by the interviewer – English-language version also applied to other nationals   263
 A.3 Multiple-choice questionnaire for Japanese nationals – designed in French, translated into Japanese for on-site self-completion by Japanese participants   266
 A.4 Semi-structured anonymous questionnaire for the Petit Trianon security personnel (self-completed)   272
 A.5 Film list used for the survey (* denotes official English film titles, according to IMDb)   276

References   277
Index   319

Illustrations

Figures

0.1	Eighteenth-century architectural narrative of the Petit Trianon – indicator for the objective assessment of the role played by Marie Antoinette (C.-L. Châtelet 1786)	2
2.1	Defining heritage authenticity through its meanings (Ashworth & Howard 1999)	43
3.1	The qualitative inquiry continuum (Butler-Kisber 2010)	56
3.2	Marie Antoinette merchandise at Château de Versailles	62
3.3	Observation of the different ways tourists 'consume' the Petit Trianon	63
3.4	Factors responsible for distortions of Marie Antoinette's role since the eighteenth century, deciphered through contemporary visitor discourses at the Petit Trianon	75
4.1	Marie Antoinette, an adulated queen at the beginning of her reign	91
4.2	Marie Antoinette, a hated queen (1780s)	92
4.3	Caroline Sihol as Marie Antoinette – 1993 theatrical remake of the queen's trial	93
4.4	A replica of the infamous necklace, which contributed to the fall of the French Monarchy	95
4.5	Norma Shearer, in the 1938 Hollywood biopic *Marie Antoinette*	98
4.6	Poster of the film *Farewell, My Queen*	102
4.7	The Royal Family in 1782, gathered around the first Dauphin, Louis Joseph Xavier François (French School 1782)	107
4.8	Count Hans Axel von Fersen (P. Dreuillon 1798)	109
4.9	Poster for the film *Marie Antoinette* (2006)	111
4.10	Image from promotional trailer scene for *Marie Antoinette* (2006)	112
4.11	Cabinet des Glaces Mouvantes at Petit Trianon	113

4.12	Filming *Marie Antoinette* (2006) on-site at Château de Versailles	113
4.13	*Marie Antoinette* (2006) and unsuitability to the Republican school curriculum	116
4.14	Marie Antoinette and Fersen, Versailles love scene (*Rose of Versailles* 1972)	120
4.15	Petit Trianon (*Rose of Versailles* 1972)	121
4.16	Marie Antoinette and Fersen, Tuileries love scene (*Rose of Versailles* 1972)	122
4.17	Marie Antoinette and Lady Oscar (*Rose of Versailles* 1972)	122
4.18	Marie Antoinette in tragic scenes (*Rose of Versailles* 1972)	124
4.19	Marie Antoinette full of courage and dignity (*Rose of Versailles* 1972)	125
5.1	La Salle des Gardes at Petit Trianon	129
5.2	Visitor numbers at the *Domaine de Marie-Antoinette*	130
5.3	The remains of Marie Antoinette's oak, which led to funding of the 2008 restoration of the Petit Trianon	132
5.4	'Commodification of the Past', based on Tunbridge and Ashworth (1996)	133
5.5	*Marie Antoinette à la rose* (É. Vigée Le Brun 1783)	136
5.6	Renaming Petit Trianon – the main entrance displaying the new name	137
5.7	*Marie Antoinette en gaulle* (É. Vigée Le Brun 1783)	140
5.8	Eighteenth-century architectural plans for Petit Trianon (R. Mique 1786)	141
5.9	Derelict interiors at Le Hameau de la Reine	142
5.10	Eighteenth-century reception at Petit Trianon (N. Lafrensen le Jeune, dit Lavreince 1785)	144
5.11	Marie Antoinette and her children at Petit Trianon in 1789 (F. Dumont)	145
5.12	Empress Eugénie exhibition room at Petit Trianon	150
5.13	Marie Antoinette, Dauphine of France (J. Krantzinger 1770)	152
5.14	Marie Antoinette in front of the Temple of Love at Petit Trianon in the 1780s (J.-B. A. Gautier-Dagoty)	153
5.15	Marie Antoinette's active role of mother in the heritage narrative of Petit Trianon (*Le Pavillon Français* by F.-D. Née after L.-N. Lespinasse circa 1788)	154
5.16	Royal cultural capital – a charitable event organised in 1901 by French aristocracy	158
5.17	Petit Trianon, part of today's main visit at Château de Versailles	158

6.1	The flight to Varennes, eighteenth-century revolutionary cartoon	165
6.2	Nineteenth-century Republican cliché of Marie Antoinette playing the shepherdess at Petit Trianon (C. Delort 1891)	167
6.3	Nineteenth-century Royalist representation of Marie Antoinette and her family at Petit Trianon (C. L. Müller circa 1860)	168
6.4	A brave Marie Antoinette in her attempts to rescue the royal family (T. F. Marshall 1854)	169
6.5	Michèle Morgan on set at Petit Trianon in September 1955 for Jean Delannoy's 1956 film *Marie Antoinette, Reine de France*	170
6.6	*Les Chouans* at La Chapelle Expiatoire – a counter-memory event	171
6.7	Petit Trianon in 1901, setting for an aristocratic charitable event	172
6.8	Kirsten Dunst in Sofia Coppola's updated version of *Marie Antoinette* (2006)	176
6.9	Madonna as Marie Antoinette at the 1990 MTV awards	184
6.10	La Conciergerie, a nostalgic discourse	186
6.11	George W. Bush depicted as Marie Antoinette in an 'imaginary social interaction' with contemporary Americans (M. McParlane 2008)	191
6.12	Artist Riyoko Ikeda – pictured in 2008 with Taiwan fans in the guise of Marie Antoinette and Lady Oscar	193
6.13	Visitor perceptions of Marie Antoinette and the Petit Trianon	197
7.1	The hermeneutical paradigm applied to the study's data collection	203
7.2	Izis' 1953 mise en scène of the famous 1901 apparition sighting of Marie Antoinette	205
7.3	*Le Loup-Garou – Le Temple* (J. Becket-Griffith 2010)	207
7.4	The legendary shoe purportedly worn by Marie Antoinette to the scaffold	208
7.5	Most recent cinematic 'Cinderella' image – Coppola's *Marie Antoinette* (2006) film	209
7.6	Poster advertising *M.A. Sillage de la Reine*	211
7.7	Authentic eighteenth-century hand-coloured engraving of Marie Antoinette from *La Galerie des Modes* (Le Clere 1776)	214
7.8	2007 Christian Dior Haute Couture design using a replica of the notorious necklace	215
7.9	Royalist representation of Marie Antoinette at her trial: 'J'en appelle à toutes les mères!' (Bouillon 1851)	216

xiv *Illustrations*

7.10	At Petit Trianon, the goat-drawn carriage of the first Dauphin	217
7.11	*Marie Antoinette* (2006) and 'Let Them Eat Cake!'	219
7.12	Original photo featured in 'All the Riches a Girl Can Have' – Ymre as Marie Antoinette in *Vogue Japan*, October 2012	222
7.13	Ladurée retail shop at Château de Versailles	223
7.14	Marie Antoinette merchandise at Château de Versailles – a pink theme	223
7.15	Hall (1997) and the commodification of Marie Antoinette's historical character	224
7.16	*Point de Vue* (2009) article negatively likens Carla Bruni to Marie Antoinette	227
7.17	Marie Antoinette in art photography representations incorporating the colour pink and macarons (V. Ielegems circa 2011)	228
7.18	Lady Gaga's 'Marie Antoinette' at the Brit Awards 2010	230
7.19	Marie Antoinette and her contemporary cliché image in art (C. Comyn 2010)	231
7.20	Hall (1997) and the cliché reproduction detected through the Petit Trianon survey	234
7.21	Petit Trianon, the cube that inspired countless copies	237
7.22	Madame Élisabeth's room at Petit Trianon	238
7.23	In the queen's bedroom at Petit Trianon	239
7.24	Le Temple de L'Amour at Petit Trianon	239
7.25	Le Belvédère at Petit Trianon	240
7.26	Le Moulin at Petit Trianon	241
7.27	La Ferme at Petit Trianon	242
7.28	Le Petit Théâtre de la Reine at Petit Trianon	243
7.29	Foundations of the former La Laiterie de Préparation, highlighting a nostalgic absence at Petit Trianon	244
7.30	La Maison de la Reine at Petit Trianon	245
7.31	All in a shop window! The entire conflated repertoire of Marie Antoinette images (A. Corrons 2008)	246
8.1	Nostalgic 'Places of Memory' for that which is lost – Marie Antoinette at Petit Trianon	257

Tables

2.1	The range of sites aimed at tourist consumption	41
3.1	Main clichés associated with the historical character of Marie Antoinette	56
3.2	The structure of the respondents' samples over 15 months of fieldwork research	68

3.3	The main groups detected by the interpretation of respondent discourses	71
4.1	'Bestseller' biographies of Marie Antoinette (2010–2012) at Librairie des Princes	83
4.2	The key moments contributing to the portrayal of Marie Antoinette's controversial image	87
6.1	A representative discourse on fascination with Marie Antoinette	178
6.2	Evidence and negative evidence, respectively, for American minority- and majority-group perceptions at the Petit Trianon	181

Preface

The interdisciplinarity of the present book brings contributions on both a theoretical and an ontological level, overarched by the critical heritage perspective which defines its analysis. It addresses current issues relevant to contemporary visual theory intrinsic to museology, tourism and popular culture, and at the same time offers a rehabilitative view of Marie Antoinette, one of the most important yet misunderstood (and misused) figures of the eighteenth century. Recent American (Goodman 2003b) and French (Berly 2011) academic sources on the subject acknowledge that an objective portrayal of Marie Antoinette could only be achieved through an analysis of her role in direct relation to the French Revolution. This task is also acknowledged to be unfulfilled, either because of the controversial historical character's conflicting representations in the Anglo-American academic literature ranging from 'Burkean hagiography to Jeffersonian demonization' (Lanser 2003), or the French Revolution historians' prejudice, prone to depicting a negative image of the queen (Martin 2011). This book adopts an innovative approach which does not rely on historical data but rather sheds light on the past through an analysis of eighteenth-century art history and current curatorial practices at the Petit Trianon. Contemporary visitor perceptions, collected on site, contribute equally important perspectives to this study. In short, the book's research benefits from the rare double perspective of curators and visitors. This unique approach was made possible by two doctoral research internships over a total period of 15 months at the Château de Versailles, including privileged access that permitted in situ visitor and staff surveys at the Petit Trianon, as well as participant observation conducted within the curatorial culture of the museum. Last, but not least, an academic affiliation with a British institution (Plymouth University) ensured a constant distancing from the French cultural and political milieus, necessary in the context of the ethnographic methods used.

Beginning in the 1980s, notable revisionist historical studies have emerged from within Anglo-American and French academia (Hobsbawm & Ranger 1983; Hunt 1989, 1991, 2004; Nora 1984–1992). There are no published monographs, however, which challenge the French Republican agenda through a critical heritage approach. Given the complexity and controversy of the subject, this book makes an original contribution to scholarship by clarifying important heritage issues of the modern era through the case study of the Petit Trianon. The reason for focusing the argument through a heritage analysis is that the chosen historic architectural site represents, above all, a unique case of cultural heritage with an intricate narrative structure. Analysing the causes, implications and forces behind the narratives involved offers not only a better understanding of the Petit Trianon, as well as its famous former owner, but also a better grasp of French cultural heritage and the construction of national identity during the French Third Republic based on myths that persistently surround the French Revolution, a topic of universal relevance to modern history. From this perspective, the book brings an innovative contribution to the explanation of a paradox stemming from the self-construction of modernity and self-contradiction by means of manipulation, re-creation and distortion of history. Finally, through Marie Antoinette's heritage commodification at the Petit Trianon, the book analyses the effects of this paradox in postmodern times: an uncontrolled, perpetual multiplication of representational images having escaped the authority of their creators.

From a critical heritage studies perspective, the originality of the book resides particularly in its first aim of revealing the diverse range of contemporary images portraying Marie Antoinette's historical character, showing how they affect the interpretation and perception of the Petit Trianon. By considering both producers and receivers of these cultural heritage exponents – Marie Antoinette's historical figure and the historic house museum of the Petit Trianon – the book expands current understandings of twenty-first century cultural heritage perceptions in relation to tourism and popular culture. This is a fresh approach, of benefit to museum professionals and heritage academia. The need for this is perhaps best revealed by the highly contradictory images of the last Queen of France, due to divergent readings of the French Revolution, which in turn influence the understanding of the modern concept of heritage, so much of which is born from the sweeping changes triggered by this event. Given that heritage studies were among the first postmodern academic subjects to gain momentum in recent decades, the nature and subject of this monograph are overdue. Not incidentally, the 2008 restoration of the Petit Trianon, the first since the French Revolution, in attracting new audiences, has made this research even more significant and has afforded the unprecedented opportunity to assess the full breadth of perceptions of Marie Antoinette.

Acknowledgements

Many individuals helped me, professionally and personally, in undertaking the research for this book and bringing it to publication, for which I am deeply thankful:

My former European Heritage Masters tutor, Professor Peter J. Howard, who supported my PhD enrolment, together with Professora Ascensión Hernández Martínez, under whose supervision I completed museology studies at the University of Zaragoza (Spain).

At the Château de Versailles, where I conducted my doctoral research, and elsewhere in France: Jérémie Benoît, Marie-Laëtitia Lachèvre, Philippe Baudin, Pierre-Xavier Hans, Gwenola Firmin, Karine McGrath, Laure Chedal-Anglay, Olivier Delahaye, Gérard Robaut, the late Silva Forapani (who is greatly missed), Patricia Bouchenot-Déchin, Michèle Lorin, Cécile Coutin, Professor Annie Duprat, Simone Bertière, Chantal Thomas, Jean Sévillia, Yves Carlier, Géraldine Bidault, Lionel Dupont, Caroline Gaillard, Delphine Valmalle, Yann Le Petit, Makiko Ichikawa, Nadia Francaviglia, Alexandre Laval, Françoise Billoux, Lena Kamoise, Marie-Lynne Délbès, Cyril Duclos, Béatrice de Parseval. In addition, I express my gratitude to Marieline Hoarau, Concetta Conti and the security staff members at the Petit Trianon who always showed me kindness during the long hours spent interviewing visitors. Their devotion to Marie Antoinette is to be commended; they are true keepers of her legacy at the Petit Trianon.

In the United Kingdom, the United States, Mexico, Australia and Japan: Professor Paul Brunt (who, in a crucial moment, encouraged me to write this book), Dr Graham Busby, Professor Robert Brown, Professor Daniel Maudlin, Dr Charlie Mansfield, Dr Kevin Meethan, Professor Mike Robinson, John Barnes, Christopher Davies; Joseph Vigliotti, Cardozie Jones, Elena Maria Vidal, Hélène Demeestere; Martin Foley; Dr Linda Young, Dr Matthew Rofe; Hitoshi Onodera, Mark Tramontana and last but not least, Atsuko Tanaka. Also to all my students at Plymouth University.

At Routledge and Apex CoVantage: Dominic Shryane, Heidi Lowther, Louisa Vahtrick, Marc Stratton and Autumn Spalding.

The image artists/professionals who generously supported my book: Philippe Baudin, Sheryl Scott, Guy Marineau, Jasmine Becket-Griffith, Viona

Ielegems and Dirk von Heinrichshorst, Christine Comyn, Anne Corrons, Michael McParlane, *Point de Vue*, Nelly Dhoutaut and *Paris Match*, Ymre @ VDM Model Management and Ferry Korver, Miho Yamagishi and *Vogue Japan*, Glenn Bradie, Doug Fallone and Everett Collection, Patricia Touzard and Musée de Beaux-Arts Caen, and last but not least, Jim Löfgren and Östergotlands Museum.

My family and friends: *Tuturor familiilor mele iubite*, Maior, Boată, Barron, Dincu, Stuparu and Botta; Marina Samoilă, Cristiana Scutaşu, the friends of my youth Ana, Dana and Dănuţ, Ioana Popovici (proofreader and editor of my thesis), Willa Wirth, Graeme Davies, Kathy and David Bennett, Adrian Rozei, Pilar Bernad Esteban, and, of course, Richard Maior-Barron who was my nurse, cook, driver, IT consultant and a true support in most difficult times during my doctoral research years. Finally, my husband and colleague, as well as copy-editor of this book, Edward R. Bosley, director of The Gamble House in California.

Denise Maior-Barron
Pasadena, 2018

Introduction

The key concerns of this book lie in the visual production and appropriation of cultural heritage, with analyses operating within an interdisciplinary field pertaining to museology, art history, history, popular culture and tourism. This in turn provides support for charting the contemporary commodification of Marie Antoinette's historical character at the Petit Trianon, a process which encourages uncanny memories (Ricoeur 2004) of the last Queen of France. The eighteenth-century art history appraisal vis-à-vis contemporary heritage practices and visitor perceptions are analysed here within the groundbreaking postmodern academic field of critical heritage studies.

The Petit Trianon and Marie Antoinette are examined in this book in the context of four major narratives that are relevant to the contemporary heritage interpretation of the *Domaine de Marie-Antoinette* (Estate of Marie-Antoinette) as well as its perception by the majority of its visitors. Fieldwork research has detected these to be the historical, cinematic, architectural and heritage narratives of the Petit Trianon and Marie Antoinette.[1] The Estate is part of the Château de Versailles UNESCO heritage site, and has recently been restored, and renamed *Domaine de Marie-Antoinette*, a transformation envisioned to strengthen its identity as home to the last Queen of France.[2]

UNESCO inscribed the heritage site of the Palace of Versailles in 1979. The second most visited museum in France after the Louvre,[3] Versailles remains a symbol of the French Monarchy, primarily represented by two historical characters: Louis XIV, or the Sun King, founder of the Royal Court of Versailles at the end of the seventeenth century, and Marie Antoinette, also known as the last Queen of France, who reigned at the end of the eighteenth century. Both figures belonged to the Ancien Régime, and while the first is generally regarded in a positive light, the latter is renowned as the notorious historical character best remembered for uttering the (falsely attributed) words 'Let Them Eat Cake!'. This ubiquitous cliché image of the last Queen of France, deeply rooted in the French collective memory, was the initial instigator of the present study, which attempts to dispel numerous myths surrounding this perception by analysing the narrative of the Petit Trianon, the residence identified as the home *par excellence* to Marie Antoinette.

Themes and aims

Themes: Marie Antoinette, the Petit Trianon, the French Revolution, the French Third Republic, National Identity,[4] Cultural Heritage,[5] Media,[6] Tourism,[7] Hermeneutics, Qualitative Research, the Romantic Tourist Gaze, Narratives,[8] Visitor Perceptions, Postmodern Visual Cultural Consumption, Heritage Authenticity, Dissonant Heritage, Heritage Commodification

The originality of the book resides particularly in its first aim: to reveal the diverse range of contemporary images portraying Marie Antoinette's historical character and to show how they affect the interpretation and perception of the Petit Trianon and its former royal owner. The evaluation intrinsic to this process is set against an understanding of the living environment she created – the eighteenth-century estate of the Petit Trianon (Figure 0.1). Although the working concepts that will make this evaluation possible constantly refer to the 'image' of Marie Antoinette, the analysis, in attempting to objectively portray this Enlightenment (Todorov 2009) monarch, intends to establish the factual reality behind the image.[9] The evaluation further supports the fulfilment of the second aim: to expose the heritage commodification of Marie Antoinette's historical character at the Petit Trianon – its

Figure 0.1 Eighteenth-century architectural narrative of the Petit Trianon – indicator for the objective assessment of the role played by Marie Antoinette (Claude-Louis Châtelet 1786)

Biblioteca Estense, Modena, Italy © Alfredo Dagli Orti/courtesy Art Resource, NY production and consumption. Last, but not least, the third aim of this book is to challenge the French Republican agenda's portrayal of Marie Antoinette.

As earlier noted, the controversy surrounding the historical character of the last Queen of France provided motivation for the research project. To fulfil the first aim, the book needs to analyse the representations of Marie Antoinette. In order to achieve this on a practical level, all collected data[10] are filtered via assessment, in Chapters 6 and 7, against the impact of each of the four investigated narratives on visitors at the Petit Trianon, along with the emergent images of Marie Antoinette. The results of the assessment establish the ranked prevalence of these main narratives within visitor perceptions at the Petit Trianon, enabling not only the detection of the range of contemporary images associated with Marie Antoinette but also an explanation for the existence of these images, which is key to understanding the complex process of heritage commodification of Marie Antoinette at the Petit Trianon.

The analysis establishes first the historical parameters which led to this commodification. Furthermore, as this proved to be of a dissonant nature (Tunbridge & Ashworth 1996), the book highlights the dissonance aspects generating this commodification, as well as its production and consumption supported by an 'alchemical' process, which renders it highly lucrative. As revealed by fieldwork research, the cultural heritage associated with the French Revolution is in dissonance with the cultural heritage defining Marie Antoinette's historical figure, the two impinging on each other. Nevertheless, it is also true that the heritage dissonance overarching the case study of the Petit Trianon and Marie Antoinette has an alchemical nature, with the meanings of the past having undergone a transformation in order to be treated as cultural capital meant to later be appropriated successfully. 'Alchemical dissonant heritage', the generator of Marie Antoinette's commodification at the Petit Trianon, is coined here for this purpose, a term that highlights the paradox of modernity's self-construction, which is in contradiction to itself by means of manipulation, re-creation and distortion of its history. This is explored throughout the book, at an ontological level, via the cultural heritage represented by the Petit Trianon as home to Marie Antoinette. It should be emphasised that the entire research project is placed under the sign of this paradox of modernity, which, from the point of view here, could be explained through (Brown pers. comm. 2011):

> the inherent nature of the modern nation state whose birth is attributed to the French Revolution by following the idea according to which the Enlightenment equally gave rise to a cultural and political agenda which increasingly found acceptance within the European aristocratic and royal environment of the 18th century, as well as to the anti-aristocratic/anti-royalist aims and movements that would ultimately bring down these archaic institutions across most part of Europe.

4 *Introduction*

To this end, it is necessary to examine the duality of acceptance/rejection of the Enlightenment, persistent in contemporary French collective memory (Todorov 2009; see also Baker & Reill 2001) by primarily assessing how Marie Antoinette's historical character became, and continues to embody, the negative image of the French Monarchy/Ancien Régime since the 1780s. Given that her role has been highly debated, and has been even before her reign as a consequence of the Austrian-French alliance treaty of 1754 coupled with the French phobia of Austrians (Austrophobia, see Kaiser 2000, 2003a, 2003b), the manipulation of her image begins to become clearer already. In fact, it was Austrophobia which created the premises for a rejection of a queen whose legitimacy has been continuously undermined – initially by the court, and finally by public opinion – through means of violent propaganda (Gruder 2002). Equally, Marie Antoinette's own endeavours in challenging some of the old precepts of the Court of Versailles etiquette (de Nolhac 1898a, 1899a, 1925, 1927; de Nolhac & Hirschauer 1927), no longer in alignment with the social changes brought by the Enlightenment (Furet & Richet 1973; Furet 1978), are grossly ignored or continue to be misinterpreted and criticised as a result.

The identification of Marie Antoinette with the French Monarchy and, ironically, with an Ancien Régime whose social rules she sought to break (via emancipation of the role of Queen of France), led to revolutionary agents labouring to dismantle the ruling institution by targeting and destroying its most potent symbol: Marie Antoinette. In this context, her self-created environment at the Petit Trianon further completes the symbolic negative role attributed to the queen through misinterpretation as a typical image of the royal/aristocratic disregard of a people whose living conditions contrasted markedly with their own. This study will demonstrate that this image stems from a revolutionary propaganda strategy, further illuminating the image manipulation mentioned above, and consequently, the 'alchemical dissonant heritage' commodification of Marie Antoinette's historical character. To this end, the main focus lies in the analysis of visitor perceptions at the Petit Trianon, assessed through fieldwork research. This is underpinned by the analysis of the images of Marie Antoinette and of the Petit Trianon at their conception at the end of the eighteenth century, and their re-creation by the nineteenth-century nationalist agenda of the French Third Republic.

Finally, the evidence provided by the research highlights the direct impact of modernity's paradox on the fiction-reality relationship, within which operates, more than ever, a reversal: fiction into reality, and vice versa. This effect could also be construed as another (this time postmodern) paradox: following the incessant re-creation and distortion of political images during the modern nationalist era, the contemporary corporatist and consumerist West is witnessing a constant multiplication of all images pertaining to diverse spheres – political, cultural, social and/or economic. As controversy and martyrdom have placed Marie Antoinette's image within a spectrum of cultural caricatures that range from taboo to iconic, through the heritage interpretation given to the site of the Petit Trianon, and by charting the commodification of Marie Antoinette's historical character, this paradox of modernity, translated into postmodern terms, is examined and found to be an uncontrolled perpetual multiplication of representational images having escaped the authority of their creators.

Chapter content

For theoretical background, this book considers the Petit Trianon to be a highly representative 'place of memory' as defined by Pierre Nora (1984–1992). Subscribing to a rehabilitative history narrative, Chapter 1 represents contextual theoretical background for the analysis of the four major narratives (historical, cinematic, architectural and heritage) of Marie Antoinette and the Petit Trianon. To this end, the chapter clarifies the wider context of the evolution of 'places of memory' throughout history, using nationalist theories to analyse the rift between the Royal/Christian tradition and the new 'religion' of nineteenth-century nationalism. In addition to Nora's 'places of memory', the views of Benedict Anderson (1991); Eric Hobsbawm (1983) and Pierre Bourdieu (1984) generate the classic testimony for this particular argument.

Chapter 2 links the concept of 'places of memory' with authors whose views anchor them in the present (Lefebvre 1991; Urry 1990, 1995, 2002). The chapter also contains a literature review related to important theoretical issues discussed in the book: heritage commodification and authenticity in the context of heritage industry. The definition of heritage authenticity used here originates in Gregory Ashworth and Peter Howard (1999) and was chosen over other definitions because of its correspondence to principles adopted by the heritage authorities in charge of the Petit Trianon's interpretation and its 2008 restoration. The literature review concerning the heritage industry is supported by the book's research: fieldwork evidence and observations concerning the perception of authenticity by the majority of visitors at the Petit Trianon. Last, but not least, the chapter includes an overview of a range of sites aimed at tourist consumption, an overview essential to completing the picture of the status reserved nowadays for 'places of memory' such as the Petit Trianon.

Chapter 3 – the methodological framework of this book – is structured into four sections as follows: the hermeneutical methodology used for analysing the representation, interpretation and perception of the Petit Trianon; methods of investigation used for constructing the project's working hypothesis; qualitative research conducted at the site of the Petit Trianon, including the author's fieldwork research ethnographic elements (2010–2012); and finally, a critical model developed as an overview of the discussion built upon the academic field, literature review and methodological framework.

The hermeneutical principles of intersecting diverse meanings support the book's methodology, including the library and archive research selection and interpretation (Scott 1990). Furthermore, through thematic analysis (Boyatzis 1998; Saldaña 2013), a hermeneutical research paradigm underpins the methodology for interpreting visitor discourses at the Petit Trianon. This research paradigm is complemented at a theoretical level by Paul Ricoeur's (2004) hermeneutical analysis of the uncanniness of Pierre Nora's (1984–1992) 'places of memory' in conjunction with Maurice Halbwachs' (1980; see also 1992) 'collective memory', the two key theories supporting the analysis of production and consumption of Marie Antoinette's heritage commodification through the power of clichés.

Chapter 4 synthesises data collected through the hermeneutical analysis of the relevant sources composing the historical and cinematic narratives associated with the historical figure of Marie Antoinette. This chapter analyses first the public image of the last Queen of France as conveyed by relevant French historical works to date, including an evaluation of eighteenth-century revolutionary pamphlets and their effect on Marie Antoinette's image. Central to this chapter's analysis are twentieth- and twenty-first century biographers of Marie Antoinette, who have had a direct influence over cinematic narratives as sources of inspiration. The chapter continues by investigating the cinematic narrative surrounding Marie Antoinette. Field research proved this study to be fundamental, since American and Japanese visitors in particular use popular culture media sources as reference points for their perception of the site and its former owner. The cinematic productions considered are Sofia Coppola's *Marie Antoinette* (2006) and, albeit a cinematically illustrated book rather than a film, Riyoko Ikeda's manga, *Rose of Versailles* (1972). The former has been significant to the process of promoting the Petit Trianon to new audiences since 2006, and the latter has had an important influence over Japanese visitor perceptions.

Chapter 5 provides data collected through the hermeneutical analysis (Mugerauer 1995) of the architectural and heritage narratives of the Petit Trianon contained in its contemporary heritage interpretation since the 2008 restoration. The chapter focuses, in parallel, on the principles guiding the heritage interpretation of the site as well as various issues connected to the heritage industry and its links with tourism. Furthermore, through the analysis of the extensive 2008 restoration, which marked a definite change in the ways in which the site was interpreted as well as its perception by the visiting public, the chapter elucidates two major issues from a heritage interpretation perspective: how dissonant heritage was handled by those in charge of the interpretation of the Petit Trianon, and where this restoration has placed it within the range of sites – analysed theoretically in Chapter 2 – which spans 360 degrees of heritage authenticity aimed at tourist consumption. Within this analysis, the term 'alchemical dissonant heritage' is coined, which not only refers to fitting a piece of counter-memory into the official national discourse, but moreover, through an alchemical process, also refers to rendering the heritage commodification of Marie Antoinette a highly lucrative commercial proposition.

Chapter 6 evaluates the findings of the fieldwork research method at the Petit Trianon (a survey conducted on site over a period of 15 months) through an assessment of visitor discourses from within and without French borders. The chapter focuses on French, American and Japanese perceptions of the site by building on the fieldwork research results supported by the ethnographic study on 'imaginary social worlds' (Caughey 1984). Particular attention will be given to the artificial types of memories primarily induced through 'collective memory' (Halbwachs 1980) but also to a specific form of false, and time-line independent recollections introduced by the imaginary social interaction of contemporary individuals with media and historical figures. 'Imaginary social memories' are thus coined in this chapter. Nora's (1984–1992) 'places of memory', uncanny memory constructs which, under the sign of nostalgia, could embody what is lost, also play an important role in the analysis of visitor discourses. From the perspective of the hermeneutical paradigm interpretation underpinning the methodology, Chapter 6 provides perspectives on the cultural conditioning and 'prejudice' manifested by contemporary visitors at the Petit Trianon.

Chapter 7 contains the comparative assessment of the historical, cinematic and architectural narratives against the heritage narrative, thereby discovering the emerging range of images associated with the last Queen of France at the Petit Trianon. Furthermore, the chapter identifies the reasons behind the formation of such images as well as the processes that led to the unintentional strengthening of some of these, which resulted in the 'alchemical dissonant heritage' commodification of Marie Antoinette's historical character at the Petit Trianon. At the same time, Chapter 7 assesses the postmodern paradox – the subject of the ontological analysis of the book – by referring back to some of its underpinning theories and complementing them with semiotic, structuralist and post-structuralist approaches concerning the encoding and decoding of postmodern images (Barthes 1972; Baudrillard 1994, 2001; Eco 1986; Hall 1997).

The analysis of the four main narratives of the book collectively illustrates a better picture for drawing conclusions for the entire study of the range of images associated with Marie Antoinette at the Petit Trianon. It is through the assessment of the incessant manipulation of these images of the last Queen of France, since her reign, that this study reveals the misconceptions surrounding the historical character best known as Marie Antoinette.[11]

Notes

1 The book assesses the image of Marie Antoinette as generated solely by the four noted narratives, which field research evidence has indicated to be relevant in the production and consumption of the 'alchemical dissonant heritage' commodification of Marie Antoinette's historical character at the Petit Trianon. Negative evidence confirming the validity of focusing the analysis primarily on these selected

narratives is provided by observations punctuating the analyses contained in Chapters 4 and 5. Accordingly, the image of the queen conveyed by Romantic literature of the nineteenth century, such as Alexandre Dumas' novels, was found to have no direct impact on the majority's perception. Nevertheless, it did serve as source for various later media productions that added to the ambiguity of this historical character's portrayal today. Equally, Marie Antoinette's image found in painting history has only influenced a minority, such as specialists in the field and individuals with art history knowledge.

2 The research analysis results are evaluated for validity against the eighteenth-century architectural narrative of the Petit Trianon, sourced from architectural history in order to unearth the objective truth surrounding Marie Antoinette's historical character. The architecture narrative's indicator is identified in the Petit Trianon at the time of its creation as the eighteenth-century home to Marie Antoinette, which includes the building of the Petit Trianon, the Jardin Anglais with all its *fabriques* designed during Marie Antoinette's time including Le Théâtre de la Reine, Le Hameau de la Reine and La Ferme.

3 According to official French statistics, see DGE (2016).

4 The concept of National Identity refers to the modern notion of national identities formed as a result of the nineteenth-century nationalism movements defined from a modernist perspective (Gellner 1993a), rather than to the mediaeval understanding of the term, better known as the primordialist theory of nationalism (Llobera 1996).

5 The term 'cultural heritage' is used in line with the UNESCO definition. Accordingly, the study adopts the 1972 UNESCO World Heritage Convention acceptation of the term, which includes monuments, groups of buildings and sites (Jokilehto 2005). It also takes into account the added dimension of the national level through the 1970 UNESCO Convention (Illicit Property) defining cultural heritage as a national state's cultural property. This refers not only to moveable, immoveable, tangible and intangible aspects of cultural heritage but also to the lives of national leaders (Jokilehto 2005).

6 The concept of media refers to all media channels, from pamphlets and newspapers (Anderson 1991) to film and social media (Watson & Hill 2006). Each chapter will specify which form of media is employed for each particular step of the analysis.

7 The concept of tourism is understood here as 'cultural tourism', found in the 1976 ICOMOS Charter for Cultural Tourism (Jokilehto 2005): in essence, the form of tourism concerned with the discovery of monuments and sites.

8 Following Barthes' (1966) structuralist approach adopted by the field research methodology informing the book (Maior-Barron 2011), narratives are threads of a storyline rather than a compilation of multiple stories.

9 The book will not identify the image of Marie Antoinette with the image of the site, the latter being only incidentally used as supporting evidence in proving the artificial construction of the former. Consequently, the image of the site of the Petit Trianon provides data for the research analysis, being one of the research variables along with the historical, cinematic and heritage narratives concerning the Petit Trianon and Marie Antoinette. Moreover, as the book examines the commodification of Marie Antoinette's historical figure at the Petit Trianon, resulting from the array of conflicting images of the last Queen of France (their production and consumption), the image of the Petit Trianon assists this assessment by substituting the physical site inasmuch as the commodification of Marie Antoinette substitutes her historical figure within the process.

10 It must be stressed that the analysis of the historical, cinematic, architectural and heritage narratives provides data for the research rather than being a literature review of the sources relating to these subjects. This is why Chapters 4 and 5, in dealing with these narratives, only draw on certain sources. The choice of criteria was based on the relevance which these sources have to the contemporary perception of the Petit Trianon and Marie Antoinette.
11 For the many names used for this historical character, see Seth (2006).

1 'Places of memory' in the nationalist era of the French Third Republic

The modern concept of cultural heritage, and the French national identity to which this is affiliated, are regarded here as being artificially constructed through manipulation of historical discourse, starting with the very events of the French Revolution. For a better illustration of this process, Chapter 1 leans on theories supporting the point of view of the imagined and respectively artificial construction of national identities (Anderson 1991; Hobsbawm 1983). These complement each other and offer a sound analytical basis. Moreover, in order to explain the manipulation of cultural heritage by national identities in a bid for legitimation, this chapter focuses on the most relevant element involved in this manipulation process: the 'cultural capital' as found in the work of French sociologist Pierre Bourdieu in his seminal study *Distinction* (1984). It is by integrating his theory into the analysis that this book establishes the mechanisms behind the political, yet abusive, appropriation of a certain 'cultural capital' by the French political elite of the Third Republic in an exercise of self-legitimation.

This chapter also represents a contextual theoretical background for historical, cinematic, architectural and heritage narratives of Marie Antoinette and the Petit Trianon. The differing agendas and their underlying causes require the following analysis, which subscribes to the stance of a rehabilitative history narrative. This is construed through the prism of well-established British and French theories on nationalism (Hobsbawm 1983; Nora 1984–1992; Anderson 1991; Gellner 1993a, 1993b) which, in the past four decades, challenged previous readings of dogmatic historical discourses. This theoretical background is relevant to cultural heritage studies which explore the relationship between heritage and power. With this relationship identified as the root of the heritage commodification for tourist consumption detected at the Petit Trianon, the analysis of the present chapter prepares the way for the theoretical background relevant to issues of heritage commodification and authenticity analysed by Chapter 2.

Founding *les lieux de mémoire*

The Petit Trianon is considered here to be a highly representative example of historian Pierre Nora's theory of *'lieux de mémoire'* (hereafter 'places of memory'), with Nora's magisterial study, interspersed throughout the academic field covered by Chapters 1 and 2, providing the main theoretical background. Nora's contribution to the understanding of the modern concept of cultural heritage represents a pivotal theoretical source, chosen for its brave challenging of modern French historical and heritage paradigms. The author's lifetime commitment to the development of an alternative approach to French-culture representation earned him widespread recognition and a nomination at the French Academy (Nora et al. 2002), which confirms this contribution to be a cornerstone of modern cultural heritage studies (Howard 2001).

When history seems to have stopped in its natural course in order to make way for an interpretation or even reconstruction of the past (stemming from the need to legitimise a present mainly defined in contrast to the past in term of political ideologies and circumstances), then history itself becomes heritage in the making – the main idea illustrated by Nora's theory presented here. This point of view circumscribes opposing theories regarding the legitimate birth of the modern concept of heritage, seen as a culmination of the Enlightenment's ideas crystallised into the French Revolution itself.

Nora attributes the existence of 'places of memory' to the end of what he describes as 'memory-history' (Nora 1984a:XVII). The chapter '*Entre Mémoire et Histoire – La problématique des lieux*'[1] explains how, through an acceleration of history and an increasingly rapid swing back to a past with little connection to the present (a past irretrievably lost), the natural equilibrium of history's course was shattered. The French Revolution was, in fact, the marker of the rift which occurred between the lived traditions – the natural development of history preceding the Revolution – and the artificial structures of the historical 'traditions' created in its aftermath. This argument is illustrated through Anderson's views on the imagined nature of national identities as well as Hobsbawm's theory on the artificial creation of the French national identity by the Third Republic.

Nora observes: 'Places of memory exist because there are no other environments left in which memory can manifest itself' [translation mine] (1984a:XVII). The disappearance of traditions, customs and ancestral norms gives the individual an acute sense of self without any continuity or affiliation to the past. Therefore, the memory of history becomes lost. Once this happens, places representing a concentration of memory provide a source of fascination for the past but also a material link, which gives the hope of a possible reincarnation of all that was lost. As the feeling of continuity becomes residual to places, the 'places of memory' come to life because there is no other remaining environment where memory can manifest itself.

Maurice Halbwachs' *Collective Memory* (1980) approached within Paul Ricoeur's hermeneutical paradigm of history (2004) in Chapter 3, supports Nora's position on the separation between tradition and history itself. As Halbwachs' (1980:78) classic quote states: '[H]istory starts where tradition ends'. In fact, Ricoeur (2004) considers Halbwachs' work on collective memory based on tradition as antithetical to historical memory.

Furthermore, Nora (1984a:XVIII–XIX) points out that once memory becomes detached from history, the latter transforms into an artificial construction itself, having been emptied of its 'affective and magical' dimension. This process is best understood through the differences between the 'lived-in' history of traditional societies and the dogma-ridden history of modernity. What Nora calls the 'history of history' – or the awakening of a historiography consciousness – is the most visible sign of this process. As the author astutely observes, in a country such as France the 'history of history' cannot be an 'innocent operation'. Nora points out that once a national, constitutive event, namely, the French Revolution, comes under question and critical analysis, even if only by a small number of French historians, the nation no longer completely identifies with the heritage defined by the French Revolution, which in fact equates with French tradition itself. By extension, it is argued here that a 'tradition'-generating event coming under question could be indicative of the event's initial, artificial construction.

For a nation state built on the basis of its cultural heritage, this situation indicates a genuine crisis. Furthermore, the last incarnation of this now-lost 'memory-history' was the 'nation memory'. Once this 'nation memory' was challenged by the French society's ideological crisis of the 1930s (shifting the accent placed by history from the right to the left of the political spectrum), nationalism, as a determinant attribute of the bourgeoisie, also fell under the challenge of an increasing proletarian internationalism. A new focus on the societal level rather than national level heralds the transition from Nation State to the Society State (see Nora 1984b).

Hobsbawm's views on the invention of traditions fully support the above arguments. Nora himself acknowledged the important contribution brought by Hobsbawm's essay to the understanding of 'places of memory' (Nora 2011a). Regarding the particular inventions of traditions by the Third Republic on the basis of the French Revolution, Nora (1984b) observes that the Republican memory created as such, was authoritarian, unitary, exclusivist, universal and intensively retrospective.

Another important factor confirming the artificiality of the creation of national identities through manipulation of cultural heritage is counter-memory (see also Koselleck 2004), to which Nora dedicates a separate section in his first volume, *La République* (1984). Counter-memory (see also Erll 2011) highlights the discordant aspects that dominant ideology needs to eliminate by reinterpretation of dissonant heritage (Tunbridge & Ashworth 1996).

Although the creation and artificial construction of national identities involve many aspects and processes, at a schematic level, two main theories in the field fittingly complement each other, providing a linear model of explanation for the case of the French Revolution. As this has, in turn, provided the nationalist model for later centuries, the Revolutionary/Republican alchemy of firstly forging political realities and secondly transforming the historical past sheds light on how modern totalitarian regimes were able to come into being, legitimate themselves and ultimately operate.

Imagined communities

In this respect, the first theoretical source is that of *Imagined Communities* (Anderson 1991). Anderson's analysis shows clearly that written messages, conveyed through the press and the educational system, were the main tool used in creating nation states at the end of the eighteenth and throughout the nineteenth century. Consequently, nineteenth-century nationalism and national identities developed thanks primarily to the press. In the case of the French Revolution, libellous pamphlets of revolutionary propaganda fuelled this nationalism. In effect, it was the printing press which enabled the considerable impact of the media on the public's consciousness.

Moreover, nationalism replaced the cultural systems that had defined the preceding eras of religious community and the dynastic realm. Anderson (1991:12) explains how nationalism would be better understood in a cultural rather than a political context 'by aligning it, not with self-consciously held political ideologies, but with the large cultural systems that preceded it, out of which – as well as against which – it came into being.' In fact, nationalism became the nineteenth-century religion.

Anderson's key concept in explaining the 'artificiality' to which this book refers, lies in the imaginative process which, once generating bonds between the members of an otherwise virtual community, would create the basis of a strong community. But his views differ from other modernist nationalist theories (Hobsbawm 1983; Gellner 1993a, 1993b), Anderson (1991:6) specifying that, although he favours the idea of modern nations' 'invention', in his opinion this does not equate with 'fabrication' and 'falsity' but with 'imagining' and 'creation'. However, when comparing Anderson's own description of the earlier cultural systems which nationalism replaced and of nationalism itself, in the case of the latter a definite degree of fabrication can be detected. In the case of the dynastic realm, the imagined link between the members of its corresponding community was provided by the legitimacy of kingship, deriving from divinity rather than popular support, and organised around a 'high centre' (Anderson 1991:19), not a fully demarcated territory. Naturally, the religious background of the society models corresponding to the dynastic realm facilitated 'the ease with which pre-modern empires and kingdoms were able to sustain their rule' (Anderson 1991:14). Although the decline of the automatic legitimacy of the Western European dynasties started with the seventeenth century and the English Revolution (with the resulting beheading in 1649 of King Charles I), it is only 'after 1789 [that] the principle of Legitimacy had to be loudly and self-consciously defended' (Anderson 1991:21).

The above fact supports, indirectly, the idea of a clear break marked in the perception of historical time by the French Revolution. Moreover, Anderson also perceives the 'lived-in' history of traditional societies contrasting with the dogma-ridden history of modernity mentioned by Nora. In the chapter 'Apprehensions of Time', Anderson (1991:22) points out that in addition 'to the decline of sacred communities, languages and lineages, a fundamental change was taking place in modes of apprehending the world, which, more than anything else, made it possible to "think" the nation.'

But whilst it is true that modernity would have favoured a different perception of historical time, the crucial moment for the creation of the rift within historical discourse is the French Revolution, an event favoured by the advent of print capitalism and bearing the responsibility of the modern nations' official birth. Anderson (1991) signals that the novel and newspapers were the most representative examples illustrating and explaining the transformation leading to the process of 'imagining'.

Bringing this theory to reflect on the subject of Marie Antoinette's eighteenth-century images resulting in her contemporary commodification, it is revealed that the impact of print capitalism is fully represented by the case of certain novels, such as those of Jean-Jacques Rousseau, and the pamphlets directed against the French Monarchy, particularly Marie Antoinette. As Professor Annie Duprat (pers. comm. 2012), specialist in the caricatures of the French Revolution's propagandistic pamphlets, observes:

> The French Revolution could not have happened without the pamphlets! Marie Antoinette, by having ignored them – meaning not reacting against and not realising their damaging permanent effect to her image – has indirectly allowed the collapse of the French Monarchy through the pamphlets' successful attacks to her image in the public opinion of the time. [translation mine]

Moreover, the fact that the queen's image was always portrayed by the pamphlets out of any clear specific context (Duprat pers. comm. 2012), such as the Court of Versailles or the Petit Trianon, yet fabricating for these absent contexts an aura of promiscuity (particularly the Petit Trianon, which acquired an image of its own), allowed an even greater degree of 'imagining'[2] to take place in the readers' consciousness. This intentional ambiguity led to the public opinion's identification of the French Monarchy with Marie Antoinette and promiscuity. In fact, as Duprat (2006) noted in her work on Marie Antoinette, a second queen was created, namely, a 'paper queen'. The manipulation operated through the pamphlets' distorting messages is considered here to be one of the most effective tools that the masterminds of the French Revolution used in destroying the monarchy.

Anderson (1991:36) described the wider context of print capitalism as the most precipitating and fruitful way of allowing 'rapidly growing numbers of people to think about themselves, and to relate themselves to others', highlighting the mechanisms operating behind the creation of modern nations. Despite advocating the importance of the mediaeval national legacy, Llobera (1996:103) also recognises the 'tremendous impact of print capitalism' signalled by Anderson, and does not dispute the fact that, ultimately, the bourgeoisie has 'used nationalist ideologies to further its economic objectives and political domination.'

On the one hand, Anderson's analysis clearly shows that the main tools used in creating the nation states of the end of the eighteenth and nineteenth centuries, were the written messages conveyed through the press and educational system. Where the French Revolution is concerned, this was mostly achieved through pamphlets of assiduous propaganda. On the other hand, the paradox of acceptance/rejection that this book examines ontologically through its analysis is reflected by Anderson's (1991) observations on the discourse delivered by Renan, who asked the 'nation' to both remember and forget key events such as the massacre of *Saint-Barthélemy's* night, massacres of French by the French, which in his opinion shaped what came to be the French nation. By analysing this discourse in his chapter aptly called 'The Reassurance of Fratricide', Anderson (1991) elucidates the creation of the French modern national identity, as well as the reason for its success in perpetuating an artificially constructed notion. These were achieved through the acceptance and rejection of the Enlightenment's values by the political elites of the Third Republic, thereby becoming fixed as such in the French collective memory.

The invention of tradition

With regard to the Third Republic's essential input into the artificial construction of France's contemporary national identity, Hobsbawm's (1983) views further refine Anderson's theory. According to Hobsbawm, 1870 was the crucial political moment in European history to crystallise the new states' national identities. The 1870 French defeat at Sedan witnessed the rise of France's Third Republic, and marked the beginning of the re-creation of France's historical past through a political agenda concerned with forging a strongly defined national identity (see also Gérard 1970).

Hobsbawm (1983:263) reviewed the motives behind the assiduous invention of what he coined 'political and social traditions', in Europe between 1870 and 1914. His analysis reveals that the main cause for the 'mass-producing traditions' of this period lies in the 'profound and rapid social transformations', which consequently determined the invention of political traditions. This idea brings further depth to Anderson's theory of imagining the nation by explaining how a social context – once prepared and ultimately created – facilitates its own political manipulation, thus providing a mutual reinforcement of the two aspects of a 'tradition', social and political. Out of the array of such inventions of the period, Hobsbawm's analysis revealed that the middle classes of all European nation states were the ones to relate (and/or identify themselves) in the strongest manner to nationalism-supporting traditions. Through the example of the bourgeois Third Republic, the case of France is particularly relevant.

Referring to the importance of studying the 'invention of traditions', Hobsbawm links this invention directly to the evolution of modern nationalism. For Hobsbawm (1983:12–13), the invented traditions 'are highly relevant to that comparatively recent historical innovation, the 'nation', with its associated phenomena: nationalism, the nation state, national symbols, histories and so on. All these rest on exercises in social engineering'. As a result, it is clear that the national phenomenon could not be adequately investigated without careful attention given to the 'invention of tradition'. In this respect, Hobsbawm (1983:14) emphasises the subjectivity of the elements constructing the modern nations which are associated with 'appropriate, and in general, fairly recent symbols or suitably tailored discourse (such as "national history")'.

Placing the arguments above into the wider context of Hobsbawm's views as presented in his later work, Hobsbawm (1992) suggests that the French Revolution – and the propaganda preceding and preparing the ground for upheaval – was chiefly responsible for a masterminded break with a certain undesirable political past.

Concerning the Third Republic and its construction on the basis of the French Revolution's tradition, Hobsbawm (1983:269) distinguished three main routes used to achieve the successful implementation of 'invented traditions'. The first and most effective was 'the development of a secular equivalent of the church, notably primary education imbued with revolutionary and republican principles and content' (Hobsbawm 1983:271) mediated by *instituteurs*, the equivalent of one-time priests or friars. The second path was the invention of ceremonials such as 'Bastille Day', known in France as 'jour de la fête nationale' or simply *'le 14 juillet'*, established in 1880. The third path was the mass production of public monuments, mostly embodying the symbolic image of the Republic itself: the bare-breasted Marianne. The choice was not accidental. Given the highly debated historical figures of the French Revolution, such as Robespierre, the Third Republic had to steer away from an explicit depiction of its actual past. Hobsbawm (1983:278) unpacks the French context which facilitated such a choice, in contrast with Germany:

> A comparison of the French and German innovations is instructive. Both stress the founding acts of the new regime – the French Revolution in its least precise and controversial episode (the Bastille) and the Franco-Prussian war. Except for this one point of historic reference, the French Republic abstained from historical retrospect as strikingly as the German Empire indulged in it. Since the Revolution had established the fact, the nature and the boundaries of the French nation and its patriotism, the Republic could confine itself to recalling these to its citizens by means of a few obvious symbols – Marianne, the tricolour, the 'Marseillaise', and so on – supplementing them with a little ideological exegesis elaborating on the (to its poorer citizens) obvious if sometimes theoretical benefits of Liberty, Equality and Fraternity.

Distinction

Hobsbawm's views on the inculcation of invented traditions through education link Anderson's theory of print capitalism with Bourdieu's (1984) 'cultural capital' theory. The classic sociological study *Distinction* proved the salience of the value placed by the political and social elite on cultural capital, which once appropriated or acquired becomes a form of 'distinction' and thus legitimation for political elites.

Through the formula [(*habitus*)(capital)]+field=practice, from the perspective of the present analysis, Bourdieu (1984) explains the underlying divisive phenomena to class condition, social conditioning and, ultimately, the ways in which each class manifests itself in practice where economic, cultural and symbolic capital are concerned. According to Helena Webster (2010), Bourdieu's concept of *habitus* is paramount to understanding the appropriation of cultural capital by social classes. In fact, it is argued here that *habitus* is the main responsible factor in creating the distinctions between social classes.

Bourdieu's concept of *habitus* facilitates a sociological understanding of the bourgeois French educational system. This provided privilege to the *haute bourgeoisie* by equipping the offspring of the elite with skills necessary for cultural capital accumulation, whilst isolating and discouraging other groups. But more importantly, Bourdieu's *habitus* proves the existence of uncontested attributes which are passed on from generation to generation within the same class system, and which ultimately differentiate the social classes. Up to postmodern times, education alone would not have sufficed for the acquisition of a complete and socially recognised cultural capital. This is why, beginning with the nineteenth century, the bourgeoisie felt the need to legitimate themselves by ostentatious mimicry and overcompensation for the cultural conditioning and limitations of their class.

Furthermore, Bourdieu (1984) observes that the aristocracy has mastered the ease and naturalness of inherited manners, the passage of time proving to be essential in authenticity of taste. By contrast, Bourdieu (1984:312) defines the *haute bourgeoisie* through adjectives such as 'up-tight' and 'stuffed-shirt'. In fact, due to the conscious efforts of the bourgeoisie to replace the aristocracy within the class system, including attempts to appropriate its aesthetic taste, the bourgeois manifestation of the aesthetic disposition and associated cultural values remained 'self-conscious' (Bourdieu 1984:208), a copy unable to naturally evolve, as was the case of aristocratic taste in England, for instance. This view is congruent with Lefebvre's (1991; see Chapter 2).

Nevertheless, it is important to note that throughout Bourdieu's study, the distinction found in each class operates at a conceptual level given that, in reality, the boundaries between classes and sections of classes were already blurred in the 1970s at the time of Bourdieu's field research, and this state of affairs has dramatically accentuated since. Whilst the aristocracy's earlier-noted attributes could well be recognised historically, the French social reality proved, through the trauma suffered by this class after the events of the French Revolution, that it had never regrouped and recovered the status of a social class (Doyle 2009). Given the absence of the aristocratic social class, Bourdieu could not undertake empirical studies on the subject as he was able to in the case of bourgeois and working classes, as well as intellectuals and artists. In fact, Bourdieu (1984) considers intellectuals to be the contemporary aristocratic class of culture.

Consequently, Bourdieu (1984) assessed the distinctions found between all the studied classes against the two types of taste central to the essay: the 'pure' and the 'barbarous' taste. Webster (2010:52) observes that Bourdieu heavily criticised Kant's classic study on taste by considering that the:

> Kantian notions of 'pure' aesthetics, and its foil 'vulgar' aesthetics, were nothing more than the illusory constructions of a cultural elite, which had the effect of reifying the distinction between the dominant and the dominated groups in society. Bourdieu followed this accusation with an attack on intellectuals [the aristocracy of culture] for their self-serving complicity with this situation.

At this point, one of the subtle differences between the French and German Enlightenment principles regarding the function of art must be highlighted, as it significantly contributes to concluding arguments. If, for Diderot, the French Enlightenment's main art critique exponent, art should be made accessible and target the masses in an educational manner, for Kant the appreciation of art through sublimation of senses and forgoing of ordinary considerations, such as pleasure, is paramount. This continuous cultivation of taste by the elite, disregarding popularisation of taste, led and imposed cultural standards. Although Bourdieu's work is generally in greater kinship with Diderot's than with Kant's in this respect, Bourdieu has been criticised for not taking into account the importance of popular culture. Moreover, Bourdieu contradicted his own attack against Kant by valuing the dominant taste of an elite over popular taste (see Webster 2010). However, rather than bringing criticism to Bourdieu's stance on taste (on this subject, see also Bourdieu & Saint-Martin 1976), it is argued here that this contradiction constitutes further support for the argument that the Enlightenment itself, through some of its principles and ideas, generated confusion regarding taste. Finally, by extending the appreciation of art to all other forms of cultural production and practices, and by taking into consideration the mechanism elites used to impose their domination (see 'symbolic violence' in Weber 2001), Bourdieu's work ultimately explains the self-legitimation of the bourgeois class, reinforcing and perpetuating a political discourse based on the events of the French Revolution.

The French Revolution and its cultural heritage

To achieve a better understanding of the views informing the book's theoretical background, the conceptual context of the French Revolution, and the modern nationalism associated with it, must be outlined next, since these underpin the book's arguments. What follows is a brief overview of the principal analysts and various theories covering the French Revolution and its sociopolitical and economic reverberations until present times. Fieldwork research and evidence revealed that the cultural heritage associated with the French Revolution is in dissonance with the cultural heritage defining Marie Antoinette's historical character, the two impinging on each other. A central argument here, then, concerns the mechanisms behind the manipulation, for nationalist purposes, of cultural heritage, including the French Revolution itself as well as the monarchic tradition embodied by the Bourbon dynasty of the Ancien Régime, in particular the last ruling couple: Louis XVI and Marie Antoinette.

Due to the event's historiographical complexity – directly linked to the contrasting left and right ideologies in France – what is commonly acknowledged as the 'orthodox' tradition of the French Revolution historiography consists of the views of 'a cohort of leftist writers including Jean Jaurès, Albert Mathiez, Georges Lefebvre and Albert Soboul' (Davies 2006:3). This canon has, in Peter Davies's view, hijacked what is known as the 'Great Tradition' of the political, right-winged Third Republic's historical discourse. This is a direct reflection of the 1930s political crisis in France, when the political movements of the left challenged the structures underpinning Republican legitimacy.

The dogmatism of this view was contested by soft and hard revisionist theories, which were in turn expanded on by post-revisionist historical discourses, further classifiable into various other categories. William Doyle (1980), one of the key hard-revisionist figures amongst the plethora of French Revolution historians, offered an overview of this complex situation, analysing the developments in the historiography and research of the event since 1939, the year marking a crucial change in the perception of its origins and interpretations.

Lefebvre's *Quatre-Vingt-Neuf* (1939) triggered this shift whilst still remaining one of the most important classic 'orthodox' studies of the French Revolution, whose origins the Marxist author attributes to the rise of the bourgeoisie. However, with the changes brought by World War II to European and American political ideologies, the 1950s saw the emergent rewriting of a far more complex history than previously perceived (see also Cobban 1964). But, as Doyle (1980:1; see also Doyle 2002; Kafker & Laux 1989) established, there is still no clear conclusion, and 'to close the case on the origins of the French Revolution [would be] an impossible task in any event.'

Roger Chartier's (1991) political-philosophical history of the French Revolution reassesses the origins and confirms the intricacy of the phenomenon (see also Baker & Kaplan 1991). This essay is one of the French Revolution's bicentenary re-evaluations of the direct links between the eighteenth-century cultural sphere and the political arena. In reviewing Daniel Mornet's (1933) assessment of the Enlightenment's implications for the French Revolution, Chartier raises new questions which, if extensively answered, would support the present view on the manipulation and even 'invention' of the event by certain political groups. This is in line with similar American and English hard-revisionist scholarship such as Baker's (1990) or the critical review of the Republic and the Terror as depicted by Simon Schama (1989). Nevertheless, one of the most daringly challenging analyses (Furet & Ozouf 1989) came from French academia around the bicentenary. The views of François Furet (with Richet 1973; 1978; see also Dalberg-Acton 2000), who is considered the most notable French hard-revisionist author, and Mona Ozouf, were criticised by Marxists (see Nora 2011a; Blanning 1986, 1987) for minimising the role of the French Revolution and denying the role played by the class struggle in the course of the events (Kates 1997). However, given that Furet, in particular, drifted from Marxism to hard-revisionism because of his disillusionment with Communism (which in his view is the twin of Fascism), it could be argued that his work benefits from a wide range of political insights rather than being based on one political stance.

American historians Keith Michael Baker (1987a, 1987b, 1992, 1993, 1994), also a hard-revisionist, and Steven Laurence Kaplan (1995), have since brought considerable contributions to the subject. Furthermore, regarding the political context of the bicentenary, Davies (2006:170) observes that François Mitterand's 1981–1995 presidency succeeding a lengthy governmental supremacy of the Conservative right, had 'self-consciously aligned itself with the revolutionary legacy of the 'rights of man' and the triptych, *'liberté, egalité, fraternité'*. This confirms the appropriation of the French Revolution's cultural heritage by both right and left movements, each selecting and emphasising the aspects best suited to its respective political discourse.

Based on his review of the main theoretical stances vis-à-vis the event, Bailey Stone (2002) attributes to the French Revolution a beneficial role in universal history. Nevertheless, Stone (2002:266) acknowledges that it represents 'a "transitional upheaval" in the history of modern sociopolitical revolutions' through a cataclysmic link between the English and American Revolutions of the seventeenth and eighteenth centuries, respectively, and the twentieth-century Russian and Chinese Communist Revolutions. Stone's point of view further supports the present argument concerning the 'legitimised' violence instilled by the French Revolution into the modern political arena. Furthermore, from the perspective of historical discourse continuity, all interpretations of the French Revolution adhere to views of the event either as a violent break with the past or as a natural historical progression. Martyn Lyons (1994 cited in Stone 2002:259) declared, with reason, that 'The French Revolution [. . .] was a "decisive historical rupture" that placed Louis XVI and his eventual successor, Napoleon I, in "totally different spheres"' (see also Mason & Rizzo 1999).

Contemporary readings of the event also benefit from notable French and American scholarship, particularly stemming from feminist studies aiming to illustrate the violent, anti-feminist traits of the French Revolution (Rendall 1984; Pateman 1988; Landes 1988; Fraisse 1989; Marrand-Fouquet 1989; Outram 1989). Concerned, in a more general context, with re-writing traditional historical discourses, American academic Lynn Hunt (1989, 1991, 1992, 1993, 2004; see also Fort 1991; Appleby et al. 1994; Revel & Hunt 1995) has extensively analysed revolutionary propaganda and the actual unfolding of events.

In contrast, and drawing from further current contributions to elucidating the real dimensions of the French Revolution (Wasserstrom et al. 2000; Burrows 2006; Fureix 2005; Brown 2006; Pastorello 2010), recent scholarship (Armenteros et al. 2008; Edelstein 2009) seeks alternative interpretations to the Jacobin thought and action during the Reign of Terror. This line of theoretical enquiry sets out to rehabilitate even controversial actors such as Maximilien Robespierre and radical ideals of the French Revolution, which suggests that the field is far from reaching agreement on the interpretation of events.

Concerning the historical rehabilitation of Louis XVI and Marie Antoinette, Jöel Félix's (2006) study, focused on the roles and attributions of the royal couple, successfully assesses issues generated by political forces leading up to and operating during the Revolution. Importantly, Félix is among the authors currently aiming to objectively review (and thus rehabilitate) the French dissonant past.

Lastly, amongst the array of conservative to liberal political positions assessing the events of the Revolution, Edmund Burke's (O'Brien 1986; see also Macleod 1998) insights are particularly visionary. The eminent Irish political thinker, statesman and parliamentarian is considered the classical founder of the Conservative political discourse on the French Revolution (Kafker & Laux 1989), despite having been a liberal thinker himself. This is because authors who regard the event as a negative break with the earlier dynastic and religious traditions are considered to have adopted a conservative view, whilst the liberal stance implies that the event is a progressive, beneficial step into modernity. The value of Burke's discourse lies in his acute perception of the historical rift between the dynastic and religious traditions triggered by the French Revolution. Burke, in comparing and contrasting the English and French Revolutions, noted that the former preserved, whilst the latter destroyed, 'key elements of the past' (Davies 2006:11).

Burke expressed particular concern for the fate of Marie Antoinette, who became the victim not only of violent attacks in the written press but also of an attempted murder during the storming of the Palace of Versailles in October 1789. Burke's ardent speech for the protection of the Queen of France placed the Irish political thinker under much criticism, ultimately undermining his credibility. In fact, it was Burke's defence of Marie Antoinette that led to his discourse being criticised as subjective, despite its undeniable coherence and value (see Blakemore & Hembree 2001). This criticism provides evidence for the considerable impact French public opinion had on the international perception of Marie Antoinette.

Public opinion's decisive role leading up to the French Revolution has been previously described via the theory of print capitalism and the construction of the paper image of the queen through revolutionary pamphlets. Where revolutionary propaganda is concerned, recent studies have begun to acknowledge the pivotal role played by Marie Antoinette in the evolution of events by her mere existence as an Austrian female figure in the political arena (generating continuous attacks in the press against the monarchy itself). Furthermore, the impossibility of assessing the French Revolution and its agenda without taking into consideration its connections to Marie Antoinette is now also recognised (Berly 2011). Susan Lanser (2003) also points out an as-yet unmet objective – in American academia – to place Marie Antoinette within a new historiography of the French Revolution.

Finally, it must be clarified that, despite all of the above-noted controversy surrounding the French Revolution, debate is confined largely to academic circles, whilst the heritage of the event still constitutes the basis of the French national identity. In fact, this identity which was crystallised by the Third Republic – with its 'traditions' deeply seated in the French collective memory – corresponds to modern nationalism, which itself has its roots in the French Revolution.

The context of modern nationalism: A rehabilitative history narrative

The theoretical context of modern nationalism can be found in Ernest Gellner's (1993a, 1993b) theory which considers nationalism to be a necessary pre-condition to nations and nation states. The main counterargument to this is Josep R. Llobera's (1996) theory of primordialist nationalism, which considers nationalism to occur through natural, cultural conditioning. The aim is not to delve into an exhaustive analysis of theories of nationalism, nor to assess the pros and cons of opposing theories; however, it is Gellner's theory around which gravitate all the nationalist theories considered here. Modern nationalism – later to be copied or adapted – was instilled by the French Revolution which, in replacing the old order of monarchical institutions, subsequently triggered the first major shift in the historical discourse away from religious and dynastic traditions.

From this perspective, it is irrelevant whether nationalism is forcedly inculcated through indoctrination or occurs through natural, cultural conditioning. The following analysis does not contradict the above opposing theories where its own arguments are concerned, benefitting in fact from the objectivity of widely accepted views concerning the modern nationalism originating in the events of the French Revolution. The fact that the successful creation of modern national identities was ultimately determined by the

French Revolution supports this. Furthermore, the analysis below leans on mechanisms which all theories (Hobsbawm 1983; Nora 1984–1992; Anderson 1991) underpinning the theoretical background agree on.

Gellner's views best synthesise the nationalist position argued here, this author being one of the leading anthropological modernist analysts of nationalism (Hall 1998). Anderson and Hobsbawm, whose theories were previously outlined in this chapter, subscribe to the idea of modern identities germinating from nationalism. If Hobsbawm's views are in line with Gellner's, Anderson's theory complements and enhances this theoretical position by attributing the process of 'creation' not to 'artificiality' but to 'imagination'.

The 'artificiality' of national identities is a topic on which nationalist studies stand divided in two opposing positions: the anthropological primordialist theory claiming natural origins for nationalism, and Gellner's modernist theory sustaining its artificiality. The latter is criticised (Hall 1998:3) as too modernist, optimistic and 'at a more formal philosophical level, [. . .] having a too instrumental view of human motivation and [. . .] relying excessively on functionalist argumentation'. This criticism is convincingly called into question by more persuasive theories, namely, those of Nora (1984–1992) and Hobsbawm (1983). Primordialist theory is nonetheless also cited here for helping in determining the convergence points that reinforce the modernist arguments.

Llobera (1996:xiii), one of Gellner's and Hobsbawm's main critics with regard to their hypotheses on the artificiality of modern national identities, admits that the French Revolution, 'the single most important historical event in terms of nationalist effects [. . .] is a nationalist watershed and marks a frontier of no return'. Furthermore, Llobera (1996:218) acknowledges that 'it is difficult to imagine what its [the nation's] future would have been without the French Revolution and its aftermaths.' Also, Llobera (1996:103) does not criticise but in fact supports Anderson's theory of 'print capitalism', the major factor responsible for the imagined character of the nation.

Gellner (1993a) reinforces the idea that national identities are constructed and chosen rather than already existent, which logically segues into the idea that nationalism determines nations, rather than vice versa, as maintained by the primordialist theory (Hall 1998:2). The artificial construction of national identity implies that high culture (Kant 1781) imposes itself from the top, replacing/displacing the 'previous complex structure of local groups, sustained by folk cultures' (Gellner 1993a:57).

Gellner (1993a:124) further considers that 'nationalist ideology suffers from pervasive false consciousness. Its myths invert reality: it claims to defend folk culture while in fact it is forging a high culture; it claims to protect an old folk society while in fact helping to build up an anonymous mass society.' In fact, Gellner (1993a) explains how high culture reinvents low culture, nationalist ideology sustaining a self-deception from which it nevertheless draws strength. When analysing the power of nationalism, Gellner (1993a) concludes that, it stems precisely from the artificial and forced construction of national identities. Although Llobera is the advocate of an uncontested mediaeval heritage of the modern nation states, he does indirectly support Gellner's idea in his analysis of the construction of Western national identities after 1870.

It is precisely this artificiality of national identities which elucidates the paradox of the Enlightenment highlighted in the Introduction. This paradox of modernity can be explained through the nature of the modern nation state, whose birth is attributed to the French Revolution. In fact, this paradox applies to a far deeper and wider context than could perhaps be perceived at a first glance: not only was the Enlightenment embraced by royalty, aristocracy and middle-classes alike, having led to the conflictual situation signalled above, but it also generated, through some of its idealized and politically untested notions, the core problem of later totalitarian regimes in Europe.

This propagation was indirectly achieved, firstly, through the French Revolution's adaptation and interpretation of the Enlightenment's ideals (Priestland 2010) and, secondly, through the nineteenth-century Enlightenment-inspired Romanticism and its contradictions (Llobera 1996; Gellner 1993b), which in turn served as a starting point for the ideology of Fascism. It should be stressed that French (McMahon 2001) and German Enlightenment are quite different in terms of key concepts and subsequent political consequences (see Gadamer 2004).

Paul Ricoeur (2004:308) also emphasises the paradox of modernity, modernity which in fact 'has gone a long way in defining itself in opposition to itself. Along this trajectory, Germany and France occupy very different positions, the great break occasioned by the French Revolution prolonging itself in a rupture on the level of mores and taste.'

Burke (O'Brien 1986) intuited as early as 1790 that the French Revolution, in the name of some theoretical Enlightenment principles, led to an irreparable calamity. We must also recognise and underline the lack of clarity – in terms of political translation – evidenced by Enlightenment ideals. Consequently, when confronted with historical reality, these ideals manifested their political weakness and fell prey to the ideatic degeneration triggered by the French Revolution and the violent precedent it set.

Referring to the increasingly degenerating distortion of ideas since the time of the Enlightenment, Gellner (1993b) makes it abundantly clear that Enlightenment ideals of equality – which during the time of the Enlightenment itself operated mostly at a cultural and social level – would degenerate in the following centuries through political interpretation. Ideals such as the return to humanity's roots left certain ethnic groups in a conundrum regarding which roots to choose (see also Heuer 1998). As a result, during the twentieth century, these groups became the target of either racial purification, as in the case of Nazism, or of forced displacement enacted by Communism.

France's dissonant past

Finally, a literature review of the main French authors attempting a rehabilitation of the past, dissonant from the Republican agenda's portrayal of French history, is necessary not least because France's dissonant past is at the root of the contemporary commodification of Marie Antoinette's historical character which has been detected through field research at the Petit Trianon. Amongst the most notable authors to initiate the effort to rehabilitate France's dissonant past are the contributors to *Les lieux de mémoire* (Nora 1984–1992). These are classified below along with recent contributions to the subject based on criteria underpinned by Hobsbawm's theory on the three avenues used by the late nineteenth-century political elites in the manipulation of cultural heritage for nationalist purposes. Nora's explicit approval of Hobsbawm's idea (see also Nora 2011a) is fully reflected in the structure of his most prominent work.

The first of Hobsbawm's three main paths devised for the successful invention of traditions was the manipulation of education in the formation of the future population of France. Nora dedicated a whole section to this important manipulative process in his first edited publication on *les lieux de mémoire*, namely, *La République* (see Ory 1984a; Nora 1984c, 1984d; Ozouf & Ozouf 1984; Marie 1984).

The second avenue signalled by Hobsbawm concerns the creation of new ceremonials and commemorations, also noted in Nora's publication (see Goulemot & Walter 1984; Amalvi 1984; Ory 1984b; Ageron 1984). At a later stage, Mona Ozouf (1988) contributed work on the festivals devised by French revolutionaries with the aim of replacing Christian/monarchic tradition. Such festivals inspired the Third Republic's own forged traditions. The invention of traditions in turn provided the abstract symbols – the national flag (Girardet 1984), revolutionary calendar (Baczko 1984) and national anthem (Vovelle 1984) – necessary to make acceptable the breakaway of French history from its past.

Hobsbawm's third avenue of successful national-identity creation refers to monuments and their general use by the new nineteenth-century European elite to strengthen their image and secure legitimation. The most important monuments reflecting the French Third Republic's need to identify with the revolutionary past include the Panthéon (Ozouf 1984), the *Mairie* office buildings in all French towns (Agulhon 1984), and national monuments to the dead (Prost 1984; Ben-Amos 1984).

Jean-Yves Andrieux (2011) is another notable French heritage author who recently compiled an edition of articles concerning the manipulation of cultural heritage (from written language to architecture) by the European nineteenth-century political elite. Andrieux's selected articles reflect the paradox of modernity – self-construction based on denial of the immediately preceding period, coupled with a reinvention of cultural identity based on new nationalistic ideologies.

Dominique Poulot (see 1997, 1998a) is an established academic figure of high visibility in francophone academic circles for his overt efforts to rehabilitate France's dissonant cultural heritage. In Poulot's (1998b) article 'Versailles, lieu de mémoire' (paraphrasing Nora's 'places of memory'), the author dispels from the start the popular misconception that the palace was a site of class-based social exclusion during the Ancien Régime. For instance, access to the king and queen was far easier then than it would be today to gain access to the president at the Elysée Palace.

The initiative to dismantle history and popular culture myths, about both the Ancien Régime and the French Revolution's real parameters, is found in Jean Sévillia's (2010, pers. comm. 2011) work aimed at the wider public. Journalist and editor for *Le Figaro*, this author also contributed a rehabilitative piece (Sévillia 2006) in the special issue of the magazine dedicated to Marie Antoinette for the release of Coppola's film (*Le Figaro* 2006). Although the issue did not appear as an effort to balance the image induced by the media launch of the movie, Sévillia (pers. comm. 2017) believes that the historical inaccuracies of the film have been rectified by the issue.

From a heritage perspective, the aforementioned authors deal with a case of dissonant heritage directly related to the concept of counter-memory, to which Nora (1984) specifically dedicated a part of his publication. Jean-Clément Martin (1984), dealing with counter-memory stemming from the events of the French Revolution, refers to the region of La Vendée. In fact, Martin (2006, 2007, 2010, 2011) is one of the French historians to devote extensive analysis to the violence of the French Revolution. However, as a French Revolution historian, the author finds himself obliged to partially justify that same violence as necessary to maintaining the French Revolution's status as the legitimate founding myth for the French Republic. As shown earlier, the official Republican discourse is prone to explaining and justifying such massacres as ultimately necessary.

Dissonant heritage is one of the most sensitive political, cultural and social issues which authorities in charge of conveying the heritage narrative of 'places of memory' must resolve. More complex than conflict heritage (Uzzell 1989a, 1989b; Uzzell & Ballantyne 2008; Forbes et al. 2009), dissonant heritage is defined by John Tunbridge and Gregory Ashworth (1996) as the discordance or lack of agreement and consistency regarding the meaning of heritage. The general conflict generated in such circumstances lies in the differences between an official discourse – or 'authorised heritage discourse' (Smith 2006) – and a minority's narrative (usually found imprinted in the collective memory of that particular group) or between the contrasting historical discourses of various political regimes. It is however the dominant ideology's discourse which has the ultimate authority over the heritage interpretation of a site of national value. The works of Ashworth and Peter Larkham (1994) and Brian Graham et al. (2000) illustrate the manipulation to which cultural heritage was subjected due to nationalist ideologies and the contemporary repercussions of this process on heritage interpretation.

A crucial aspect of dissonant heritage relevant to the analysis here, and which leads Tunbridge and Ashworth's (1996) analysis of dissonance,[3] was condensed by Graham et al. (2000) as the zero-sum characteristics of heritages. More recently, Graham and Howard (2008a:3) further emphasised the initial contribution of the original two authors, summarising that 'dissonance arises because of the zero-sum characteristics of heritages, all of which belong to someone and logically, therefore, not to someone else'. This 'zero-sum' trait is tested in later chapters, with intellectual authorship attributed to Tunbridge and Ashworth (1996), whilst adapting the term used by Graham et al. (2000) to the research focus here. Indeed, one of the key findings of the research is that the cultural heritage of Marie Antoinette impinges on the cultural heritage of the French Revolution and vice versa, an apt example of the zero-sum trait. Further, the dissonant heritage theory (Tunbridge & Ashworth 1996) was chosen over other more recent theories on problematic heritage (with a variety of terms having developed: e.g. 'difficult heritage', see Macdonald 2009) due to its considerations on how dissonant heritage relates to heritage commodification, an important topic discussed in Chapter 7.

Laurence Gouriévidis' (2010) heritage analysis of the Highland Clearances further supports the points above on dissonance in relation to heritage interpretation through a review of various interpretations given to this traumatic event. The dominant discourses reflecting different perspectives confirm the vital role played by the dominant political ideology of a nation in heritage interpretation. Particularly relevant to the present research, and supporting it with further evidence, is the fact that the collective memory of a nation is imbued with notes of the official discourse of history. Furthermore, dissonant narratives can only be found within the confines of the collective memory of certain minority groups, and require collection by rehabilitative history researchers working towards making these stories known (see the Popular Memory Group in Olick et al. 2011). In exceptional cases (see the Petit Trianon), such expert knowledge could hint at alternatives to official discourse through carefully considered heritage interpretations (see Chapter 5).

Finally, it must be stressed that the main authors, whose work carved out a path for the rehabilitation of various debated historical periods and characters, were Nora (1984–1992, 2011a, 2011b, 2013), Todorov (1995, 2009) and Ricoeur (2004). Nevertheless, Halbwachs' (1980, 1992) analysis of the French collective memory remains the definitive work in this particular field, serving as the cornerstone for theoretical frameworks of numerous subsequent studies. It was his posthumously published study that marked a definite contrast with the previous era's perception of the past, of its history and memory.

In conclusion, this section of the book has illuminated the mechanisms of manipulation through which the nationalist elites of the nineteenth century secured political hegemony. It also clarifies the wider context of the evolution of 'places of memory' along the historical course of late nineteenth-century history. As it has been demonstrated, nationalism developed its own imagined or invented traditions through the abusive appropriation and manipulation of the old order's values by the new political elite. This theoretical background is required for an understanding of the differing agendas (which originate in the relationship between heritage and power) underlying the four major narratives of the book. In analysing these theories, the historical, cinematic, architectural and heritage narratives of Marie Antoinette and the Petit Trianon are understood in the context of the manipulation of cultural heritage by national identities, a process at the root of the contemporary heritage commodification of Marie Antoinette's historical character at the Petit Trianon.

Notes

1 For the English version, see Nora (1996–1998). Throughout the present book, I have used the French version, in my own translation.
2 Here, 'imagination' refers to Anderson's idea of the solidarity of a group as created by imagining the existence of other members belonging to the same group, but even more specifically to a form of imagination which created the perceived conflict between Marie Antoinette and the 'French people'. As such, the 'threat to the French nation' posed by the 'infamous' queen implied by the pamphlets' messages, was the basis of a strong, adverse public opinion. Thus, my analysis extends Anderson's 'imagination' in creating the nation to an explicit consideration of this process as causing an effect on the members of a group by forging a solidarity reaction against the 'enemy'. One of the main manipulation techniques perfected by twentieth-century totalitarian regimes was the creation by the political elite of an 'imaginary enemy' which, once targeted and depersonalised, would facilitate the solidarity of the masses in a common cause. This was the case with the 'Jewish threat' to Nazi Germany, or the 'enemy of class fight' in Communist Russian politics. For Hobsbawm's notes on the cohesion created through an 'imaginary enemy', see Hobsbawm (1983); for the role played by rumours as one of the most powerful media forms, see Kapferer (1990); for the particular French context referred to in the book, see Renard (2010).
3 In the authors' discussion, a very important issue generated by dissonance lies in the sphere of cultural property; for various stances on the subject, see also Carman (2005); Greenfield (2007); Fairclough et al. (2008); Cuno (2009) and Gillman (2010).

2 'Places of memory' anchored in postmodernity

In contrast to the historical analysis of the evolution and symbolically acquired value of 'places of memory' developed in the previous chapter, here Pierre Nora's views on the commemorative trait of 'places of memory' are scrutinised whilst linking the term with other theories which provide conceptual anchorage in the present. This is achieved by providing the means to read, decode and ultimately interpret 'places of memory' politically and culturally by taking into consideration the new 'class' of place appropriation: the postmodern visitors. This analysis is given here as theoretical background and literature review for the process of heritage commodification detected through field research at the Petit Trianon.

In addition to Nora's analysis, the chapter provides a key to the understanding of the Petit Trianon as a 'place of memory' through a 'reading' and 'decoding' of its inscribed messages, informed by Henri Lefebvre's (1991) philosophical views on the production and interpretation of space. The theory of political appropriation present in Lefebvre's work recommends him over other authors for the purposes of this study and is complemented by John Urry's (1990, 2002) classic analysis of tourism, focused on the concept of the 'tourist romantic gaze'. Despite critiques that the 'gaze' is not representative of tourism's primary drivers, this theory is incorporated into the following analyses, as it represents the main factor responsible for the appropriation of places which are highly popular with the contemporary tourist. A process of 'absorption' mediates the appropriation, enabled by photographic devices and the equivalent psychological and subliminal 'appropriation' in which tourists engage. Imagination plays a decisive role in appropriation, as Chapter 6 reveals.

It is considered here that the image is responsible for globalised contemporary tourism, a consideration which complements the theories on space appropriation underpinning the analysis. From this theoretical standpoint, the development of the 'romantic gaze' theory feeds into the explanation of the postmodern paradox of uncontrolled image multiplication. Through the individual appropriation of images, tourists and the public in general are now able to devise their own interpretation of someone else's private material, released publicly with no clear explanation of its true meanings (see Chapter 7).

The last part of the chapter concludes the theoretical background of the book by developing a classification of the postmodern range of sites based primarily on two criteria of distinction: heritage authenticity and the 'tourist romantic gaze'. Whereas the former determines a certain differentiation between sites considering their intrinsic value, the latter concerns the extrinsic level of their perception by the majority of visitors. The heritage authenticity definition from Gregory Ashworth and Peter Howard (1999) was chosen over other types of authenticity, such as the form of existential authenticity detected by tourism studies (Cohen 1972, 1979), because of its correspondence to principles adopted by the heritage authorities in charge of the Petit Trianon's interpretation and its 2008 restoration (see also Chapter 5).

Commemorating *les lieux de mémoire*

To begin with, Nora's analysis of 'places of memory', in conjunction with national commemorative issues informing the theoretical background of the book, expose definite symptoms of the present-day crisis stemming from the incongruence between French national identity and the cultural heritage upon which it was built. Confirming these symptoms, as Nora (1984a) points out, are 'places of memory' and their very nature, which essentially consist of attempts to ritualise a society without rituals and introduce fleeting moments of sacredness into a world bereft of sacred dimension.

The multitude of manifestations assumed by 'places of memory' ranges from material to symbolic. To name just a few, they can be museums, archives, cemeteries, various collections, festivals and anniversaries; the main trait that links them all resides in what became the current phenomenon of registering, cataloguing and ultimately commemorating (Nora 1984a).

The commemorative trait is a very important factor in explaining the existence of 'places of memory' today, as there exists a direct relationship between the two: an increase in commemoration determines the loss of the authentic historical value of a 'place of memory', thus giving it its absolute form as a place dedicated to memory as opposed to a historical place. This view subscribes to British theories (Hewison 1987) of heritage seen as freezing the natural course of historical evolution by overpowering historical places.

As a result of the commemorative trait, Nora (1984a:XXIII) considers that the study of 'places of memory' finds itself at the intersection of two main movements, one of a reflexive history and the other of a purely historical nature, the latter, however, depicting the end of the tradition of history read as memory. This situation leads to a reconstituted history materialised in a very 'solid' idea of heritage – equating with tangible heritage – which is nevertheless representative of a distant past that translates only into symbols today.

Commemoration through the 'solid' idea of heritage determines monumentality. Anderson (1991) observes that modern monuments are in fact

'Places of memory' in postmodernity   31

intrinsically linked with nationalism, due to its transcendental claims replacing religion at the end of the eighteenth century. For Lefebvre (1991), the value of monumental space – entirely representative of the society which produced it – can be further expanded through processes specific to psychoanalysis and linguistics.

Furthermore, the increasing tendency of contemporary society towards this 'commemorative' dimension indicates a real need to accurately interpret messages conveyed by the past. One of the main characteristics of 'places of memory' is what Nora (1984a:XXXV) describes as their 'Moebius strip' quality, a perpetual reinforcing of symbols through their very own symbology. However, since 'places of memory' are also able to generate another history – their own – there is danger of self-perpetuation, which could thus create images increasingly distanced and, eventually, dissonant from the symbol which they would have related to in the first place (see Chapter 7). In this context, the Petit Trianon, as home to Marie Antoinette, represents a symbol yet to be decoded so that its original history may be told, along with an accurate story of its former owner.

For a possible reading of this space and the messages originally inscribed within, Nora's theory of 'places of memory' is applied to the Petit Trianon by considering that the absolute form of this historical architectural context is defined as the home to Marie Antoinette. This argument further uses Lefebvre's (1991) philosophical views on the spatial triad of space.

The production of space

This section focuses on Lefebvre's explanation of the production of space from a political and cultural perspective in order to facilitate the understanding of all the past and present parameters defining the space of the Petit Trianon. Lefebvre's spatial triad model and the consequent effects of this interpretation, presented below, are the main elements selected from this classic essay to further expand the book's theoretical foundation.

According to Lefebvre's (1991) spatial triad, there are three main adjacent values of social space: the 'spatial practice', or 'perceived' space; the 'representation of space', or 'conceived space'; and the 'representational space', or 'lived space'. The 'perceived space' is defined through the 'spatial practice' (Lefebvre 1991:38) of 'a society [which] secretes that society's space [. . .]. From the analytic standpoint, the spatial practice of a society is revealed through the deciphering of its space.' The 'representation of space' or the 'conceived space' (Lefebvre 1991:38) is the 'conceptualised space, the space of scientists, planners, urbanists, technocratic subdividers and social engineers, as of a certain type of artist with a scientific bent'. Thirdly, the 'representational space' or 'lived space', consists of (Lefebvre 1991:38–39):

> the space as directly *lived* through its associated images and symbols, and hence the space of 'inhabitants' and 'users', but also of some artists and

perhaps of those, such as a few writers and philosophers, who *describe* and aspire to do no more than describe. This is the dominated – and hence passively experienced – space which the imagination seeks to change and appropriate. It overlays physical space, making symbolic use of its objects.

According to the above, today the heritage site of Petit Trianon is a 'representational space'. Therefore, in analysing and interpreting the contemporary heritage site of the Petit Trianon, it is important to constantly refer back to the qualities associated with 'representational space'. However, the main indicator of the analysis – the architectural context of Petit Trianon at the time of its creation as home to Marie Antoinette – has evolved in essence from a social space to an absolute space. This clear distinction is paramount in understanding the comparative analysis of the four key narratives of this book: historical, cinematic, architectural and heritage.

When defining 'absolute space', Lefebvre (1991:236) makes a clear distinction between the dimensions of such a space and those of the 'abstract (or Euclidean) space'. By analysing the concept within the history of Western culture, Lefebvre (1991:238) notices that in this context 'the absolute space has assumed a strict form: that of volume carefully measured, empty, hermetic, and constitutive of the rational unity of 'Logos' and 'Cosmos.' It is 'made up of sacred or cursed locations: temples, palaces, commemorative or funerary monuments, places privileged or distinguished in one way or another' (Lefebvre 1991:240).

From this perspective, the Petit Trianon as home to Marie Antoinette includes not only the cultural model of an eighteenth-century art landscape created by two of the most representative architects and artists of this era – Richard Mique and Hubert Robert – but also a royal residence. Therefore, it is an 'absolute space' reuniting two sets of codes, of art and political nature. In this light and further defining the architectural narrative (see above), the Petit Trianon becomes an indicator which does not need interpretation but rather serves as supporting evidence against which the other three narratives are assessed, in search of the objective truth.

Given the characteristics of 'absolute space', there is a clear differentiation between the ways a 'user' belonging to the 'absolute space' and its associated time will read or decode the space, and the analogous ways of tourists perceiving the same space as found today. Whereas for the former, 'time contained the spatial code and *vice versa*' (Lefebvre 1991:241), for the latter the experience is constructed mainly through the prism of an added layer of visual means. As Lefebvre (1991:96–97) observes, this modernist emphasis on visual means poses a further problem:

> One wonders just how many errors, or worse, how many lies, have their roots in the modernist trio, triad or trinity of readability-visibility-intelligibility. [. . .] Take images, for example: photographs, advertisements, films. [. . .] After its fashion, the image kills [the real space].

Emphasis should now be placed on the fact that 'Logos' and 'Cosmos', respectively narrative and space, are intrinsic to 'absolute space' but are separated in the case of 'representational space'. In order to comprehend the ways in which the historical, cinematic, architectural and heritage narratives are perceived by contemporary visitors at the Petit Trianon, it is vital to understand the essence of Lefebvre's views on the production of 'social space' in general, which hinges on the differentiation that has to be made between 'Logos' and 'Cosmos'.

Lefebvre (1991) favours the idea according to which the 'Logos', in its Western Cartesian meaning of discourse, is compromised by having evolved separately from its content and having become a superfluous structure, independent of the reality that it should transcribe. This situation enables images, signs and all manner of narratives to express their own reality, different from the intended message of the space they refer to. This idea links with further analyses in Chapters 6 (Caughey 1984) and 7 (Barthes 1972; Baudrillard 1994, 2001; Hall 1997), which reveal through the commodification of Marie Antoinette's historical character – a representation with no connection to the content – the postmodern paradox of an uncontrolled multiplication of images.

Therefore, the architectural narrative of the Petit Trianon, as defined in the form of 'absolute space', in conveying its message throughout all chronological and cultural layers subsequently added, represents the fixed marker against which other narratives must be assessed in order to arrive at a better picture of the objective truth. In turn, the historical, cinematic and heritage narratives require interpretation, as they have been separated by the initial *'true space'* (Lefebvre 1991:236) through time as well as other added layers, all of which are separately analysed by the chapters dealing with each narrative. Lefebvre's philosophical views on the political and cultural appropriation of space are complemented next by Urry's (1990, 1995, 2002) classic theory of the 'tourist romantic gaze'.

The romantic gaze

Urry's (1990, 1995, 2002) classic sociological study on the evolution of tourism over the past two centuries explains trends in tourism as well as the 'consumption' of tourist destinations. Urry's theory of the 'tourist gaze' – its 'romantic' version – presupposes conditioning by preformed images, which instils a visit anticipation of heritage sites usually in contrast to the actual visit experience. Kevin Meethan (2001) contributes valuable criticism of the limitations of the 'tourist gaze'. Urry (1992, 1999, 2002; with Larsen 2011) also revisited his own theory by acknowledging the role of the 'embodied gaze' in the perception of tourist spaces. Further studies on this subject suggest that embodiment associated to 'representation' leads to the 'non-representational' appropriation of tourist spaces (Crouch 1999, 2004, 2009, 2012).

Despite the 'gaze' not being the primary driver for contemporary tourism, it is largely responsible for the appropriation of places sought by contemporary tourists. In the case of the Petit Trianon, the 'tourist romantic gaze' (hereafter 'romantic gaze') is proven by field research to induce the dissonant commodification of Marie Antoinette's historical character (see Chapter 7). The 'romantic gaze' also helps to explain how postmodern authenticity values informed the 2008 restoration of the Petit Trianon and its heritage perspective issues (see Chapter 5).

Urry (1990) posits that organised travel for pleasure and cultural purposes goes back to Imperial Rome, although these were exclusive activities accessible only to the elite. Pilgrimages became a widespread phenomenon in the thirteenth and fourteenth centuries, combining religious purposes with the earlier cultural and leisure aspects of travelling. Urry (1990:4) observes that by the end of the seventeenth century, the 'Grand Tour had become firmly established [. . .] for the sons of the aristocracy and the gentry, and by the late eighteenth century for the sons of the professional middle class.' The nature of the Grand Tour evolved from a classical to a romantic appreciation of the spaces visited, in direct relation to the type of gaze involved. During the nineteenth century, the romantic Grand Tour was the apogee of the 'romantic gaze', which eventually became the most prominent gaze of postmodern tourism. Nevertheless, it was between 1600 and 1800 that 'treatises on travel shifted from a scholastic emphasis on touring as an opportunity for discourse, to travel as eyewitness observation' (Urry 1990:4). Starting with the end of the sixteenth century (Urry 2002:146), the visual observation in general 'came to be viewed as the basis of scientific legitimacy [. . .] [which] subsequently developed into the very foundation of the scientific method of the west, based upon sense-data principally produced and guaranteed by sight.'

The romantic connotations of the Enlightenment, which encouraged this shift, are best illustrated by a new perception of landscape in the context of travel. Furthermore, garden landscape design of the last quarter of the eighteenth century was in turn transformed by this new perception (see John Dixon Hunt 2004). This facilitates a better understanding of the context enabling the creation of the English Garden of the Petit Trianon. Moreover, the cultural importance of tourism in the perception of the Petit Trianon building is accounted for by its brief function as an *auberge* immediately after the French Revolution, and as a museum since 1867 (see Chapter 5). Nevertheless, in order to decipher the contemporary perception of the Petit Trianon and Marie Antoinette, a major factor which needs to be analysed is the effect of the shift from tourism as individual travel during earlier centuries to the mass tourism of postmodernity.

Mass tourism is, in fact, responsible for the emergence of stereotypical images, which in turn generate a certain type of visit anticipation, usually far removed from reality (Urry 1990, 1995, 2002). Not only is this 'staging' (Gottlieb 1982; MacCannell 1999; Robinson 2001; AlSayyad 2001a) deliberately created and encouraged by both tourist operators and those in charge of tourist hotspots – from indigenous populations to museum curators – but the majority of tourists seem to subconsciously *prefer* such fabrications to the genuine reality behind the image.

Although admittedly there are various categories of tourists in search of different destinations and experiences (Cohen 1972, 1979, 1988a, 1988b; MacCannell 1999; Meethan 2001), naturally opening the previous statement to debate, evidence from field research undertaken at the Petit Trianon shows this view to be valid with respect to the majority of visitors at this site. Indeed, research evidence confirms that Urry's 'romantic gaze' applies appropriately to the heritage site of the Petit Trianon, as a former royal residence associated with a notorious and highly debated historical character.[1]

Urry (2002) highlights an opposing theory (MacCannell 1999) to the above, which equates tourists with modern pilgrims engaged in a quest for authenticity equivalent to the pursuit of the sacred dimension of the religious pilgrimages of yore, sought in other times and other places. Whilst this holds true for a certain category of tourists or certain aspects of a visit, research evidence from the Petit Trianon suggests that such quests are problematic because they are ruled by an 'image' of other times and other places (see Chapter 6). This view is supported by Lefebvre's theory on the modernist trio of visibility, according to which the image kills the real space, and further reinforced by his views on appearances (versus reality; see Lefebvre 1991:96) being determined by other times and other spaces.

Nevertheless, the analogy as well as the direct link between pilgrimage and tourism cannot be ignored, as it sheds light on the process, conferring paramount importance on images in contemporary tourism. The pilgrimage trait of tourism is also particularly relevant to cultural tourism, or the visiting of heritage sites. In order to illustrate the analogy between the two cultural manifestations of pilgrimage and tourism, Urry leans on Dean MacCannell's (1999 cited in Urry 2002:10) analysis:

> [T]here is normally a process of sacralisation which renders a particular natural or cultural artefact a sacred object of the tourist ritual [. . .]. A number of stages are involved in this: naming the sight, framing and elevation, enshrinement, mechanical reproduction of the sacred object, and social reproduction as new sights (or 'sites') name themselves after the famous. It is also important to note that not only are there many attractions to which to pay homage, but many attractions are only gazed upon once. In other words, the gaze of the tourist can be amazingly fickle, searching out or anticipating something new or something different.

Urry further employs Donald Horne's theory, which also discusses this analogy, seeing tourists as modern pilgrims carrying guidebooks as devotional texts and for whom the only thing that matters is what they are told they are seeing. Moreover, Horne (1984 cited in Urry 1990:129) emphasises that the 'fame of the object [of gaze] becomes its meaning. There is thus a ceremonial agenda, in which it is established what we should see and sometimes even the order in which they should be seen.'

The search for authenticity – as a founding factor of tourism (see above references to pilgrimages) – is also contested by the view that, in fact, tourists embarking on trips mainly seek escape from the ordinary. It could be summarised that tourists consume heritage either as an 'escape to fantasy' or an 'escape to reality' (Tunbridge & Ashworth 1996:64). In line with this, it has also been argued (see Gottlieb 1982 cited in Urry 1990:11) that tourists would seek contrasting experiences to their habitual existence by an inversion of values, such as the middle-class tourist wanting to be 'peasant for a day' whilst the lower middle-class aspires to be 'king/queen for a day'. In addition, differences between the distinct 'liminal zones' of ordinary life versus holiday life lead to suspension and/or inversion of ordinary obligations.

Victor Turner and Edith Turner (1978 cited in Urry 2002:11) consider that a change in liminal boundaries encourages 'licence for permissive and playful "non-serious" behaviour'. Whilst this newly added element can link into many aspects of a holiday, from the point of view of experiencing authenticity, it offers insight into the deliberate choice made by tourists to experience inauthentic sights and sites, consciously preferring the hyper-reality induced by images to an authentic reality.[2] Umberto Eco's (1986:44) examples of Disneyland best illustrate this situation: 'Disneyland tells us that faked nature corresponds much more to our daydream demands [. . .] Disneyland tells us that technology can give us more reality than nature can.' Urry (1990:146) aptly assimilates the hyper-reality described by Eco to Debord's (1994, 1998) 'society of the spectacle' or Lowenthal's (1985/2015) observations on the 'habituation to replicas [which] tends to persuade us that antiquities should look complete and "new".'

Eco's (1986) quest for the inauthentic in the United States discovered that inauthenticity could even be preferred to authenticity. In the case of the Getty Villa museum in Los Angeles, California, for example, to reinforce a feeling of authenticity, museum professionals created period settings for original artefacts, which by nature found themselves outside their original context. (Ironically, the created settings remain whilst many of the original artefacts have returned to Italy and Greece; see Gill 2015.) Derived from Baudrillard's (1994) theory of simulacra which also informs the analysis developed in Chapter 7, Eco's theory on hyper-reality befits the present discussion.

It must be stressed that simulacra are not a safe 'reality', as the images derived from hyper-reality have complex implications for the consequent defining of spaces to be gazed upon. Analysing David Harvey's theory on 'time-space compression' (1989 cited in Urry 1995:177), which also contributes to the analysis in Chapter 7, Urry reveals that the broader changes in contemporary economic and social life were influenced by the uniformity of space brought about by the change of capitalist labour-time. Amongst the five main effects of time-space compression on contemporary society, the fourth is concerned with the fact that signs and images prevail, a worldwide industry producing and marketing images 'not only for products, but also for people, governments, places, universities and so on'. The fifth directly indicates images resulting from the time-space compression, and which involve production of simulacra.

The collapse of barriers induced by this compression of time-space accentuates the need for distinctiveness, each place striving to achieve it especially when competing with others (Urry 1995). This situation leads to propagation of simulacra at all levels, including the commodification of heritage sites, meant to increase their popularity and cultural accessibility by no longer exclusively associating with 'high culture' (Kant 1781). Moreover, even authentic sites such as the Petit Trianon are forced to consider a re-invention in order to appeal to a wider market characterised by fierce competition. In addition, the collapse of barriers is also directly linked to the 'de-differentiating' character of postmodernity itself, which works against the above-mentioned need for distinctiveness. This complicates the position of heritage sites even further, as they find themselves in need of integrating the fulfilment of visitor anticipation into their aims.

Urry (1990:83) also recognises the difficulty in addressing the topic of postmodernism (see also Featherstone 1991), since the signifier 'postmodern' seems to be 'free-floating, having few connections with anything real [and] no minimal shared meaning of any sort'. For capturing the essence of postmodernity, Urry (1990) leans on Scott Lash (1990:11) who defines the term in contrast to modernity, as 'a regime of signification whose fundamental structuring trait is "de-differentiation"'. Furthermore, the de-differentiation relates to an important observation made by Walter Benjamin (1973 cited in Urry 2002:84) on the 'anti-auratic' character of postmodernist culture, where the aura of a cultural phenomenon refers to the uniqueness which would have separated it from social aspects. Given the dissolution of all barriers, de-differentiation further implies that postmodern cultural forms are not consumed in a state of contemplation any longer, but of distraction. Moreover, postmodern culture affects audiences through immediate impact, which ultimately undermines any strong distinction between the high culture of the elites and the popular, low culture of the masses (Urry 2002).

Museums, in particular, have been affected by the anti-auratic character of postmodernity, as their aura would have distinguished them previously in their exclusive, cultural role. Postmodernity has led to a situation where museums are on a par with theme parks and shopping malls, culture and commerciality merging. Urry (2002) attributes most of the blame on the booming heritage industry (see also Hewison 1987), which is in line with Nora's theory on the commemorative trait, further discussed below.

Furthermore, Urry (2002) remarks on tourism's innate postmodern traits (the visual prominence in sightseeing and the 'spectacle' element) accentuated by postmodernism to the extent that currently, what tourists consume are representations of places and not the places themselves. This consumption of representations makes for the subject of other notable visual culture and heritage studies (Lash & Urry 1994; Selwyn 1996; Rojek 1997; Kirshenblatt-Gimblett 1998; Morgan & Pritchard 1998; Crouch 1999; Crouch & Lübbren 2003; Crouch et al. 2005; Robinson & Picard 2009b, 2009a; Waterton 2010; Watson 2010; Korstanje & George 2014). The counter-views, despite acknowledging the role of visuality, also recognise the existence of phenomenological elements in visual consumption through tourist practices, performance and identity (Edensor 2001, 2009; Meethan 2001, et al. 2006, 2011; Knudsen & Waade 2010; Selby 2010; Selwyn 2010; Crouch 2004, 2012, 2015).

The transfer phenomenon – from place to representation, which thus becomes the new object of tourism consumption – is facilitated by images. This explains the seemingly paradoxical situation of tourism reverting to the earlier, elitist form of romantic sightseeing, which Urry's theory on anticipation links with the tourists' preformed images. In testing this theory through field research at the Petit Trianon, an incongruence was revealed between preformed images stemming from tourist anticipation and the actual reality experienced. Urry's (1990:3) assessment of visit anticipation is condensed as follows:

> Places are chosen to be gazed upon because there is an anticipation, especially through daydreaming and fantasy, of intense pleasures, either on a different scale or involving different senses from those customarily encountered. Such anticipation is constructed and sustained through a variety of non-tourist practices, such as film, TV, literature, magazines, records and videos which construct and reinforce that gaze.[3]

Urry also reviews previous theories (see Campbell 1987) which consider visit anticipation to be related exclusively to contemporary consumerism. According to Colin Campbell (1987), anticipation itself provides the satisfaction which otherwise would be provided – in Urry's own theory – by the actual visit experience when it coincides with the anticipation. Nevertheless, Campbell (1987) does not deny the importance of the imagination process. He considers, as a key characteristic of modern consumption, the paramount role played by emotion which he sees as the link between mental images and physical stimuli, with imagination enabling this emotional interaction (like being in love).

Regarding visit anticipation, Urry (1990:83) stresses that the 'daydreaming is not a purely individual activity [. . .] [but] socially organised, particularly through television, advertising, literature, cinema, photography and so on.' Photography, in particular, is the element through which the transition from the romantic *flâneur* of the nineteenth century to the contemporary postmodern tourist occurs, both appropriating spaces via photographs. However, the main trait as well as the mastered art of the *flâneur*'s gaze is seeing without being seen, which arguably is not the case with the tourist gaze.

Nevertheless, it is true that photography acts in both instances as a desire to appropriate – that is, to make new sense of – the places 'gazed at'. With Charles Baudelaire considered the 'progenitor' of *flâneurism* in literature, later adapted by Walter Benjamin through an ethnography research strategy used in urban studies (Jencks & Neves 2000), the subject of the contemporary tourist seen as the romantic *flâneur* has garnered special research within visual culture and heritage and tourism studies (Tester 1994; Jokinen & Veijola 1997; Wood 2005).

In addition, for the tourist, photographs are the main incentive and determining element of the visit, prior to it taking place. Thus, photography is directly linked to the postmodern tourist gaze, by pre-conditioning it as well as fulfilling it. More recent contributions further analyse the role of photography for the 'tourist gaze' (Taylor 1994; Selwyn 1996; Crawshaw & Urry 1997; Crang 1997; Osborne 2000; Lenman 2003).

In fact, the visual practices discussed earlier 'provide the signs in terms of which the holiday experiences are understood, so that what is then seen is interpreted in terms of these pre-given categories' (Urry 1995:132). This is further explained by one of the main characteristics of the tourist gaze, which Urry draws from Jonathan Culler (1981 cited in Urry 1990:3):

> The gaze is constructed through signs, and tourism involves the collection of signs. When tourists see two people kissing in Paris what they capture in the gaze is 'timeless romantic Paris'. When a small village in England is seen, what they gaze upon is the 'real olde England'. As Culler argues: 'the tourist is interested in everything as a sign of itself [. . .]. All over the world the unsung armies of semioticians, the tourists, are fanning out in search of the signs of Frenchness, typical Italian behaviour, exemplary Oriental scenes, typical American thruways, traditional English pubs'.

As shown by the quote above, apart from signs themselves, the tourist gaze also looks for distinct elements to be drawn from unique objects, unfamiliarity, unusual contexts, unusual visual environments as well as (see Culler 1981 cited in Urry 1990:12) from:

> particular signs which indicate that a certain other object is indeed extraordinary, even if it does not seem to be so. [. . .] The attraction is not the object itself but the sign referring to it that marks it out as distinctive. Thus the marker becomes the distinctive sight.

This view has particular relevance here, as the majority of visitors at the Petit Trianon (based on the research sample), do not visit out of interest for neoclassical architecture but because of the association with Marie Antoinette. The re-naming of the site as the *Domaine de Marie-Antoinette* in 2006 aimed to capitalise on this tourist trait as further shown in Chapter 5.

40 'Places of memory' in postmodernity

When considering the 'gaze' itself, Urry (1990:83) classifies it as three pairs of a dichotomous nature: romantic/collective; authentic/inauthentic; historical/modern. It is the 'romantic gaze' which 'has become considerably more significant and is part of the mechanism by which contemporary tourism has been globalised', an increased significance facilitated by traits of postmodernity analysed earlier, in particular the prominence of images within their cultural paradigm. Although Urry (1999) later expanded this classification, the above attributes of the 'romantic gaze' remain unaffected.

The nature of this particular type of gaze places 'the emphasis [. . .] upon solitude, privacy and a personal, semi-spiritual relationship with the object of the gaze' (Urry 1990:45), thus leading to a seeming paradox of postmodern mass tourism. In fact, the situation *can* be explained through a transfer of values. This transfer theoretically aligns with the assessment of class taste by Bourdieu, Urry (1990) himself having applied Bourdieu's views in explaining social class-based differences in tourism trends. For instance, the intellectuals' 'ascetic' type of sightseeing resonates with the exclusivity of former aristocratic visiting trends, whilst the middle class is more ostentatious in its travelling and visiting habits.

However, it is argued here that the globalisation of tourism through the 'romantic gaze' does not originate from the preponderance of the intellectual or middle-class visiting public but from the very process of place appropriation via images as it applies to the majority of postmodern tourists. This argument is based on the fact that the 'romantic gaze', as Urry aptly noticed, is indeed the main agent through which tourism has become globalised. However, the exact process enabling this transformation remains relatively unclear. The evidence uncovered by the field research at the Petit Trianon (see Chapters 6 and 7) suggests that, rather than the object or the nature of the classic eighteenth-and nineteenth-century 'romantic gaze' leading to globalisation, it was the very process of place appropriation through a hijacking/requisition of images which was instrumental to the shift. It is a key finding that, whereas a certain elite would have travelled during the eighteenth and nineteenth centuries, increasingly enticed to appropriate the visited spaces through a solitary, reverie-travelling fashion to absorb the picturesque value of the visited landscape, contemporary 'absorbing' is enabled by the tourist devices of taking photographs and/or by its equivalent psychological and subliminal 'appropriation'. Furthermore, it is irrelevant whether tourists are travelling alone or in groups, to quiet or crowded spaces. What matters is the act itself of appropriation of a certain anticipated image.

Following this idea, the globalisation of contemporary tourism was made possible not by the object or nature of the 'romantic gaze' but by the image which this type of gaze would seek. Urry himself makes no clear note of the aforementioned transfer of values, although he implies it through the revision and updates of his original theory (Urry 2002). The discussion here contributes this clarification of Urry's sociological analysis: tourism, which has started in antiquity as a practice reserved to the elites for social and economic reasons and progressively became available to the masses, came to

'Places of memory' in postmodernity 41

be experienced in similar individualistic ways – on a subliminal, rather than physical level – through the mediation of images allowing the tailoring of individual anticipations. Imagination plays a decisive role in the process. To explain public perception of environments visited through the mediation of imaginary social interaction, Chapters 6 and 7 employ the theory of 'imaginary social worlds' as found in John L. Caughey (1984).

Postmodern heritage authenticity and commodification

Finally, this chapter applies the above theories to the postmodern heritage industry – whose emergence is due to the commemorative trait of 'places of memory' signalled by Nora – by classifying the range of sites spanning 360 degrees of heritage authenticity aimed at tourist consumption. As found on a self-generating cycle between authenticity and commodification of heritage (see Table 2.1), the classification of sites employs two distinction criteria. The first criterion is a heritage authenticity definition found in Ashworth and Howard (1999) in conjunction with a literature review concerning the heritage industry. This definition (see Figure 2.1) was

Table 2.1 The range of sites – spanning 360 degrees of heritage authenticity – aimed at tourist consumption

---

1. Natural heritage sites such as national parks or reserves and heritage gardens, tending to aim for authenticity respecting all sources of authority but sometimes conveying narratives superimposed onto the intrinsic value of the site to become accessible to all visitors (Tilden 1957).

2. Cultural heritage sites relying on authenticity at all levels and trying to convey it and interpret it as such; e.g. churches, cathedrals, religious and worship spaces in general (Ashworth & Howard 1999).

3. Museums possessing a great deal of authentic material displayed through traditional and New Museology methods of exhibiting; e.g. national museums, art museums, community museums, eco-museums. This category also includes historic house museums which themselves display a wide range of models, from the most authentic examples such as the Gamble House to the less faithful (see Young 2017). All of these institutions aim to attain and/or convey authenticity from the perspective of several defining meanings, as defined in Figure 2.1. On the one hand, there is a threat to the authenticity of the material or ensemble, posed by the use of new media technology and its hyper-reality effects. Museums mainly using new media displays are audience led, with participatory traits being their strength (Graham & Cook 2010). New media technology enables innovative interpretations which are nevertheless criticised for placing museums on a par with shopping malls (Urry 1995; Cuno 2004). Another common denominator for the New Museology interpretation lies in the acknowledged aim of museums to become accessible to all through an overarching communication or 'Translation' (Bhabha 1994) of their messages (Hooper-Greenhill 1992, 1995, 2004, 2007; Roberts 1997; Hein 1998; Henning 2006; Dudley 2010; see also Chapter 5). On the other hand, the manipulation of cultural heritage by nationalist,

---

(Continued)

Table 2.1 (Continued)

> ethnic and/or cultural agendas still plays an important role which cannot be ignored, since it threatens the 'concept' and 'history' authenticity principles as defined in Figure 2.1 (Vergo 1989; Karp & Lavine 1991; Walsh 1992; Karp et al. 1992; Pearce 1989, 1994, 1995; Hooper-Greenhill 1994, 1995, 2000; Kaplan 1994; Bennett 1995; Macdonald & Fyfe 1996; Barker 1999; Boswell & Evans 1999; Fladmark 2000; Dicks 2000, 2004; Crooke 2000, 2001, 2007; McLean & Cooke 2003a, 2003b; Carbonell 2004; McIntyre & Wehner 2001; Simpson 2001; Macdonald 1998, 2003, 2006; Witcomb 2003; Kreps 2003; Brocklehurst & Phillips 2004; Cuno 2004; Corsane 2005; Littler & Naidoo 2005; Watson 2007; McLean 2008; Gouriévidis 2010; Waterton 2013). Furthermore, the tendency derived from New Museology principles to evoke feelings at the expense of material authenticity leads to settings which could not be technically classifiable as museums in this category (see House of Terror in Budapest; Rátz 2006).

4   Heritage sites exuding authenticity of 'material' (Figure 2.1), such as heritage gem cities (see Ashworth & Howard 1999) or cities rich in cultural heritage. This authenticity is often in competition with – to the extent of being overshadowed by – superimposed features deriving from literary (Augé 1997; Hollis 2009), film (Beeton 2016) or other media sources; e.g. Amsterdam with its Bantjer tour, Oxford with its Detective Morse trail (Reijnders 2010); Madrid with its Cervantes Train emphasising Don Quixote as much as the author's presence (Busby et al. 2011); Bran Castle in Transylvania with its Dracula myth (Mureşan & Smith 1998).

5   Sites with less historical or architectural notoriety or value, but benefitting from outstanding natural heritage features and using cultural, artistic and historical myth connections together with literary or film tourism in a bid for increased popularity; e.g. Concarneau, which enhanced its heritage package by alluding to a built heritage connection with Vauban, the Brittany circle of artists and with the Maigret series of crime novels, such as *Le Chien Jaune* (Mansfield 2015); Cornwall with its myths, St Ives or Newlyn art circles and literary/film associations (Busby & Laviolette 2006) such as the Cornish location of Port Isaac with its history of smuggling, as well as popular television connection with *Doc Martin* (Busby & Haines 2013). These sites, even when associated with literary tourism, are different from literary places which do not have heritage value other than their connection to a literary source granting and protecting their status of cultural tourist sites (see Robinson & Andersen 2002). Nevertheless, cultural tourist sites could also be considered heritage sites according to other criteria not used here (see Herbert 2001; Fawcett & Cormack 2001).

6   Heritage sites trying to induce authenticity by depicting a certain historical period by inauthentic means (Howard 2003); e.g. Williamsburg, Virginia, the archetype model of colonial re-enactment and heritage interpretation, uses costumed guides and a carefully reconstituted setting, all inauthentic but depicting authenticity for educational reasons.

7   Heritage Centres – a hybrid between heritage sites and theme parks; e.g. Wiggan Pier in UK (Urry 1995) – mainly combining the authenticity of the 'function', 'concept' and 'history' (Figure 2.1), nevertheless packaged in commodified form for tourist consumption.

8   Theme Parks (Davis 1996; Hollinshead 2009) authentic from the perspective of 'function' and 'concept' (Figure 2.1), but using inauthentic materials to depict certain heritage elements; e.g. Disneyland (Eco 1986; Fjellman 1992; Zukin 1993; Marling 1997; Byrne & McQuillan 1999) with its 'Sleeping Beauty' castle, inspired in part by Viollet le Duc's restoration of Carcasonne castle (Binh 2010), and by another nineteenth-century mediaeval re-invention, Neuschwanstein in Bavaria. Viollet le Duc's nineteenth-century restoration ethics are questionable in terms of heritage authenticity values (Jokilehto 1999) as shown by his 1864 restoration of Notre-Dame under the influence of Victor Hugo's 1831 novel (Hollis 2009), later adapted in film (see *The Hunchback of Notre-Dame* 1911, 1923, 1939, 1956, 1986), including by Disney (1996). Nevertheless, theme parks such as Disney's catering to the heritage of childhood tales spanning generations are arguably as authentic as any other fairy tales of the past, both instances embodying aspects of cultural heritage. Another notable type of theme park comprises those models staging foreign places by attempting to accurately represent famous heritage landmarks through the lens of commodification; e.g. Japanese theme parks depicting other cultures (Hendry 2009; Schlehe et al. 2010). Although not overtly a theme park of 'otherness', due to legitimate diaspora connections, the architecture of the 'Polish villages' in Curitiba, Brazil, also exhibits such theming, a complex case of authenticity and commodification through identity re-invention for tourist purposes (Irazábal 2004).

9   Entertainment, tourist and even residential sites that are inauthentic, but meticulously copying authentic heritage sites. The latter are increasingly dimmed by the hyper-reality; e.g. Las Vegas' copies of Venice or of the Pyramids, the Japanese copies of European heritage towns such as Amsterdam, residential town replicas such as Disney's *Celebration* or copies of heritage sites manufactured with the occasion of the Great Universal Exhibitions in the past (AlSayyad 2001a; Roy 2004).

10 Shopping Malls depicting famous heritage sites – mingled with hotels, shops, etc. – the peak of the postmodern consumerist market (Eco 1986; Urry 1995; Coles 2004). Crawford (1992) analyses the threats posed by the shopping mall classification subset, determining an annihilation of public space through hyper-reality. For several analyses of the same effects of the hyper-reality of theme parks, see also Sorkin (1992).

CREATOR	MATERIAL	FUNCTION	CONCEPT	HISTORY	ENSEMBLE	CONTEXT
'The hand of the master'	'The original material'	'The original purpose'	'The idea of the creator'	'The history of the artefact'	'The integrity of the whole'	'The integrity of the location'

Figure 2.1 Defining heritage authenticity through its meanings (Ashworth & Howard 1999)

chosen over others due to principles matching those considered by the heritage authorities in charge of the Petit Trianon's interpretation and its 2008 restoration. The literature review is supported by the fieldwork evidence and observations concerning the perception of authenticity by the majority of visitors interviewed at the Petit Trianon. The second criterion is Urry's 'romantic gaze', which was chosen because field research at the Petit Trianon demonstrated this to be one of the main factors responsible for the contemporary commodification of heritage detected at this site (see Chapter 7).

It must be stressed that the classification of sites in Table 2.1 does not consider other definitions of authenticity other than the above. This represents one of the limitations of the research. Valuable analyses consider other tourist authenticity types (Hughes 1995; Selwyn 1996; McIntosh & Prentice 1999; Taylor 2001; Chhabra et al. 2003; Hyounggon & Jamal 2007; Lau 2010), some of which include a reappraisal of 'staged authenticity' (MacCannell 1973, 1976) and Cohen's (1972, 1979) 'existential authenticity' which relates to Heidegger's phenomenological theory (see Steiner & Reisinger 2006; also Macleod 2006). This classification is essential in completing the picture of the position reserved today for 'places of memory' such as the Petit Trianon, as ultimately it is the perception by their most important consumer, the contemporary tourist, which anchors them in postmodernity. This overview paves the way for a better understanding of the 2008 restoration of the Petit Trianon with its strategies, demands and issues, as presented in Chapter 5.

Although postmodernity might in essence refer to, aim for and even induce de-differentiation and individuality, the opposite also holds true due to the inherent ambiguity of postmodernism. Postmodernism's hostility to authority stems in part from the reaction of individuals against being seen as a mass, yet postmodernity's main trait is de-differentiation. Linda Hutcheon (1986–1987 cited in Urry 1990:87) explains this apparent contradiction by seeing postmodernism as 'a model that is profoundly implicated in, yet still capable of criticizing, that which it seeks to describe' (see also Hutcheon 2002).

Given the nature of the 'romantic gaze', and given that many media images create a high expectation of exclusivity, an even more contrasting clash intervenes between the anticipated image of a tourist site and the actual visiting conditions of mass tourism, such as overcrowding. In addition, the presentation and even commodification of heritage sites for tourist purposes can feed into this contrast. Commodification is an inherent trait of any postmodern heritage site, but despite being aimed at increasing attractiveness for the mass visitor, it can also work against the fulfilment of visitor anticipation.

Regarding the literature review grounded on the commemorative trait of Nora's 'places of memory', the postmodern *patrimonialisation* signalled by Nora's theory finds a British equivalent in 'heritigisation' (Hewison 1987; Walsh 1992). Ben Cowell (2008) also contributed a valuable heritage case study basing his discussion on this phenomenon. Robert Hewison (1987) decries the trend of the past overtaking present and future to transform

Britain into a static museum. His views are countered to a point by Raphael Samuel's trilogy *Theatres of Memory* (1994), which does not consider the increasing appreciation for the past as negative. Another notable author concerned with this heritage analysis is the American scholar David Lowenthal (1996, 2015), whose views are cohesive with Nora's stance on the obsession with the past, adding that the representation of the past in each epoch is conditioned by various factors, not least political, leading to an altered understanding of history. Australian heritage academic Rodney Harrison (2013) also provides an important contribution to the idea of Nora's *patrimonialisation* by building on Renan's discourse on the paradoxical idea of 'forgetting to remember' fed back into the context of the over-preservation trait of cultural heritage.

The turning point for heritage studies, which crystallised the new understanding of the concept, as well as the process of heritage for the twenty-first century, comes from the millennium publication *A Geography of Heritage* (Graham et al. 2000; see also Tunbridge et al. 2013; Howard 2013). All aforementioned stances, along with other notable contributions, are reviewed by David Harvey's (2001, 2008) historical analyses of cultural heritage as a process (see also Pearce 1998). Other valuable contributions from Australian scholarship (Smith 2013; Winter 2013) further the understanding of the concept and process values of cultural heritage. In line with this, Emma Waterton and Steve Watson (2013) distinguish the notable recent contributions to some of the main topics of this book, including the role of heritage in creating identity and values of authenticity, and the dissonance intrinsic to this creation process, by identifying the work of Laurajane Smith (2006); David Crouch (2012) and Rodney Harrison (2012). Waterton and Watson (2013) also review the main heritage debates of relevance today (see also Harrison et al. 2008; Schofield 2008) and the challenging questions tackled over the past few decades by the theorists mentioned in this chapter, whilst proposing a framing theory for moving the discussion forward.

Furthermore, Australian academic Tim Winter (2014a, 2014b; see also 2015) highlights the unprecedented current crisis of heritage studies, mainly caused by globalisation and a postmodern shift of values contending with the previously hegemonic Western Eurocentrism. The Western European agenda of the nation state faces increasing criticism, as pointed out by authors such as Robert Mugerauer (2001). This illuminates the flaws plaguing the concept of cultural heritage due to its manipulation by Western European nineteenth-century nationalism. At the same time, it must be noted that the nineteenth-century nationalist recipes for 'imagining' the nation have been undermined by the global cultural flows which are best defined by Arjun Appadurai's (1996) theory of 'scapes', with migration (including tourism), new technologies, finance corporatism, media and governmental political ideologies changing the ways in which the 'imagining' of nations takes place in postmodernity. Nevertheless, in line with Anderson's imagined communities which were conditioned by nationalism and print capitalism coagulating national identities, the postmodern social imaginary is also conditioned by its corresponding social phenomenon, that of globalisation. By pointing to mass migration and electronic mediation to characterise globalisation, Appadurai (1996) shows how these factors can create new consumption patterns with images of lifestyles, popular culture and self-representation circulating internationally through the media. He further shows how these same images are borrowed in ways that are inventive and might be surprising to their originators. From the perspective of contemporary heritage tourism, Waterton (2013) argues that heritage representations are still defined by national agendas (see also classification subset 3 in Table 2.1). Yet within the interconnection of heritage with tourism, the encounter between authorities and visitors is also acknowledged to display bivalency inasmuch as both sides represent authorities in creating meaning, the former through interpretation, the latter through engagement (see Laurajane Smith 2012). This suggests that the intersection between the producers and receivers of messages at heritage sites is bound to negotiate the encoding and decoding of images, as analysed in Chapter 7 (see Figure 7.1).

Lastly, paramount in establishing the classification in Table 2.1 are cultural heritage and tourism studies focused on the relationship between the concepts of authenticity and tourism-driven commodification of heritage. Relevant to the discussion here, valuable scholarship on these subjects is provided by Nezar AlSayyad (2001b); Peter Howard (2003); Melanie Smith and Mike Robinson (2006) and Waterton and Watson (2010). The representational and non-representational (performing) aspects of heritage in relation to tourism have also garnered notable contributions from David Crouch and Nina Lübbren (2003); Brian Graham and Peter Howard (2008b); Tazim Jamal and Mike Robinson (2009); Charles Mansfield and Simon Seligman (2011); Crouch (2011); Smith et al. (2012) and Russell Staiff et al. (2013). (For a valuable reappraisal of heritage tourism, see Light 2015). From the perspective of the 'romantic gaze', authenticity would be defined and established via visual means, which evidence amassed by field research at the Petit Trianon proves to be in stark contrast with the definition of authenticity in Figure 2.1, which matches the principles followed by the heritage authorities in charge of the Petit Trianon's interpretation and its 2008 restoration. Consequently, by intersecting the sources of authority of those in charge of the site and of the visitors, a converging picture of authenticity generated by various types of sites can be synthesised as shown in Table 2.1.

Gottdiener (2001) analyses the social implications of theming, referring to the last three classification subsets: theme parks, sites such as Las Vegas and shopping malls (also see Paradis 2004). With hyper-reality having infiltrated public space and having changed modes of social interaction, physical presence is no longer as important as it once was. Presence as derived from *telepresence* (Minsky 1980) and induced by virtual reality (VR) is acknowledged to have found an important niche in cultural heritage interpretation (Pujol & Champion 2012) to the extent that the term 'virtual heritage' has been coined.[4] (For an overview of the term and its applications, see Ibrahim et al. 2011; in line with the term is also 'new heritage', see Kalay et al. 2008). The last three classification subsets, based on theming, exclusively rely on hyper-reality as initially analysed by Eco (1986) in the context of museum presentation, and which seems to have garnered increasing popularity even with some traditional museums. For example, the use of holograms, three-dimensional displays and digital applications are now favoured by a majority of the visiting public according to the literature review supporting the above classification (see also Gretzel & Fesenmaier 2009). In fact, the increased popularity of VR in museum interactions, is believed to redefine (see de Groot 2010) the relationship between 'historiography and virtuality', which in turn redefines (even questions) the authority of the museum discourse since the individual agency is becoming its competitor in creating meaning. From the perspective of the interpreting authorities of royal and aristocratic heritage, three-dimensional reconstructions of particularly problematic collections such as the Petit Trianon, lost palaces and/or architectural alterations increasingly find their applicability (Martens 2016; Hoppe & Breitling 2016).

It is worth noting that the above classification subsets contain a degree of heritage authenticity which decreases in inverse proportion to their popularity, suggesting that less authentic sites appeal to the majority of the visiting public. Also, despite heritage authenticity decreasing from classification subsets 1 to 10, Table 2.1 indicates that even the least authentic models aspire towards portraying authenticity by copying the originals with painstaking care. Given the character of postmodernity, the copies have displaced the originals. Nezar AlSayyad (2001a) offers a personal anecdote about the American academic at the University of Nevada who was disappointed to see that the real Sphinx in Egypt was much smaller than its three-times-enlarged replica in Las Vegas, to which he had become accustomed. AlSayyad also discusses the difficulty of establishing what is authentic or not. Disneyland could hence be considered more authentic than a heavily restored heritage monument, as the former honestly states its 'fakeness'. Assessing the values attached to these types of sites is not the object of this study. However, it is undeniable that all of these forms of authenticity have their own legitimate function. Furthermore, since these forms of authenticity sustain and reinforce each other, they all contribute to the complete picture of a classic notion of heritage authenticity in the context of postmodern society (Ashworth & Howard 1999).

This chapter set out to complete the academic field introduced in Chapter 1 by discussing Nora's views on the commemorative trait of 'places of memory', with commemoration being responsible for their very existence. This theory was linked with two other significant views (Lefebvre 1991; Urry 1990, 1995, 2002) anchoring 'places of memory' in the present whilst taking into account the new 'class' of the postmodern visitor which appropriates places through the intermediary of images. This chapter also provided theoretical background necessary to the analysis of the uncontrolled (yet

48 *'Places of memory' in postmodernity*

alchemical) dissonant commodification of Marie Antoinette's historical character and to the identification of its producers and consumers at the Petit Trianon. Further analyses in later chapters complete the understanding of this process and its underlying causes.

The dimensions of authenticity discussed above underline the need for a better understanding of visitor perceptions at heritage sites. To this end, the next chapter focuses on the hermeneutic method of interpreting built environments, applied in conjunction with Lefebvre's interpretation of space, which also underpins the assessment of the architectural and heritage narratives of the Petit Trianon site.

Notes

1 The majority of respondents (except the Japanese majority group) discovered the Petit Trianon because of its promotion associated with the 2008 restoration (see also Chapter 5). Moreover, for these visitors (and the Japanese majority group) the anticipation was constructed through media images.
2 An example for this preference is the recent concept of the trendy Museum of Ice Cream, see www.museumoficecream.com/.
3 Inglis (2000) contributed a study on the pervasiveness of contemporary television programmes in the anticipation of a holiday; see also Kim et al. (2009).
4 Of particular relevance to the discussion on the reversal of reality and fiction, central to this book's analysis, is that *telepresence* slid from reality into fiction. Whereas Marvin Minski's research was aiming to take the real self to the real environment through the intermediary of VR (for repairing nuclear reactors safely, from a distance, for example), in the new context, the real self is absorbed into a VR environment.

3 Methodology and fieldwork research at the Petit Trianon

The methodological framework is structured into four sections as follows: the hermeneutical methodology used for analysing the representation, interpretation and perception of the Petit Trianon; methods of investigation used for constructing the project's working hypothesis, amounting to a data collection review; qualitative research conducted at the site of the Petit Trianon, including the author's fieldwork research ethnographic elements (2010–2012); and finally, the presentation of a critical model developed as an overview of the discussion built upon the academic field, literature review and methodological framework of the book.

The hermeneutical principles of intersecting diverse meanings support the book's methodology, including the library and archive research selection and interpretation (Scott 1990). Furthermore, through thematic analysis (Boyatzis 1998; Saldaña 2013), a hermeneutical research paradigm underpins the methodology for interpreting visitor discourses at the Petit Trianon. This research paradigm is complemented at a theoretical level by Paul Ricoeur's (2004) hermeneutical analysis of the uncanniness[1] of Pierre Nora's (1984–1992) 'places of memory' in conjunction with Maurice Halbwachs' (1980) 'collective memory', the two key theories supporting the analysis of production and consumption of Marie Antoinette's dissonant commodification through the power of clichés, crucial to understanding the perpetuation of artificial images of the last Queen of France.

Hermeneutical paradigm of interpreting the Petit Trianon

For a refined decoding of the mechanisms underpinning the creation of the image of the Petit Trianon as home to Marie Antoinette, in connection with the factors contributing to the dissonant commodification of this historical character, the methodological framework uses as a starting point Robert Mugerauer's (1995) comparative study for the interpretation of built environments, praised in heritage studies (Howard 2003:47) as 'a particularly useful text about ways of understanding historical architecture'. Mugerauer (1995) contributed a valuable analysis of the traditional, hermeneutic and deconstruction paradigms of cultural heritage interpretation.[2]

This book consciously focuses on the hermeneutic paradigm of interpretation of the Petit Trianon, making use of Mugerauer's guide,[3] in turn based on Martin Heidegger and Hans-Georg Gadamer. This framework is complemented by the views of Ricoeur (2004), perhaps the most quintessentially hermeneutical author. The focus falls on Ricoeur's analysis of Halbwachs' 'collective memory' in conjunction with his observations on Nora's 'places of memory', both necessary to fully grasp contemporary French visitor perceptions at the Petit Trianon.

As outlined in the Introduction, the methodology of hermeneutics was chosen due to its congruence with the theoretical corpus assembled in support of this book's arguments. Given the controversial nature of both historical site and figure, the hermeneutical paradigm is particularly suited to a decryption and understanding of the heritage narrative of the Petit Trianon as home to Marie Antoinette. Moreover, the main principles of the hermeneutical paradigm lend themselves to a direct application onto the case study of the Petit Trianon. This hermeneutical approach is fully realised in Chapter 7, which juxtaposes the narratives analysed by previous chapters into a theoretical and practical assessment of the range of images associated with Marie Antoinette that led to the dissonant contemporary commodification of her historical character.

Traditionally associated with the academic discipline of philosophy, the process of interpretation has undergone a shift towards other modes of investigation and other disciplines, mostly due to the ideological crisis of the postmodern era. Thus, from humanities to environmental sciences, the new interpretational approaches of hermeneutics and deconstruction (see Derrida 1997) have become increasingly accepted and used as views essentially complementary to the traditional approach, which maintains as a basic foundation of interpretation that any artefact has meaning because of its extrinsic relations (Mugerauer 1995). Both hermeneutics and deconstruction stem from the traditional approach, inasmuch as the first aims not to develop a new take on the traditional interpretation but rather 'to clarify how understanding takes place' (Mugerauer 1995:xxvi), while the second is formulated in total opposition to the paradigm of Tradition, accepting its 'position – the positing' but aiming to undo it (Mugerauer 1995:xliii).

In comparison with the traditional approach, which considers the message of the author as fixed and unique, hermeneutical interpretation must establish the confluence of the meanings emerging from all traditions involved, such as that of the creator as well as that of the public's perception of the creation in a later time frame. Heidegger (Mugerauer 1995:xxviii) sees this confluence as well as the hermeneutical accent placed on the importance of the interpreter through the 'hermeneutical circle': understanding of any part of one's world 'depends on a prior connection with or preunderstanding of the whole, and any understanding of the whole can proceed only from an understanding of, or projection from, the parts.' Whilst also emphasising the need to consider prejudice in hermeneutical interpretation, Gadamer further streamlined Heidegger's concept, by explaining that:

> in the process of understanding, the hermeneutical circle is expanding concentrically [. . .] [and in] interpreting phenomena it is crucial to open new meaning by uncovering still-efficacious meanings from the past that bear on the present in ways that have been concealed by naturally shifting intermediate horizons (that is, over time) or by partial and derivative meanings that have come to act as blinders, restricting and monopolising our focus.
>
> (Mugerauer 1995:xxviii)

The method of hermeneutical interpretation outlined above next integrates the case study of the Petit Trianon as home to Marie Antoinette, linking the broader analysis with the next sections concerning the fieldwork research method and evidence. By directly applying the hermeneutical principles outlined below, what is highlighted here is the convergence of the theories analysed thus far, and the narratives presented in the following chapters, into a body of knowledge fully addressing the main arguments.

Hermeneutics takes into consideration a polysemic structure of meaning as found at the meeting of the past world of the creator, of the intermediate worlds of those who intervened later at different levels and in different ways, and finally of the present world of the public perceiving a historical and architectural artefact. Hermeneutical interpretation is found at the intersection between conveyor and receptor, as well as interim users, creators and interpreters, and thus each of their agendas must be analysed in order to deliver an accurate interpretation.

As highlighted by the Introduction, to unearth the objective truth surrounding Marie Antoinette's historical character, the research analysis results were evaluated for validity against the eighteenth-century architectural narrative of the Petit Trianon sourced from architectural histories. Consequently, the architectural narrative of the Petit Trianon as defined here suggests that the messages inscribed into the space of this eighteenth-century royal residence were not a manipulation of existent material as a statement of legitimation, but an expression of its own legitimate position. This is the marked difference between the conception (creation) of Marie Antoinette's Petit Trianon and ulterior, unsuccessful attempts at appropriation by subsequent users. Further reflecting this, is Nora's observation that 'places of memory' come into being once the 'lived-in' tradition disappears, and are replaced by self-conscious attempts to create new traditions culminating in 'commemoration'. Marie Antoinette's choice to feature a Norman village – as quintessentially French vernacular architecture – at the Petit Trianon, even if only in a symbolic way, was the result of an innate need to be in touch with a country which had never fully accepted her. Still, the queen did not intend this to be a conscious expression of national identity. It was only in the late nineteenth century that it became fashionable for political elites to display connections with the folk culture of their national audience.

The hermeneutical interpretation also aims to uncover what is hidden and usually overlooked because of its nearness and purposeful concealment (Mugerauer 1995:118): '[A]s Heidegger insisted, we need to reflect on what is nearest, on what is so close that we do not see or think it.' This principle of the 'near' (Heidegger 1971), frequently utilised in the investigation and assessment of historical and heritage narratives, also applies, to varying degrees, to this analysis of narratives centred on Marie Antoinette and the Petit Trianon. As such, despite clear indications that a closer look at the obvious would dispel many persistent popular myths, the majority of historical authors, whose works are analysed in Chapter 4, base their studies on already established 'facts' and views, without questioning or challenging their authority. Paradoxically, the minority of authors who do focus on dismantling these myths have felt the need to purposefully disguise their findings in the form of historical fiction.

Similarly, even when faced with the simplicity and restrictive/Spartan space of the Petit Trianon, a part of the contemporary public still prefers to take the mental leap of imagining it as the promiscuous/lavish setting popularised by myth. In the same way, the May 1789 revolutionaries who inspected the Petit Trianon for evidence of the opulent luxury the queen allegedly lavished upon her estate were disappointed by the simplicity of the place and concluded that all the 'treasures' must have been hidden before their arrival. What they found was not gilded décor or precious gems but rather sparsely furnished, pale interiors of modest scale. The major factor responsible for the misperception evidenced in both cases lies in the dominance of images, as discussed through Urry's theory. Consequently, the image is what becomes unanimously accepted, whereas the content – the building itself – devolves from main image generator to mere hidden message, ultimately and ironically becoming insignificant in the perception of the Petit Trianon by the majority of contemporary visitors.

Finally, the hermeneutical interpretation of the Petit Trianon takes into account the prejudice of each of the parties involved in the creation, interpretation and perception of this space as home to Marie Antoinette. This is crucial, since the power of prejudice is a significant force on both individual and societal levels. Therefore, each narrative and its assessed impact, as shown in later chapters, uncovers and highlights the prejudices imposed by each different context, such as Marie Antoinette's Catholic faith; the cultural background of historical authors from the nineteenth, twentieth and twenty-first centuries; Sofia Coppola's self-confessed 'spoilt teenagehood'; Riyoko Ikeda's Japanese feminist attitude; the French curatorial approach to the museum of the Petit Trianon; or the various sections of the contemporary visiting public's cultural conditioning.

The final part of the present section looks at Ricoeur's observations on Halbwachs' 'collective memory' in conjunction with several aspects generated by Nora's 'places of memory'. Ricoeur's hermeneutical acceptations of these two concepts are essential in drawing research conclusions on the entirety of the study, particularly in connection to charting the commodification of Marie Antoinette's historical figure, which is produced and consumed through the power of clichés inscribed in French collective memory but also through an artificial remembering process typical to 'places of memory'. Responsible for this is modernity's fracturing of the historical discourse, which Ricoeur (2004:301) sees as 'a fault-line fissuring from within the presumed encompassing, totalising idea of world history' with the French Revolution considered to be 'the mother of all ruptures'. Moreover, the author observes that the role of 'teacher of life', which the 'ancient *topos* of history' would have previously played, has been subverted into many uncanny manifestations, including 'collective memory' and 'places of memory'. Analysing these two concepts, Ricoeur (2004:393) emphasises the fracture anew, sourcing his usage of 'uncanny' from Freud's *Unheimlichkeit*: 'the painful feeling experienced in dreams revolving around the theme of pierced eyes, decapitation, and castration.' The author investigates the themes of 'death in history', 'historicity and historiography', and 'the dialectic of memory and history', the latter being the focus of the present analysis.

Halbwachs makes a clear distinction between 'collective memory' and historical memory. As Halbwachs places the individual memories themselves within the structure of a group,[4] Ricoeur critiques the externality which, in these circumstances, would control the internal process of individual memory. Although Ricoeur maintains a critical view against this 'external gaze', the philosopher also admits that Halbwachs' particular use of the notions of place and change of place is what in fact defeats 'a quasi-Kantian use of the idea of framework, unilaterally imposed on every consciousness'. (Ricoeur 2004:124). Halbwachs observes that history is first learned in school by mechanical means of memorisation, thus inducing an external encounter with a narrative taught within the framework of a nation. The externality factor, acknowledged to be polemic by Ricoeur (2004), actually plays a special role in Halbwachs' theory of 'collective memory'.

Ricoeur (2004:394) notices that it is through this externality that Halbwachs was in fact able to explain the process of a 'progressive disappearance of the gap between the history taught in school and the experience of memory, a gap that is itself reconstructed after the fact.' Most importantly, externality is the main factor – in the discovery of historical memory – of gradual familiarisation with the unfamiliar. Familiarisation consists of an initiation process that is mostly supported by a transgenerational tie: 'As the family elders become uninterested in contemporary events, they interest the succeeding generations in the framework of their own childhood' (Ricoeur 2004:394). Ricoeur sees in the phenomenon of transgenerational memory the essential element ensuring the transition from learned history to living memory.

Halbwachs' theory reflects Lefebvre's views on the difference between 'Cosmos' and 'Logos'. Moreover, it links with Nora's and Hobsbawm's observations, bringing clearer insight: if the national identity of a country does not fully coincide with its cultural heritage – as reflected by the invented traditions of nationalism – factions of different 'collective memories' from groups bridging the gap between individual and nation start to evolve. In addition, the generations themselves seem to act as separate layers amidst the dialectic of memory and history, thus inducing clear distinctions between collective and historical memories.

Nora's views on generations – which could themselves be seen as 'places of memory' and consequently generators of history – complete Halbwachs' reticence to arrive at a clear conceptual delimitation for either the memory or the history of the modern era. Nevertheless, Nora's theory on 'memory-history' distances him from Halbwachs, as he does not clearly differentiate between the collective and historical memory. Instead, as Ricoeur (2004:403) notices, in Nora's theory these two concepts would have been linked by the nation: 'History was holy because the nation was holy. The nation became the vehicle that allowed French memory to remain standing on its sanctified foundation.' Therefore, when Nora considers the rupture between history and tradition, he perceives the nation's role in linking memory to history in the nationalist era. The nation was the last embodiment of memory and the national historical discourse was the generator of collective memory itself (see also Nora 2011a, 2011b, 2013).

In addition, generations have contributed to the understanding of 'places of memory' and their relation to heritage. In the third and last volume of *Les France* (1992), which completes the entire series, *Les lieux de mémoire* (1984–1992), Nora dedicates his chapter to exploring memory and history in connection to the succession of generations. Although in theory the sequence of generations should have countered *patrimonialisation*, it is argued here that the very crisis of identification with the nation has generated an endless loop of identification with an increasingly divided and reconstructed past, as demonstrated by the competition between contemporary media imagery and the images imprinted on 'collective memory'. This is illustrated through fieldwork research findings at the Petit Trianon (see Chapter 6).

Data collection review

Following the presentation of the 'uncanny' theories which contribute to the interpretation of results from the survey undertaken at the site of the Petit Trianon, the preparatory field research carried out within the context of a thematic analysis is detailed next. This section thus reviews the methods behind the construction and testing of the working hypothesis of the fieldwork.[5] Crucial in establishing the course and goals of the research strategy, the theoretical methods were complemented by practical ones, as outlined below.

Methodology and fieldwork research 55

The fieldwork research was based on two consecutive doctoral internships at Château de Versailles: October 2010 to May 2011 and October 2011 to August 2012. Having been granted the official authorisation of '*Chargée de recherches – Conservation*', I undertook historical documentation research and conducted my own survey investigating the public perceptions of the Petit Trianon and the impact of its 2008 restoration. The survey work was approved and supported by Mr Jérémie Benoît (head curator, *Domaine de Marie-Antoinette*) and Château de Versailles specialists: Mr Pierre-Xavier Hans (curator of eighteenth-century decorative arts), Mr Philippe Baudin (heritage architect in the restoration department) and Ms Marie-Laëtitia Lachèvre (head librarian of the curatorial documentation department). Following data collection during the first placement period, it became clear that immersion into the French culture was vital for a better understanding of the French public's perception of the controversial historical figure of Marie Antoinette. Thus, further methods of interaction and observation were devised and applied during the second placement period.

The following data sets were used inductively within the context of a thematic analysis. Typically, this type of analysis is most compatible with phenomenology (Giorgi & Giorgi 2008) and is applied successfully in psychology research such as Interpretative Phenomenological Analysis (IPA; see Smith & Osborn 2008; also Braun & Clarke 2006) and grounded theory (see Auerbach & Silverstein 2003), as well as arts research (see Butler-Kisber 2010; Saldaña 2013). However, thematic analysis is used here in line with recent ethnographic research by employing its definition as an intersection of analytical coding and hermeneutical interpretation (Kozinets 2010; Saldaña 2013), and was chosen due to its characteristic of focusing on themes/patterns (Boyatzis 1998). The themes that are the subject of analysis here (see Table 3.1; also Table 4.2) relate to the representation and interpretation of Marie Antoinette's historical character, whilst the patterns searched for relate to its perception. Identification of these themes/patterns was data-driven – as opposed to theory-driven – determining an inductive approach (see Boyatzis 1998). Furthermore, rather than as a specific method, thematic analysis is considered here as a tool used across different methods (Boyatzis 1998; Braun & Clarke 2006), representing an overarching approach to the archival/library research and the ethnographic methods of informal interviews and participant observation.

The ethnographic methods of the research were carried out not only in my role as intern and doctoral researcher at Château de Versailles, but also as a resident of France (2010–2012) and as a waitress in a restaurant next to the Château de Versailles (April – August 2012). From this perspective, my position of researcher belongs to critical realist ethnography approaches (Smith pers. comm. 2012; see also Brewer 2000; Van Maanen 2011), as my interpretation of data pertains to qualitative inquiries found on the border between modern and postmodern ethnography (Figure 3.1). Furthermore, by searching for patterns (typical for modern ethnography) and by drawing

Table 3.1 Main clichés associated with the historical character of Marie Antoinette used for the hypothetical theming tested through the survey at Petit Trianon

Cliché	Connotative meaning
Uneducated Arch-Duchess	Supposedly poor childhood education received at the Court of Vienna; emphasises superiority of French court over its Austrian counterpart
Queen of Fashion/ Overspending	Favoured luxury and leisure over the fulfilment of royal duties; bankrupted France
A 'tête à vent'; 'frivole' and 'nulle en politique'	Not inclined to serious matters; hinting at stupidity rather than lightness of spirit and/or an artistic personality
Playing the shepherdess	Completely cut off from the reality of the society she lived in; substituted reality with her own version, Le Petit Trianon, derogatorily named La Petite Vienne, reinforcing the idea of Marie Antoinette's rejection of France and French people on the grounds of her Austrian nationality
Unfaithful spouse of depraved morality/ sexuality	Attributing to Marie Antoinette a countless series of lovers – men and women – ranging from close companions to revolutionary figures (Barnave, Mirabeau, even La Fayette) who supposedly changed their minds about the Revolution's ideals under the influence of their 'lover'
Austrian spy and traitor	Supposed disloyalty to France and the French people; '*L'Autrichienne*', a nickname favoured by detractors
'Let Them Eat Cake!'	Supposed disregard for the poor (arrogance), cruelty, stupidity (see Campion-Vincent & Shojaei Kawan 2002)

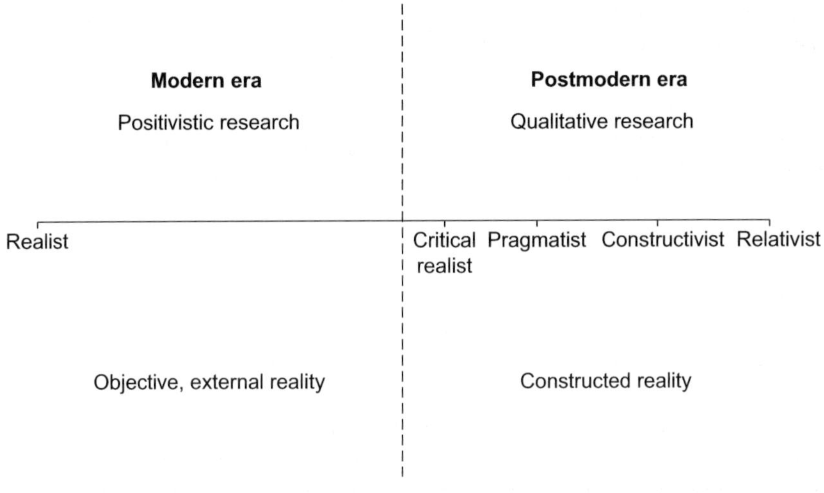

```
                    Modern era              |   Postmodern era
              Positivistic research         |   Qualitative research
                                            |
    ────────────────────────────────────────┼────────────────────────────────────────────────
    Realist                                 |   Critical    Pragmatist  Constructivist  Relativist
                                            |   realist
                                            |
           Objective, external reality      |          Constructed reality
```

Figure 3.1 The qualitative inquiry continuum (Butler-Kisber 2010)

causal conclusions (see Silverman 2007; Butler-Kisber 2010) whilst accepting at the same time a confluence of meanings derived from many perspectives which are all accounted for, this ethnographic approach falls within the hermeneutical interpretation underpinning the entire methodology. Where reflexivity is concerned, in line with critical realist approaches, my 'voice' (see Hertz 1997) and my 'identity' (see Van Maanen 1995; Denzin 1997; Coffey 1999; Butler-Kisber 2010; Denzin & Lincoln 2013) are representative of the theoretical rehabilitative stance presented in Chapter 1, providing the research legitimation in relation to the contested notions discussed throughout.

The hermeneutical principles of intersecting a polysemy of meanings supported my choice of library and archive sources used to assess the architectural and historical narratives. The hermeneutical interpretation was also extended to the cinematic and heritage narratives when analysing the data corpus related to these (see Chapters 4 and 5). Scott (1990:31) highlights the importance of hermeneutics in extracting meaning, particularly as a vital aid to documents researchers, by allowing them to enter 'into a dialogue with the author of the document being studied'. Thus, further understanding is facilitated by examining the hermeneutic circle in which the document was composed. Following Scott's (1990) representativeness, a sociological principle essential in extracting meaning from consultation of records, it must be noted that the documents consulted were always considered for their representativeness to the total amount of extant artefacts/documents and all other related sources. The 'deliberate destruction or removal' (Scott 1990:25) of various documents is an equally important aspect of representativeness. The scarcity of Marie Antoinette's original artefacts, due to destruction and dispersal, further reinforced the validity of the decision to use a visitor perceptions survey at the Petit Trianon, to compensate for lack of evidence. Finally, the hermeneutical principles of the 'near' and the 'prejudice' (Heidegger 1971; Gadamer 2004) highlighted earlier, play a vital role in the aforementioned analyses of the four narratives – architectural, historical, cinematic and heritage.

There are fifteen data sets used in the research, which are presented next in sequential order. This order subscribes to the stages of an inductive approach consisting in data collection, construction of the working hypothesis, and analysis. Data Sets 1–3, in particular, gathered knowledge about the general perception of Marie Antoinette, which was later used for constructing the working hypothesis (in conjunction with Data Sets 4–7). This hypothesis was subsequently tested through the questionnaire-led survey at the Petit Trianon (2010–2012). A particular trait of the methodology used in this study is the outline of a working hypothesis (Chelcea et al. 1998) through hypothetical coding. This is characteristic to qualitative research such as thematic analysis (Saldaña 2013). Furthermore, the hermeneutical interpretation intrinsic to thematic analysis, with the hermeneutic circle playing a central role in extracting meaning (Thompson et al. 1994; Arnold & Fischer 1994), further legitimates the choice of this method over other approaches. Thompson et al. (1994) also highlight the fact that a good hermeneutical interpretation must delve into the social and historical contexts of the data to provide a nuanced cultural interpretation. This was achieved through the intersection of the different data collected for the four aforementioned major narratives.

The hypothetical coding employed, as themes, the clichés detected by the data collection (Table 3.1) in the representation of Marie Antoinette's historical character. Not only were these clichés matched by the coding of the visitor discourses at the Petit Trianon (see Chapter 6) but the power of clichés also proved to be at the root of the dissonant commodification of Marie Antoinette's historical figure, further explaining the production and consumption of this commodification at the Petit Trianon (see Chapter 7).

Finally, it should be stressed that the samples of the historical works on Marie Antoinette, supplied in Chapter 4, as well as the sources at the Librairie des Princes, are 'theoretical/purposive' (Mason 2002). The cross-referencing of these two types of sampled populations against academic analyses focused on the construction and manipulation of Marie Antoinette' image. Chapter 4 is pivotal in understanding the relationship between Republican clichés themed in the book, and their influence on the heritage commodification of Marie Antoinette's historical character at the Petit Trianon, elaborated upon in Chapter 7.

Data Set 1

Hermeneutical analysis of the major, up-to-date historical works, mémoires and novels focused on Marie Antoinette was required to assess the general message conveyed to the public by these sources, a message which coincided in essence with the narrative perpetuated by the Revolutionary/Republican agenda.

Communication with authors (Chantal Thomas and Patricia Bouchenot-Déchin) whose work helps to balance the Revolutionary/Republican agenda, ultimately shaped my analysis, which subscribes to a historical rehabilitation narrative. These discussions also helped to refine the focus of my fieldwork questionnaire. Chapter 4 contains the hermeneutical analysis of the historical narrative of Marie Antoinette – a data collection related to the analysis of all the above-mentioned sources.

During this first stage, the research revealed the common themes typically connected with the historical figure of Marie Antoinette. These were the Republican clichés (Table 3.1) hypothetically coded/themed and detected later in the visitor discourses gathered at the Petit Trianon, thus confirming the working hypothesis. These clichés' origins are in either the French court's slander or in revolutionary pamphlets, all later appropriated by the Third Republic discourse. These themes were found through later data sets (12 and 15) also to be pervasive in the contemporary press and other media channels, sources considered in support of the argument in Chapter 7 relating to media as an external subliminal influence to visitor perceptions at a heritage site.

Data Set 2

Informal interviews starting October 2010, with Jérémie Benoît, head curator at the Petit Trianon; Pierre-Xavier Hans, eighteenth-century decorative arts curator; heritage architect Philippe Baudin; head archivist Karine McGrath; and head librarian Marie-Laëtitia Lachèvre yielded evidence that within art history elite circles, opinions converge at the opposite pole to that of majority public perception. Interestingly, opinion sources differ, with many specialists 'reading' into historical facts or the details of the queen's habitation, rather than interpretations based on historical narratives. The interviewed subjects were also aware of the persisting 'negative' image of Marie Antoinette engraved onto the French national collective memory.

Data Set 3

Hermeneutical study of relevant exhibition catalogues, press and internet sources, as well as of other relevant French libraries and archive databases (see Maior-Barron 2015b), was also needed to assess the general public opinion towards the last Queen of France. To understand Japanese visitor patterns, particular attention was paid throughout November and December 2010 to catalogues concerning exhibitions on Marie Antoinette in Japan. These sources helped construct the multiple-choice Japanese questionnaire (Appendix A.3).

Press and internet releases on the exhibition held by Takashi Murakami at the Château de Versailles (14 September–12 December 2010), through the artist's own statements, suggested the paramount importance of the manga, *Rose of Versailles*, in Japanese perceptions of Marie Antoinette:

> It's very surreal to be here [at the Palace of Versailles] [. . .]. As a kid growing up in Japan I learnt about Versailles through the girls' comic book Rose of Versailles, which was such a big hit that it became a musical and a TV show. Everyone in Japan wants to talk to me about this particular commission, not because they're interested in me or my work or even art – they're just mad about Rose of Versailles. But, you know, I don't have a problem with that.[6]

Press sources (see Data Set 12) concerning *Rose of Versailles* revealed that Riyoko Ikeda would be in France for *Le 38e Festival International de la Bande Dessinée d'Angoulême* (27–30 January 2011). Ikeda also gave a soprano recital at the Petit Trianon,[7] and a conference talk which I attended (Data Set 4). Ikeda's fascination with Marie Antoinette and the eighteenth century was particularly investigated (Chapter 4). By extension, given her immense public following (see Oka 2008; Brethes 2011), I tested through the Japanese questionnaire whether this fascination is shared by Japanese visitors at the Petit Trianon. This was subsequently confirmed by research evidence (Chapter 6).

60 *Methodology and fieldwork research*

In January 2011, I attended a film exhibition at La Conciergerie (29 October 2010–13 February 2011; see Binh 2010), a valuable source of information on filming historical sites in general and the Petit Trianon in particular. The exhibition conveyed the extreme popularity of Marie Antoinette's historical character in media as one of the most often portrayed feminine figures of French history. This data collection informs the analyses of the historical, cinematic and heritage narratives analysed in Chapters 4 and 5.

I attended the International Heritage Show (3–6 November 2011, Carrousel du Louvre) to review and record the main French heritage publishing houses and their publications in the field. I followed this line of inquiry to the heritage library of the École de Chaillot, where, in May 2012, Mr Cyril Duclos kindly granted me full access to consult their publications and documents. The resulting data collection deepened my understanding of contemporary French heritage studies. In turn, this understanding informed the critical reviews in Chapters 2 and 5. Established in 1887, École de Chaillot has provided formation courses for heritage architects ever since. Today, heritage architects in France have the greatest authority in terms of managing/restoring heritage buildings.

Data Set 4

Attendance at conferences and colloquiums complemented the above data sets. At annual history conferences – held each November since 2008 – at the Hôtel de Ville of Versailles, in 2010, I met contemporary historians, including the late Jean Favier (French Mediaeval rehabilitative history) and Patricia Bouchenot-Déchin (rehabilitative history of the image of Marie Antoinette through historical fiction); and in 2011, I met authors Jean Sévillia (rehabilitative history of the French Old Regime) and Simone Bertière (Marie Antoinette biographer). Each author confirmed the definite trend of misunderstood historical-character rehabilitation. At the colloquiums held by Château de Versailles in 2011 to raise public awareness of the complexity of Marie Antoinette's historical character, I attended the talks of biographers/historians Chantal Thomas, whom I met, and Cécile Berly. All of this contributed to the data collection outlined in Chapter 4.

To better understand the agenda of Japanese *mangaka* Riyoko Ikeda, I attended her presentation at La Maison de Culture du Japon (2 February 2011, Paris; see Ikeda 2011). While still a teenager, she was greatly moved by Stefan Zweig's biography of the last Queen of France, developing a lifelong admiration for the courage and dignity of Marie Antoinette, whom she believes to be a figure of heroic yet tragic destiny. While still in her twenties, Ikeda created the manga *Rose of Versailles* from this particular perspective. These facts helped me to understand the Japanese public's perception and

Methodology and fieldwork research 61

consequently to refine the multiple-choice Japanese questionnaire implemented in fieldwork in February 2011. Ikeda's work forms part of the data collection provided in Chapter 4.

Data Set 5

Communication with the security guards of the Petit Trianon was also needed. Discussions with key members of the surveillance team of the Petit Trianon shed more light on visitors' ways of 'consuming' heritage. These discussions suggested that long-term employees, through an increased understanding of the space encompassed by the Petit Trianon, also had a better understanding of the last Queen of France (Chapter 7). This hypothesis was tested and confirmed in April 2011 via a questionnaire for Personnel (Appendix A.4) out of whom 20 (10 on permanent, 10 on temporary contracts) participated. A majority of the 10 respondents with permanent contracts had senior positions. The respondents preferred to remain anonymous.

Data Set 6

Further consultation of the Château de Versailles visitor statistics was essential in order to establish the impact of the 2008 restoration and new presentation of the *Domaine de Marie-Antoinette*, as well as the connection between the 2006 release of Sofia Coppola's film and the increase in visitor numbers (see Chapter 5).

Data Set 7

Enquiries and field observation at the Palace's boutiques and book shops proved that Marie Antoinette is the heritage commodity that 'sells the most' at the Château de Versailles (Figure 3.2). Printed images of the queen range from the pink *princesse* crayons/colouring books to life-size reproductions of one of her most famous sculptures, a bust by Boizot priced at 2900 euros or replica perfumed leather gloves at 3900 euros. The best-selling books also relate to Marie Antoinette, although statistics were not available (see Chapter 4).

Data Set 8

The empirical research hypothesis reached through a synthesis of the methods above required adjacent observation of the ways visitors engage with the Petit Trianon (Figure 3.3) combined with observations of the site's curatorial interpretation through didactic panels, and its packaging through management decisions. Furthermore, attending the guided tours of various

62 *Methodology and fieldwork research*

Figure 3.2 Field observation of all Château de Versailles boutiques indicates Marie Antoinette merchandise is the highest selling, from the cheapest souvenir to the most expensive products

Author photo 2014/courtesy Château de Versailles

guide-conférenciers – whose delivery of information is independent of Petit Trianon curatorial authority – helped to establish whether narratives of the queen and her *Domaine* were cohesive. Chapter 5 incorporates the various types of observation and informal interviews on which I built my assessment through reflexivity (see my researcher position in regards to reflexivity as defined earlier).

Figure 3.3 Observation of the different ways tourists 'consume' the Petit Trianon
Author photo 2011/courtesy Château de Versailles

64 *Methodology and fieldwork research*

Data Set 9

In parallel with the above, following the initial meeting in December 2010 with heritage architect Philippe Baudin (Department of Architects of Historical Monuments, Château de Versailles), an in depth study (January – March 2011) of the architectural interventions since 1805 found at the archives of Château de Versailles proved to be essential in establishing the interest of the later elites in preserving (or not) the *Domaine* of Marie Antoinette by adopting and/or adapting it according to their political agendas. I have compared the building works which the three main parts of the Estate (The Palace, the Grand Trianon and the Petit Trianon) underwent until 1837, when the Palace became a museum (Gaehtgens 1984; Gervereau & Constans 2005), as my doctoral thesis was initially going to include the development of the relationship between cultural heritage and national identity during the nineteenth century (Maior-Barron 2014). This part has been excluded following the focus on the contemporary perception of the site.

Finally, relevant to this data set, from an architectural point of view, is the analysis of the state of the *Domaine* before, during and after Marie Antoinette's historical period, which clarified the queen's careful stewardship of the Petit Trianon. This was achieved by consulting the conservation plans for the 2008 restoration together with other relevant sources (see Chapter 5), as well as publications issued by the archaeological department of Château de Versailles (see Chapter 7).

Data Set 10

As an adjacent method of traditional library research which supported the second stage of fieldwork, I consulted relevant documents and publications relating to the French Revolution (see Chapter 1) at the Institut d'histoire de la Révolution française (Université Paris I/Panthéon-Sorbonne), where I was granted unlimited access for eight months from March 2012, with the support of historian and author Professor Annie Duprat and of head librarian Marie-Lynne Délbès.

Data Set 11

During the first and second stage of fieldwork, my understanding of the visitor perception of Marie Antoinette was enhanced through meetings with subjects representing minority visitor groups detected through field research. These respondents' discourses were gathered outside the ordinary course of interviewing conducted at the Petit Trianon. An overview of their opinions (Chapter 6) refines the definition of the wider perceptions of Marie Antoinette at the Petit Trianon. In 2011, I also attended the commemoration for Louis XVI and his family, held every year on the first Sunday following the 21 January (date of his execution in 1793) at La Chapelle Expiatoire in Paris.[8]

Data Set 12

Analysis of French press releases throughout the duration of field research in France, as well as an analysis (2010–2014) of the prevalent image of Marie Antoinette in international popular culture sources, contributed to shaping the argument of Chapter 7, which relates to media as an external subliminal influence to visitor perceptions at a heritage site. As a result, I learned about and attended, on 4 November 2011, the French premiere of the first European[9] ballet about Marie Antoinette (Vienna Volksoper; choreography by Patrick de Bana, commissioned by the 2010-appointed director, French ballet star Manuel Legris), at the Royal Opera, Château de Versailles.

I also became acquainted with the most recent French film production on Marie Antoinette: Benoît Jacquot's *Les adieux à la reine*. Launched on 29 March 2012, in Versailles, where I was based at the time of the film's premiere in France, the first week's screenings were boycotted by Royalist and Catholic groups (see also Duprat 2013). Certain French Revolution historians see the film in a positive light (de Baecque 2012), whilst others, such as Berly (*Zéro de conduite* 2012), only comment on the reduced connection which the film makes between Marie Antoinette and the French Revolution. This production is incidentally examined in Chapters 4 and 7.

Data Set 13

Financial constraints required that I seek employment during fieldwork in 2012. I worked two to three days a week as a waitress (April – August 2012) in an American-style tourist restaurant (Sisters' Café, 15 rue des Réservoirs) near the East entrance to the Château de Versailles, next to Théâtre Montansier and opposite the Japanese-owned shop Renaissance, at 24 rue des Réservoirs. My field observations whilst living and working in Versailles revealed that this shop was one of the main stops of the organised Japanese group visits at Versailles.[10] During my work as a waitress, I met a considerable number of American tourists whose casual comments (prompted by my various questions investigating their interest in Château de Versailles and Marie Antoinette) further confirmed my field research findings. Other habitual restaurant customers included performers at the Royal Opera of Versailles and Théâtre Montansier, as well as local families. During the week, many members of the Château de Versailles staff also preferred it to their official *cantines*. This method pertains to ethnography. Inasmuch as being a 'survival job' rather than an undercover placement (see Ehrenreich 2005), it brought a valuable contribution to the interpretation of visitor discourses, as this job experience afforded valuable insight into both the tourist and local culture through reflexive observations and inside knowledge.

Data Set 14

In August 2014, I returned to Versailles to update inside knowledge related to the curatorial and heritage architectural projects at the Petit Trianon. Conclusions from my discussions with experts Jérémie Benoît, Philippe Baudin and Marie-Laëtitia Lachèvre are included in the relevant chapters. I also analysed boutique merchandise and books stocked at Librairie des Princes (Chapter 4). Furthermore, I met key members (who preferred to remain anonymous) of the Association Marie-Antoinette to check my findings against the expressed opinions and inside knowledge of French historical academics, as well as Royalist and Marie Antoinette fan circles. In August 2014, I also gathered information at three retail locations of Ladurée, a high-end confectionery, through informal interviews with their shop assistants (Anon. 3,4,5; pers. comm. 2014). This information was needed for assessing the contemporary dissonant commodification of Marie Antoinette's historical figure through the intermediary of the candy pink macarons sold by this retailer, as analysed in Chapter 7.

Data Set 15

During the last stages of my doctoral research (2013–2014), after returning from France, I analysed several internet sources concerning the images of Marie Antoinette which contributed to her dissonant commodification at the Petit Trianon. This method was required under the premise that media sources have an external subliminal influence on visitor perceptions at a heritage site (see Chapter 7). Sampling for these sources through the nature of webgraphs equates here to snowball sampling (due to intertextuality, see Krippendorff 2013). I base this equivalency on the nature of the hypertext of internet images (Sturken & Cartwright 2009) and its coding, which automatically selects the images according to the rules of this method of sampling. Snowball sampling is a reliable representative method when there is a clear research question, thus ensuring validity for the interpretation given in Chapter 7 when analysing the dissonant commodification of Marie Antoinette's historical figure at the Petit Trianon.

Marita Sturken and Lisa Cartwright (2009), who lean on Hall (1997) and his use of Barthes' (1977) theory referring to denotative, as opposed to connotative meaning of photographs, observe that postmodern visual culture relates mainly to connotative meanings. Concerning the dissonant commodification of Marie Antoinette's historical character, this confirms that, regardless the form of assimilation of images (dominant-hegemonic, negotiated or oppositional; see Hall 1997), the images of Marie Antoinette are perceived first and foremost under the rule of Hall's circle of representation: the connotative meaning of images, being culturally specific, determines that the cultural conditioning of each individual is the main element responsible for the ultimate perception of her historical character (see Chapter 7; also Figure 7.15).

Fieldwork research method at the Petit Trianon

This section details the qualitative questionnaire-led survey at the heritage site of the *Domaine de Marie-Antoinette*, conducted over a period of 15 months (2010–2012).

Field research goals

- To register and assess the image of Marie Antoinette in the perception of visitors at the Petit Trianon from within and without French borders
- To evaluate the origin and background of that image
- To establish the existing links between the perceived images and the corresponding visitors' political and cultural background

Field research was initially focused solely on library and archive[11] research methods. However, discussions with Château de Versailles experts Jérémie Benoît and Marie-Laëtitia Lachèvre suggested that this project would require an in-depth investigation of visitor perceptions at the Petit Trianon, and of French public opinion regarding the Ancien Régime in general, and Marie Antoinette in particular. Consequently, I expanded my research with qualitative investigation methods and devised a questionnaire to record visitor perceptions on site.

This analysis, set against a complex background reading of historical facts and imagery pertaining to popular culture, draws information and evidence from data collected specifically for this research project. The analysis is further assessed against factual evidence related to the Petit Trianon in the context of architectural history. This research strategy was determined by a lack of new, relevant and insightful material. Nevertheless, careful review of the various narratives related to the researched topic clearly showed a manipulation of primary sources. This finding indicated a potentially new way of reading such interpretations by assessing the facts objectively, taking as a point of reference the eighteenth-century architectural narrative of the Petit Trianon as home to Marie Antoinette.

In total, there were 307 valid responses (Table 3.2; see also Table 3.3). The first 52 respondents (including 22 French nationals) were interviewed throughout November – December 2010 in what amounted to a pilot test (Brunt 1997; Chelcea et al. 1998). Interpretation of their discourse allowed further refinement of the open-ended questionnaire, and helped to construct the multiple-choice questionnaire for Japanese visitors. The pilot test revealed that the majority of Japanese respondents did not speak English; therefore, a translation and redesign of the questionnaire were required.[12]

The following 199 respondents, interviewed from February through April 2011, belong to the following nationalities: French – 84; American – 34; Japanese – 26; Other – 55. For the second stage of the investigation, carried

Table 3.2 The structure of the respondents' samples over 15 months of fieldwork research

Date	Respondent nationality	Respondent numbers	Respondent gender	Respondent age group	Respondent declared art history knowledge/ background
Pilot test November – December 2010; Total Respondents: 52					
Sat.13/11/10;20/11/10; 27/11/10; 4/12/10; 18/12/10 Sun.14/11/10;21/11/10; 28/11/10; 5/12/2010; 19/12/10	French	22	14 F 8 M	36-59 60+	18 No 13 F; 5 M 4 Yes 1 F;3 M
Sat.13/11/10;20/11/10; 27/11/10; 4/12/10; 18/12/10 Sun.14/11/10;21/11/10; 28/11/10; 5/12/10; 19/12/10	American	12	7 F 5 M	26-35 36-59 60+	9 No 6 F, 3 M 3 Yes 1 F, 2 M
Sat. 20/11/10;18/12/10 Sun. 28/11/10	Japanese	3	3 F	26-35 36-59	3 F – Yes
Sat. 27/11/10; 18/12/10 Sun. 5/12/10	Spanish	4	2 F 2 M	26-35	No
Sat. 27/11/10;11/12/10 Sun 28/11/10; 5/12/10	Italian	5	3 F 2 M	36-59	No
Sun. 28/11/10; 5/12/2010	Hungarian	3	1 F 2 M	– 25 26-35	No
Sat. 27/11/10	South Korean (Canadian)	1	M	36-59	No
Sun. 5/12/10	French Canadian	2	1 F 1 M	36-59	No

First Stage February – April 2011; Total Respondents: 199

Fri. 8/04/11; 15/04/11 Sat. 19/02/11; 12/03/11 19/03/11;26/03/11; 2/04/11; 16/04/11 Sun.6/02/11; 20/02/11;13/03/11; 20/03/11;27/03/11; 17/04/11; 24/04/11	French	84	46 F 38 M	−25 26–35 36–59 60+	67 No 39 F, 28 M 17 Yes 7 F, 10M
Sat. 12/02/11;19/03/11; 26/03/11; 2/04/11 Sun 13/02/11;20/03/11; 3/04/11;10/04/11; 17/04/11; 24/04/11	American	34	18 F 16 M	−25 26–35 36–59 60+	29 No 14 F,15 M 5 Yes 4 F,1M
Sat. 5/02/11; 12/02/11; 5/03/11 Sun. 6/02/11; 13/02/11; 6/03/11	Japanese	26	16 F 10 M	−25 26–35 36–59 60+	21 No 11 F 10 M 5 F Yes
Sat. 12/02/11;12/03/11; 26/03/11 Sun.13/02/11;27/03/11; 24/04/11	Spanish	14	10 F 4 M	26–35 36–59	No
Sat. 12/02/11; 26/03/11 Sun. 27/03/11 Fri. 8/04/11; 15/04/11	Italian	14	8 F 6 M	26–35 36–59	No
Sun. 27/03/11	Colombian	4	2 F 2 M	26–35	No
Sat. 12/02/11 Sun. 13/02/11 Fri. 8/04/11	French Canadian	5	3 F 2 M	36–59 60+	No
Sun. 27/03/2011	Kuwaiti	4	4F	−25	No

(Continued)

Table 3.2 (Continued)

Date	Respondent nationality	Respondent numbers	Respondent gender	Respondent age group	Respondent declared art history knowledge/ background
Sat. 9/04/11	Iranian	3	3F	−25	No
Fri. 8/04/11; 15/04/11	Belgian	3	2F 1M	36−59	No
Sun. 10/04/11	Saudi Arabian	2	2 F	−25	No
Sat. 23/04/11	British	4	2 F 2 M	36−59	No
Sun. 24/04/11	Egyptian	2	2 F	−25	No
Second Stage November 2011 – July 2012; Total Respondents: 56					
Sat 19/11/11; 21/01/12 Sun. 22/01/12; 12/02/12; 25/03/12; 15/07/12	French	16	6 F 10M	36−59 60+	No
Sat 10/12/11 Sun 12/02/12; 25/03/12; 1/04/12; 22/04/12; 29/04/12; 20/05/12;27/05/12; 24/06/12; 1/07/12; 15/07/12; 22/07/12	American	16 valid 28 invalid	9 F 7 M	−25 26−35 36−59	No
Sat 10/12/11 Sun12/02/12; 25/03/12; 22/04/12; 29/04/12; 20/05/12;27/05/12; 17/06/12; 24/06/12; 1/07/12; 8/07/12; 15/07/12; 22/07/12	Japanese	24	15 F 9 M	−25 26−35 36−59 60+	23 No 14 F, 9 M 1 F Yes

Table 3.3 The main groups detected by the interpretation of respondent discourses

Group identification	Nationality	Size	Gender	Age group
Group 1	French	51	26 F; 25 M	36–59 / 60+
Group 2	French	43	32 F; 11 M	26–35 / 36–59
Group 3	French	21	8F; 13M	–25 / 26–35 / 36–59
Group 4	French	2	2M	36–59 / 60+
Free Sunday Group	French	5	5F	36–59 / 60+
Group Majority	American	54	29 F; 25 M	–25 / 26–35 / 36–59 / 60+
Group Minority	American	8	5 F; 3M	26–35 / 36–59
Group Majority	Japanese	44	25 F; 19 M	–25 / 26–35 / 36–59 / 60+
Group Minority	Japanese	9	9 F	26–35 / 36–59
Other European Group	Italian	19	11 F; 8 M	26–35 / 36–59
Other European Group	Spanish	18	12 F; 6 M	26–35 / 36–59
Other Middle East Group	Kuwaiti Iranian Saudi Arabian Egyptian	11	11 F	–25

out between November 2011 and July 2012, additional interviews were completed during several days of peak visitor numbers, to gather a total of 100 French, 50 American and 50 Japanese visitor discourses. Because saturation had been reached by the end of the first stage of the survey, I decided with my supervisory team at the time that the last part of the investigation should focus on three nationalities: French, American, Japanese. Their opinions on Marie Antoinette and perceptions of the Petit Trianon were the most relevant to the research in terms of exposing links between the cultural background and political agendas (if any) of the visitors, and their manner of decoding messages at a heritage site. Apart from on-site interviewing, I also investigated the perceptions of other specialist sections of the public – avid collectors and 'fans' of Marie Antoinette – through informal meetings and communication (see Chapter 6). These discourses, however, are not included in the aforementioned sample, but the fascination with Marie Antoinette which they represent will form the subject of exclusively ethnographic further research.

The initial sampling for the pilot test and the first stage was random,[13] whilst the second stage excluded respondents with an art and art history educational background, given that results from the previous stages indicated a strong association between educational-related variables (see Chelcea et al. 1998; Mason 2002; Robson 2002; Richards 2009; Marshall & Rossman 2011) and responses. These respondents constituted a niche minority, with a perception of Marie Antoinette contrasting to that of the majority. Therefore, the nationality-based selection for the second stage eliminated these respondents prior to application of the questionnaire.

The second stage, also carried out during peak season months (May, June, July 2012) confirmed the opinion held by the majority of visitors, which had begun to take shape after the first stage. However, it was particularly challenging to gather valid responses, with many potential respondents refusing to participate or bringing the interview to a close before completion. American respondents were particularly reluctant to participate, as they were either in a hurry, disinterested in being part of such research or sometimes even intimidated by the idea of expressing their own ideas about the site and all its associated values, including the image of the queen. Twenty-eight American respondents chose to terminate the interview early in the questionnaire, resulting in invalid responses. Those who participated fully were assigned to the American majority group. Japanese respondents were equally difficult to approach during these months, as they were mostly part of guided-group visits. Following discussions with several guides, it emerged that organised groups run on too tight a schedule to accommodate for the time necessary for visitors to fill in the questionnaire (see also Data Set 13).

The interpretation of responses was based on coded answers for each topic approached by the investigative questions (see Saldaña 2013; also Richards 2009), which allowed me to establish the main patterns of visitor perception. Once the detected patterns reached saturation for each nationality (by the end of the first stage of the survey), the responses provided by the second stage were used as confirmation of the validity of the working research hypothesis (Chelcea et al. 1998). Richards (2009:144) summarises saturation as: the 'arrival at a stage when nothing new is coming up'.

The methodology developed for the book and the preliminary results of the fieldwork research (see also Maior-Barron 2011) established the prevalence of all the narratives associated with the Petit Trianon and the mechanisms behind their construction. Furthermore, as the Petit Trianon is indissolubly associated with the figure of the last Queen of France (despite being built for and having belonged to various other famous historical characters), this association was also investigated.

Through the analysis of the architectural, historical, cinematic and heritage narratives of the Petit Trianon, it emerged that very different agendas are involved, with commercial, political and academic interests leading to disparate interpretations. More than two centuries after the French Revolution, the historical figure of Marie Antoinette continues to be highly debated, and discrepancies abound in the portrayal of her image even by official and well established sources. Consequently, the essay focused on the image of Marie Antoinette as generated by the four different narratives mentioned above, with the Petit Trianon interpreted as an indicator of their validity.

The assessment was based upon the evaluation of comments by the French and non-French visitors at the Petit Trianon, in an effort to establish the prevalence of the four main narratives in visitor perceptions, as indicated by visitor discourses. In fact, the ranked prevalence of the four major narratives of the Petit Trianon, within visitor perceptions, supported the charting of the dissonant commodification of Marie Antoinette's historical character. The methodology employed qualitative research methods (Chelcea et al. 1998; Mason 2002; Richards 2009; Marshall & Rossman 2011; Saldaña 2013) reinforced by a heritage concept put forward by Howard (2003:45): messages 'received at heritage sites [. . .] depend as much on the prejudices of the recipient as on the content of the message'. Prejudices have a direct, distinct influence on the individual perception of information in general (Chelcea et al. 1998).

The research working hypothesis was formulated by intersecting findings provided by Data Sets 1–7 with those provided by Data Set 8. Once associated and streamed into a strategy specifically devised for this research project, the methods employed by the qualitative research were complemented by the construction and in-field application of three types of questionnaires, with the Japanese version comprising multiple-choice questions to facilitate interpretation, and all others being semi-structured. I conducted the semi-structured questionnaires myself, recording respondent comments.

The version designed for the French public included questions meant to identify the political orientation of the respondents (Questions V, XIX), and to attempt to gauge overall nationalist inclinations (Questions V, XIX – XXIV). The latter turned out to be an unrealistic goal. The English version – also translated into Spanish and Italian – excluded questions of a political nature. The Japanese questionnaire had two additional questions, the first meant to investigate their perception of real versus mythical space under the influence of media sources and the second to specifically investigate traits of pilgrimage tourism, which theorists (Guichard-Anguis 2009) suggest

74 *Methodology and fieldwork research*

are particular to this public. The media influence over tourist perceptions and the pilgrimage trait of tourism were also tested for other nationals during the semi-structured interviews. In addition, all questionnaires included a specific question meant to identify the degree of interest of the respective respondents/tourists for historical sites in general.

The first four questions for all nationals were designed to clearly gauge their interest in the Petit Trianon, as opposed to other focal points of the entire estate of Versailles, as well as to assess their knowledge about the place. Furthermore, the second question (except the Japanese version) was meant to investigate whether the interpretation aim of the 2008 restoration was achieved, namely the Petit Trianon projecting the feel of a home rather than a museum, whilst also placing Marie Antoinette's ownership period in the historical continuity of previous and later ownerships. Although the second question for the semi-structured questionnaires was worded to avoid influencing the answers (i.e. I did *not* ask 'Do you think this feels like Marie Antoinette's home?'), my step-by-step prompting, which was aimed at detecting this identification, revealed that the interpretation aim of the restoration had been only partially achieved: the majority of the visiting public identifies the Petit Trianon exclusively with Marie Antoinette and not with other owners, as confirmed by answers to Question XII. For the Japanese public, this also proved to be the case, as reflected by their answers to Question 12.

Questions V-XI investigated the image and opinion that the public had formed about both the Petit Trianon and Marie Antoinette, also analysing whether the visit had any bearing on these perceptions. The evidence disproved this in relation to the majority of the public, but confirmed it for particular categories of tourists, such as Japanese nationals and a segment of the American nationals. The reason behind this shift of opinion proved to be the simplicity of the Petit Trianon, as opposed to the luxury respondents had expected. Other possible factors, such as nostalgia, are analysed in Chapter 6.

Questions XIII-XVIII (14–19 for the Japanese version) examined the degree of interest in and knowledge about the place. An additional question for Japanese visitors (13) assessed their perception of the site through preformed images acquired via media channels, by asking whether they would also like to visit the home of Lady Oscar, a fictitious character in the manga *Rose of Versailles*. The positive answers of the majority group proved the significant degree to which popular culture influences the perception of the Japanese audience. As aforementioned, the other added question (23) for the Japanese version refers to the pilgrimage tourism characteristic of this public, which the answers confirmed.

For Question V, respondents of all nationalities (except Japanese) were shown a separate list of films featuring Marie Antoinette as either the main or secondary character (Appendix A.5). A wide range of films was chosen, from those abounding in Republican clichés to those containing few or none, with the objective of eliciting responses used to analyse the respondents' political views. In this case, the aforementioned clichés served as indicators. After selecting the films they had seen, respondents were asked to rank them on a scale from 1 to 5, with 1 being the closest to historical truth. After detecting the initial source of the respondents' opinions about Marie Antoinette, this proved to be an effective way to further identify their historical beliefs, by comparing responses with film narratives.

Results demonstrated that media sources play an important part in forming the visitor perceptions of Marie Antoinette, with the exception of a few nationalities. For the majority groups of American and Japanese respondents, both school education and media sources – which generally perpetuate and reinforce Republican clichés – were found to have shaped the perception of the historical figure of Marie Antoinette (see also Figures 3.4 and 7.15).

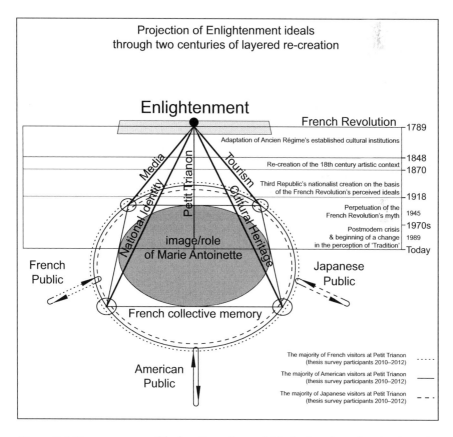

Figure 3.4 Factors responsible for distortions of Marie Antoinette's role since the eighteenth century, deciphered through contemporary visitor discourses at the Petit Trianon

Author 2012

Synthesis of the academic field, literature review and methodological framework

This last section presents a synthetic model, developed on the basis of the theoretical background, by associating the literature review in Chapters 1 and 2 with the methodological framework of the book, including the fieldwork research method and the evidence detailed in Chapter 6. This model[14] (Figure 3.4) is critical to illustrating the methodology of the book in relation to its academic background. Furthermore, it elucidates the manner in which the theories underpinning the book contribute to its arguments. The model is also essential in bringing together all elements required by the analysis of the four major narratives of Marie Antoinette and the Petit Trianon.

First, it must be stressed that, on a timeline between the transformation of the Enlightenment to the present day – from its conception in Marie Antoinette's Enlightenment vision through to the contemporary public's viewpoint – many distortions are revealed within the perception of the Petit Trianon. Further, these distortions have contributed to the dissonant commodification of Marie Antoinette's historical character. As shown, the main factors responsible for the distorted projection of the Enlightenment throughout the following centuries are: cultural heritage, national identity, tourism and media. The layers of distortions reside within the space created by these four factors of manipulation. Whilst the first two factors are directly linked to the French collective memory, the latter two are analysed through the prism of their mutual reinforcement of each other in contemporary society, as demonstrated in later chapters.

The 'Cultural Heritage' factor is mainly defined through Nora's 'places of memory' (1984a), and regards cultural heritage – in the absence of history's 'real' course – as a continuously and assiduously appropriated element of modernity. The theory explaining how places in general are produced spatially, and could be understood in a political context, is adapted from Lefebvre's (1991) theory on human political geography. Bourdieu's 'cultural capital' (1984) further supports these theories, highlighting the antithesis of cultural heritage and economic capital as well as its ability to legitimise new political and social elites.

The 'National Identity' factor is explained through the combined theories of Anderson (1991) and Hobsbawm (1983), framed in Gellner's (1993a, 1993b) wider context of the modernist anthropological theory of nationalism (Chapter 2). Accordingly, I conceive of national identity as an artificial construct which manages to define and project itself to the present day by manipulating cultural heritage.

Urry's theory of the 'romantic gaze' informs the 'Tourism' factor. His prominent sociological study of the evolution of tourism over the past two centuries analysed trends in tourism and the ways in which the contemporary public 'consumes' tourist destinations. It is important to note that tourism in its eighteenth-century form, a mode of travel reserved to the elite, represents one of the generating factors of the eighteenth-century picturesque landscape. Nevertheless, the distortion of the image of the Petit Trianon – and consequently of Marie Antoinette – enacted by Tourism, lies in the preformed images that contemporary visitors unwittingly bring to their visit.

By integrating the 'Media' – the model's last factor responsible for the distortion of Marie Antoinette's and the Petit Trianon's images – we can discern between the real parameters of the French Revolution and its self-projection onto the French collective memory. As Anderson (1991) explains, the self-generation of nationalism and its subsequent production of the national identities of the nineteenth century owe much to the written form of messages conveyed, and that media impact on the public began with eighteenth-century pamphlets of revolutionary propaganda (on media influence in public opinion of the late eighteenth century, see Habermas 1989; also Darnton 1995).

The transversal sections of the model represent the layers of re-creation and consequent distortion of Enlightenment ideals, through interpretation according to various agendas. The understanding of these layers is underpinned by all previously mentioned theories. In addition, Hobsbawm (1983) determined that the 1870s were the political decade in European history crucial to crystallising Western modern states' national identities – a view providing the model with a watershed point for its timescale.[15]

The period up until 1848 saw many reversals and upheavals in the succession of political regimes. In terms of cultural heritage, there were known attempts to replace the old institutions of the Ancien Régime through conservation and preservation, with variable (and debatable) degrees of success (O'Connell 1989). In fact, a closer examination of new legislation and institutions emerging from the fall of the Ancien Régime revealed a surprising adaptation of the old structures and an import of ideas from England. By contrast, a further analysis of the 1848–1870 historical period indicated a clear re-creation of eighteenth-century artistic tastes and trends through an overt appropriation of the period's artistic sensibility, prized by key political and cultural personalities such as Empress Eugénie and Prosper Mérimée (Ball 2011). Setting the tone of this appropriation for their French contemporaries through public as well as personal examples, they initiated a trend responsible for elements of the discourse of Enlightenment that became inspirational for nineteenth-century French Romanticism. Furthermore, Empress Eugénie's own fascination may have inspired the cult-like following around Marie Antoinette's historical figure. The focus of this book puts the period between 1789 and 1870 beyond the remit of the analysis.

The period encompassed by this study begins with the defeat of France at Sedan in 1870, which heralded the rise of the Third Republic. This date marks the beginning of an institutionalised re-creation of France's historical past through a political agenda designed to create a strongly defined national identity within a carefully organised programme, as attested by Nora (1984); Hobsbawm (1983) and Anderson (1991). This process of re-creation is an

78 Methodology and fieldwork research

important contributing factor to the contemporary dissonant commodification of Marie Antoinette's historical figure at the Petit Trianon.

The base of the model is represented by the French (national) collective memory, having at its centre the true role of Marie Antoinette, developed through the projection of the initial eighteenth-century creation of the Estate of the Petit Trianon, a site which subsequently serves as an analysis indicator. In these circumstances, within the graphic layout of the model, the Petit Trianon represents the axis of projection. It is argued here that the true role of Marie Antoinette was successfully obscured through juxtaposition with the queen's perception in the French collective memory. In other words, her perceived image had subverted historical truth.

This juxtaposition was determined by many chronological layers continually interpreting this role, with the first source of distortion originating in the French phobia of Austrians, which predated Marie Antoinette's reign. Evidence gathered at the Petit Trianon illustrates to what extent the French collective memory's perceived image of Marie Antoinette has influenced locals as well as visitors from abroad. For the American and Japanese majority groups partaking in the field study, results indicate that an essential source contributing to the preformed images of the majority of non-French visitors is the media factor – that is, popular culture disseminated through media channels (films, novels, manga). Although the media factor per se was not specifically indicated to have influenced the French groups, and although Halbwachs' (1992) own theory does not explicitly state that the media factor is responsible for the creation of individual memories (via collective memory), this is actually implied by his observations on the importance of social frameworks in creating the collective memory from which individual memories are drawn. (Astrid Erll contributes an outstanding analysis of Halbwachs' work – including the way through which media infiltrate social frameworks – in the wider context of 'memory in culture'; see Erll 2011). Returning to the survey at the Petit Trianon, these observations are further validated by the fact that the particular element linking French collective memory to these other nationals' (American and Japanese) perception of Marie Antoinette at the Petit Trianon was identified in revolutionary-propaganda clichés perpetuated by the French Third Republic's political agenda. The libellous eighteenth-century pamphlets/media – from which the clichés originated – are therefore responsible for the image distortions of Marie Antoinette's historical character.

Finally, 'Tourism' is the element requiring a differentiation between various sections of the contemporary visiting public. The general contemporary perception of Marie Antoinette and the Estate of the Petit Trianon, relevant to the three main nationalities analysed here, is depicted through concentric circles circumscribing the base of the model (Figure 3.4). The circles represent the preformed images of these different sections of the public and refer to the majority, not the minority, groups identified by the research evidence. The circles' positioning was not determined by visitor statistics at the Petit

Trianon. Instead, they represent the lenses through which the image of Marie Antoinette is perceived today by the majority of French and non-French visitors, and the order was naturally dictated by the logic of this perception.

This chapter defined the methodological framework of the book and the research method developed specifically for this case study, whilst also taking into consideration the evidence further analysed in Chapter 6. The synthetic model brings them all together and places them in the context of the theoretical background. It must be reiterated that the research principles established in this section operate throughout the analysis of the narratives of the Petit Trianon and Marie Antoinette in later chapters. Furthermore, an analysis of the research findings in Chapter 6, and the final assessment of the prevailing narrative of the Petit Trianon in Chapter 7, reveal the emerging images of Marie Antoinette at the site. These images, in turn, amount to the dissonant commodification of this controversial historical figure at the Petit Trianon.

Notes

1 Ricoeur analyses these two forms of historical memory and considers them to be uncanny based on Freud's (1919) term of 'Unheimlich'. Although both processes suggest a familiarity of values to start with, in fact they induce artificially constructed 'recollections', and are thus false.
2 Through his heritage and tourism relationship analyses, Australian academic Matthew W. Rofe establishes the basis for the philosophical paradigm of Reconstruction; see Rofe (2006, 2013, 2016).
3 Robert Mugerauer (1995) successfully applies this paradigm in the interpretation of American natural landscape perceptions since the nineteenth century. Cultural heritage studies relevant to the present argument utilise the hermeneutic paradigm either to reveal opinions prejudiced by nationalist purposes (see Collins 2011) or to detect the confluence between curatorial interpretation and visitor perceptions in museums. Particularly successful contributions come from Hooper-Greenhill (2000), and from Davey (2012), who provides an appraisal of the hermeneutical method by highlighting its advantages.
4 In Halbwachs' (1992) theory, the social frameworks encompassing literal and metaphorical elements, from social groups to cognitive schemata, play a central role in the creation of individual memories.
5 Chelcea et al. (1998) distinguish between 'theoretical' and 'working' hypotheses in qualitative research. In line with hypothesis coding used in qualitative research (see also Saldaña 2013), I have used this type of hypothesis, which was tested and validated by field evidence at the Petit Trianon.
6 See http://cashtrackingclub.com/index.php?do=/blog/10794/let-them-eat-manga-how-takashi-murakami-launched-japanese-kitsch-to-the-pal/ [Accessed: 8 November 2010]. For a recent alternative perspective on the connections between Murakami's work, *Rose of Versailles* and a Japanese imaginary aesthetic construction, see Lee (2017).
7 Riyoko Ikeda, who trained as a soprano at the age of 40, saw a personal dream come true by performing in 2011 at Le Petit Théâtre de la Reine where Marie Antoinette once acted and sang. The *mangaka's* notoriety turned her recital into a VIP event organised by CVS (Château de Versailles Spectacles) with ticket prices starting at 1500 euros.

80 *Methodology and fieldwork research*

8 La Chapelle Expiatoire is a commemorative site for Louis XVI and Marie Antoinette, built on the actual premises of the Madeleine cemetery where all the victims of the *guillotine* were initially buried in communal graves. On 21 January 1815 the remains of the two monarchs were transferred to Basilique (Royale) de Saint-Denis, the French Monarchy's legitimate place of rest. The altar at La Chapelle Expiatoire is allegedly positioned on the exact spot where Louis XVI and Marie Antoinette were exhumed. Initiated by Louis XVIII (Comte de Provence) the construction was finished during the reign of Charles X (Comte d'Artois) in 1826; www.chapelle-expiatoire.monuments-nationaux.fr/. In attendance at the 2011 event were cadet branch descendant Charles-Xavier de Bourbon Parme and his wife, as well as Royalist minority groups such as *Les Chouans*.

9 Performed with eighteenth-century music, the production of *Marie-Antoinette* premiered at the Vienna Volksoper on 20 November 2010. The production was later updated for their 2015/2016 season. The very first ballet about Marie Antoinette, however, premiered in the United States in 2009 (*Marie*, performed by the Houston Ballet, with choreography by Stanton Welch) and received mixed reviews. It was praised (Glentzer 2009), though also criticised for both choreography and music choice (Macaulay 2009). Interestingly, Glentzer (2009) references Sofia Coppola's *Marie Antoinette* (2006).

10 See www.societe.com/societe/renaissance-414819763.html. Beginning in 1997, Renaissance sold Louis Vuitton and other European luxury brands favoured by the Japanese market. Prior to touring the Palace of Versailles and the Petit Trianon, Japanese guided groups visited *Renaissance*.

11 Source materials at the Documentation Library and the Archives – La Petite Écurie (departments of Château de Versailles where I conducted research) can be classified under 'Restricted' access (see Scott 1990:14), as they are available only to staff and academic researchers from Master level onwards. The Documentation Library and the Archives moved to the Grand Commun, in 2013 and 2016, respectively.

12 After initial design and structure feedback from head curator Jérémie Benoît, the final translated version of the questionnaire was ready at the beginning of February 2011. A sample of 26 respondents completed it during February weekends and the first weekend of March 2011. During the fall of 2010, Japanese visitor numbers rose, according to Château de Versailles staff observations (Benoît pers. comm. 2010c). Takashi Murakami's exhibition at the Palace, which was highly controversial, may have contributed to this increase. In February 2011 Japanese visitor numbers at the Petit Trianon increased again, perhaps due to the presence of Riyoko Ikeda in Paris and Versailles, following her appearance at the Angoulême International Comics Festival (see Data Sets 3 and 4). The earthquake and tsunami that struck Japan on 11 March 2011 affected the frequency of Japanese visits to the site. The Château de Versailles displayed posters throughout the Estate expressing sympathy and support for one of their most devoted audiences. I personally stopped approaching the few Japanese visitors with requests to fill in the questionnaire, as I felt this would have been inappropriate at the time.

13 The sampling was done randomly according to Veal (2006). As soon as I finished completing one questionnaire I would approach other potential respondents passing by. During the cold months I was stationed by the exit next to the Cour d'Honneur. Another exit by the Farm of the Hamlet is open and used in the summer by local families and foreign tourists, usually if they get lost. I used the latter exit point during the spring months in order to obtain answers representative of local visitors. During the cold months I approached respondents by the former exit, and invited them inside the building of the Petit Trianon. I made arrangements with the security personnel of the Petit Trianon to allow me to return through the door which otherwise serves only as an exit towards the gardens.

14 Model designed by Denise Maior-Barron (2012). I would like to thank heritage architect Philippe Baudin (Château de Versailles) for the professional visual rendition of the model. Disclaimer: Please note that the model does not represent the stability of a pyramid. Its four sides are not in equilibrium but quite the opposite, rising to and falling from prominence depending on the time's dominant agenda of each political era. This instability represents the source of the image distortions analysed.
15 For a recent historical analysis of the complexity of Versailles as a 'place of memory' incorporating multivalent meanings from the seventeenth century to the present, and appropriated accordingly by different international historical and political agencies, see Pestel (2017).

4 Historical and cinematic narratives encoding Marie Antoinette's contemporary perception

This chapter synthesises data collected through the hermeneutical analysis (Scott 1990) of the relevant sources composing the historical and cinematic narratives associated with the historical figure of Marie Antoinette. The chapter further analyses, first, the public image of the last Queen of France as conveyed by relevant French historical works to date, including an evaluation of eighteenth-century revolutionary pamphlets and their effect on Marie Antoinette's image. Central to the analysis are twentieth- and twenty-first century biographers of Marie Antoinette, who have had a direct influence over cinematic narratives as sources of inspiration.

Further, the chapter continues to investigate the cinematic narrative surrounding Marie Antoinette. Field research proved this study to be fundamental, since American and Japanese visitors in particular use popular culture media sources as reference points for their perception of the site and its former owner. The first cinematic production considered is Sofia Coppola's *Marie Antoinette* (2006). Interestingly, while Coppola's film was arguably not appreciated by the French public, it has attracted much interest in the queen's *Domaine* and life. The Château de Versailles management foresaw and seized on the opportunity to strengthen and further promote the site's image, whilst planning a restoration of the Petit Trianon, completed in 2008. The other media source composing the cinematic narrative of the book, albeit a cinematically illustrated book rather than a film, is Riyoko Ikeda's manga *Rose of Versailles* (1972), which has had a significant influence on the way the Japanese public regards the Petit Trianon and Marie Antoinette. Such was its force, in fact, that the manga became part of a social phenomenon of women's emancipation in 1970s Japan.

Historical narrative

The present historical narrative is understood through Roland Barthes' (1966) structuralist approach and used accordingly in the field research methodology of the book (see also Maior-Barron 2011). Following Barthes, 'narratives' are threads of a storyline rather than a compilation of multiple stories. From this perspective, a definition of the concept used in social science research belongs to Denning (2000; see also Polkinghorne 1988), who refers to narrative as something told or recounted in the form of a causally linked set of events, be they true or fictitious. The research of the book is also concerned with the associated element of 'narrative meaning', which according to Denning is created by establishing that something is a part of a whole, within links of causation. The meaning of each event is therefore produced by the part it plays in the narrative. This chapter, as well as Chapter 5, assembles the presentation of the four major narratives of the Petit Trianon and Marie Antoinette from the particular perspective of 'narrative meaning'.

The historical narrative elements are paramount in understanding the representation, interpretation and perception of Marie Antoinette's historical character relevant to the majority of contemporary visitors at the Petit Trianon. Consequently, the selection of historical sources was based on their direct or indirect influence over the encoding and the subsequent decoding of the historical character of Marie Antoinette for Petit Trianon visitors, with a focus on the majority groups. Royalist, Romantic, rehabilitative and feminist historiographies underpin the data collection relating to the minority visitor groups, thus representing negative evidence for the Republican views of the majority.

The source selection was cross-referenced with the stock of the main bookshop of Château de Versailles (Librairie des Princes) and their bestsellers, according to testimonials gathered from shop assistants during 2010–2012 (Table 4.1). To construct a comprehensive view of the most up-to-date

Table 4.1 'Bestseller' biographies of Marie Antoinette (2010–2012) at Librairie des Princes (in alphabetical order, including original year of publication)

Cécile Berly and Jean-Clément Martin	*Marie-Antoinette* (2010)
Simone Bertière	*Marie-Antoinette l'insoumise* (2002)
Madame Campan	*Mémoires de Madame Campan, Première Femme de Chambre de Marie-Antoinette* (1823/1988)
André Castelot	*Marie-Antoinette* (1953)
Jean Chalon	*Chère Marie-Antoinette* (1988)
Benedetta Craveri	*Marie-Antoinette et le scandale du collier* (2006/2008)
Élisabeth de Feydeau	*Jean-Louis Fargeon, Parfumeur de Marie-Antoinette* (2005)
Antonia Fraser	*Marie-Antoinette: Biographie* (2001/2006)
Évelyne Lever	*Marie-Antoinette: La dernière reine* (2000a/b)
	Marie-Antoinette: Correspondance (1770–1793) (2005a)
Chantal Thomas	*La Reine scélérate: Marie-Antoinette dans les pamphlets* (1989a)
	Les Adieux à la Reine (2002) (novel)
Stefan Zweig	*Marie-Antoinette* (1932/1933a)

tendency in the portrayal of Marie Antoinette, a few recent publications authorised by Château de Versailles, and identified during the final field research trip in August 2014, are included in a later section of the chapter. It is relevant that the majority of visitors do not buy books at Librairie des Princes. Field research suggests that book-sale trends are representative only of a minority of visitors with a degree of art history knowledge.[1]

The premises of the present chapter's analysis establish, based on field research evidence, that school education in France, the United States and Japan, bears Republican connotations, Marie Antoinette being generally represented in a negative light, if at all. An analysis of French or other nationals' school curriculum is not included here, the complexity of the topic recommending it for a future study. Despite school education forming an important source of information on the subject of historical figures in general, and of Marie Antoinette in particular, its role is acknowledged here exclusively in conjunction with the concept of 'collective memory' (Halbwachs 1980, 1992) – the one element to conclusively shape public perception – through the intermediary of clichés circulated by popular culture.

In addition, field research evidence revealed the absence of a single or clear source which the majority of visitors would consider formative for their opinion about Marie Antoinette. For the majority of French and American visitors, multiple sources are found in school education as well as books, novels, television programmes and films. With few exceptions, respondents were unable to list these sources. Chapter 6 analyses this particular aspect of unidentifiable sources of information in the context of the 'imaginary social worlds' theory (Caughey 1984). In the case of the majority of Japanese visitors, apart from school education, the two sources contributing to their opinion of Marie Antoinette were Ikeda's *Rose of Versailles* and Coppola's *Marie Antoinette*.

In French academic circles, the postmodern tendency of reassessing 'tradition' (Figure 3.4) has led to attempts to integrate the truncated passages of French history (Le Goff & Nora 2011; Le Goff 2014) and to invest the role of historian with the duty and ability to objectively portray the past (Le Goff & Nora 2011; Darwin Smith 2012). This is based on the recognition of otherwise old problems (Bloch 1997) which become, in the 'making of history', new and stringent problems, new approaches and new objects (Le Goff & Nora 2011). Moreover, the role of the public historian, which is of particular concern here, was recently acknowledged by Nora (2011a:15) as the key to successfully placing French history into the 'heart of French culture and identity'.

All of the above has led to the appearance of various recent biographers of Marie Antoinette (some of whom come from academic backgrounds not restricted to history) submitting their work to the 'nouvelle histoire'. This chapter establishes how successful this aim of rewriting history can be, given the deeply rooted misconceptions surrounding the French Revolution and Marie Antoinette. In fact, field research revealed a peculiarity surrounding Marie Antoinette and, intrinsically, the Petit Trianon, in terms of historical narrative. The misrepresentation that has defined the image of the queen for so long determined a reversal of reality into fiction, and vice versa. The results of vehement propaganda, and all the issues raised by it until the last hours of Marie Antoinette's life (when one of the incriminations was famously to do with the 'great expenses' incurred for building works at the Petit Trianon), positioned the queen's estate in a reprobate but also fantasy dimension in the eyes of the public. The Petit Trianon became synonymous with the luxury and decadence of the Ancien Régime itself.

Reality became fiction, and fiction became reality again – a constant, long-established process clearly translated into the vast literature written about the last Queen of France. Following extensive analysis of the major historical works and historical fiction surrounding Marie Antoinette, a clear conclusion can be drawn: on one side there are historians who intend to be objective in giving their own interpretation to already established historical material. However, this material, after two centuries of misrepresentation, sets traps for present-day interpretations. On the other side, there are historians doing painstaking research outside of the historical dogmas who often arrive at conclusions in opposition to common beliefs which are so well rooted in the French collective memory that they cannot be overtly challenged. Therefore, their work can only be published without being discredited if reclassified as fiction. According to Dorrit Cohn (2001), the difference between historical and historical fiction narratives lies in the higher probability of the latter being associated with 'untruth' despite the possibility of their truthfulness with regard to real events as historical narratives. Furthermore, there is another crucial aspect to consider when truth comes into question. As Darwin Smith (2012) suggests through his study on the professional position in which French contemporary historians working with/at CNRS[2] find themselves, research projects aiming for an accurate depiction of France's past are not only hampered financially but also politically. Having witnessed the highly politicised milieu of French journalism, the historian seems to observe similar patterns within the CNRS.

Leaning on the observations above, in the case of research on the historical character of Marie Antoinette, political and financial considerations converge in two possible ways. First, they can restrict the presentation of alternative ways to understand Marie Antoinette's historical character due to the well-established historical discourses and associated historical dogmas espoused by the majority of historians. Second, and perhaps worse, they can favour the sensationalistic works about Marie Antoinette due to the lucrative potential and incentive for monetary gain. Marie Antoinette sells well, creating a veritable industry of biographies – more or less romanced and ranging between fiction and history – which have flooded the market, especially since the 2006 release of Coppola's *Marie Antoinette* (see also Seth 2006; Biard & Leuwers 2007). Furthermore, Marie Antoinette's fate makes her popular with a wide range of audiences, to whom she appeals on different

86 *Historical and cinematic narratives*

levels, regardless of their opinion of her. In turn, this popularity encourages the ever-increasing avalanche of literary and cinematic productions.

Other relevant contributions to the historical narrative analysis derive from American and British authors. In fact, Marie Antoinette seems to be a popular subject for American academia, befittingly illustrating their counterarguments to a French Republican historical thesis. Perhaps due to the competitive nature acknowledged by Nora (2013) in an up-to-date analysis of the tandem of forces existent between the two models of modern democracy (see also Kuisel 1993), American and French historical discourses stand in disagreement with regard to France's dissonant past. If Marxism may have been at the root of the antithesis, recent postmodern reconsiderations of history (on both sides), have made strides to reconcile the previously disparate approaches. The reconciliation between American and French views over French history translates into the revisionist French trends aligning the two perspectives. Nevertheless, for the majority of American visitors at the Petit Trianon, their opinion of Marie Antoinette is similar to that of their French counterparts.

Susan Lanser (2003:277) also observes that within the American/Anglo-Saxon milieu, the views on Marie Antoinette emerged from a 'marked contrast between Burkean hagiography to Jeffersonian demonization', but that, however, the negative extreme is starting to be challenged by recent contributions to the subject (Goodman 2003b). In fact, challenging old historical precepts is currently restricted to academic circles. Furthermore, American popular media sources, such as Sofia Coppola's film (or British author Antonia Fraser's biography, on which the film is based), despite attempting a fairer portrayal of the queen, only reinforced old Republican clichés (see Table 3.1), a fact decried by both sides of the aforementioned history academia circles (Hunt 1991; Goodman 2003b; Duprat 2006, 2007, 2011, 2013; Lever 2006b; Berly 2006, 2012; Berly & Martin 2010). Chantal Thomas (1989a); Catriona Seth (2006); Annie Duprat (2006, 2013) and Cécile Berly (2012) extensively review the clichés associated with Marie Antoinette in the French milieu, whilst Thomas Kaiser (2000); Vivian Gruder (2002); Dena Goodman (2003b) and Caroline Weber (2006) provide the American counterpart of this perception. Véronique Campion-Vincent and Christine Shojaei Kawan (2002) contribute a French rehabilitative review of the 'Let them Eat Cake!' cliché, identifying three associated connotative meanings to this: arrogance, cruelty and stupidity.

There are key moments in Marie Antoinette's life, reign and death which are constantly reproduced and debated (Table 4.2). Whilst the early life and final moments are generally agreed on, it is the period following the accession of Louis XVI to the throne in 1774 until 1792 (the fall of the French Monarchy) which divides opinions between Republican and Royalist sympathies. According to the hermeneutical paradigm and its principles of the 'near' and the 'prejudice', such a division confirms the manipulation of Marie Antoinette's image by various parties.

Table 4.2 The key moments contributing to the portrayal of Marie Antoinette's controversial image by the historical narrative of the book

2 November 1755	Birth of Maria Antonia Johanna Josepha de Loraine-Habsbourg, Archduchess of Austria, youngest daughter of their Most Catholic Majesties, François I (of Lorraine) and the Austro-Hungarian Empress Maria Theresa.
1755–1770	Childhood at Schönbrunn Palace: relatively 'etiquette free' royal Austrian upbringing, closely resembling the French Bourgeois milieu.
1770	Child bride married to Louis-Auguste, Duc de Berry, Dauphin of France, future Louis XVI; the Dauphine is well received by the French people but not as well by various factions of the Court of Versailles due to her Austrian nationality; the two teenagers belonging to previously enemy countries are thrown together into a game of circumstances which, despite keeping them apart in the beginning, gradually forged their union as a devoted couple united in political views.
1770–1774	Dauphine of France at Versailles Palace; continuing to be a well-loved princess by the French people as she is actually seen in contrast with the declining morality of the Court of Versailles; unanimously praised for her generosity and charitable nature, inclined to helping the poor.
1774	30 January 1774 – The Masked Ball at the Opera in Paris: Marie Antoinette, incognito, converses with the Swedish Count Hans Axel von Fersen, historical character upon whom rests the proof of fidelity or infidelity of the queen towards her royal husband, and even the proof of Marie Antoinette's alleged treason due to help received from this 'foreign' national in the course of later events.
	10 May 1774: Death of Louis XV, the ascension to the throne of Louis XVI and Marie Antoinette, both in their teens.
	Marie Antoinette enters into possession of the Petit Trianon, and initiates works on the garden that would become one of the most accomplished models of Jardin Anglais, but would also be vehemently criticised for being one of the main causes for France's bankruptcy.
1774–1778	Early-reign years and childless marriage: the 'Queen of Fashion and Balls' image takes root in the public imaginary through the influence of eighteenth-century pamphlets; in the absence of other targets (previously, the kings' mistress/*favorite*) due to Louis XVI's fidelity, Austrian-born Marie Antoinette becomes the ideal political figure to embody the negative image of the French Monarchy and the Ancien Régime.
1778	20 December: Birth of Princesse Marie-Thérèse-Charlotte of France, first child of Marie Antoinette and Louis XVI, future Duchess of Angoulême. This event intensifies the defamatory libels against Marie Antoinette, proving the underlying intention to decrease her popularity as soon as it was on the mend. The queen proved to be an exemplary mother to all her children.

(*Continued*)

Table 4.2 (Continued)

1780	29 November: Death of Empress Maria Theresa, Marie Antoinette's mother and mentor; despite the overpowering maternal presence (even from the great geographical distance separating them), Marie Antoinette deeply cherished her mother who she held as a moral model in crucial moments for the rest of her life.
1781	22 October: Birth of the Dauphin of France, Louis-Joseph-Xavier-François; the official seal of legitimation for Marie Antoinette's role of Queen of France, previously uncertain in the absence of a male heir; the event intensifies the calumny against Marie Antoinette, derogatory pamphlets alluding to illegitimate paternity.
1785	27 March: Birth of the second son of Louis XVI and Marie Antoinette, the future Dauphin of France (after the death of his eldest brother in 1789) and later Louis XVII, King of France following the death of his father; the calumny against Marie Antoinette continues.
	15 August: The outburst of the Affair of the Diamond Necklace (*L'Affaire du Collier*) which arguably sealed the negative image of the queen, easing the way for the final blows towards the French Monarchy through calumny; a web of intrigues surrounding the secret purchase by a high-standing religious official of one of the most expensive pieces of jewellery ever made, allegedly on behalf of Marie Antoinette. The dimensions of the affair surpass credible reality, making this episode one of the most popular topics of fiction work on Marie Antoinette.
1786–1787	Birth and death, before the age of 1, of the fourth and last child of the royal couple: Princess Sophie-Hélène-Béatrix of France. Marie Antoinette together with the king and their eldest child in particular (Madame Royale who was old enough to acknowledge this death) are very affected by the loss.
1789	4 June: Death of the first Dauphin which greatly affects Marie Antoinette and Louis XVI; the fall of the Bastille and the French Revolution's first events occur against the backdrop of the couple's bereavement.
	The night of 5 October: Château de Versailles invaded by an alleged 'spontaneous' mob action led by Parisian 'women' (later many proved to be men) seeking the death of the queen. The queen escapes and dominates the mob by appearing at the royal balcony (attesting her charisma and courage in key moments).
	6 October: The royal family leaves Château de Versailles, forced to move to Tuileries Palace in Paris; last day spent at Versailles.
1790	The royal family helplessly witnesses the rising chaos engulfing France; attempts to reinstall order through unsuccessful negotiations with various parties; the public opinion against Marie Antoinette culminates in hatred.
	26 December: Louis XVI signs the Civil Constitution.

1791	18 April: The royal family is prevented from leaving the Tuileries for Saint Cloud with the occasion of Easter; confirmation of their unofficial status of prisoners. Marie Antoinette is increasingly being targeted as a figure of hatred, to the point of her life becoming endangered.
	20 June: the flight organised by Marie Antoinette with Count von Fersen, aiming to take the royal family out of Paris (destination Montmédy; see also Figure 6.1); episode that bears high political relevance for the Republican historical discourse trying to prove the disloyalty which Marie Antoinette has shown to the French people (see Tackett 2003).
	21 June: the royal family captured at Varennes and brought back to Tuileries; the failed Montmédy flight becomes known as the Varennes flight.
	25 June: The king's official attributions are suspended; the Legislative Assembly is formed as a temporary ruling body.
1792	20 April: The Legislative Assembly declares war on Austria in the name of France, whilst Louis XVI stood against plans involving any French bloodshed.
	20 June: Attack of the Tuileries Palace, as a commemorative threat to the Varennes flight; serious concerns for the safety of the royal family mounting amongst royal supporters from abroad (for a valuable account of the context and attempts to rescue the French Monarchy by the royal family and their supporters abroad, see Price 2002).
	25 July: the Brunswick Manifesto (see Barton 1967; Cross 2011) is signed by Duke Brunswick at Coblenz – The Austrian-Prussian coalition recognises Louis XVI as sole legitimate ruler of France, pressing threats onto the Revolutionary Committee for guaranteeing the safety of the French royal family; crucial moment used by the revolutionary factions for the final dissolution of the monarchy, under the pretext that Louis XVI conspired with the enemy (as some of the Royalist supporters from abroad, such as Count von Fersen, were involved in the planning of the Manifesto in a last desperate attempt to rescue the royal family); the event was later used against the royal family in charges of conspiracy with foreign powers.
	10 August: Invasion of Tuileries Palace and massacre of the Royal Swiss Guards charged with the protection of the royal family who escaped by finding refuge with the National Assembly – Official date for the fall of the French Monarchy.
	13 August: The National Assembly decides to imprison the royal family at Le Temple.
	22 September: The First French Republic is formed.
	11 and 26 December: Trial of Louis XVI by the Convention who finds him guilty of treason.

(Continued)

Table 4.2 (Continued)

1793	16–18 January: Death sentence for Louis XVI voted and irremediably decided on, following the rejection of Thomas Paine's plea for reprieve on the 18.
	21 January: Louis XVI's death – execution by guillotine (for a contemporary account of the events that led to this moment, see de Montjoie 1814).
	1 July: 8 year-old Louis XVII (as the Royalists proclaimed the Dauphin, Louis-Charles, after his father's execution) is separated by the Revolutionary Committee from his mother, Marie Antoinette.
	2 August: Marie Antoinette is moved to La Conciergerie, known as the last stop for death-sentence prisoners.
	14–15 October: Marie Antoinette's Trial; following lack of evidence for treason, the accusation of incest is brought on the second day leading to the moment which sealed Marie Antoinette's symbolic role of female victimisation by the French Revolution. Marie Antoinette is sentenced to death.
	16 October: Marie Antoinette's death – execution by guillotine; birth of a modern (and postmodern) legend.

The stark contrast revealed by the images of Marie Antoinette in official representations of the 1770s (Figure 4.1; see also Duprat 2013) and analogous public opinion images of the 1780s (Figure 4.2), reflects the replacement of the court's sphere of influence with that of public opinion – the effect and/or the cause of the monarchic decline (see Habermas 1989). However, surprisingly, Royalist and Republican sympathies towards the historical character of Marie Antoinette are not always linked (paradoxically perhaps) with political connotations. Royalist writers (Girault de Coursac 1962, 1990), in wanting to rehabilitate the image of Louis XVI, choose to denigrate Marie Antoinette, seeing the two historical characters in a conflict of interests.[3] The defamatory discourse on Marie Antoinette can be traced to Catholic contemporaries to the events of the French Revolution (Soulavie 1801). Equally, there are sections of the public today, such as members of Association Marie-Antoinette, a French NGO concerned with the rehabilitation of Marie Antoinette's image, who do not all consider themselves to have Royalist political inclinations. What prevails is the members' fascination with the figure of the last Queen of France (Lorin pers. comm 2014b). This attests to the fact that Marie Antoinette transcended her political, social and cultural dimensions, having acquired the status of symbol, whether criticised or highly admired. The variations found in the perception of her historical character reinforce this symbolic value in different ways, appropriated by different identities.

Establishing an external validation to the results of the survey at the Petit Trianon makes for the subject of future research. However, using the

Figure 4.1 Marie Antoinette, an adulated queen at the beginning of her reign, as depicted in this official vignette honouring her as patron of the arts (C. N. Cochin 1776)

Courtesy Bibliothèque nationale de France

Figure 4.2 Marie Antoinette, a hated queen by the late 1780s as depicted by the revolutionary pamphlet caricatures of the time, such as this image of a harpy trampling the Constitution (Anonymous)

Courtesy Bibliothèque nationale de France

historical narrative in this chapter to evaluate whether these authors' views are integrated in the visitor discourses gathered in the survey at the Petit Trianon (2010–2012), the analysis confirms this to be the case. This could also suggest representativeness of the survey sample for the wider French public when corroborated by the further evidence of the 1993 theatre spectacle directed by actor Robert Hossein (historical advisers Alain Decaux and André Castelot),[4] which was dedicated to the bicentenary commemoration of Marie Antoinette's death (Figure 4.3). This spectacle revisited the queen's trial, whilst showing flashbacks of her life, and gave 4,000 spectators each night for five months a chance to act as the jury by voting to potentially

Figure 4.3 Caroline Sihol as Marie Antoinette – 1993 theatrical remake of the queen's trial, directed by actor Robert Hossein

© Paris-Match

change the course of 'History' at each performance.[5] The queen was most often exiled to Austria, her country of birth (Franck 1993; Berly 2006; Seth 2006). The vote to exile – significantly to Austria – could suggest that the French public still considered Marie Antoinette an unwelcome foreigner who brought prejudice to their country significant enough to warrant exile to her homeland. Even more significantly, one of the members of the public who attended the *'spectacle'* on 16 October 1993, the date marking the actual bicentenary commemoration, commented that the queen had been 'sentenced to death *once again'* (Lorin pers. comm. 2014b). The significance of the date likely attracted a greater number of Republicans wishing to express their opinions, as much as it attracted the queen's supporters. Between the two parties, the Republican views prevailed. Nevertheless, despite the long-lasting effects of revolutionary propaganda on contemporary French citizens, it must be highlighted that there is also a powerful fascination with Marie Antoinette, which usually associates with admiration in circles of art lovers/specialists who have access to alternative sources of information other than Republican history.

Nineteenth-century authors

The analysis of historical sources is introduced by a brief review of the main nineteenth-century historical authors, as they were the primary drivers of misconceptions surrounding the historical character of Marie Antoinette. Albeit having suffered countless distortions since the eighteenth century, through revolutionary propaganda and the clichés it disseminated about the queen, field research shows that it was the nineteenth-century historical discourse of the Republican agenda which sealed the perception of Marie Antoinette for the majority of contemporary visitors to the Petit Trianon.

Firstly, the Republican agency and its history written by Jules Michelet (1847–1853, 1867) during the nineteenth century (see also Durand 2001; Duprat 2013), constitute a major cause of distortions to the perception of Marie Antoinette. Secondly, but arguably of more importance (Berly & Martin 2010), the nineteenth-century French Romantic literature developed around her historical character added to the multitude of confusing stories. Notable in this respect are the novels of Alexandre Dumas *père* (1845, 1846–1848, 1849–1850, 1851, 1852–1855).

The son of a general who fought against the monarchy during the French Revolution, Dumas' Republican sympathies clearly shine through in his portrayal of Marie Antoinette. Starting from a subtle depiction of negative traits in his early novels, he fully depicts the queen in a negative light in the last novel, *La Comtesse de Charny* (1852–1855), which is based, perhaps not fortuitously, on very little historical evidence. Hailed as the 'King of Romance' (Hemmings 1979), and having undeniably enjoyed great popularity in his time, often even surpassing that of Victor Hugo, only *Le Chevalier de Maison-Rouge* (1845) and *Le Collier de la reine* (1849–1850) proved to

Figure 4.4 A replica of the infamous necklace, which contributed to the fall of the French Monarchy, is exhibited at the Palace of Versailles in the queen's private chambers, accessible through guided visits

Author photo 2010/courtesy Château de Versailles

be still fairly well known, based on the survey sample. The former, which depicts a neutral image of Marie Antoinette seen in the context of the Reign of Terror just after Louis XVI's execution, was remembered by a few French and Italian survey respondents because of its 1963 Franco-Italian television series adaptation. The latter novel, based on the 'necklace' (Figure 4.4) scandal of 1785, is unsympathetic to Marie Antoinette and in fact prejudiced her image without any solid basis in reality (Table 4.2).[6] It also inspired several other novels and films (Seth 2006; Petitfils 2011), including the most recent Hollywood production on the subject (*The Affair of the Necklace* 2001), which chose to portray Marie Antoinette in a negative light, taking a sympathetic view of the actual perpetrators (see also Mason 2003). These two novels by Dumas are sold at the Librairie des Princes but were not reported amongst their bestsellers (Table 4.1).

The nineteenth-century sources above have been notably counteracted by Royalist biographies such as that of the brothers de Goncourt (1858) and de Lescure (1866, 1867b; see also Geffroy 1866). However, due to the panegyric tone of the former and the official Royalist discourse of the latter, it is doubtful whether these sources competed successfully against the negative portrayal of Marie Antoinette, or inadvertently reinforced the Republican message by overtly challenging it. They may have even contributed to further confusion in the perception of Marie Antoinette.

The mémoires of Marie Antoinette's contemporaries, including her close entourage (de Ligne 1814; Campan 1823; de Tilly 1828; Vigée

Le Brun 1835–1837; de Waldner de Freundstein 1853; Karamzine 1867, 1885; d'Hézecques 1873; de Croÿ d'Havré 1883; Léonard 1905; de Croÿ-Solre 1906–1921; de la Tour du Pin 1920), tend to be placed by Republican historians – who dismiss them as biased – on a par with the array of fabricated mémoires published after the brief restoration of royalty during the first half of the nineteenth century. In fact, not all of these contemporary sources are entirely credible given the political choices of their authors during the events of the French Revolution. For example, Mme Campan, whose mémoires are amongst the bestsellers at the Librairie des Princes, entered the service of Napoléon I. Regardless, these works (all available at the Librairie des Princes) represent valuable testimonials to the end of the eighteenth century.

Further evidence, provided by the mémoires of eighteenth-century English political figures (Burke 1790; Walpole 1823), objectively reinforces a positive portrayal of the queen, which is counterintuitive given the historical enmity between France and England. Even more significantly, contemporary French political figures who supported principles opposed to those of the royalty, tried at the time to expose the injustices brought to the queen's image as well as to her person. In fact, the *Declaration of the Rights of Woman and Female Citizen*, published in 1791 by the female revolutionary figure Olympe de Gouges (see de Gouges 1970) was dedicated to Marie Antoinette, as the author well understood that the queen was used as a scapegoat of the failing Ancien Régime by most of her revolutionary male counterparts (for more supporting perspectives from prominent female thinkers of the time, see also de Staël 1793, 1818; Cottret 1994).

Twentieth- and twenty-first century authors

Amongst the historical sources examined here, the work of the Austrian novelist Stefan Zweig deserves special attention. His biography of the queen represents one of the most important contributions to the cult-like following that began in the nineteenth century. Also reviewed is British author Antonia Fraser, whose biography inspired Sofia Coppola's 2006 film *Marie Antoinette*. Contributions on the subject of Marie Antoinette from American academia are also briefly considered, since their cumulative historical narrative is relevant to a rehabilitative discourse, based on either feminist or political readings of history.

Zweig's *Marie-Antoinette: Bildnis eines mittleren Charakters* (1932)[7] initiated a process of moral rehabilitation of the queen, in contrast with the general perception of his contemporaries stemming from the Republican agenda's negative portrayal. However, his work interprets the material found and, even more importantly, the missing material, in a Freudian manner. Although innovative at the time, the psychoanalytical interpretation minimises one's personality to one's sexual life – a view that discounts an individual's conscious self-censorship, particularly strong in the Catholic tradition. Zweig depicts an unlikely psychological and intellectual portrait of the queen, reducing her to the sum of the most common Republican clichés (Table 3.1). The crucial difference to Republican portrayals lies in Zweig's appraisal of the manner in which Marie Antoinette faced her tragic end. Stressing that she would have been an unremarkable figure otherwise, the author nonetheless acknowledges Marie Antoinette's sublime overcoming of her 'average' nature. Such an approach, however, denies to Marie Antoinette a positive contribution to either the history of the Queens of France, or of art history, yet it appeals to readers through a feeling of closeness to her elusive historical character (Ikeda 2011).

Zweig's focus on the tragic episodes, and especially on the supposed affair of the queen with Count Axel von Fersen – to which the author devotes an important part of his psychoanalytical approach – was reflected to a point in the first Hollywood biopic on Marie Antoinette (1938, starring Norma Shearer; Figure 4.5) inspired by the book. Based on the literature review providing the sample for this chapter's data collection, Zweig's biography remains the cornerstone of all other twentieth-century cult-revival sources, the author's expressed desire to understand and discover the real queen setting the tone for similar attempts, regardless of their views towards Marie Antoinette. Apart from the undeniable quality of his literary style, Zweig's contribution lies in his review of frequently quoted sources, acknowledging or dismissing them according to authenticity of authorship. His work was signalled as one of the bestsellers at the Librairie des Princes.

André Castelot's historical analysis of Marie Antoinette has established his reputation since 1953 as a French biographer enjoying popularity with a wide public as well as with French television producers and cineastes. With an array of publications on the subject of Marie Antoinette and her royal family (Castelot 1947, 1950, 1953, 1971, 1989), abundantly re-edited and translated into other languages, his work is a hybrid between Zweig's engaging literary style and critical observations regarding the earlier part of the queen's life, infused, however, with a good dose of personal fascination with Marie Antoinette. His public – circles of admirers of the queen and those just starting to learn more about her (Lorin pers. comm. 2014b) – shares his fascination. Although certain Republican clichés are present, this source has a definite rehabilitative agenda.

In a completely admirative vein, another biography of the queen comes from Jean Chalon (1988). Highly criticised for biased views by historians of the French Revolution (Berly 2006), the author nevertheless brings a fresh approach to previous analyses by anchoring Marie Antoinette's story into the political context of the French Revolution, which he incidentally likens in violence and abusive treatment to totalitarian regimes such as German Nazism. Furthermore, the author makes use of astrological readings, meant to clarify the context that allowed the dramatic development of events in the queen's life and death. Despite its nonconventional and highly subjective approach, Chalon's biography is one of the

Figure 4.5 Norma Shearer, in the 1938 Hollywood biopic *Marie Antoinette*, pictured here as the frivolous young queen

Courtesy Everett Collection

bestsellers at the Librairie des Princes, its readers presumably being devoted admirers of the queen (see also Delorme 2011).

Two other bestsellers target a specific, narrow segment of the specialist audience. Élisabeth de Feydeau (2005; see also 2011, 2012) provides a valuable study of Marie Antoinette's *parfumeur* and his recipes. Benedetta Craveri (2008) analyses the Affair of the Diamond Necklace (Table 4.2; Figure 4.4), one of the most popular topics for historical fiction on Marie Antoinette. The complexity of this case, and its importance in sealing the negative image of Marie Antoinette in the public opinion of her time, required academic analysis. Craveri's contribution aligns with earlier American studies on the subject (Maza 2003), which attempt to clear remaining misconceptions. Despite her proved innocence in the matter (Funk-Brentano 1901; Mossiker 1961), such misconceptions still linger even in analyses by the principal biographers of the queen (see Lever 2004). Furthermore, a recent British publication (Beckman 2014) proves that the episode continues to fascinate through sensationalist intrigues involving crooks, prostitutes and the clergy, a perfect recipe for popular fiction plots.

Évelyne Lever, research historian and specialist in the Ancien Régime and the French Revolution, has contributed many publications on the subject, and in many editions (see for example, Lever 1991, 2000a, 2000b, 2002, 2004, 2005a, 2005b, 2006a, 2006b, 2006c; with Garcia 2008), and is quite possibly the principal French contemporary biographer of Marie Antoinette. After Sofia Coppola's initial consideration of using Lever's work on Marie Antoinette as inspiration for her own film, yet eventually deciding in favour of Antonia Fraser's book, the French author was chosen instead as historical consultant for Coppola's 2006 biopic: 'A consultant never consulted' [translation mine], as the French author declared in an interview for *Le Figaro* at the time of the film's release at Cannes (de Montety 2006). The French historian did not approve of Coppola's final production (Lever 2006b; see also de Montety 2006). Nevertheless, Lever's work did inspire a theatre play which toured the United States in 2013.[8] Although this particular piece could be considered as revisionist in essence, Lever's tone generally oscillates between an ostentatious impartiality, however, interspersed with Republican clichés along with sympathy. Unintentionally, in excusing the queen, the author incriminates her in the process. When attempting an examination of historical facts from an objective perspective, Lever's work attests to the cultural and political conditioning of historians belonging to the Republican school. Moreover, the author gives a highly subjective interpretation to missing facts, reinforcing Republican clichés. Most of Lever's books are also sold at the Librairie des Princes, some counted among its bestsellers.

Simone Bertière (2002), the other major contemporary French biographer of the queen, maintains a clear position in her work, though she wages constant battle against the deeply rooted misconceptions of public opinion in trying to disprove them. This situation confirms, once again, the persistence and incredible power of this unfounded negative image in the French collective memory, which causes even informed researchers to venture cautiously into the topic. Bertière had to leave many questions unanswered regarding the private life of the queen, due to lack of documents and to a confusing amount of contradictory testimonies. Bertière (pers. comm. 2014) stresses the importance of not adding any personal judgements into a biography, as so often is the case:

> Literature can teach us a lot on the subject. When I write biographies, I try above all to understand the characters of the past, simultaneously close, but different to us. I have no sympathy for colleagues who happily dish out moral judgements based on their own reactions. I respect my characters. [translation mine]

Bertière (pers. comm 2011, 2014) displays a particular sensibility in using her literary background for clear depiction, despite not having any personal affinity for Marie Antoinette. In fact, the author admits the contrary, and also that her interest lies in French social history in general and in trying to arrive at a clearer picture of past political contexts. Furthermore, having written only one book on the subject and refusing to make of Marie Antoinette's subject a lucrative business by continually churning out material for fans (Lorin pers. comm. 2014b), the author could perhaps be considered one of the most objective contemporary French biographers of Marie Antoinette.

A further important contribution to a revised reading of the Republican historical discourse on Marie Antoinette is brought by the research of Professor Annie Duprat (2006). A specialist in the role played by caricatures in late eighteenth-century propaganda, she brings valid observations and explanations of how a 'paper queen' was actually created by public opinion, clearly revealing that it was in fact this painstaking and lengthy propaganda process – concurrent with Marie Antoinette's reign – which finally destroyed her as the embodiment of the monarchy, which it indirectly targeted. The queen's Austrian nationality provided reasons and means for violent attacks culminating in the events of 1789 (Duprat pers. comm. 2012). Furthermore, in her most recent work focused on Marie Antoinette, which includes the perception of contemporary popular media channels, Duprat (2013:14) notes that not only is the image of Marie Antoinette seen mainly through 'her double, this paper queen of the propaganda, stuck to her skin like Nessus' lethal tunic', but also that 'we all bear within us a Marie-Antoinette forged by passions, by readings and films'. [translation mine]

Another notable author writing about Marie Antoinette from a rather different perspective is Chantal Thomas. Having studied Philosophy and Literature with Roland Barthes, the author began her work on the eighteenth century by studying the artistic characters of the Enlightenment. As the image forged by the media of the time (pamphlets) did not match the character that Thomas knew through the artistic channels to which she was accustomed, she investigated further. Thus, her first work (Thomas 1989a) studied this 'pamphlet' image and the underlying reasons for its existence. The author concludes that Marie Antoinette, as favourite target of eighteenth-century pamphlets, became their victim, just as the Marquis de Sade became a victim in his role of pamphlet author.

Thomas' approach is notable for attempting to assemble the real character of the queen from the analysis of her letters (see Thomas 2011a). A subtle understanding of Marie Antoinette's character as well as of her life, allows Thomas to depict, in a much more accurate manner, the essence of historical events. The author was also historical adviser for a 2007 'docu-fiction' series (see Schifano 2009), which is very likely to have been produced as a reaction to the previous year's release of Sofia Coppola's film (Thomas pers. comm. 2011b). Thomas has also contributed chapters and articles to both French and American academic publications (Thomas 1989b, 2003; see also 1999, 2004). Her historical novel, *Les Adieux à la Reine* (Thomas 2002), was awarded the prestigious *Prix Femina* and adapted for French cinema. Released in 2012, the film of the same name, directed by Benoît Jacquot, portrays a mostly conventional Republican image albeit within a contemporary visual narrative. Paradoxically perhaps, the film had excellent critiques but was a public flop (Duprat 2013). The narrative of the film (see Figure 4.6) was in fact a misportrayal of the novel's narrative: the lesbian relationship of the queen was Jacquot's own addition. Despite not claiming this to be the historical truth, the film director confessed to picking up the idea from eighteenth-century pamphlets.[9] Considering that Thomas was trying to dispel the distortions brought to Marie Antoinette's image by these same pamphlets, the message of the author and its popular media representation are revealed to be at odds.

Catriona Seth (2006) is another author with a French literary background[10] who brings a considerable contribution through her dictionary on Marie Antoinette, which covers a wide range of topics, making this a valuable document for a clearer portrayal of the queen. Thus, it seems that a literary sensibility is required for rewriting Marie Antoinette's history. Literary authors Bertière and Thomas have become equally reputable biographers of the queen, as much as those with a historical background, such as Lever.

Having been the subject of Royalist as well as Republican perspectives during the nineteenth century (de Alméras 1907, 1935; Fleischman 1908), Marie Antoinette was also the subject of eighteenth-century pamphlets – most of them pornographic – which continue to generate further reviews (Darnton 1982, 2010; Darnton & Roches 1989; de Baecque 1988, 1997; Revel 1991; Price 1992; Mason 1998; Kaiser 2000, 2003a, 2003b; Gruder 2002; Hunt 2003; Colwill 1989, 2003; Burrows 2006). What is important to the debate is whether the pamphlets were the cause of the decline of the monarchy (Thomas 1989a; Farge 1994; Kaiser 2000; Biard 2009; Duprat 2013) or whether, as Gruder (2002) argues, these were only an effect of the decline which had occurred by 1789, following continual attacks

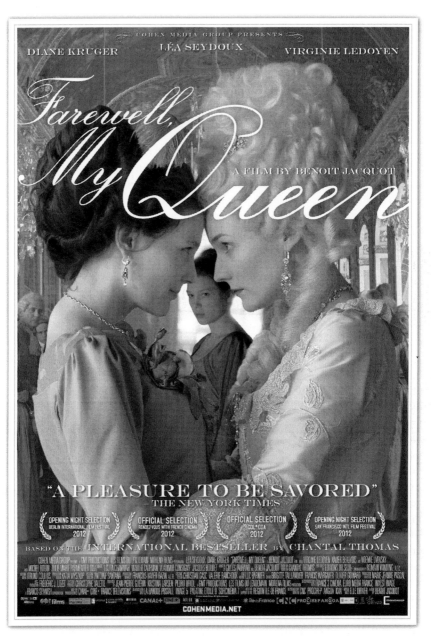

Figure 4.6 The 2012 edition of Chantal Thomas' novel *Farewell, My Queen* depicts on its cover the promotional poster of the film (pictured here) which worked against the initial message of the author

© Cohen Media Group/courtesy Everett Collection

against the queen issuing from higher levels of society, including the court (see also Habermas 1989; Goodman 2003a). Either point of view once again confirms the manipulation of the queen's image, which ultimately destroyed her and the monarchy – the indirect target of the attack. Furthermore, a common conclusion to most of these studies is that Marie Antoinette represents a unique case of an individual having been both tried and sentenced to death on the basis of 'crimes' (see Seth 2006) committed by a 'paper' double. Fiction became reality – and continues to be so.

British historian Antonia Fraser (2001, 2006) provides a sympathetic and psychologically nuanced account of the queen's life. However, the author followed, to an extent, the example of Zweig by arriving at crucial conclusions to otherwise unknown facts through personal interpretation. Fraser looked at the historical reality of the eighteenth century through the lens of the contemporary society to which she belongs today – progressive and permissive, a time of 'sexually liberated' women. The main misleading fact in her biography of Marie Antoinette (also featured in Coppola's film inspired by Fraser's work) is the alleged affair of the queen with Count von Fersen. The relationship remains as debated as the very image of the queen herself, the two being closely interrelated. Furthermore, the affair usually acts as one of the variables determining the polarity of the image of Marie Antoinette in the perception of the majority.

Last, but not least, a French biographer of Marie Antoinette, particularly notable due to her revolutionary history background, is Cécile Berly (2003, 2006, 2012, 2013, 2015a, 2015b; with Martin 2010), increasingly known for re-evaluating the role played by Marie Antoinette. The author tries, to an extent, to rehabilitate the queen's image and, indirectly, that of Louis XVI, whose historical character she feels has been unjustly misportrayed for too long (Berly 2011; on the subject of Louis XVI's misportrayal, see also Chéry 2011, 2015). But Berly's essential contribution lies in an attempt to reconcile the French Revolution and its violence vis-à-vis Marie Antoinette. However, Berly's work confirms that contemporary French historians are not yet able to fully depict the true role played by the queen, due to the French Revolution's value as founding myth of the French nation. To objectively understand and reveal the queen's role still implies adopting a critical stance towards the real dimensions of the French Revolution: devotion to the latter precludes objectivity towards the former. Still, Berly's and Jean-Clément Martin's contribution (2010) – one of the bestsellers at the Librairie des Princes – is notable for trying to break with profession-specific patterns of thought and research. Other French Revolution historians such as François Furet (with Richet 1973; 1989; with Ozouf 1989) further attest through their work to the zero-sum trait of heritages, expressed at its clearest: the cultural heritage of the French Revolution's events impinges on the cultural heritage of Marie Antoinette's historical character – seen as a symbol of the French Monarchy – and vice versa.

Librairie des Princes bookshop was used to cross-reference the historical sources reviewed, in order to obtain a clearer picture of the contribution brought by the heritage site of Château de Versailles to the perception of Marie Antoinette's image from a historical narrative perspective. Having analysed the main points of incidence between the vast literature written about the last Queen of France and the stock sold at the Librairie des Princes, this section concludes with a selection of relevant educational sources available at the bookshop, whose review reveals a mixed discourse.

First are image-driven publications aimed at making the character of Marie Antoinette better known to the wide public, mostly by liaising with popular culture trends, fashions and demands (e.g. Maral 2012, 2016; Delalex et al. 2013; Delalex 2015). Given their nature, these sources are mixed and diluted versions of the main texts discussed earlier in the chapter, touching upon key moments in Marie Antoinette's life, without providing a high scholarly content or clear historical and/or art history stances. By contrast, *Marie-Antoinette For Dummies*, a guide by Marion F. Godfroy (2013) – member of the Institute of the French Revolution – is a richly detailed account of the queen's life. Aimed at adult visitors seeking more historical information on Marie Antoinette, and lacking a solid historical knowledge about the subject, this source attempts to demystify cliché-generated misconceptions surrounding this historical character. However, the zero-sum trait of heritages regarding the French Revolution and Marie Antoinette limits the scope for change in perception. This source also confirms the list of clichés persisting in the French collective memory (see Table 3.1).

The review of a recently published book addressed to 9–12 year olds (Le Loarer & Bouvarel 2014), proves this source to be a Republican portrayal of Marie Antoinette constructed negatively in antithesis to the French Revolution. A recent *bande dessinée*, edited in collaboration with the Château de Versailles (Adam et al. 2013), also perpetuates Republican clichés of Marie Antoinette through a mix of fiction and history. These publications reconfirm the zero-sum trait of heritages. By contrast, throughout the other publications aimed at younger readers (under the age of nine), the tone is so sympathetic as to be Royalist. On closer examination, the reason can be found in the nature of these publications. They are essentially art history essays for a young audience and which, moreover, stop their narratives before having to deal with the events of the French Revolution (see Cullen & Young 2006). These events are too violent and complex to be explained to young audiences. At the same time, such publications – addressed mainly to young girls – lend themselves perfectly to Marie Antoinette's mythical image of a fairy-tale princess.

Finally, a recent *shōjo* manga by Fuyumi Soryo (2016) published by Château de Versailles in collaboration with Glénat under the main supervision of heritage curator Alexandre Maral and Jean-Vincent Bacquart, draws from many of the above authors as references, taking, however, a clear stance. This particular source is impressive in its scope of rehabilitating not only

Marie Antoinette's image but also that of Louis XVI, and with them, that of the Bourbon dynasty. The Petit Trianon plays a central role in the visual narrative.

Fiction or history? Attempts to rehabilitate Marie Antoinette through historical fiction and social media

Having reviewed sources relevant to the historical narrative of Marie Antoinette, this section focuses now on several examples of published or internet discourses attempting to rehabilitate the image of Marie Antoinette. The common denominator for the published sources lies in the use of fiction to convey, more or less successfully, historical facts whilst the social media referred to clearly aims to challenge and disprove the Republican historical discourse.

The first example is found in a literary genre of fictional personal diaries of Marie Antoinette. In fact, this is the only source indicated by fieldwork evidence to have had a clear impact on a segment of American visitors at the Petit Trianon – young women under the age of 25. However, titles and authors of such 'diaries' were not recalled by the respondents. Although the opinion of the respondents apparently improved after the reading, their image of Marie Antoinette remained negative. The message conveyed through such sources starkly contrasts with general beliefs instilled by official channels, the readers thus finding it difficult to believe that the historical discourse of these novels could be reflecting the truth. Respondents also confessed embarrassment once they realised that their opinion of the queen had become more positive, given their perception of how decadent she was at a time of great suffering for the poor French people. Again, the zero-sum trait of heritages acts fully in these instances.

For a better illustration of these particular sources and their influence, in the absence of clear sources cited by the above respondents, a review of 50 internet comments regarding three examples of such diaries (Lasky 2013; Erickson 2005; Clegg 2010) was undertaken (see Maior-Barron 2015b).[11] The conclusion based on this cross-referencing of the data collection is that the diaries addressed to teenagers seem to have a greater impact in changing opinions on Marie Antoinette because these diaries endear her to young readers. Yet what was expressed by the visitors at the Petit Trianon who mentioned this type of source as being relevant to them, was the general assumption that the Marie Antoinette they came to know and like must have changed in later life for the worse, becoming 'mean', since the diaries only covered the teenage years of the Dauphine of France. There were also exclusive positive comments among the internet reviewers, some readers even finding these diaries 'illuminating'. By contrast, Marie Antoinette 'diaries' aimed at an adult audience, given their focus on sensationalist 'confessions' such as illicit love, only reinforce Republican clichés, and do not seem to make any difference to the readers' opinion on Marie Antoinette.

Although the expressed intentions of such authors to endear Marie Antoinette's historical character to the readers might not always be successful for various reasons, this genre has also been adopted with the same aim by reputable French historians. Besides Lever (2002), the prolific French biographer of the queen, whose 'intimate journal' of Marie Antoinette is sold at the Librairie des Princes, another relevant example for the contrasting Republican and Royalist views on Marie Antoinette is a contribution by the late Countess of Paris: *Moi, Marie Antoinette* (d'Orléans-Bragance 1993).[12] Published on the eve of the bicentenary of the queen's death, the book was clearly meant to reflect as closely as possible the queen's own perspective on her life. The personal kinship of the author with Marie Antoinette ensured a sympathetic view. Yet, as in the case of Royalist biographies, this kinship could for some readers undermine the historical discourse's credibility. This particular source is not sold at the Librairie des Princes, although it is not out of print.

It is not possible to statistically evaluate the effect of historical novels on the image of Marie Antoinette, yet there is a possibility that this type of rehabilitative discourse contributes towards a gradual change in perceptions. A notable example is provided by the work of Elena Maria Vidal (pseudonym), an American historian and author of a historical novel (Vidal 2010). This book is relevant for its genre but more importantly for the Catholic faith of its author. Indeed, Elena Maria Vidal tries to dispel Republican clichés in light of Marie Antoinette's Catholic faith; the royal family is seen as a close unit, with Louis XVI playing an important part which the Republican discourse usually denies to him (Figure 4.7).[13] Vidal is perhaps the only author on the subject of Marie Antoinette who looks at the queen's destiny strictly from a Catholic perspective. If her religious views could be considered to influence the objectivity of the discourse (in the same way as the Royalist views could be suspected to), what is essential is their ability to bring the reader closer to an important trait of the analysed subject, a trait otherwise ignored by other contemporary studies, as Vidal (pers. comm. 2014a) suggests:

> I do write historical novels which in the USA are regarded as being the same as historical fiction. I see my novels as windows into the past and a way to make historical persons come to life. The novel is an art form. Yes, I think that my Catholic background gives me an understanding of Marie-Antoinette's own Catholic perspective of the events in her life. There are recent novels about the queen by non-Catholics which are sadly lacking the understanding of sacrifice and martyrdom in union with Christ. Martyrdom is the key to understanding Marie-Antoinette at the end of her life.

Richard Lee (2013) confirms that one of the most important reasons for lack of objectivity in historical fiction lies in the secularised views of their authors who refer to a deeply religious past. I argue that this is the case also for

Historical and cinematic narratives 107

Figure 4.7 The Royal Family in 1782, gathered around the first Dauphin, Louis Joseph Xavier François (French School 1782)

Photo Christophe Fouin. Château de Versailles et de Trianon Collection © RMN-Grand Palais/ courtesy Art Resource, NY

historical biographies. Very importantly, Vidal (pers. comm. 2014a, 2014b; see also Horvat n.d.) stresses that even within the Catholic milieu, there is division, and many misconceptions surrounding Marie Antoinette, akin to Republican clichés. Whether Marie Antoinette was indeed a martyr, as Vidal and other Catholic scholars suggest (Horvat n.d.), is beyond the authority of this book. However, given the hermeneutical paradigm underpinning the methodology, it is crucial to acknowledge the religious and monarchic conditioning which acted upon Marie Antoinette's decisions. Following the model of her mother, the queen was a staunch Catholic. Indeed, her faith transcended the appearances of a monarch required to play a role at one of the most sophisticated courts of Europe, as well as of an eighteenth-century adept of Enlightened ideas, and even of an emancipated woman. Marie Antoinette's decisions and attitudes in key moments – not least concerning devotion to her royal consort and when faced with the events of the French Revolution – indicate that her Catholic faith entwined with monarchic tradition. Following the success of her novel, first published in 1997, Vidal believed it necessary to further reiterate her message by creating the *Tea at*

108 *Historical and cinematic narratives*

Trianon blog in 2006, not least because of the release that year of Coppola's film, which Vidal (pers. comm. 2014b) felt to have reinforced the usual clichés detrimental to Marie Antoinette's perception.

It is debatable whether the contribution of such internet blogs[14] can be construed as competition for the prevailing Republican historical discourses. However, Cécile Berly expressed fears regarding such internet portrayals of Marie Antoinette, since, in her opinion, the internet seemed to be flooded with the biased views of the queen's admirers. Berly's (2003) belief is that these views could skew the perception of the younger generations, who are increasingly using the internet as an educational tool.

Listed among the sources causing concern, Association Marie-Antoinette founded in 1996,[15] is the only official, non-governmental body in France overtly aiming to rehabilitate the image of Marie Antoinette. The work of the association is divided between managing the social media generated by their forum and organising various events. Counting approximately 100 members, including Japanese nationals, the Association's Forum – where all members post under the name of Marie Antoinette – generates various discussions about the queen, her royal family and the French Monarchy in general, trying constantly to reveal new facts. The founders also organise colloquiums on the subject of Marie Antoinette and have taken part in television programmes (Lorin pers. comm. 2014b). Rehabilitative contributions also come from Académie des Sciences Morales, des Lettres et des Arts de Versailles et d'Ile-de-France (or Académie de Versailles), an official organisation founded in 1834. This body, with 31 branches throughout France, is concerned with continuing and promoting the work of cultural institutions founded by the Ancien Régime.[16]

Patricia Bouchenot-Déchin, researcher and historian at Centre de recherche du château de Versailles (CRCV) and titular member since 2002 of the Académie de Versailles, has authored historical fiction concerning the nature of the controversial relationship between Marie Antoinette and Count von Fersen (Figure 4.8). The publication of the Count's diary and letters (Fersen 1878/1902; see also Söderhjelm 1930), triggered a great deal of interest and speculation around the real foundations of the Swedish noble's strong attachment to the queen and her family. Bouchenot-Déchin thoroughly reviewed extant documents in Sweden and France in order to shed light on this debated relationship. The groundbreaking findings were published for the first time in 1998 in the form of a novel (see Bouchenot-Déchin 2006; also 2004), as this seemed the only effective claim to plausibility when the fresh historical findings contrast so much with the commonly known clichés (Bouchenot-Déchin pers. comm. 2010, 2011). The historian's findings revealed a devoted friendship and a platonic love on both sides.

In this respect, the analysis makes further use of sources (Webster 1936; Chalon 1988; Bertière 2002; Delorme 2011) that made a good case for the reasons this relationship could not have been anything other than either pure devoted friendship or a platonic love at the most: the Catholic faith of the queen and the devotion and respect of the Count to the French royal couple.

Historical and cinematic narratives 109

Figure 4.8 Swedish Count Hans Axel von Fersen's Royalist loyalties led to his tragic end on 20 June 1810. The date, coincident with the Varennes flight that eventually brought about Marie Antoinette's end, is often used to cast their relationship in a romantic light

Peter Dreuillon 1798. Courtesy Östergötlands Museum

Moreover, Count von Fersen is acknowledged to have been one of their most important political advisers (Bertière 2002).

Visitor discourses analysed in Chapter 6 showed that members of the French and American majority groups who were aware of and elaborated on the relationship consider the 'consummation' of this love differently

110 *Historical and cinematic narratives*

from historical authors (Zweig 1932; Lever 2000a; Fraser 2001; Farr 2013, 2016), who depicted it in a romanticised fashion, or in a sympathetic and wishful way to somehow compensate for the queen's misfortune, with at least some moments of complete surrender to her feelings. In fact, for the above respondents, even a mere insinuation of an affair adds to the incriminations formulated by the eighteenth-century revolutionary propaganda, later integrated into the Republican history agenda, from whence they were disseminated into the French national collective memory.

Cinematic narrative

To build a comprehensive view of the essential factors of Marie Antoinette's portrayal and the commodification of her historical character, this section analyses cinematic narratives relevant to the perception of Marie Antoinette by the majority of visitors at the Petit Trianon. Field research proved that American and Japanese nationals use cinematic media sources as reference points. These sources do not influence Marie Antoinette's image imprinted into the French national collective memory but through a perpetuation of Republican clichés are responsible for its perception by these other nationals.

Despite a complex and numerous filmography featuring Marie Antoinette as main or secondary character (estimated at 50 films, although only three biopics), the present chapter is narrowed down to two sources proven to be influential for visitor perceptions at the Petit Trianon. Based on the field research evidence, they are Sofia Coppola's *Marie Antoinette* (2006) and Riyoko Ikeda's *Rose of Versailles* (1972). Whereas Ikeda's contribution is in the form of a manga, its pages have a definite cinematic quality. The relevance of Sofia Coppola's 2006 film lies in its connections with the promotional strategies used by the Château de Versailles. Although highly controversial, the film attracted considerable national and international interest in the queen's *Domaine*, to such an extent that Château de Versailles foresaw and seized the opportunity to strengthen and further promote the site's image whilst also planning the refurbishment of the Petit Trianon structure, completed in 2008. A comparison of Petit Trianon visitor figures before and after the revival sparked by Coppola's film revealed an increase of more than 100%.

Sofia Coppola's Marie Antoinette *(2006)*

On 18 May 2006, the Cannes Film Festival opened with the viewing of *The Da Vinci Code*. The year's most anticipated production, however, was Sofia Coppola's *Marie Antoinette* (Figure 4.9), the young director's third film, after *Virgin Suicides* (1999) and *Lost in Translation* (2003). A recurrent theme of troubled teenage years/young womanhood runs through all three. The queen is seen to be divided in spatial terms between the suffocating etiquette which ruled at Château de Versailles and her beloved Petit Trianon, where a haven

Figure 4.9 A postmodern-anachronistic portrayal of Marie Antoinette in the poster for the film *Marie Antoinette* (2006)
© Sony Pictures/courtesy Everett Collection

Figure 4.10 Image from promotional trailer scene for *Marie Antoinette* (2006), shot off-location, depicting Marie Antoinette at the Petit Trianon in the Cabinet des Glaces Mouvantes

© Sony Pictures/courtesy Everett Collection

of peace and tranquillity contrasts with the rigid life at court. However, the director chose to give this refuge an added dimension of frivolity and libertinage by transforming it into the setting for the queen's supposed love affair with the Count von Fersen. The exterior scenes at the Petit Trianon were exclusively shot on location. The interior spaces, however, being too small, did not lend themselves to filming the scenes depicting a world of excess (see Figures 4.10; 4.11).[17]

Despite many other notable cinematic productions, the analysis of the visitors' responses showed no direct influence from any of these films on their perception of the site, nor an incentive to visit. By contrast, despite its controversy, and despite not being the reason for visiting the Petit Trianon, Sofia Coppola's film was known by the majority of visitors, though not always from first-hand viewing. This demonstrates the effectiveness of the film's publicity strategy and, at the same time, the impact it made on the public image of the site as it succeeded in subliminally linking to it. The filming (Binh 2010), almost entirely on location (see Figure 4.12); the prize-winning period costumes (2007 Academy Awards); and the meticulously researched décor – all supported by the director's notoriety – made the release eagerly

Figure 4.11 The small proportions of the actual Cabinet des Glaces Mouvantes could not accommodate the film's extravagant scenes of excess

Author photo 2011/courtesy Château de Versailles

Figure 4.12 Coppola marvelled at the generosity of the Château de Versailles in granting her access to film: 'I was given more access to Versailles than I was to the Park Hyatt in Tokyo for *Lost in Translation*' (Willis 2010)

© Sony Pictures/courtesy Everett Collection

anticipated and contributed further to its wide publicity. The director's father, Francis Ford Coppola (present on set in his role of executive producer, see Hohenadel 2006) half-jokingly commented on Marie Antoinette's popularity today: 'Marie Antoinette is Lady Di' (Poirson 2007). However, the film's release sparked controversy and heavy criticism in the press, with wide-ranging reviews from glowing to utterly negative (O'Hagan 2006; Bradshaw 2006; Dobbins 2013; Fauth & Dermansky n.d.; French 2006; Murray 2006a, 2006b; Poirier 2006a, 2006b; Lichfield 2006). Film analyses (Poirson 2007, 2009; Mendelsohn 2009) further confirm criticism in France as well as the United States. Worldwide, Coppola's *Marie Antoinette* seems to have enjoyed its greatest success with the public in Japan, given that box-office figures showed viewing rates for this country to be statistically as high as domestic figures, and double of those registered in France (see IMDb 2006). This is presumably due mainly to Marie Antoinette's popularity through Riyoko Ikeda's work,[18] which is later analysed in this chapter. Field research evidence revealed that for the majority group of the Japanese visitors, Coppola's film acts as a source of opinion about Marie Antoinette, after the manga, *Rose of Versailles* (1972; see Chapter 6).

The postmodern approach of the director, through an anachronistic portrayal of Marie Antoinette, was appreciated for capturing clear similarities between eras of social and cultural crisis (Citton 2009). Anglo-American feminist film authority Pam Cook (2006, 2014) considers Coppola's use of anachronism (see also 'travesty') particularly ingenious for inviting viewer participation and, on a whole, Coppola's impressionistic approach to history is innovative in eliciting emotional response. Further, Cook believes that Coppola successfully contributes to a new 'auteurism' for the biopic genre: one that is comfortable with the postmodern commodity culture to which it belongs, yet, whose deeper purpose is 'to confront accepted ways of seeing, hearing, and understanding' (Cook 2014: 224). From a semiotic perspective, Pamela Flores (2013) suggests that the film successfully managed to capture the emancipation of Marie Antoinette, who asserted herself at the Court of Versailles through fashion. This point of emancipation through fashion resonates with recent historical research on the subject (see Weber 2006). Also, in creating a hybrid between a heritage film and a costume drama, as opposed to a historical film (Poirson 2007, 2009), Coppola succeeded in depicting a female protagonist trying to surpass the condition assigned to her by a declining system. She also succeeded in depicting the extent to which Marie Antoinette achieved this within limitations imposed by both the Ancien Régime and the mounting Revolution which targeted her so mercilessly. However, Poirson (2007, 2009) in particular, places the film's merit within a wider negative critique, considering it symptomatic of the American license (especially through Hollywood) to change French history, and relevant to the persistent ambiguity surrounding Marie Antoinette's perception. Yet it must be noted here that this license is not exclusive to Hollywood and extends in fact to most cinematic biographies.

Coming back to Coppola's film, there are further conflicting reviews and analyses: whilst an anthropological reading of the film (Backman Rogers 2012) praises its value as a document for feminine rites of threshold with deep transcendental connections surpassing the eighteenth century or even contemporary femininity, Mendelsohn (2009) critically reviews the film (from an American perspective) as unsuccessful, due to its one-sided recounting of events. Nevertheless, the script of the film, inspired by Fraser's biography of Marie Antoinette, purposely looked at the past through the queen's own eyes, aiming to elicit sympathy by focusing on the feelings of the unhappy sovereign: a 'history of feelings' in Kirsten Dunst's words (O'Hagan 2006). Twenty-first century moral principles and attitudes guide both Fraser's and Coppola's versions of Marie Antoinette's life, yet they defeat the purpose of causing the public to empathise with the sovereign. Ironically, the surreptitious 'product placement' of a pair of bubble-gum pink Converse (trainers) in one of the film's scenes clearly shows this failed attempt. Rather than placing the viewer in mind of the eighteenth century, the gesture instead brings Marie Antoinette into the twenty-first. This temptation to 'update' Marie Antoinette is by no means exclusive to Coppola but is a postmodern trait well reflected in other popular culture representations of the queen.

Despite historical inaccuracies, Sofia Coppola's *Marie Antoinette* was nonetheless acknowledged by French historians and scholars as a valuable artistic vision of the queen's life (Lever 2006b; Berly & Martin 2010; Duprat 2013). Furthermore, because of its first-person perspective, according to some respondents to the survey, the biopic succeeded to a certain extent in giving viewers an idea of 'what it must have been like to be the queen'. Kirsten Dunst's charmingly teenage demeanour contributed to this appeal, and French and American respondents belonging to the minority groups of the survey attested to have appreciated her acting, although, in their view, Marie Antoinette herself exuded much more dignity and refinement. The historical accuracy of the film narrative was also considered lacking, yet these same respondents indicated that they would not have expected historical accuracy from a film that they regarded as an anachronistic interpretation of the eighteenth century.

On the other hand, from the perspective of a Republican teaching of history, Briand (2013; see also Besson 2014) does not consider the film fit for showing to students as a source of reliable information about French history, as it would give the impression that Marie Antoinette was a victim of the French Revolution (Figure 4.13). This view is supported by Duprat (2013), Poirson (2007, 2009) and Ozouf (2011), inasmuch as they also disapprove of the idea of Marie Antoinette being shown in the role of the victim of villainous masses. Within the context of a wider filmography, with Coppola's film highlighted, Berly and Martin (2010:436) only remark that it is difficult to identify the historical character of Marie Antoinette under the many layers of mythical representations given to her by a cult of *dévots*,[19] some of whom, they comment, do not portray her in a very orthodox manner. The

Figure 4.13 The unsuitability of the film in teaching French history within the Republican school curriculum lies in sympathetic scenes such as this

© Sony Pictures/courtesy Everett Collection

unsuitability of the film in teaching French history within the Republican school curriculum is not due to Coppola's raunchy scenes (depicting Marie Antoinette's alleged affair with Count von Fersen), as one would expect. Instead, the problematic scenes would be those which depict the royal family falling under the attack of the people. Significantly, Coppola's film ends with the queen's bedroom vandalised by the Revolutionaries in October 1789, over the music track of 'All Cats Are Grey' by *The Cure*, ominously evoking incarceration and death.

Coppola's film deliberately attempted to omit the political and adjacent social implications of the years before the outbreak of the French Revolution – for which it was criticised by French historians. However, the film reinforced the Republican historical agenda (albeit unintentionally) by portraying the queen, with few exceptions, as an embodiment of Republican clichés. This is attested by having been awarded, in 2006 at Cannes, the 'grand prix de l'Éducation nationale' (Poirson 2009) – conclusive proof that the narrative conformed to the official French historical discourse. Nevertheless, the film's narrative was criticised for conforming to a wider Anglo-Saxon and American tradition of opposing the French Revolution values and historiography (Mazeau 2008; Biard 2006; Biard & Leuwers 2007; Dupuy 2007; Duprat 2007; Dallet 2007; see also Vovelle 2012). It is important to note that, despite the noted contra-revolutionary tendency, Republican clichés are circulated particularly within the Anglo-Saxon and American popular culture milieus (see also Dallet 2007). As it will be shown later in Chapter 7, film is central to this circulation.

Thus, while Sofia Coppola tried to 'defend' the queen sympathetically– according to Poirson (2009:243), she identified with the 'spoiled child' behaviour – she did not manage to rewrite history. Paradoxically perhaps, Coppola meant to purposely dispel one of the most widespread of the clichés: 'Let Them Eat Cake!'. Yet despite her having explained that what is taught at a basic level about the Ancien Régime in American schools is a conglomerate of clichés (Poirson 2009), the message sent by the promotional trailer of the film, and the lavish décor painstakingly staged with the help of Ladurée, worked against this aim. An 'imaginary' scene, meant to show the public what the pamphlets would have claimed the queen to be, was intentionally depicted in contrast to Coppola's 'real' Marie Antoinette. According to the internet use of this image, its intended meaning is completely lost.

These observations may seem contradictory, but they reveal that the producers of both the Republican and Royalist historical discourses each appropriate differently the historical knowledge relating to Marie Antoinette generated by popular media such as film. Not only is this particular film director (Coppola) restricted by the hermeneutical circle that applies to her own milieu of historical knowledge, but the circle also acts on audiences and critics, which in turn affects the assessment of the film's objectivity. When knowledge translates into images, the hermeneutical circle shifts into the circle of representation (Hall 1997). Moreover, the volatility of images removes them from the control of their creator, confirming that films are destined to be read on many levels, some lost in the wake of commerciality and entertainment.

Coppola's film further reveals that the 'real' Marie Antoinette is still raising passions in France with the same intensity as over two centuries ago. Both fascination and hate are perhaps best described by Coppola's own comments to her film's conflicting *accueil* at Cannes (O'Hagan 2006):

> 'It's very French', she says, shrugging, when I bring up the catcalls at Cannes, 'Afterwards, I had a lot of French journalists saying, "I like your Marie Antoinette but I still hate the real Marie Antoinette". I guess she's still kind of a loaded subject there.'

The impact of Coppola's biopic over the general perception of the Petit Trianon and the character of Marie Antoinette (Duprat 2007), even if indirect, cannot be ignored. Following the earlier, black-and-white Hollywood biopic of Marie Antoinette, filmed in 1938 exclusively in the studio (Figure 4.5), and despite its influence over twentieth-century film representations of Marie Antoinette (Mason 2003; Poirson 2009), Coppola's hyper-reality film inaugurated, through its narrative and star actress, a new form for this

118 *Historical and cinematic narratives*

representation. The eclectic mixture of accurate eighteenth-century costumes with updated versions became Coppola's contribution to high fashion, further reinforcing the representation of Marie Antoinette in popular culture. By bringing Marie Antoinette's character to the fore in the media, Coppola's biopic inadvertently generated an invitation, or challenge, to other authors as well as cineastes, actors and performers to further explore Marie Antoinette's historical character. In conclusion, it cannot be ignored that Hollywood, through these two visually contrasting twentieth and twenty-first century biopics of Marie Antoinette, set the trend for a certain image of Marie Antoinette in film (Poirson 2009; Binh 2010). In turn, these images spilled into media and popular culture representations of Marie Antoinette with Kirsten Dunst becoming Marie Antoinette's new avatar (Goetz 2006). Lastly, it must be highlighted that Coppola's film was not on sale in any of the boutiques of Château de Versailles during 2010–2012, but in 2014 was part of the main display at the Librairie des Princes.

Riyoko Ikeda's Rose of Versailles *(1972)*[20]

This section analyses Riyoko Ikeda's manga (1972), which has had a great influence not only on the Japanese public's perception of the site of Petit Trianon, and Marie Antoinette in particular, but also played an important role in the social phenomenon of female emancipation in 1970s Japan (Ikeda 2011). In 2009, Ikeda was awarded the Legion of Honour 'for playing a major role in promoting French culture in Japan' [translation mine] (Brethes 2011). Japanese visitors at the Petit Trianon are second in numbers only to the French, and this largely due to Ikeda.[21]

The *shōjo* manga (manga aimed at teenage females) *Rose of Versailles* was adapted for television as a series of cartoons (anime), *Lady Oscar* (TMS 1979–1980), and even as a film produced and directed in Japan in 1979 by Jacques Demy (Binh 2010; Shamoon 2007). Coppola's film is the other source that Japanese majority group respondents noted as having influenced their opinion on Marie Antoinette, and the present section assesses the common ground between the film and the *shōjo* manga. This assessment provides further data collection for the analysis of Japanese visitor perceptions at the Petit Trianon (see Chapter 7).

Ikeda was inspired to design her manga when she was in her twenties, after reading as a teenager Zweig's biography of Marie Antoinette. Ikeda (2011) was greatly impressed by this and developed a deep, long-lasting admiration for the queen and for the courage and dignity she proved capable of when faced with her tragic yet heroic destiny. Ikeda also 'loves' Marie Antoinette for having been a rebel (Mauger 2011). *Rose of Versailles* faithfully adopted the historical discourse found in Zweig's novel, thus having, in essence, the same Republican historical narrative as Coppola's film (see also Vovelle 2012). However, Ikeda 'excuses' the queen not only because of her own sympathy for the sovereign but also due to Japanese fascination with the eighteenth century (Oka 2008). Members of the French minority group, as detected by the field research, were acquainted with and – unanimously – were also fans of the manga. Ikeda's illustrations, as well as her interpretation of the queen's tragic destiny, appeal to respondents with an art history background. The manga was also known to Italian respondents.

Another shared trait between the American film director and the Japanese *mangaka* is the portrayal of Marie Antoinette's history/story as a result of their own agendas: Coppola has an attraction for 'lostness' and young womanhood, while Ikeda (2011) is focused on femininity in all its forms, representations and manifestations, including transgender issues (Ikeda 1978). The fictitious main character of *Rose of Versailles* is Marie Antoinette's captain of the *Gardes du corps*, Oscar de Jarjayes (familiarly referred to as Lady Oscar), an androgynous figure who thus strengthens the idea of female emancipation to which the storyline is also dedicated.

Given the social position of women in Japan until not long ago, authors such as Ikeda felt admiration for women who broke social patterns, as Marie Antoinette incontestably did in her time: the queen was an emancipated woman who managed to shatter conventions, but not by libertinage, as common misportrayals would have it. Marie Antoinette was the first queen to play both the role of sovereign and that of royal mistress, Louis XVI being totally devoted to her. Being in charge of the court's *fêtes*, Marie Antoinette became quickly known for her exquisite refinement and taste in matters of music and theatre, at the same time 'daring' to express herself by either simple, overt support of musicians and artists of the time, by taking part in theatre plays (see Maisonnier et al. 2006; Oka 2008), and even by commissioning major art and architectural works – mostly at the Petit Trianon. By taking the lead within the political couple that she was forming with the king, amidst the turmoil of their last years, Marie Antoinette became a symbol of early feminist empowerment, appealing even more to the Japanese culture, where the role of women has always been secondary to that of men (Ikeda 2011).

What needs to be highlighted regarding the cinematic narrative associated with *Rose of Versailles* is the tremendous impact it had on the Japanese public perception of the character of Marie Antoinette. This, however, must be considered in relation to the perception of the fictitious character of Lady Oscar, who has taken on real dimensions in the public imaginary, as revealed by field research evidence. The two characters, and their fictitious, entwined destinies as imagined by Ikeda, could not exist separately.

Indeed, their story lines support and complement each other, creating a setting for the Japanese interpretation of the French Revolution's events – essentially a Republican narrative focusing on the poor living conditions of the French people as the main legitimiser of the violence and abuses of the events.

The third of the three main characters presented in the manga's introduction is Count Hans Axel von Fersen, who plays a particularly important role in the narrative. Ikeda (2011) confessed to having been shocked at first, when she read Zweig's account of the affair between the queen and Fersen. Yet she came to feel sympathy for the love they could not fulfil through marriage. In the manga, she introduced a particular scene meant to legitimate an otherwise illegitimate relationship, thus making it acceptable to Japanese mores: during one of their secret encounters, Marie Antoinette asks Fersen to promise that he will marry her in another life (Figure 4.14). This is, in fact, the key to understanding why the majority of Japanese visitors at the Petit Trianon have a positive image of Marie Antoinette. Despite any other Republican clichés (Figure 4.15), Ikeda's manga depicts Marie Antoinette's destiny as being in essence tragic. In the same manner that Coppola does not rewrite history, but gives a sympathetic look into the queen's life, Ikeda adapts Marie Antoinette's tragic circumstances to a Japanese understanding, eventually making her into the victim that the majority of Japanese visitors at the Petit Trianon see her as.

Lastly, this section explores the significant role *Rose of Versailles* played in shaping Japanese opinions on Marie Antoinette, filtered through the analysis of the appeal that this manga had, and continues to have, over generations of Japanese fans. According to Deborah Shamoon (2007), *Rose of*

Figure 4.14 'Oh, Fersen, promise that you will marry me in another life!' 'I promise!' (*Rose of Versailles* 1972)

© Ikeda Riyoko Production

Historical and cinematic narratives 121

Figure 4.15 Petit Trianon seen through Republican clichés, as in Zweig's biography – the costly whim of a queen, which sent France into ruin
© Ikeda Riyoko Production

Versailles revolutionised the modern genre of *shōjo* manga by shifting the genre focus from *dōseiai* (same sex love) to heterosexual romance depicted explicitly (Figure 4.16). This is common ground with Coppola's biopic of Marie Antoinette, the relationships depicted in the manga referring primarily to the same characters: Marie Antoinette and Fersen. Ikeda (2011) acknowledged her intention of providing female emancipation to Japanese girls, previously accustomed to the concept of heterosexual relationships equating female submissiveness with male power. Ikeda de-(re)constructed these traditional views by introducing adult heterosexual romance between equals (see Shamoon 2007). Masami Toku (2007) considers *Rose of Versailles* as a defining part of the *shōjo* manga golden era which revolutionised patterns of expression and illustration.

Nevertheless, Ikeda confessed to having been conditioned by the genre to gradually introduce this new idea of heterosexual romance, building upon *dōseiai* (which was accepted and encouraged by Japanese Meiji culture as necessary before marriage) by setting up a budding romance between Marie Antoinette and Oscar when in their early teens (Figure 4.17). However, Oscar is dressed as a man, whereas *dōseiai* is based on sameness of the girls'

Figure 4.16 Marie Antoinette and Fersen consummate their love at the Tuileries after Fersen risks his life coming to see the queen; the episode is faithful to Zweig's biography

© Ikeda Riyoko Production

Figure 4.17 An allusion to a budding romance between Marie Antoinette and Oscar – all the ladies at the Court are jealous despite knowing that Oscar is a woman dressed as a man

© Ikeda Riyoko Production

appearances, underlined by mythical relationships such as Castor and Pollux (Shamoon 2007). Duprat (2013) considers this imagined relationship to be an allusion to the lesbian portrayal of Marie Antoinette in eighteenth-century pornographic pamphlets, which, however, was not confirmed by Ikeda herself (2011). From the complexity of the genre as subject of anthropological studies (Napier 1998; Suzuki 1998; McLelland 2000; Kenji Tierney 2007), the manga's acknowledged contribution to shifting boundaries between genders should be noted.

Consequently, Marie Antoinette's historical character became, in part, a symbol of female emancipation in Japan through an imaginary relationship. This is an addition to the real dimensions of her role, as Ikeda did not avoid depicting poignant moments of the queen's life (Figure 4.18) and death, including the understanding that Marie Antoinette remained faithful to the monarchic order – narrative elements directly inspired by Zweig.

On a background of 'the lush, rococo setting and sweeping epic scale [which] certainly appealed to girls' sensibilities' (Shamoon 2007:3), all of the aforementioned narrative and visual elements made *Rose of Versailles* highly popular, shaping Japanese opinion on Marie Antoinette. Equally, the tremendous mourning effect on manga readers at the news of Lady Oscar's death (see Ikeda 2002, 2011) suggests that the character at least matches, or potentially surpasses, Marie Antoinette's popularity (see also Japanese costume play, or cosplay[22]). When considering that Marie Antoinette is seen in antithesis with the events of the French Revolution, and Oscar, despite being an aristocrat, changes sides during the events, it becomes clear that the zero-sum trait of heritages is again in operation, this time through the intermediary of symbolic fictional characters. The central role that Marie Antoinette continued to play within the narrative of *Rose of Versailles* is attributed to Ikeda's (2002:preface) own extreme fascination with Marie Antoinette:

> I remember with great nostalgia that period of my life, and a time passed at debilitating speed. I remember being besieged by work to the point of growing painfully thin and having to receive nutrients via injection, receiving injurious letters from certain literary female figures, falling into depression because I lacked ideas, drawing with a 40° fever and ice cubes on my hand . . . At the time, I had a passion to which I was capable to sacrifice everything, without regret, a once in a lifetime fixation – like the 'explosion of a star', to use Stefan Zweig's expression – a moment of revelation I wouldn't exchange for anything, and also, the youth of being 24. [translation mine]

According to Osamu (1995 cited in Toku 2007), the *shōjo* manga of the 1970s went beyond simple entertainment, having shifted to the self-expression of its authors, as confirmed by Ikeda.

Figure 4.18 Ikeda depicted tragic moments, amongst which the queen's separation from the Dauphin and her majestic defence in court, crowned by the moment known as 'J'en appelle à toutes les mères!'

© Ikeda Riyoko Production

Historical and cinematic narratives 125

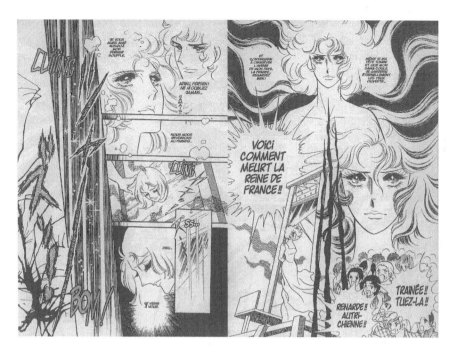

Figure 4.19 A Marie Antoinette full of courage and dignity, a symbol of the monarchic order itself
© Ikeda Riyoko Production

Within the process of appropriating Marie Antoinette's image, through the authors' personal fascination as well as their own agendas, Ikeda's work confirms (along with most other authors presented in the chapter) the hermeneutical circle which acts throughout their narratives. The zero-sum trait of heritages is further seen at its clearest through the final captions of Marie Antoinette's last thoughts (Figure 4.19):

> [addressed to the masses insulting her] Even if my head rolls and my blood gushed forth, I will always keep my eyes open . . . and will continue to watch over the future of my country, France . . . You look! [addressed to Fersen] Know I would have loved you till my last breath. Farewell, Fersen! Never forget me . . . We will meet again in Heaven . . . [her dying thought the moment her head is severed] God . . . I come to Thee. [translation mine]

The lines above clarify the reasons for which a supporter of the French Revolution's ideals cannot approve of the last Queen of France and vice versa

126 *Historical and cinematic narratives*

(the zero-sum trait of heritages) unless ways to reach compromise between their true stories are found. Ikeda also highlights the main traits that define the role of the queen, the woman and the Christian, all embodied by Marie Antoinette: devotion to her country of adoption which she considers as hers, the love for a man that she chose and was not chosen for her and finally, her deep connections to a religion that was made obsolete by the French Revolution. These conflicting roles have made her the most cherished historical character of contemporary Japan, albeit through the intermediary of another woman: Riyoko Ikeda.

Notes

1 Selection indicated by the Librairie des Princes shop assistants, based on observations, in the absence of statistics, which could not be provided by the RMN (Réunion des musées nationaux) representatives in charge of merchandise order stock. The selection includes only historical biographies (except Chantal Thomas' 2002 novel), thus indicating a specialist target audience. It also reflects, to a point, the preferences of the minority public French visitors, the group more likely to purchase books when visiting. For the other books sold at Librairie des Princes (English, Italian, German, Spanish or Russian in a smaller proportion), shop assistants could not provide a pattern of bestsellers.
2 Centre national de la recherche scientifique; the largest governmental research organisation in France.
3 The conflict-of-interests theme can also be found in the work of major biographers of the two consort monarchs (Bertière 2002, 2006; Hardman 2016; see also Petitfils 2006).
4 See www.youtube.com/watch?v=GcoBWn9z790;www.youtube.com/watch?v=it7VH57Az18.
5 The play was based on a historical discourse that reiterated certain Republican clichés but also focused on Marie Antoinette's nobility and dignity in facing a tragic end.
6 For a textual reading of this novel which highlights Dumas' Republican, anti-Royalist agenda in reconstructing the 1785 plot of events, see Peters (2012).
7 *Marie Antoinette: The Portrait of an Average Woman* (1933b).
8 Lever's (2005a) work on Marie Antoinette's private correspondence was first adapted for the Grignan Festival in 2007, with a mise en scène by Sally Micaleff (see www.grignan-festivalcorrespondance.com/editions.html), and has been performed periodically since, with the latest representation as recently as 2017. A one woman-show, *Marie Antoinette, In Her Own Words* was developed on this idea and toured the United States in 2013 under the direction of Katherine Adamov and starring Molière Award-winning actress, Barbara Schulz.
9 In line with the pamphlets' content, film director Jacquot chose to portray Duchesse de Polignac as Marie Antoinette's lover (see also Chapter 7). She was one of the female figures from the queen's entourage targeted by libelous pornographic media.
10 Academic of British nationality; Professor Seth has taught at Oxford since 2015.
11 Internet analysis also revealed an abundance of novels written in the form of Marie Antoinette's personal diaries aimed at teenagers and adults. The genre is not exclusively reserved to the last Queen of France, but generally to royalty surrounded by intriguing circumstances (e.g. Princess Anastasia's diary, sold on Amazon paired with Marie Antoinette's in bulk).
12 Princess Isabelle of Orléans-Braganza, Countess of Paris (1911–2003), historical author and consort of the Orléanist pretender, Henri, Count of Paris, was a direct descendant of Marie Antoinette's sister, Marie Caroline of Naples.

Historical and cinematic narratives 127

13 Louis XVI's historical character is nevertheless garnering increased attention, with alternative readings being offered; for a recent contribution to this attempt, see Fiquet (2015).
14 For relevant examples of contributions to social media editorial on Marie Antoinette's subject, see also http://vivelaqueen.blogspot.com/; http://laparigidimariaantonietta.blogspot.com/2013/10/.
15 This is the official accreditation, the Association having been active much prior to this date (Lorin pers. comm. 2014a). One of the NGO's notable founders, Cécile Coutin, has an impressive profile in the field as former curator of spectacles at the BnF (Bibliothèque nationale de France). Secretary and Co-Founder of the Association, Michèle Lorin, works diligently to counter the misrepresentation of the queen (see Lichfield 2006). One recent point of contention (see Chazan 2014) was that former call-girl Zahia Dehar was depicted as Marie Antoinette at Le Hameau by kitsch artists 'Pierre et Gilles'. Interestingly, this piece of popular culture art was chosen to be exhibited two years later at the Royal Academy of Art, London. www.bbc.co.uk/programmes/articles/JtW1WN7SrctP3RF9sK7qQ8/the-royal-academy-summer-exhibition-sees-double-for-the-first-time.
16 See www.academiedeversailles.com/.
17 When not shooting on location, Château de Millemont stood in for both the Palace of Versailles and the Petit Trianon (see Binh 2010).
18 Relevant to this is a Japanese blogger's (see *Rucca-Lusikka* 2007) account of the film, at the time of its release:

> I wanted to watch the movie Marie-Antoinette directed by Francis [sic] Coppola because the story is well known through manga, Berusaiyu no Bara. Like many of us, I have a series of manga books of Beru-Bara and an animation DVD. In addition to the influence of Beru-Bara, I was interested in the fashionable, gorgeous and picturesque images of this movie. [translated by Atsuko Tanaka]

19 *Dévots* were historically staunch defenders of the Catholic faith.
20 *Rose of Versailles* (*shōjo* manga) was serialised between April 1972 and December 1973 (Shamoon 2007) in the *Margaret* Comics; it is sold in Europe in a French translation by Kana (Ikeda 2002, 2011), and since 2016 in America and Canada by Udon Comics. The image analysis contained in the text is based on the French 2002 version of *La Rose de Versailles* sold at the Librairie des Princes.
21 This information cannot be confirmed statistically since no formal studies on criteria of visitor nationality exist specifically for Petit Trianon. Observation based on personal communication had with security personnel at Petit Trianon and other on-site research.
22 Within Japanese cosplay trends, Oscar's popularity, along with that of Marie Antoinette, is attested by contemporary costumes sold alongside recent manga merchandise; www.cosplayfantasy.com/rose-of-versailles-c-99/?sort=20a&page=1 [Last Accessed: 18 September 2017].

5 Eighteenth-century architectural and heritage narratives of the Petit Trianon

This chapter looks at data collected through the hermeneutical analysis (Mugerauer 1995) of the eighteenth-century architectural and heritage narratives of the Petit Trianon contained in its contemporary heritage interpretation since the 2008 restoration, when significant changes were made in how the site is interpreted to the public. The chapter equally focuses on the principles guiding this shift in heritage interpretation as well as on various issues connected to the heritage industry and its links with tourism. Furthermore, through an analysis of the extensive 2008 restoration and the shift in both interpretation and visitor perceptions, the chapter elucidates two major issues from a heritage interpretation perspective: how dissonant heritage was handled by those in charge of the interpretation of the Petit Trianon, and where the 2008 restoration places it within the heritage industry and its range of sites – spanning 360 degrees of heritage authenticity – aimed at tourist consumption (analysed in Chapter 2).

Managerial vs. curatorial and heritage architects' agendas

The following compares the managerial agenda with those of expert teams (curatorial, heritage architects) by analysing messages encoded in the 2008 restoration of the Petit Trianon building (Benoît 2016; see Figure 5.1).

The 2008 restoration: Political and economic considerations

The life of the historic house museum of Petit Trianon started on 22 February 1867, when *Le Moniteur* announced its opening under the patronage of Empress Eugénie, the opening coinciding with the Exposition Universelle held in Paris the same year (de Lescure 1867a; Desjardins 1885, 1894; see also Mahler 1887). Historic house museums, generally dating back to the second half of the nineteenth century in both Europe and the United States,[1] were created due to a wave of appreciation and desire to commemorate the lives of important political and cultural figures (Christensen 2011; Young 2017).

Due to the deep admiration of Empress Eugénie for Marie Antoinette, the Petit Trianon was founded as a memorial and house museum dedicated

Figure 5.1 La Salle des Gardes at the Petit Trianon – the post-restoration layout and visit flow were designed to better convey the intrinsic values of the historic house museum
Author collection/2008 photo courtesy Philippe Baudin

to the last Queen of France. Eugénie related to the queen via links other than strictly historical: her artistic sensibility was the main factor prompting the perceptive understanding of the former sovereign and her artistic contribution at the Petit Trianon (Bigorne 1998; Granger 2005; Chapman et al. 2007). In the wake of this understanding, at the end of the nineteenth century Pierre de Nolhac – through his research and writings – established a rehabilitative curatorial tradition concerning the Petit Trianon as home to Marie Antoinette (de Nolhac 1899b, 1906, 1925, 1927; de Nolhac & Hirschauer 1927; Montupet 2006).

However, the Petit Trianon remained shrouded in an aura of remoteness and did not garner the attention of mainstream visitors until recently. Its sudden popularity was triggered by Coppola's filming of *Marie Antoinette* during 2005, which was encouraged by Christine Albanel, who at the time was president of Château de Versailles. In fact, Albanel carefully constructed a marketing promotion around the notoriety of the American film director, which, though questionable from a traditional curatorial point of view, has had the anticipated effect of increasing visitor numbers at the Petit Trianon.

130 *Architectural and heritage narratives*

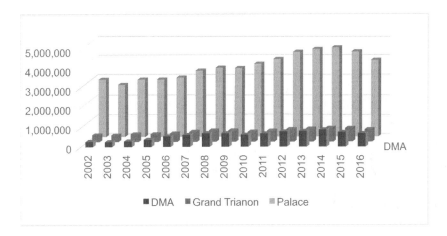

Figure 5.2 Visitor numbers at the *Domaine de Marie-Antoinette* (DMA), the Grand Trianon and the Château de Versailles (Palace) – total of paid and free entries

Statistics courtesy Château de Versailles

A study of all the figures relating to visitor numbers at the Petit Trianon since 2002[2] (see Figure 5.2) reveals an increase in excess of 100% from 2004 to 2007, with the comparison between 2005 and 2006 alone showing an increase of 46.3%. In 2008, a further increase of 13.1% was seen, after which figures stabilised until 2010, when a decrease of 10.3% was registered compared with 2009. This drop might be attributed to the general economic situation, but visitor numbers for the Château de Versailles actually increased by almost the same amount that year, suggesting that the drop at the Petit Trianon was more likely a softening after the initial impact of the film's marketing promotion (Busby & Klug 2001). Visitor momentum at the Petit Trianon returned in 2011 with an increase of 9.6% over 2010. This was followed by another jump of 15% in 2012, a further increase of 3% in 2013 and another increase in 2014 of 7.8%. That year, there were 883,906 visitors, a record for the Petit Trianon, although this is likely to stem from the sponsorship of Christian Dior SE of the most recent restoration at the *Domaine de Marie-Antoinette*, that of La Maison de la Reine. Dior intensively marketed and promoted the sponsorship, especially through their new makeup range, Trianon, released in 2014 (see Chapter 7). The effect was not long-lasting, however, as 2015 saw a drop of 12.9% versus 2014, and 2016 saw a further decline of 8.6%. Significantly, visitor figures at the Palace also increased during the period of increase for the Petit Trianon, though not as dramatically, demonstrating a proportionally stronger rise in popularity of the *Domaine de Marie-Antoinette* relative to the main Palace. By 2013 (the year before Dior's potential impact), the Petit Trianon was attracting 20% of the total number of visitors to the Palace, compared with only 10% in 2002.[3] Since one of the goals of the 2008 restoration was to improve visit-flow distribution at the Palace, these statistics confirm this to have been achieved.

On 13 June 2006, Montres Breguet, the Swiss company founded by Abraham-Louis Breguet, became the official sponsor of the restoration of the Petit Trianon. Monsieur Breguet was the queen's watchmaker, renowned for manufacturing the perpetual watch, *Marie-Antoinette*, commissioned in 1783 by an unknown admirer of the queen and finished 34 years after her death. It is perhaps surprising that the Petit Trainon building had never undergone a refurbishment on this scale (Lablaude et al. 2006a, 2006b, 2007) prior to 2008. However, this sponsorship contract raised concerns among some of the curators of the Petit Trianon about the potential for accelerated deterioration due to increased visitor traffic attracted to the site after the completion of such a high-profile project (Benoît pers. comm. 2010b; Baudin pers. comm. 2010, 2011a, 2011c).

Montres Breguet had its own agenda and narrative: promoting and enhancing the company's image by association with royalty through the historical figure of Marie Antoinette. The 1983 robbery of the *Marie-Antoinette* watch from the L.A. Mayer Museum of Islamic Art (Jerusalem), eventually led to Montre Breguet's decision in 2005 to remake the watch from the detailed technical blueprints of the original (Hayek & Aillagon 2009).[4] The manipulation of certain events for marketing purposes is confirmed by the fact that, despite the recovery of the original watch in 2007, the new watch came to surpass it in fame through closer association with contemporary Versailles, as part of a new narrative. One crucial part of this new narrative was Marie Antoinette's oak tree, under which she had often rested while at the Petit Trianon. This venerable tree was struck down by lightning in 2005 (Figure 5.3). For Montres Breguet, led at the time by Nicolas G. Hayek (d. 2010), the lightning strike was providential, coming on the heels of the decision to rebuild the original watch. Montres Breguet imaginatively asked permission of Château de Versailles to use wood taken from the downed tree to create the display case of the new watch. Château de Versailles generously made a gift of the wood, and Montres Breguet would ultimately donate the 5.5 million euros needed for the restoration of the building of Petit Trianon.

Domaine de Marie-Antoinette: *Heritage commodification vs. authenticity*

All manner of narratives serve as background not only for heritage interpretation, but also for heritage financing (Ashworth & Howard 1999). This implies aspects of heritage commodification, a hotly debated issue impinging on the loss of heritage authenticity. Possibly an effect of the *patrimonialisation* of the contemporary society (Nora 1984a), heritage commodification engages complex theoretical and philosophical discussions. The postmodern commodification of culture covers a wide range of motives and implications (Appadurai 1986; Bhabha 1994; Edson 2004; Misiura 2006), focalising

Figure 5.3 The remains of Marie Antoinette's oak, which led to funding of the 2008 restoration of the Petit Trianon, is exhibited near the visitor entrance

Author photo 2011/courtesy Château de Versailles

extensive scholarship on the endangering of authenticity by tourist consumption (MacCannell 1999; Meethan 2001; Robinson 2001; Macleod 2006). Still, the very existence of authenticity is as debated as its loss, many authors forwarding a different understanding of the concept and thus influencing its evaluation (Cohen 1988b; Bendix 1997; Phillips 1997; Wang 1999; Waitt 2000; Upton 2001; Roy 2004; Reisinger & Steiner 2006; Orbaşli & Woodward 2009; Knudsen & Waade 2010; Crouch 2011; Silverman 2015).

The term 'heritage commodification' has acquired a wide range of meanings: from a sophisticated form of cultural representation as defined by Stuart Hall (1995, 1997) translated into heritage parameters by Gregory Ashworth and Brian Graham (2005) – in this instance, representation is a discourse vital to conveying the intrinsic values of heritage – to the most basic of commercial products, such as a mass-produced souvenir (Ashworth & Howard 1999). Souvenirs are invested at the same time with a symbolic value (Goss 2004; see also Schouten 2006; de Azeredo Grünewald 2006), which makes the commodification process even more complex in terms of rivalry to authenticity. Moreover, heritage discourse manifests through a wide range of milieus: from the personal level to that of the media, or from local to

Architectural and heritage narratives 133

international dimensions, and/or from the popular discourses of television programmes and films to professional discourses such as prizes and awards (Groote & Haartsen 2008). With regard to the images associated with all the above discourses, opinions are again divided between those who consider the nature of identities created through images to be arbitrary, such as marketing of certain tourist places (Urry 1995; Meethan 2001), and those who believe them to be deeply rooted in cultural phenomena (Anholt 2010). This particular association between image and place is analysed in Chapter 7, associating the fieldwork research evidence with the effects of the commodification of Marie Antoinette's historical character at the Petit Trianon, which proved to be uncontrolled.

Heritage commodification (Figure 5.4) is an inherent trait of, and essential factor in, the subsistence of heritage sites. As long as it is controlled by those in charge of the heritage interpretation of the site, it can be a source of much needed financial revenue (Ashworth & Howard 1999; Howard 2003). This study argues against the uncontrolled commodification of heritage which is a result of managerial decisions (discussed in Chapter 7). The discussion here focuses next on the curatorial team's attempts to control the image of Marie Antoinette through heritage interpretation. As demonstrated by the 2008 restoration negotiations held between the managerial and the curatorial and heritage-architects expert teams, conflicts of interest often lead to compromises. Once the sponsorship contract was signed with Breguet, a meeting took place between the managerial team, represented by President Christine Albanel and Director Pierre Arizzoli-Clémentel, and a team of Petit Trianon's specialists: head curator Christian Baulez; head of the Heritage Architectural Department, Pierre-André Lablaude and one of his main collaborators, heritage architect, Philippe Baudin (pers. comm. 2012, 2013).

At this point, it must be stressed that the president and the director of Château de Versailles are both politically charged positions (see also Rykner

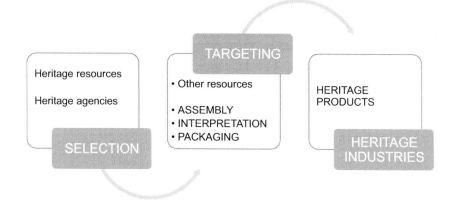

Figure 5.4 'Commodification of the Past', based on Tunbridge and Ashworth (1996)

2010a, 2010b), which is perhaps unsurprising given the previous role of the current museum. With nomination for these posts indirectly supervised by the President of the Republic, the personalities elected for a four-year mandate typically come from prior ministerial or governmental positions. As a result, sponsorship contracts, and any other projects undertaken by holders of these positions, have a double role: firstly, securing a prominent legacy for their mandate and, secondly, attracting increased funds.

The position of head curator (in any French museum, and especially at Château de Versailles) in the context of a restoration process, is limited by two main aspects, quite in opposition to the managerial agenda outlined above. Firstly, the nature of traditional conservation principles is purist, giving priority to, first, the authenticity of material[5] over induced feelings of authenticity (Crouch 2012; Schorch 2014) and second, to the classic material representation over the induced visual representation favoured within New Museology interpretation, such as the widespread use of new digital technologies (see Vergo 1989; Edensor 2002; Appleton 2006; Waterton & Watson 2010; Watson & Waterton 2010; Graham & Cook 2010; Light 2011; Waterton & Watson 2013). The Petit Trianon has had the theoretical status of a historic house museum since its founding in 1867. Therefore, the pronounced feel of a home conferred by the 2008 restoration layout clearly differentiates the museum presentation of the Petit Trianon from that of the classic European art museum, based on the European tradition of collecting (Pearce 1995) – a particularly Western approach imposed on other cultures, such as the Japanese, since the nineteenth century (Morishita 2010; Tythacott 2012). This classic Western tradition is best exemplified by the Louvre Museum, much criticised for the 'death of the experience' generated by the removal of artefacts from their context (Hetherington 2014).

The second factor impinging on curatorial decisions is the implication in the restoration process of the heritage architect, who has, in France, the authority to make final decisions on the course of restoration projects (but not interior furnishing). Although historically, the Western European tradition equally favoured historians/art historians as well as architects in the creation of heritage discourse (theoretically and practically – see Jokilehto 1999; Graham et al. 2000; Hernández Martínez 2008), the French tradition values architectural expertise, possibly as a result of the restoration ethos of architect Eugène Viollet-le-Duc (Foucart 1986; Ball 2011; Baudin pers. comm. 2011a, 2011b).

Despite some rivalry between the heritage architect and curator professions, confirmed through fieldwork research, the authority of the former over the latter in built restoration decisions remains uncontested due to tradition. Nevertheless, more recently, management has gained increasing authority over the decisions of both aforementioned professions. With these clarifications in mind, one can easily understand the conflict of interests behind the negotiations of a large-scale restoration like the 2008 Petit Trianon project. Although Christian Baulez (head curator at the Petit Trianon at the time) had worked over a period of approximately 30 years to accurately restore furniture and other features of the Petit Trianon to historical periods, and had conducted extensive curatorial research throughout his career (see Baulez 2007), he opposed the 2008 large-scale restoration, as it implied dramatically increased visitor access. Under contractual obligation to Breguet, and faced with the inevitability of the project, Baulez devised preventive measures against potential future damage. Consequently, the general curatorial restoration outline successfully impressed upon the managerial team the need to limit visitor numbers to the second and third floors. This was achieved by strict scheduling of a limited number of guided visits for small groups at certain times of day, as opposed to the free-flow visits available on the ground and first floors. Since 2010, guided visits to the upper floors are no longer available on a daily basis, and require advance booking.

From the specialist expertise point of view, the restoration sought to strengthen the association between Marie Antoinette and the Petit Trianon whilst also achieving a better coherence of the heritage narrative by placing the site into a historical continuity (Baudin pers. comm. 2011b). A clear shift away from old museology exhibition trends particular to historic house museums, and towards contemporary – New Museology – principles (see Vergo 1989; Walsh 1992; Hodge 2011; Christensen 2011), was undoubtedly achieved. The challenging museographic project consisted in preserving and strengthening the identity of the Petit Trianon as Marie Antoinette's 'home', as well as making clear references to all the later-period inhabitants through a modified collection display. Nevertheless, the ground and first floors (Figure 5.5), open to public, free-flow visits, exclusively represent Marie Antoinette's period, with only the upper two floors also displaying other inhabitants and their periods. Potentially as a result of this decision, the field research evidence revealed that the majority of visitors do perceive Petit Trianon at least as half 'home'/half museum when asked about the feel of the place. Apparently, only the lack of more personal effects belonging to the queen detracts from the complete feel of the sovereign's home. Furthermore, the majority of visitors are entirely unaware of the details of the initial construction and estate ownership during eras preceding and succeeding that of Marie Antoinette, as well as the existence of the upper two floors. Consequently, the Petit Trianon's heritage interpretation can be described as a double-level museum presentation (Benoît pers. comm. 2010b), one dedicated to the mass public and another aimed at the informed visitor. This aspect resonates with the traits of 'personal cultural capital' (Busby & Meethan 2008). Given the loss of most of the furniture, art objects and other furnishings dating from Marie Antoinette's period, the initial museum, established in 1867, recreated the atmosphere of the eighteenth century through a mix of authentic and period pieces donated by Empress Eugénie (Pincemaille 2003). More authentic pieces have been acquired since, the retrieval of those artefacts sold during the French Revolution being one of the Palace's policies from 1938 (see Baulez 1989).

The feel of a 'home' was accentuated by reinstating the functionality of other building segments, such as the *réchauffoir* and the *domestiques* quarters. Authentic furniture and art objects dating to periods after Marie Antoinette's

Figure 5.5 Marie Antoinette à la rose (Élisabeth Vigée Le Brun 1783), one of the best-known representations of the queen in painting, is displayed on the first floor of the Petit Trianon

Photo Christophe Fouin. Château de Versailles et de Trianon Collection © RMN-Grand Palais/ courtesy Art Resource, NY

era, are now exhibited – not in their original places, but on the uppermost two floors of the Petit Trianon. Thus, the first floors, included in the general visit, could be entirely reconfigured and presented as Marie Antoinette's living spaces. The last two floors display other historical periods, also include eighteenth-century pieces, and exhibit more intimate aspects of the house. In order to convey this clearly, the Centre de recherche designed virtual tours and other media presentations of the Petit Trianon. These are available to be watched in a part of the kitchen quarters which were adapted to a media space. Field research evidence revealed that most respondents belonging to the majority groups did not take advantage of this, either because of overcrowding or being unaware of this option (despite clear signage). The compromise in interpreting the 'Golden Age' (Ashworth & Howard 1999) is typical for complex heritage sites faced with choosing a particular period to preserve over others (Kirshenblatt-Gimblett 1998; Howard 2003; Hems & Blockley 2005; Misiura 2006), the demand of the public being the final deciding factor. This 'demand' is confirmed by the total identification of the Petit Trianon with Marie Antoinette – despite prior/subsequent ownership – and further proved by the survey results of this study.

On 1 July 2006, Christine Albanel launched the concept of *Domaine de Marie-Antoinette* (Figure 5.6), inclusive of the building of the Petit Trianon,

Figure 5.6 Renaming the Petit Trianon – the main entrance displaying the new name
Author photo 2011/courtesy Château de Versailles

its gardens and the model Norman Village. Although historically incorrect (the Petit Trianon has never been officially known under this name), the designation formally signalled the opportunity seized by the Château de Versailles to revive public interest in the last Queen of France, her much debated home and its associated legends. Thus, the Petit Trianon acquired a strengthened identity.

After a year's closure for the restoration, the Petit Trianon reopened to the public on 2 October 2008. Officially inaugurated on 24 September 2008 in the presence of Nicolas G. Hayek, president of Montres Breguet SA; Jean-Jacques Aillagon, president of the Établissement Public de Versailles; and then-director Pierre Arizzoli-Clémentel, the first guided visits of the newly restored home of Marie Antoinette were conducted by the director himself, who also published the restoration layout and ethos that year (Arizzoli-Clémentel 2008a).

During the restoration closure, three main exhibitions on Marie Antoinette were held in France (Salmon et al. 2008), the United States (Chapman et al. 2007) and Japan (Bascou et al. 2008). Taking advantage of exhibit material becoming available for travel, these exhibitions were conceived to maximise the marketing impact of the new restoration in three of the countries supplying the highest numbers of visitors to the Petit Trianon. Hermeneutical analysis of the three exhibitions' intended messages addressed to their respective audiences confirmed the field research evidence regarding the image of Marie Antoinette as perceived by the majority of French, American and Japanese visitors at the Petit Trianon.

The Grand Palais exhibition of 2008,[6] whose main organiser was Xavier Salmon (at the time painting curator of Château de Versailles), was in many ways a eulogy to Marie Antoinette's contribution to eighteenth-century art, in her role as patron. Yet the first of three introductory essays to the catalogue, by historian Jean Tulard, member of the Institut de France and emeritus Professor at La Sorbonne, reveals a typical, though subtle, Republican historical stance. This is an illustrative example of the contrast between Republican readings of the historical character of Marie Antoinette and the dimensions of her character suggested by art history. In fact, assessing the narrative tone used by art historians to portray the last Queen of France, using as source exhibition catalogues as well as art and fashion history publications/articles (Tuetey 1914; de Nolhac & Hirschauer 1927; Jallut 1955, 1969; Grouvel 1964; Tapié et al. 1989; Boyer & Halard 1995; Chazal et al. 2001; Kayser et al. 2003; Choffé 2004; Boysson et al. 2005; Salmon 2005, 2008; Maisonnier et al. 2006; Weber 2006; Chapman et al. 2007; Salmon et al. 2008; Duvernois 2008; Arizzoli-Clémentel & Gorguet-Ballesteros 2009; Lanoë et al. 2011; Masson 2013; Carlier 2016; Firmin & Rondot 2016; Benoît 2016; Hennebelle 2017; Laval 2017; Hyde 2017), confirmed that art history knowledge, best supported by literary sensibility, unlocks the content behind the controversial, Republican cliché-ridden image of the Queen of France. Furthermore, the general attitude of the French public, revealed by the survey, explains why, in the introductions to all the exhibitions relating to Marie Antoinette, art historians usually employ an appeasing tone in order to cultivate in the French public an open-mindedness towards discovering a Marie Antoinette so unknown to them. It is also true, however, that even art historians harbour different attitudes depending on their cultural and political inclinations.

The second exhibition, held in 2008 at the Fine Arts Museums of San Francisco, Legion of Honor, unveiled for the public Marie Antoinette's contribution to the eighteenth-century art legacy, the Petit Trianon's outstanding architectural value and even suggested the unexplored dimensions of the historical character of the last Queen of France (Chapman et al. 2007). The same year, an exhibition held in France at the Louvre (with itinerant showcases in Tokyo and Kobe) focused on eighteenth-century court rituals in connection with Marie Antoinette (Bascou et al. 2008). The Japanese fascination with European courts, and especially Marie Antoinette, is discussed by the Japanese curator Yasumasa Oka (2008), who also highlights the lack of academic research on the reasons behind this fascination. Curated by the Château de Versailles (Firmin & Rondot 2016), another exhibition centred on the queen's life was held at Mori Arts Center Gallery in Tokyo in 2016–2017, further attesting to this fascination.

Finally, it must be stressed that exhibitions provide the main means for the curators in charge of the Petit Trianon to control, to a point, the portrayal of Marie Antoinette. Otherwise, the heritage interpretation of the Petit Trianon does not fully reflect the curatorial tradition, for reasons explained later in the chapter. The above analysis contributes to outlining the heritage narrative of the Petit Trianon as home to Marie Antoinette through a better understanding of the 2008 restoration ethos, strategies and aims. Furthermore, the agendas of all those involved in the restoration provide a clearer insight into the web of decisions behind the narrative conveyed.

Eighteenth-century architectural narrative of the Petit Trianon

This section presents the pivotal narrative of the book – the eighteenth-century architectural narrative of the Petit Trianon – against which the validity of the historical facts is assessed. This narrative highlights Marie Antoinette's vision, as supported by Richard Mique's 1780s architectural contribution (Bandiera 1985; Mique 1998) and Hubert Robert's art. The narrative conforms to the cultural heritage authenticity principles discussed in Chapter 2 from the perspective of the 'creator's concept' (see Figure 2.1) with the English Garden, its *fabriques* (e.g. Le Temple de l'Amour) and the model Norman village playing a central role (see Figure 5.8).

The following analysis determines the principles underlying this narrative, by taking as a starting point the first extensive restoration of the Petit Trianon since the outbreak of the French Revolution. This restoration, completed in

Figure 5.7 Marie Antoinette en gaulle (Élisabeth Vigée Le Brun 1783), the favourite dress style worn by the queen at Petit Trianon and Le Hameau

bpk Bildagentur/collection of Hessische Hausstiftung/courtesy Art Resource, NY

2008, sought to recreate Marie Antoinette's world in the most accurate manner possible. The aim has been achieved: the Petit Trianon looks as though the queen is due home at any moment (Figure 5.7).

But would she approve of the makeover of her much-loved former home? It is true that by not rehabilitating Marie Antoinette's model Norman village, Le Hameau de la Reine, the restoration has neglected the rural value of the Estate's outbuildings, which the queen herself favoured most. Whilst some structures were completely lost over the years, some maintenance and repairs were undertaken. Still, the interventions were limited to façadism, and restoration of the surrounding gardens – evidence of the contemporary dominance, in terms of recognised value, of the national identity expressed in the cultural heritage of the Petit Trianon. Thus, the royal neoclassical value has prevailed over a royal vernacular counterpart, which was created and preferred by Marie Antoinette. That said, curators in charge of the Petit Trianon have always been aware of this value and have long voiced support for the rehabilitation of the derelict interiors (d'Abbes 1908) of Le Hameau

Architectural and heritage narratives 141

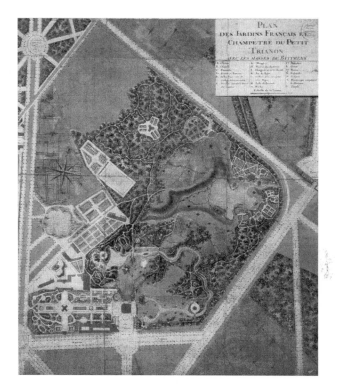

Figure 5.8 Plan des Jardins Français et Champêtre du Petit Trianon avec les masses des Bâtiments (Richard Mique 1786)
Château de Versailles et de Trianon Collection © RMN-Grand Palais/courtesy Art Resource, NY

de la Reine (Benoît pers. comm. 2011b; see Figure 5.9). Finally, in 2013, Château de Versailles signed the sponsorship contract with Dior for the restoration of the derelict interior of La Maison de la Reine (the main structure of Le Hameau), with a completion date of 2018. The period which will be interpreted inside this structure is that of Empress Marie Louise (the second consort of Napoléon Bonaparte), and not of Marie Antoinette, due to lack of information on the interior furnishings during the queen's ownership. This restoration is a complex case study unto itself, making a subject for future research.

The Petit Trianon was designed by Ange-Jacques Gabriel and constructed between 1762 and 1768, for the personal use of Louis XV and his *favorite* (royal mistress), Madame de Pompadour. After her untimely death, which took place before the Petit Trianon could be completed, Madame du Barry later enjoyed the retreat in the king's company, until Louis XVI's ascension to the throne in 1774 brought the Estate under the property of his young queen, Marie Antoinette. Between 1774 and 1789,

Figure 5.9 Derelict interiors typical of the current state of Le Hameau de la Reine buildings, such as La Maison de la Reine (first image; under restoration as of 2017) and Le Boudoir (second image)

Author photo 2011/courtesy Château de Versailles

the Petit Trianon underwent changes commissioned by the queen in collaboration with architect Richard Mique who, together with artist Hubert Robert, designed the Jardin Anglais as well as the model Norman village (see Lavedan 1944; Dams & Zega 1995; de Raïssac 2011).

An accurate description of the eighteenth-century architectural narrative of the Petit Trianon must first clearly delineate the concepts behind its creation, including its typology as a royal 'escape' from the rigid court etiquette of the Palace of Versailles, a formalised protocol purposely instilled by Louis XIV for political reasons of state centralisation (Lecoq 1986; Pommier 1986; Himelfarb 1986; Jourdan 1997). Even the great monarch, legendary for mastering his own image through the use of art and architecture, needed to balance the overpowering effect of a carefully and meticulously orchestrated court routine which employed symbolism to a particularly high degree. To 'escape' the etiquette, retreats such as Marly were built for the Sun King, who would visit from time to time in the company of a small, select group of courtiers. Louis XV followed his example, building the Petit Trianon for essentially the same purpose.

Marie Antoinette, as queen, simultaneously followed and challenged this established path by choosing to have the Petit Trianon as her own retreat, restricted to a close circle of companions, much as the earlier kings had done. Perhaps predictably, this inversion of gender roles led to high criticism, making the Petit Trianon the epicentre of constant disapproval (de Raïssac 2011). In fact, Marie Antoinette was the first queen to play both the role of sovereign and of king's *favorite*, commissioning major art and architectural works, most of which were located at the Petit Trianon (Dassas 2006). Previous French queens, such as Catherine de Medici and later Marie de Medici, who contributed similar architectural legacies (see Hill 2003; Galletti 2012; Martin 2011), were nevertheless acting within their positions as Regents on behalf of their sons. By contrast, it needs to be said that, given the Salic Law, the attributions and the limitations of the role of French queens (see Cosandey 2000) made it more difficult for Marie Antoinette to have such architectural input. (For valuable historical research on the attributions and limitations of the role of the queen, which focuses on Henrietta Maria and Marie Antoinette in the context of the English and French Revolutions, see Harris 2016.)

The Petit Trianon enjoyed a variety of practical roles supporting Marie Antoinette's endeavours. In particular, it served as a venue for protocol receptions (Arizzoli-Clémentel & Ducamp 1998) for like-minded monarchs attempting to avoid traditional court formality, to the point that they sometimes travelled incognito: in 1781 for Joseph II, Emperor of the Austro-Hungarian Empire (Marie Antoinette's brother); in 1782 for the future Russian Tsar, Paul I, alias 'Comte du Nord' and in 1784 for Gustav III, King of Sweden, alias 'Comte de Haga' (Figure 5.10).

The Enlightened ideas adopted by the Bourbon dynasty at the end of the eighteenth century are fully reflected by Marie Antoinette's education and attitude towards her children, brought up in a close relationship with their

Figure 5.10 Fête donnée au Petit Trianon le lundi 21 juin 1784 en l'honneur du roi de Suède Gustave III (Nicklas Lafrensen le Jeune, dit Lavreince 1785)

Courtesy Östergötlands Museum

parents previously unacceptable for royalty. The Estate of the Petit Trianon provided the perfect setting (Figure 5.11). It is acknowledged by historians and art historians alike (Carrott 1989; Duprat 2013; Kayser 2003) that Marie Antoinette strongly adhered to Enlightenment ideas for raising and educating children, sourced from Rousseau's novel *Émile*. The Petit Trianon landscape and buildings had an educative role for the royal offspring (de Nolhac 1899a, 1925, 1927; Martin 2011; Duprat 2013), particularly through the model Norman village and the working farm which the queen chose to build (Saule & Arminjon 2010).

The art Marie Antoinette commissioned for the neoclassical *fabriques* of the Jardin Anglais of the Estate (Dassas 2006) also aligns with Enlightenment principles. However, the French Enlightenment's art trendsetters espoused two different strands of discourse. The first was the use of art as propaganda. The *philosophes*, particularly Denis Diderot and his views as art critic for the annual *Salons* (Leith 1965), were keen supporters of this. The second was the Enlightenment model of a simplified aestheticism in accordance with the principle of the return to nature. Well portrayed by the model of Jardin

Figure 5.11 Marie Antoinette et ses enfants au pied d'un arbre (miniature on ivory, François Dumont 1789)

Photo Michèle Bellot. The Louvre Collection © RMN-Grand Palais/courtesy Art Resource, NY

Anglo-Chinois made fashionable by Rousseau's novel *La Nouvelle Helloïse*, this second principle informed the creation of the Petit Trianon (Desjardins 1885; Gromort 1928; Hazard 1946; Saudan & Saudan-Skira 1987; de Brancion 2003; Choffé 2004; Salmon 2008; Lamy 2005, 2010).

It is important to follow up an inconsistency particular to the *philosophes* strand of discourse, as it links with Gellner's reading of Enlightenment principles, which were untested by practice and also generated political confusion. Whilst Diderot criticised Boucher and the *pastorale* imagery of his paintings (for lack of educational role), he also enthusiastically praised certain still-life paintings for their purely aesthetic quality (see Leith 1965). In the end, such contradictions allowed for distortions to be brought to the message of art as propaganda which initially was not meant to be a conveyor of anti-royalty messages but rather to have a purely educative role. The numerous connections between those in power and key figures of the Enlightenment attest to this (Jourdan 1997).

Diderot's ideas were faithfully adopted by the painter Jacques-Louis David, whose artistic trajectory perfectly demonstrates the aforementioned distorted use of Enlightenment principles of art as propaganda (Clark 1999; Campbell 2006), within a new context of anti-Royalist political views. After visiting Tivoli – ancient site of Roman Emperor Hadrian's villa – David enjoyed a considerable influence over the French fashion for neoclassical art, not least because of the era's discovery of Pompeii. Seen through the lens of art and architecture manipulation in support of the revolutionary political agenda (Leith 1965), David's trajectory further contributes to our understanding of the evolution of political events towards the end of the eighteenth century. Ascending to fame through his classical compositions during the Ancien Régime, David eventually became the hero artist of the French Revolution (Priestland 2010), and later to finally become the official painter of Emperor Napoléon I (!). David's career could indicate that the artists and intellectuals instrumental to disseminating the propaganda renounced the untested ideas/ideals previously supported with such fervour. Or, it could be that their true motivation – and that of the masterminds of the French Revolution – was simply to secure power by any means, without true ideals or convictions. Regardless of David's questionable adherence to Enlightenment principles, his career highlights the bivalency and contradictions generated by the Enlightenment itself, extending into art and politics as well as science (Mauzi 2008; Stalnaker 2010), religion and morality (Mauzi 1960).

By contrast to the above, Marie Antoinette's artistic concept of the Estate of the Petit Trianon references undistorted Enlightenment ideals and messages intrinsic to the model of Rousseau's English Garden: perfecting an imperfect world through a symbolic return to nature's uncomplicated beauty (Saudan & Saudan-Skira 1987). Marie Antoinette was a declared adept of these ideals, which she followed privately through her duties as mother, in a role defined through new parameters unprecedented amongst queens of France and previously restricted by the old etiquette (Duprat 2013).

Acknowledging the transition from the seventeenth-century (overbearing) Absolutist monarchic representation to the contrasting eighteenth-century (self-effacing) monarchic aspiration to non-representation in accord with Enlightenment values (see Jourdan 1997) – corresponding to the little-acknowledged, Enlightenment rule of the last monarchic couple of the Ancien Régime – is fully evident in Marie Antoinette's legacy at the Petit Trianon.[7] This feeds into the core argument here: the creation of the Petit Trianon as home to Marie Antoinette was influenced by this climate of Enlightenment ideas. The main sources of information on eighteenth-century neoclassical architectural principles and its associated picturesque landscape are provided by the experts of the century (Laugier 1753; Morel 1776; Watelet 1774, 1777, 1784; de Lille 1782; Carmontelle 1779; Le Rouge 1776–1779; de Ligne 1781/1922; de La Borde et al. 1781–1784, 1784–1797; de Laborde 1808).

It is helpful to conclude this analysis of the eighteenth-century architectural narrative of the Petit Trianon with a contemporary translation of the Enlightenment principles mentioned above. Although the external aspects of the eighteenth-century picturesque landscape (de Andia 1978; Bigorne 1998; de Brancion 2003; de Lorme 2006; Largardère et al. 2008) garner significant attention, the differences between today's world and that of the eighteenth century are greater than appear at first glance. What to the contemporary mind may seem an evident reality was a challenging revelation more than two centuries ago.

Today, the ideas of the Enlightenment, in particular, may equate to quantum physics-cum-philosophy[8] and/or New Age religions (although the scale to which these are embraced by contemporary society is a dim reflection of the amplitude and impact the Enlightenment had on the eighteenth century). In the absence of widespread individual understanding of these contemporary trends, a considerable part of the population nevertheless tries to embrace some of the revelations conveyed, although it will take some time for these insights, once proven valid, to benefit society as the whole. Considering the Enlightenment did not refer solely to science or religion but to all the aspects of life as defined at the time, true Enlightenment ideals addressing the progress of humanity were *dans l'air du temps*, garnering legitimation from supporters among the aristocratic class and royalty (Darnton 1979). Thus, to label or criticise the espousal of these ideals as mere fanciful *divertissements* of a 'bored' aristocratic class would equate to falling into the trap of listening to classical music with contemporary ears (Ashworth & Howard 1999), that is to say, voiding the context of its meaning.

Returning to the earlier discussion of the distortion of Enlightenment ideals, an important finding of the field research revealed that respondents belonging to the majority groups at the Petit Trianon reflect this distortion through their perceptions: the majority of the contemporary public perceive the Petit Trianon as a symbol of the utter decadence of the Ancien Régime. Furthermore, the common acceptance of British art-history academia regarding the progress that 'picturesque' ideals would have eventually induced in nineteenth-century England – through the philanthropic projects of 'cottage' housing – is written off amongst eighteenth-century French counterparts as an often excessive artistic experiment (Maudlin 2015). Moreover, the eighteenth-century French picturesque was deprived of its chance to develop into a social movement (see also Garric 2014) as it was able to do in England.

It is asserted here that the Enlightenment was indeed responsible for a radical change in the perception and role of art away from the purely aesthetic course towards which the Renaissance had steered it (see Leith 1965). Despite the relevance which the picturesque in general has to today's visual culture (emitters and receivers included), its principles and representative landscapes are still misunderstood (see Macarthur 2007). From this point of view, the Petit Trianon's eighteenth-century architectural narrative reflects the perfect balance achieved by Marie Antoinette in embodying the ideals of the Enlightenment (as previously explained) in the Estate of the Petit Trianon. Research analysis carried out (Data Set 9) suggests that, while the Petit Trianon, as conceived by the last Queen of France, was a creation and reflection of its time, it was without aims of legitimation and perception manipulation, in contrast to later periods. Finally, through a restitution gesture towards Marie Antoinette and her original creation and its ethos, Empress Eugénie transformed the building into a museum dedicated to the last Queen of France.

Heritage narrative of the Petit Trianon

This section probes the details of the heritage narrative of the Petit Trianon, the fourth major narrative of the book. This narrative is seen from the perspective of the heritage interpretation given to the Petit Trianon by its expert curatorial and heritage architectural teams following the 2008 restoration. After reviewing the agendas of the teams involved, and the principles underlying the eighteenth-century architectural narrative of the Petit Trianon, the following question is engaged here: how is the heritage narrative of the Petit Trianon presented in such a complicated case of heritage management and controversial architectural narrative? The answer: mostly by omission. Field research indicates an intentional derogation of the museum's curatorial team to clearly present an opinion in conflict with the general beliefs of the public. Curatorial hesitation to adopt a clear-cut stance vis-à-vis the image of Marie Antoinette seems, for the moment, the best solution, since various factors impede a cohesive and coherent presentation in accordance with the curatorial beliefs.

Firstly, the historical character of Marie Antoinette is surrounded by controversy, both amidst the French public and French specialists. The tour guides for booked groups are not directly controlled by the museum's curatorial team but by external *guide-conférenciers* who are art historians employed by the Réunion des musées nationaux (RMN) and are not specifically designated to Versailles. My personal observations and further discussions with security staff proved that these particular guides bring their own interpretations to the Petit Trianon. In the same way that historians interpret identical material in different ways, art-historian guides also deliver presentations which differ from one to another. An 'in-house' group of guides is gradually being built up by the Petit Trianon head curator Jérémie Benoît, but lack of funds delays the implementation of the project. Eventually, some of the security staff will be able, after prerequisite training, to present guided visits with a cohesive narrative established by the curatorial team of the Petit Trianon (Benoît pers. comm. 2014).

Secondly, and as importantly, this lack of coherence can be attributed to the departmental organisation within the Château de Versailles, which is marked by a lack of close communication among the different departments which should be involved in developing heritage interpretation for the Petit Trianon. The most relevant example is that of the management of Château de Versailles, which itself is conflicted by different authorities under whose jurisdiction it must operate. For instance, although during fieldwork between 2010 and 2012 I noted the omission of certain merchandise from the boutiques of the Palace, such as Sofia Coppola's film, which could suggest an agreement in views between curatorial interpretation and managerial packaging (see Figure 5.4) of Marie Antoinette's historical character, by 2014 this particular film had taken a central place in the DVD rack at the Librairie des Princes. Judging by the stock between 2010 and 2014, the range is increasingly aimed at the non-specialist public with visually enticing and television entertainment productions gradually replacing low-budget or specialist documentaries. It is important to stress here that the authority over the choice of the merchandise and the stock of the boutiques rests solely with RMN, who are obliged to favour bestselling items. Nevertheless, unlike other French national museums, since becoming Établissement Public in 1995, Château de Versailles is no longer subsidised by the French State, having to raise its own funds. This has led to a more accentuated commodification of its historical characters, with Marie Antoinette being the highest-selling commodity. Since 2008/2009, the presence of high-end, trademarks that sell well, such as Angelina and Ladurée, was encouraged by the management of Château de Versailles. Based on field research evidence relative to the majority groups, the uncontrolled heritage commodification of Marie Antoinette, which Ladurée reinforces (see Chapter 7), is in winning competition so far with the curatorial interpretation, in regards to conveying to the public messages related to her historical character. Furthermore, perhaps unsurprisingly, another factor competing with the curatorial heritage interpretation is that of Château de Versailles Spectacles (CVS), a private enterprise in charge of event management for the wide and select public, who do not work with the curatorial departments when organising their shows and events.

Returning to the heritage narrative of the Petit Trianon as indicator for Marie Antoinette's image, the founding of the museum as a memorial

150 *Architectural and heritage narratives*

dedicated to the last Queen of France, was due to the deep admiration that Empress Eugénie (Figure 5.12) had for Marie Antoinette.[9] The Empress's artistically inclined personality related to the queen in ways beyond mere historical lineage, in particular through her artistic sensibility (Gabet 2008; Vottero 2011a, 2011b). Eugénie felt continually drawn to the period that Marie Antoinette came to represent. Not only did Eugénie become an avid collector of eighteenth-century art but she also started to increasingly emulate the figure of Marie Antoinette (Granger 2005; Vottero 2011a). As some might say, she 'had a fascination with Marie-Antoinette bordering on obsession' (Chapman 2007b). Several of the Empress's official portraits by Franz Xaver Winterhalter are acknowledged to have been specifically composed on the basis of Mme Vigée Le Brun's portraits of Marie Antoinette (Granger 2005; Salmon 2005; Chapman 2007b; Gabet 2008; Vottero 2011a, 2011b).

Pierre de Nolhac – former head curator of Château de Versailles[10] – followed in the footsteps of the Empress, consolidating the rehabilitative curatorial tradition concerning the Petit Trianon as home to Marie Antoinette. Similar to Eugénie's fascination, the most notable curator of the museum, who published the greatest amount of literature on Marie

Figure 5.12 In the *attique* room, dedicated to Empress Eugénie, the curatorial team kept parts of the original display from the 1867 exhibition

Author photo 2014/courtesy Château de Versailles

Antoinette in her role of Dauphine (de Nolhac 1898a) as well as queen (de Nolhac 1898b, 1899a, 1899b, 1925, 1927), de Nolhac became enthralled by this historical character to whom he dedicated the entirety of his eulogistic, yet precise, research (Montupet 2006). The curator's mixed background in literature and history could explain the origins of this different understanding, in contrast with the defamatory Republican historical thesis constructed at the time around the French Monarchy and Ancien Régime. De Nolhac could, indeed, be the initiator of the rehabilitative wave of literature attributed generally to Zweig (1932).

Most importantly, de Nolhac established a curatorial tradition concerning Marie Antoinette, which field research proved to be still alive.[11] Therefore, unlike historical authors who, in trying to excuse the queen, indirectly incriminate her with the usual clichés perpetuated by the Republican agenda, the curator made a de facto analysis which revealed that the real reason for the accusations brought to the queen was her feminist emancipation. By having emancipated the role of the French queens, who previously would have had a mere procreative status, Marie Antoinette attracted first the animosity of the court. Subsequently – and strategically – this animosity was adopted by the revolutionary propaganda, successfully aimed at destroying the monarchic institution.

Furthermore, de Nolhac set up a rehabilitative curatorial tradition concerning the Petit Trianon as home to Marie Antoinette by clearly establishing the real connections and role of this royal residence. Accordingly, far from being a playground, the Petit Trianon was a fitting space for a monarch who challenged the rigidity of the French court etiquette dating from a previous century and initially based on the Spanish model. Marie Antoinette's own upbringing at the Austro-Hungarian Empire's Court of the Most Catholic Empress – which displayed a far more relaxed etiquette associated, however, with very strict religious morals – favoured the young queen's intentions of politically appropriating her space. Hence, the Petit Trianon became one of the important material statements of the emerging emancipation of a French queen in the context of a planned shift away from the old etiquette.

The heritage narrative at the Petit Trianon alludes to Marie Antoinette's childhood by displaying at the start of the visit two paintings by Johann Georg Weikert which depict her theatre performances as a child (see Figure 5.1).[12] As acknowledged by the curatorial tradition launched by Pierre de Nolhac, Marie Antoinette had already started challenging court etiquette in her role as Dauphine of France by ignoring the contemporary view that riding horseback was detrimental to female fertility. This is depicted in paintings by Joseph Krantzinger, one of which, showing her in full riding habit, is in the collection of the Kunsthistorisches Museum in Vienna (Figure 5.13; see also Salmon et al. 2008). In the case of the Petit Trianon, as already mentioned, the display of material culture suffers from the scarcity of objects and furnishings related to and belonging to Marie Antoinette (see Note 5). In 2016, another painting of Marie Antoinette, now queen, in her riding outfit,

Figure 5.13 Marie Antoinette, Dauphine of France, in *Marie Antoinette avec vêtement de chasse* (Joseph Krantzinger 1770)
© Kunsthistorisches Museum Wien

Architectural and heritage narratives 153

Figure 5.14 Marie Antoinette devant le Temple de L'Amour (attributed to Jean-Baptiste André Gautier-Dagoty 1780s/photo Christophe Fouin)
Château de Versailles et de Trianon Collection © RMN-Grand Palais/courtesy Art Resource, NY

at the Petit Trianon (Figure 5.14), was acquired from a private collection by Château de Versailles (Firmin 2017a, 2017b). This particular work of art is symbolic of how appropriating the space of the Petit Trianon implied challenging old patterns which defined the role of the queen of France. A simple act such as riding horseback reflects how Marie Antoinette dared to emancipate her role – a fact little known outside a small circle of experts, the full context of which is difficult to convey to the public. Although this painting

154 *Architectural and heritage narratives*

Figure 5.15 Le Pavillon Français, Petit Trianon (François-Denis Née, after Louis-Nicolas Lespinasse circa 1788)

Château de Versailles et de Trianon Collection © RMN-Grand Palais/courtesy Art Resource, NY

will not be exhibited at the Petit Trianon (Benoît pers. comm. 2017a), its high visibility in the Palace may contribute to conveying this message.[13]

Equally, the Petit Trianon's space as a backdrop for Marie Antoinette's role as a mother is also reflected in art representations. On an upper-floor there is a copy of a gravure depicting Marie Antoinette in the French gardens of the Petit Trianon, surrounded by her three children and holding the hand of her youngest son, Duc de Normandie, born in 1785 (Figure 5.15). Judging by his height and characteristics of the other children, the date of the engraving is 1788. The simple gesture of holding a child's hand is also proof of the aforementioned emancipation. This familial closeness is further reinforced by a 1789 miniature by François Dumont (see Figure 5.11), now at the Louvre, depicting Marie Antoinette and her beloved two children – *Mousseline* and *Chou d'Amour* (the first Dauphin died that year) – all at the Petit Trianon during the last summer they spent there.

These facts of emancipation, acknowledged by de Nolhac through his research on Marie Antoinette, were transmitted to, and continue to be a certainty for, the specialists responsible for the heritage of the Petit Trianon (Baudin pers. comm. 2011b):

> The true provocation of Marie-Antoinette is to have secured autonomy from the king, which was unprecedented among any of the former

queens [. . .]. This is what the centuries to follow will hold against her: too strong a feminine emancipation in relation to the dominant figure of the king, which, of course, has served as pretext for his downfall, which she allegedly provoked through her 'debauchery'. [translation mine]

The curatorial and specialist expert opinions on Marie Antoinette's image originate in both Château de Versailles' curatorial tradition set by de Nolhac, and an ability to 'read' the queen's legacy in art through relevant art knowledge. For instance, any specialist in eighteenth-century decorative arts is aware of the style that Marie Antoinette has established by commissioning specific pieces according to her requirements (Hans pers. comm. 2010).[14] The experts' image, however, contrasts severely with the image of Marie Antoinette perceived by the majority of the visiting public.

Petit Trianon in the postmodern heritage picture

Finally, this chapter tackles the two major issues concerning the Petit Trianon from a heritage interpretation perspective. Firstly, how the case of dissonant heritage was dealt with by those in charge of its interpretation, and secondly, where exactly has the Petit Trianon been placed by the 2008 restoration within the range of sites aimed at tourist consumption when considering the full spectrum of heritage authenticity as defined in Chapter 2 (see Table 2.1).

Chapter 1 referenced the concept of dissonant heritage (Tunbridge & Ashworth 1996): the discordance or lack of agreement and consistency as to the meaning of heritage. Accordingly, the general conflict lies in the differences between an official discourse and a minority's narrative – usually found imprinted into their collective memory – or between the contrasting historical discourses of various political regimes. In the case of the Petit Trianon, there is no specific conflict between the official discourse and that of a minority group's collective memory which would influence its heritage interpretation. In fact, there is no clear minority which would appropriate Marie Antoinette as their own defining piece of history. As Chapter 4 revealed, this historical character is controversial not only in the Republican milieu but also amongst Royalists and Catholics. Furthermore, although the source of conflict would be the clash between the official Republican historical discourse and the monarchy of a different political era, in reality the conflict cannot exist, since the Ancien Régime was successfully transformed by Republican ideology into a fitting piece of its own defining history. In the case of the cultural heritage of Marie Antoinette, I am naming this process 'alchemical dissonant heritage'. This not only refers to fitting a piece of counter-memory into the official national discourse, but moreover, to the alchemy overarching this process, which, not incidentally, renders the heritage commodification of Marie Antoinette a highly lucrative commercial proposition, further discussed in Chapter 7.

Unlike other forms of dissonant heritage, in particular difficult heritage (Macdonald 2009),[15] which refers to the repudiated Nazi legacy in Germany (for a broader context of difficult heritage case studies, see also Logan & Reeves 2009), the 'alchemical dissonant heritage' detected in the case of Marie Antoinette annihilates the conflict/discordance mainly through two factors: the paradoxical self-construction of modernity – in contradiction with itself by means of manipulation, re-creation and distortion of its history – and the reduction of the historical character of Marie Antoinette to a range of symbols which can be appropriated comfortably by different identities. Thus, instead of an overt conflict that must be overcome in the heritage interpretation at the Petit Trianon, there is a minority expertise – that of curators and art specialists – growing towards a progressive, although slowly and subtly implemented, rehabilitative heritage narrative. The differences between this minority and the majority of French historians regarding the image of Marie Antoinette further contribute to the complexity of the situation. The institutional memory which seems to have influenced the minority expertise cannot rise to the level of collective memory (Halbwachs 1980), as there is not a clearly defined group which this would correspond to. Instead, the element that is decisive in establishing a set of cohesive beliefs of the minority expertise is the place itself. The Petit Trianon and a long-term acquaintance with it is what differentiates opinions even between experts.[16]

Regarding its placement within the wider context of heritage sites aimed at tourist consumption, the Petit Trianon should now be evaluated against the generic classification developed in Chapter 2. Firstly, the Petit Trianon is a historic house museum as well as a World Heritage Site, inscribed by UNESCO in 1979 (see 1972 World Heritage Convention).[17] Secondly, despite its uncontested historical and architectural value, as well as notoriety, the Petit Trianon had to recently rely on the publicity brought about by an American film director's contemporary vision of its former royal owner for attracting sponsorship and increased popularity amongst its visitors. Field research suggests that, while the film did not have a prominent direct impact on the perception of the majority of the French and international public, some of its elements did strengthen the uncontrolled heritage commodification of Marie Antoinette via promotional campaigns devised by the management of Château de Versailles. The reliance on a film's publicity denotes, to an extent, the characteristics of subset 4 of the model developed in Chapter 2, where heritage sites of rich cultural value are in competition with their media-induced images. However, in the case of the Petit Trianon, the competition does not derive from the success (or notoriety) of the film, which would have attracted initial interest after its release, but rather from the promotional strategies linking into the launch event, as masterminded by the management of Château de Versailles.

When assessing the heritage interpretation of historic house museums in general, one particular trait must be highlighted: the criticism currently faced by these particular types of museums for emphasising material culture (Young 2017) over the display of ideas, thus risking the conveyance of a false domesticity without reifying the lives and ideas of former inhabitants (Christensen 2011). From this perspective, the heritage interpretation of the

Petit Trianon is arguably not guilty of such practices. The 2008 restoration ethos was based on clearly evoking the practical context in which Marie Antoinette's time at the Petit Trianon would have been spent and the *raison d'être* and true meaning of this residence: a statement of emancipation of the role of the queen. However, the dissonant heritage values intrinsic to the Petit Trianon inhibit a full illustration of the Enlightenment ideas behind Marie Antoinette's former residence, although they are strongly suggested by the interpretation boards found at the entrance.[18] The dissonance intrinsic to heritage 'should not be regarded as an unforeseen or unfortunate by-product' (Graham & Howard 2008b:3). This is due to two main aspects: firstly, the market segmentation which occurs when heritage is seen as an economic commodity (tourist consumption by various cultures invariably leading to dissonance), and secondly, the zero-sum characteristics of heritages (Tunbridge & Ashworth 1996) – an effect of the inclusion/exclusion traits generated by the concept of heritage ownership (i.e. this is my heritage, therefore it is not yours). This is consistent with the earlier defined 'alchemical dissonant heritage' of Marie Antoinette, only inasmuch as different identities appropriate her heritage according to their own agendas.

The above observations on dissonance lead to a further point: that of heritage creating a certain identity of a place through the meaning (Hall 1997) given to the heritage associated with it by those in charge of its interpretation (Graham & Howard 2008b). The creation of identity through heritage is an essential point of the debate here, whose arguments illustrate the manipulation of cultural heritage by the nineteenth-century national identity (see, in particular, Fladmark 2000; Smith 2006; Young 2017). An analysis of the identity created by the heritage interpretation of the 2008 restoration is needed in order to conclude the discussion on the position currently occupied by the Petit Trianon within the heritage industry and the range of sites aimed at tourist consumption.[19]

The Petit Trianon was packaged by the management team of Château de Versailles into a media-generated image (see Chapter 7). From the perspective of the zero-sum trait of heritages, the identity created by the curators and the heritage architect expert teams could be evaluated as a rather politically neutral interpretation allowing a comfortable appropriation by all visitors, a fact confirmed by fieldwork research evidence. The appropriation of heritage sites illustrates Bourdieu's (1984) observations on cultural capital: heritage becomes the cultural capital that visitors acquire through their visit. Nevertheless, there is a marked contrast between the visitors to the Petit Trianon prior to the creation of the museum's new identity via its renaming as the *Domaine de Marie-Antoinette*, and the majority of those visiting since (Figure 5.17). As such, the Petit Trianon could have previously been considered a place of visit for informed visitor groups, usually art lovers, collectors and connoisseurs, as well as those with Royalist sympathies (Figure 5.16). In the same manner as Napoléon III and Empress Eugénie would have taken pride in the Petit Trianon, on the occasion of the 25 August 1855 visit by

Figure 5.16 Royal cultural capital – a charitable event organised in 1901 by French aristocracy, for the benefit and creation of the 'Nurseries of Versailles', at Le Hameau of the Petit Trianon, with Le Moulin pictured here (from Malitte-Richard albums)

Château de Versailles et de Trianon Collection © RMN-Grand Palais/courtesy Art Resource, NY

Figure 5.17 Since 2008, the Petit Trianon has been part of the main visit at Château de Versailles – the access is facilitated by visitor trains

Author photo 2011/courtesy Château de Versailles

Architectural and heritage narratives 159

Queen Victoria and Prince Albert (treating the Estate as part of their royal cultural capital), since 1867 – when the Petit Trianon became a historic house museum – its regular visitors would also have had a clear idea of the site's significance and value.

After being included and heavily advertised as part of the main visit route, following the promotional events surrounding the 2008 restoration, the Petit Trianon no longer represents a form of cultural capital as before, now often being visited 'because it is there'. From the perspective of this type of visitor consumption, the Petit Trianon turned from a form of cultural capital into a commodity consumed and appropriated accordingly. It is true, however, that material culture, once invested with a symbolic meaning through individual daily practices of any nature (de Certeau 1984), becomes cultural capital. By further considering that postmodernity turned all individuals into everyday tourists consuming the images of places surrounding them in abundance, whether at home or away (Urry 1995), the Petit Trianon, even 'consumed' in the typical postmodern state of distraction, could still be considered a form of cultural capital (e.g. 'destination-based' cultural capital, Busby & Meethan 2008). Nevertheless, it is argued here that in the absence of the intentional and conscious traits characterising Bourdieu's 'cultural capital' (1984), this cannot be the case. This further suggests that since the 2008 restoration, the Petit Trianon has entered into the tourism circuit, which Château de Versailles attracts as one of the most visited museums in France, a 'must-see' landmark due to its notoriety rather than its history/art history value.[20]

However, the redenomination – or the naming – of the Estate brings to the fore a further aspect important in the discussion of the symbolic and cultural capital value of the Petit Trianon. Given that naming 'represents a way of creating new connections between the past and the present' (Alderman 2008:195) at both the personal level of an individual as well as that of places (particularly cultural landscapes; see also Rofe & Szili 2009), it can be deduced that, the managerial point of view excepted, the redenomination nevertheless generated symbolic capital for the Petit Trianon. Furthermore, naming 'is used to fix the identity of places, often as part of larger renegotiations [. . .]. In doing so, place names can be scripted to evoke [. . .] associations with the past or to honor specific historical figures' (Alderman 2008:208). Acknowledged to be a fairly common practice in heritage management (Mitchell et al. 2001:285), naming would further serve the general goal attributed to heritage landscapes created to serve 'the demands of post-modern consumers to purchase symbolic capital in the form of unique products, and experiences that reflect a bygone era.' This confirms that the redenomination not only strengthened the connections between the Petit Trianon and Marie Antoinette but also added a new layer of distinction to the old identity of the site: a royal distinction previously obscure to the majority of visitors coming to the Château de Versailles.

Lastly, considering that the Petit Trianon represents a heritage site as well as a museum, the analysis takes into account the creation of identity by museums through their interpretation. Whilst nineteenth-century museums were a reflection of the 'Tradition' of interpretation, now they face the responsibilities of its 'Translation' (Bhabha 1994; see also Knell et al. 2007 and Table 2.1). In essence, this shift means that the modern museum interpretation, which would have fully reflected nationalist ideologies (Fladmark 2000; Smith 2006) as well as paternalist approaches to heritage – from a dominant male perspective (Smith 2008) – comes under challenge by postmodernity to such an extent that some authors even suggest that contemporary heritage is led by the agendas of losers rather than victors when referring to previously suppressed narratives belonging to a colonial past (Lowenthal 2006 referenced in Harvey 2008:32;[21] see also Lowenthal 2009). From the educational perspective of the postmodern museum representation and its reception by an audience, according to Fiona McLean (2008:283), 'there are three layers to the negotiation of identity in the museum: the identities of those encoding the representations; the identities of those decoding the representations; and the identities of those being represented.' McLean's (2008:284) analysis revealed that although the three layers are not mutually exclusive, they are 'contingent through the democratisation of the representation process'.

Regarding the first aspect of 'Tradition', the Petit Trianon proves to have been somewhat atypical since its foundation as a museum. Not only did it not reflect a nationalist ideology, but it was also dedicated to a female historical figure by another female historical figure. Taking into consideration that one of the most important reasons – together with the concepts of cultural capital and dominant ideology – for creating the national museums of the nineteenth century was the need for legitimation of the new political elite (Ashworth & Howard 1999), the Petit Trianon fully reflects this process. With regard to 'Translation', the chapter clarifies to what extent the interpretation of the Petit Trianon could entirely convey the third layer of identity considered by McLean (2008) – in other words, that of Marie Antoinette.

Notes

1 The type of historic house museums referred to are dedicated to political figures; otherwise the oldest house museums were dedicated to prominent literary figures, such as Shakespeare, as early as the eighteenth century (Watson 2007). Young (2017) provides a valuable classification of historic house museums.
2 There are no statistics dating before 2002. I have, however, had confirmation from the curators of the Petit Trianon and security personnel that the 2002 numbers matched the general average per day, according to each season, from the few years previous. It seems that prior to 1995 when the site changed its status from national museum (subsidised by the French State), the numbers were far lower.
3 My evaluation was based on analysing the paid and free entries to the Palace, based on figures provided by the Château de Versailles. It is not possible to know statistically how many visitors to the Palace also visited *DMA*, or vice versa.
4 Allen Kurzweil (2001) was inspired by this robbery to write a novel set in the eighteenth-century art collectors' world which branches into a mystical/esoteric

search. Hailed as an equivalent to Umberto Eco's *The Name of the Rose*, this novel suggests the absolute fascination that Marie Antoinette exerts in various milieus.
5 In the case of the Petit Trianon, this poses a particular problem due to the scarcity of objects and furnishings belonging to Marie Antoinette. For the auction sales during the French Revolution, see Beurdeley (1981). For the Petit Trianon's inventory, see Départment de Seine et Oise (1793–1796) and Ledoux-Lebard (1989). For later (re)-acquisitions, see Rheims (1925); Mauricheau-Beaupré (1934); Meyer (1974, 1976) and Baulez (1978, 1989, 1999, 2001). For collections found in the possession of other museums, inside and outside France, see Ephrussi (1879); Zeck (1990) and Tollfree (2006).
6 The 2008 Grand Palais exhibition catalogue has become a key reference for art historians training to be curators (Firmin pers. comm. 2014).
7 See also her choice of representation in painting (National Museum of Women in the Arts 2012) for the less formal outfits acceptable at the Petit Trianon, which nevertheless caused another stir in the public opinion of the time (see Sheriff 2003; Weber 2006).
8 Interestingly, quantum physics-cum-philosophy and its contemporary insights, could in fact be drawn from exponential Enlightenment scientists and philosophers such as Emanuel Swedenborg, whose contributions to spirituality are little known today despite having influenced the establishing of a religious sect at the beginning of the nineteenth century (see https://swedenborg.com/quantum-physics-can-tell-us-afterlife/).
9 Original exhibits of the museum included genuine Marie Antoinette artefacts, as well as nineteenth-century period reproductions and Royalist memorabilia. Amongst these, on exhibit currently, is a pair of nineteenth-century vases with the portraits of Marie Antoinette and Princesse de Lamballe, the queen's devoted confidante, whose violent death in support of the monarchy renders her a tragic figure cherished in Royalist representations.
10 Pierre de Nolhac became head curator in 1892 and retired after hosting the First World War Treaty at Château de Versailles in 1919. Paradoxically, de Nolhac studied history with Ernst Renan.
11 This evidence is based on inside knowledge of the Versailles curatorship gained during my two internships with the Château de Versailles (2010–2012). This was further confirmed by head curator Jérémie Benoît and heritage architect Philippe Baudin.
12 These were painted in 1778, commissioned by the Empress Maria Theresa as a gift to her daughter who wished to display them at the Petit Trianon.
13 See also Figure 4.7; this painting was displayed at the Petit Trianon in La Salle de Billiard (March 2011 to March 2012), and was meant to convey the value of the Petit Trianon as a family home. Since April 2012 this painting has been exhibited at the Palace within a new display for interpreting the history of Versailles (Delahaye pers. comm. 2015; see also Bossard 2001).
14 For exceptional pieces or features commissioned by Marie Antoinette, see Ephrussi (1879); Rheims (1925); Verlet (1949, 1961); Moulin (1975); Alcouffe (1999) and Carlier (2006). Rondot (2008) contributes a valuable insight by highlighting that the queen worked closely with the experts whose art she commissioned. Dassas (2008), curator of art objects at the Louvre Museum, confirms this, believing, furthermore, that Marie Antoinette did not have the time to establish a style which would become recognised by art history, such as Catherine or Marie de Medici; see also Hans (2007) and Chapman (2007a).
15 For a valuable contribution to problematic heritage and memory work, see Sather-Wagstaff (2015).
16 The concept of 'place-identity' (Proshansky et al. 1983) in relation to self-identity offers a theoretical framework for this acquaintance with, and intimation of, space.

162 *Architectural and heritage narratives*

17 The extensive expert literature on the implications of the UNESCO nominations on management and conservation of heritage sites will not be cited here, as this topic is outside the focus of the analysis since there is no evidence to suggest that the 1979 nomination itself had an impact on the site.
18 These boards are rarely read by the majority of visitors, as my own observations revealed and heritage architect Philippe Baudin (pers. comm. 2011a) concurred.
19 Sybille Frank (2016) contributes recent valuable research on the subject of the heritage industry and tourist consumption of dissonant heritage through the case study of Berlin's Checkpoint Charlie. This is considered in relation to interpretation and commercialisation, benefitting from research methodology rooted in urban discourse and its decoding.
20 For the theory defining such landmarks, see Chapter 2. An analysis of the type of tourism that Château de Versailles increasingly attracts since becoming an Établissment Public in 1995 does not fall within the focus of this study. Relevant valuable contributions come from Long and Palmer (2007), who discuss royal tourism, and Smith et al. (2012) who deal with cultural moments in mass tourism.
21 Harvey indicates that this particular, and strong, point on 'losers and victors' was the central theme of Lowenthal's (2006) lecture at the British Academy. Harvey himself notes how, today, in general, the periphery is coming to the centre (of attention) in heritage interpretation.

6 'Memories' of Marie Antoinette
Field research evidence at the Petit Trianon

The fieldwork research method used in this study was developed to answer questions regarding visitor perceptions of the Petit Trianon as home to Marie Antoinette. Moreover, it focused on ascertaining the prevalence of the four major narratives – historical, cinematic, architectural and heritage – relevant to the site's contemporary interpretation and perception. In this chapter, the evidence of the fieldwork research method at the Petit Trianon is streamed and interpreted into an assessment of the perception of Marie Antoinette and the Petit Trianon, as communicated by the visiting public. The chapter focuses on contemporary perceptions of the site and of its former owner by building on the results of the fieldwork research method, which is supported by John L. Caughey's (1984) anthropological study on 'imaginary social worlds'. Building on this theory considered in conjunction with memory theory from previous chapters further analysed here, particular attention will be given to the artificial types of memories induced mainly through 'collective memory' (Halbwachs 1980) but also will be given to a specific form of false and time-line independent recollections, introduced by the imaginary social interaction of individuals with historical figures. The term 'imaginary social memories' is thus coined in this chapter. Nora's (1984a) 'places of memory', uncanny memory constructs which, under the sign of nostalgia, could embody what is lost and also play an important role in the analysis of visitor discourses.

Given that the research methodology is qualitative, the confirmation of the empirical hypothesis of the survey was delivered by a pattern of perception instead of percentages. The interpretation focused on the answers to the questions regarding the images of Marie Antoinette and Petit Trianon in relation to historical knowledge, cultural background and, last but not least, media influences. This was achieved within a thematic analysis, in connection with a priori coding and theming based on the clichés detected in association with Marie Antoinette's historical character. The survey applied to a sample of 307 visitors, confirmed, first of all, that the prejudices of each individual are equally responsible for the perception of a heritage site as the heritage interpretation itself (Poria et al. 2003; Howard 2003). Secondly, the research further confirmed that visitors contribute to the creation of a museum's identity through their own decoding, defined as an 'active practice of untangling the multi-layered narratives, impressions, ideas and images of heritage, which visitors assimilate into their existing repertoires of historical knowledge' (Dicks 2000:219).

Republican vs. Royalist 'memories' of the last Queen of France

This section assesses Republican and Royalist discourses of French visitors at the Petit Trianon. Discourses from the majority groups, based on the survey sample, proved to be Republican. The discourses of various minority groups, detected through the fieldwork research, generally display an attitude which could equate with Royalist views, whether politically or culturally generated.

The French public, manifesting a strong nationalist character (hereafter Group 1), invariably described Marie Antoinette as *dépensière*/spendthrift, *frivole*/frivolous, totally disconnected from the harsh reality and miserable living conditions of the non-privileged French people – because she never travelled around France to witness this – and finally, an Austrian spy and traitor who even deserved her end. But whilst it is true that a small number of respondents went that far in expressing their adversity towards the queen, based on the 1993 theatre spectacle directed by Robert Hossein, the contemporary French public in general seems to exhibit a kinder attitude (see Chapter 4). Nevertheless, Group 1 expressed the belief that Marie Antoinette was against the Revolutionaries and thus was seen as the catalyst of violence in those days. This opinion was invariably linked to her 'terrible political sense' and 'unfortunate' influence over the king to agree to the *Varennes fuite*/flight (Figure 6.1), which some mentioned that she had planned with her 'lover'.

The Varennes episode is also mentioned by another group (hereafter Group 2), whose respondents are not as certain about the alleged events as members of Group 1 but still harbour thoughts of justice being done by eliminating not only the monarchy as an institution but also the king and the queen themselves. Thus, the Varennes episode legitimises the violent end of the monarchy: it was this particular instance that 'proved' the king and the queen had turned against their people. Moreover, receiving assistance from a foreign national (Count von Fersen) further cemented the ulterior course of events. It is important to note the inclination of respondents from Groups 1 and 2 to mainly blame the queen for malignant influence over Louis XVI, a king they regarded as weak, unsuited to govern and easily led by his foreign consort. These views are, in fact, straightforward translations of the historical Republican agenda's portrayal of Louis XVI and Marie Antoinette, well aligned with the French Revolution's propaganda.

The Petit Trianon is seen by members of both groups as a *prise de guerre*/ spoil of war, which they are glad to be able to visit since it is now 'in the hands of the people', despite its identification with Marie Antoinette. Paradoxically, the same respondents are also proud of their royal heritage, including Versailles,

'Memories' of Marie Antoinette 165

Figure 6.1 The flight to Varennes (destination Montmédy), organised by Marie Antoinette, is credited with as much alleged importance today (French Groups 1 & 2) for the fall of the monarchy as it was in the eighteenth century
Anonymous. Courtesy Bibliothèque nationale de France

since it has 'to do' with the French Monarchy, an arguably Royalist stance. This situation is contradictory only in appearance and confirms, in fact, the success of propaganda-led manipulation which insinuated that the French Revolution was a conflict between the French Monarchy (represented in particular by Marie Antoinette) and the French people. As such, the failings of the French Monarchy in its institutional role – reflecting the much earlier misalignment of French politics and social issues with the economic aspects of the time (Furet & Richet 1973) – came to be attributed to Marie Antoinette herself.

The successful transfer of realities achieved by revolutionary propaganda has been perpetuated by the Republican agenda down to the present day, explaining not only why the contemporary French public would nevertheless be proud of its royal heritage, but also their positive perception of other monarchic generations. The image of the Sun King is held in especially high esteem, therefore in total contrast to Marie Antoinette's image. In fact, the 'bad' and the 'good' kings/queens theory (Michelet 1867) was one of the avenues that Republican historians used in the aftermath of the French Revolution to justify the elimination of the French Monarchy (Nora 2013).

The members of Group 1 have not been influenced in their perception of the site and Marie Antoinette by any film or novel (see also Chapter 3), whilst members of Group 2, depending on their age, generally considered films to be an important source of information about a certain era, mostly at a visual level. The history learnt at school still acts as their main source of information. Belonging primarily to a younger generation than the members of Group 1, Group 2 are clearly more open to new ideas, and some even expressed confusion regarding the many contradictory stories one can hear about Marie Antoinette these days. Furthermore, Group 1 considered the Petit Trianon to be a luxurious place which for them confirmed the 'big expenses' incurred for its building, whereas the members of Group 2 expressed their surprise at the simplicity of the building and its furnishings, which contrasted with their perception prior to the visit.[1]

Even today, the eighteenth-century media image of Marie Antoinette in libellous caricatures corresponds to the perceptions held by Group 1, and partly by Group 2. The message contained seems remarkably unchanged, however, which is explained through the Republican clichés which have perpetuated this image (Figure 6.2). A closer look at history education curriculum shows that the ever-present effect of the eighteenth-century propaganda was perpetuated by the Republican agenda and the adjacent teaching system devised by Jules Ferry and other prominent figures of the French Republican nineteenth-century education system (see Nora 1984). However, despite this, a gradual rehabilitation of monarchic historical figures began at the end of the 1980s, and France has stepped onto a path of genuine reconciliation with its past, thanks to the Fifth Republic and its leader, President François Mitterrand (see also Nora 2013).

The third group (hereafter Group 3) is set apart by its members' artistic or art history academic background. Art formation seems to engender an entirely different perception of the queen and of the Petit Trianon. Among Group 3 respondents, Marie Antoinette is regarded as an Enlightened monarch, emancipated, beautiful, charitable, powerful and a fervent supporter of Music/Musicians and Arts/Artists. For Group 3, the Petit Trianon clearly reflects all her qualities and is a perfect embodiment of *l'art de vivre*/the art of living of the Enlightenment. Respondents with an art history academic background see Marie Antoinette first and foremost as a victim – even a scapegoat – of political forces, and furthermore as someone who bravely faced the events of the French Revolution. These perceptions are in stark contrast to those of Groups 1 and 2 (Figures 6.3; 6.4).

Group 3 respondents regard Sofia Coppola's film as the artistic view of an American director. For most of these respondents, anachronisms such as the 1980s music constitute a fresh approach but also affect the perception of historical accuracy, with the film rated 2 or 3 on a scale of 1 to 5, with 1 being furthest from historical fact.[2] For members of Group 3, the best cinematic portrayal of the queen (Figure 6.5) is found in Jean Delannoy's *Marie Antoinette, Reine de France* (1956). Group 3 was also well acquainted with the Japanese

Figure 6.2 Republican clichés, such as 'Marie Antoinette playing the shepherdess at the Petit Trianon' – as shown in this Third Republic publication of national history (Seignobos 1891) – perpetuate common misperceptions of the queen (C. Delort 1891)

Courtesy Bibliothèque nationale de France

Figure 6.3 Nineteenth-century Royalist representation of Marie Antoinette and her family at Petit Trianon stands in stark contrast to the derogatory 'shepherdess' image of the Republican cliché (Charles Louis Müller circa 1860)

Musée des Beaux-Arts et d'Archéologie de Libourne/Universal Images Group/courtesy Art Resource, NY

'Memories' of Marie Antoinette 169

Figure 6.4 A brave Marie Antoinette in her attempts to rescue the royal family during key moments (such as the Varennes flight) triggered by the events of the French Revolution; this nineteenth-century Royalist image corresponds to perceptions of French Groups 3 & 4 (T. F. Marshall 1854)
Courtesy Mark Tramontana

shōjo manga *Rose of Versailles*, popular in France since the early 1980s, not least through its television adaptation of the anime *Lady Oscar* (1979–1980).

Beyond the aforementioned three groups of French respondents, there is another group not included in the classification comprising visitors who usually come on the first Sunday of each month when entry is free. Insufficient responses were mostly due to either a lack of time on their part (family outings) or a reluctance to answer questions which they found too challenging once I had started the interview.[3]

The French public could also be differentiated into regular and occasional visitors, with local, Yvelines department residents visiting consistently and purposely at the Estate of the Petit Trianon, its surrounding gardens in particular. The farm of Le Hameau de la Reine is especially popular with local families, who bring their children to see and enjoy the countryside. According to the opinions expressed, these respondents belong to either Group 2, 3 or 4, with only a few fitting into Group 1.

Last, but not least, the group which further differentiated itself from amidst the residents of Versailles/Yvelines (hereafter Group 4) represents pre-Napoleonic aristocratic families. Despite having interviewed on site only

Figure 6.5 Michèle Morgan on set at Petit Trianon in September 1955 for Jean Delannoy's 1956 film *Marie Antoinette, Reine de France*
© AGIP/RDA/Everett Collection

'Memories' of Marie Antoinette   171

Figure 6.6 21 January 2011, La Chapelle Expiatoire commemoration for Louis XVI, Marie Antoinette and the royal family – a counter-memory event embodying narratives, such as that of Christian faith, represented here by *Les Chouans* and their sacrifice in support of the monarchy during the French Revolution

Author collection/2011 photo courtesy Adrian Rozei, with permission of the subjects

two respondents belonging to this group, the elaborate discussions which I initiated confirmed their views to be representative of a close-knit community sharing the same social rituals vis-à-vis the monarchy. The decision to include these respondents as forming a particular group was legitimised by further research into the validity of the conclusions drawn thus far (Halbwachs 1980; Lefebvre 1991). One of the aforementioned rituals is a commemoration held for Louis XVI and his family every year on 21 January at La Chapelle Expiatoire in Paris, which I attended in 2011 (Figure 6.6).

This group's worship of the last ruling Bourbons of the Ancien Régime equals in intensity their strong belief in the injustice brought about by the events of the French Revolution, confirming the counter-memory signalled in Chapter 2. At the same time, they feel this on a deeply personal level, one of the respondents mentioning the terrible fate of their ancestor who perished under the *guillotine*, as if it happened yesterday (M; G4; 60+; 20/03/2011). Equally, Marie Antoinette – as well as the entire royal family – is still mourned with an intensity which could be surprising. This is easier to understand, however, when considering that for members of Group 4, the Petit Trianon has always

Figure 6.7 Petit Trianon in 1901, setting for an aristocratic charitable event celebrating the eighteenth century and Marie Antoinette's legacy, for the benefit and creation of the 'Nurseries of Versailles' (from Malitte-Richard albums)

Château de Versailles et de Trianon Collection © RMN-Grand Palais/courtesy Art Resource, NY

been a part of their legitimate cultural capital, a point of identification with a social order to which they still belong (Figure 6.7). Halbwachs (1980) himself noted the particularities of the French aristocratic families and their contrasting memories to those of the bourgeoisie.

French collective memory: Animosity, curiosity and nostalgia

Following the presentation of the main French national groups identified by the field research, this section analyses the mechanisms behind the group perceptions outlined above. The observations made thus far on the various social groups' attitudes towards the historical character of Marie Antoinette fully confirm Halbwachs' 'collective memory'[4] theory, presented in Chapter 3 within Ricoeur's hermeneutical analysis of the memory/history dialectic and the relationship (mediated by externality) between an individual and the collective memory of the group he/she belongs to. Research evidence has confirmed that the individual memories of the groups' members, detected by field research at the Petit Trianon, clearly originate in the external memories of the cultural groups to which they belonged during childhood. Since socialising and further cultural development generally occurs within the same milieu (Chelcea et al. 1998), they would naturally come to regard their initial external contact with memory and history through an individually appropriated sense of memory (as well as history) which thus becomes intimately felt and lived. Exceptions come from French Group 3, their appropriation of the historical character of Marie Antoinette, based on art history knowledge and admiration all tinged with nostalgia, generates a type of remembering associated with a collective memory descendent, that of 'cultural memory' (see Assmann 2012), which could also pertain to 'places of memory' (see Nora 1984–1992; 1984a; 1984b), as explained in the last part of this chapter.

When considering heritage as the practical experience created for the visitor, the concept of 'memory work' comes to the fore (Hodge 2011:116), with heritage in general being:

> framed as 'memory work': an interdependent process of remembering and forgetting. *Memory*, whether individual or collective, is not stable. Memory *work* is not about retrieving a past truth; it is about reconstructing the past's present, shifting legacies 'in anticipation of the future' [Hallam & Hockey 2001:3].

Furthermore, Christina Hodge (2011:117) considers that: 'Material and affective mechanisms entangle individual memory with collective memory at history sites, a contested process that reproduces structured social value and meaning.' Although the definition of the concept of collective memory has been indeed criticised (Ricoeur 2004; see also Gedi & Elam 1996) as well as revised since conception (Olick et al. 2011; see also Erll 2011), recent heritage fieldwork research (Gouriévidis 2010) has confirmed my own findings relating to the present-day validity of Halbwachs' theory. In fact, Halbwachs revolutionised the understanding of collective memory by coining and theoretically developing the term. As Nicolas Russell (2006:792) pertinently notices:

> there have been many different articulations of this concept both before and after Halbwachs' work on collective memory, but a broad comparison of the most typical articulations and the most salient characteristics of the concept before and after Halbwachs reveals a general shift in the way that collective memory has been conceptualised in French literary and intellectual discourse over this period.

If early modern French theorists of the memory of groups (usually nations), such as Montaigne or Corneille, regarded this type of memory as external to and detached from individuals, due to being immanent to the group through symbolic representation, according to Russell (2006:796), Halbwachs considered 'that all remembering relies on the dynamics of groups such as families, social classes and religious communities.' One of his most prominent contributions is the emphasis on the affective dimension of collective memory,

Halbwachs stressing that it is internalised through episodic memory, a deeply personal, lived and felt, non-transferable variety of memory, in contrast with the semantic memory of early modernity (Russell 2006).

It is this particular, deeply personal nature of collective memory in Halbwachs' definition that explains the process of 'remembering' by various groups at heritage sites, which this study detected to manifest mainly through three psychological affects: animosity, curiosity and nostalgia. These emerged from within the discourse analysis of the majority as well as the minority groups of French visitors at the Petit Trianon (Figure 6.13). The three affects suggest a different perception of the same material to which visitors are exposed, thus leading to a further enquiry into heritage-generated connection of an individual to a place. Sara McDowell (2008) discusses the different types of memory present at heritage sites as being in accord with the intention of the heritage interpretation, which takes on various nuances such as 'Remembering the Past' and 'Politicizing the Past (and Present)', though both are selectively attained (see also Uzzell 1989a, 1996; with Ballantyne 2008). The remembering-forgetting process intrinsic to heritage (Harrison 2013) best reflects this selectivity. Further, selectivity is key to understanding not only the construction of a heritage interpretation but also its reception by visitors. At the Petit Trianon, it is selectivity which allows for different visitor attitudes to be triggered, although these attitudes seem to originate beyond the heritage interpretation, which at this site keeps a rather neutral tone.

Having established that the three attitudes are not stirred by the material display of the museum/heritage site interpretation, it becomes evident that they are connected to values intrinsic to 'collective memory' and 'places of memory'. Consequently, the internalisation of the images and impressions conveyed by the site into 'memories', owes as much to cultural conditioning and historical knowledge as to these more or less powerful emotional affects evoked by links with the past. Nora's theory elucidates why 'places of memory' – be they tangible or intangible – are paramount in anchoring these links with the past into the consciousness of visitors, their symbolic value conjuring feelings without which the collective memory would stagnate.

Animosity is the product of a lifelong indoctrination, constructed through 'imagined communities' (Anderson 1991) and the 'depersonalisation' of the enemy (Hobsbawm 1983), as in totalitarian regimes' techniques of mass manipulation. Curiosity is defined here as an intermediate term between the extremes of animosity and nostalgia, as it could originate in either animosity tamed by a less defined understanding of one's own beliefs or in an unclear nostalgia evoked by sheer empathy with the trials of human destiny. Regarding heritage sites with a connection to violence, Ashworth (2008) considers separately the concepts of curiosity and empathy in their role of powerful elements informing heritage consumption by tourists. Both, however, stem from a natural human instinct: the former from the attraction to anything that is spectacular, including violence, and the latter from the identification of the individual with either the victims or the perpetrators (Dann 1981, 2005; Ashworth 2008). Further, the concept of identity is linked to discussions on heritage and memory construction (see Pearce 1993; Kavanagh 2000; Prentice 2004; Sather-Wagstaff 2015).

Nostalgia was previously considered by heritage studies to originate in a conservative attitude (see Howard 2003). Research of its social functions expanded this understanding: nostalgia actually results from an affective habitus, defined as a 'structure of feeling in Western modernity' (Tannock 1995 cited in Hodge 2011:120), and reifies a subjective separation from an idealized past, simultaneously representing a bridge across that separation. As Hodge (2011:120) further observes:

> Those embroiled in nostalgia do far more than wallow in sentimental denial. By invoking a 'lost and longed for earlier period', they are 'involved in escaping or evading, in critiquing or in mobilizing to overcome the present experience of loss of identity, lack of agency, or absence of community'.
> [Tannock 1995:454]

As previously underestimated fields of study in museology, the theoretical concepts of nostalgia and empathy recently garnered valuable scholarship (Blunt 2003; Gregory & Witcomb 2007; Wetherell 2012; Clohesy 2013; Smith 2016; Smith & Campbell 2016, 2017; Campbell et al. 2017; Tolia-Kelly et al. 2017) which may eventually change current philosophies and practical approaches in heritage interpretation that view engaging affect and emotion as manipulative, thus unethical and also inaccurate (Lowenthal 2015, also 1989; Boym 2001; Bloom 2016). The current curatorial approach at the Petit Trianon does not seek to actively and purposely appeal to any of the aforementioned affects and emotions in their public's anticipated response; instead, by suggesting unknown aspects of Marie Antoinette, the heritage interpretation is meant to invite critical reflection on the subject so that visitors may review their own knowledge (Benoît pers. comm. 2014).

Visitor discourses beyond French borders and 'imaginary social memories' of Marie Antoinette

European and other nationals at the Petit Trianon

Results demonstrated that nationality does have a bearing on visitor perceptions of Marie Antoinette and the Petit Trianon. Apart from American and Japanese visitor perceptions, analysed later, the only other national groups with consistent responses were the Italian and Spanish visitors. Based solely on the samples of the survey, I observed that Italian and Spanish visitors regarded Marie Antoinette and her estate in a positive light, and manifested compassion for the queen and appreciation for the beauty of the place. For Italian respondents, this attitude possibly originates in the historical narrative taught in their school curricula, which concentrates on a negative depiction of the Reign of Terror. Spanish respondents exhibited respect for royalty, perhaps because their country still maintains its monarchy. These perceptions seemed unaffected by films or other media sources. Responses were not tested for representativeness of wider perceptions of these nationalities.

In spite of the relatively small number of respondents (11), another well-defined group comprised young Middle Eastern women (Table 3.3), all familiar with Sofia Coppola's film, which they considered to accurately depict historical reality. Although it was impossible to further test my observations, research suggests that these respondents manifest a fascination for, and worship of, Marie Antoinette similar to that of Japanese female respondents but with an added note of an uncontested approval and admiration. Moreover, the Kuwaiti respondents mentioned having been shown Coppola's film during high school history classes, apparently taught by a young female who chose the film as a perfect example of the historical context prior to the French Revolution. Rather than being criticised, Marie Antoinette seems to have gained the admiration of these young Kuwaitis, especially through Coppola's contemporary portrayal (Figure 6.8). These respondents explicitly referred to Marie Antoinette's fashion style which they admired. Prompted by my questions, it was revealed that they referred to the updated style emerging from Coppola's film. This was reinforced by

Figure 6.8 Kirsten Dunst in Sofia Coppola's updated version of *Marie Antoinette* (2006) – a contemporary inspiration to young Middle Eastern women for female emancipation

© Sony Pictures/courtesy Everett Collection

fashion shoots of iconic photographers such as Annie Leibovitz in *Vogue* (see also Chapter 7).

Whilst it was not possible to make a further distinction based on the nationality of the respondents, from the point of view of the prevalence of our four main narratives, the non-French respondents – particularly those artistically inclined, but without a formal artistic background – do change their opinion of Marie Antoinette (formed through school education and media images) once they see her estate. This change starts with the realisation that the Petit Trianon is much smaller and simpler than they imagined. Consequently, this group comes to appreciate the décor and style of the Petit Trianon, especially the Jardin Anglais and its *fabriques*, the site becoming their favourite location on the entire estate of Château de Versailles.

Formal art training has clearly distinguished another group which merits a description despite being in the minority. Although the nature of this group's views is outside the remit of this study, two of the most representative cases detected through field research are outlined below, as they suggest the vast array of contrasting images which Marie Antoinette continues to generate.

The first example is a Canadian artist/art dealer, whom I met at the inaugural specialist visits organised at the Petit Trianon as part of a series promoting a different image of the queen. Held at Le Petit Théâtre by Chantal Thomas, the inaugural session focused on the image of the queen in Thomas's novel *Les Adieux à la Reine*. During the presentation, I was intrigued by one of the participants' bohemian appearance and evident emotional interest in this author's perception of Marie Antoinette. After the talk, I approached him in order to further investigate his attitude. During our conversation he revealed that he had relocated to France five years previously without any solid employment opportunities so that he could establish, by any possible means, a link with the last Queen of France. He shared that at his residence he built – symbolically as well as physically – a shrine for the lost sovereign and is currently living in a continual search for Marie Antoinette. When asked at what point he would feel that the search would be over, he responded:

> In the same way that, when asked what brought me to France when I first entered the country, my reply was 'L'amour pour la dernière Reine de France', I can also answer you that this love for Marie Antoinette will always keep me searching for her.[5]

In this respect, for those subjects fascinated to the extreme by Marie Antoinette (respondents across all nationality groups), research evidence from the Petit Trianon suggests that such quests are problematic because they are ruled by an 'image' of other times and other places.

The second example is provided by Christopher Davies, a British respondent with an academic background in architectural history (Table 6.1), whose opinions reflect the earlier noted interest of this group, although in a slightly different manner. His views originate in empathy with Marie Antoinette's martyrdom and an appreciation of the important role he feels Marie Antoinette plays in modern art history.[6]

Although the aforementioned examples could seem isolated cases of extreme fascination with Marie Antoinette, I have had confirmation that

Table 6.1 A representative discourse on Marie Antoinette and the Petit Trianon for respondents with art/architectural history academic background who are fascinated by the last Queen of France

---

Christopher Davies, British respondent

'I [. . .] find the period after the revolution and before Pierre de Nolhac very interesting, the thought of that place in such a sad and neglected state, so romantic, stirs up all kinds of thoughts. I couldn't believe that the Trianon was once used as a tavern.'(Davies pers. comm. 2011a)

'I long for this period in history to be a reality in my life, well the period before the revolution, the music, the art, the clothing, the sensibility and the general beauty of everything the rich encountered. In my opinion there has never been and never will be another period in time like it.' (Davies pers. comm. 2011c)

'My obsession has got to the point where my house is named Trianon and all the paint colours I choose are inspired by Versailles (now I know that's crazy). I suppose my interest has gone from being about the building to being about Versailles as a place and all its connections. Once you start you can't stop [. . .]. The whole French royal family at the time of the revolution, to me should be made saints for what they went through and you can, in my opinion, still feel their presence at Versailles. Versailles has always seemed to me when walking around it, a house that has been shut up for the winter.' (Davies pers. comm. 2011b)

'My 'Pilgrimage' took place the weekend of my birthday [. . .] started at the Conciergerie and I followed the route the tumbrel had taken on that sad day with Marie Antoinette in my thoughts along every inch [of the way]. Once I had done this I did feel closer to the reality of what the Queen had gone through and felt a deep sadness for her and her family.' (Davies, pers. comm. 2011d)

'I felt that the most moving of places was the *Chapelle Expiatoire*, I took a rose and placed it at the foot of Marie Antoinette's beautiful statue and prayed for both in the chapel below. [. . .] The place I have left to visit is the final resting place St Denis, this I feel will be the completion of my pilgrimage of sorts.' (Davies pers. comm. 2011c)

'I know this is silly but I have transformed the 20ft wall on my stairs at home into a stylish MA [sic] memorial. The wall is painted her favourite grey/blue colour and the copy of her bust that sits on the fireplace in her state bedroom that I have, is on a rococo wall shelf with 'Vive La Reine' above it in silver 18th century typeface, it looks great, I don't care what my visitors think.' (Davies pers. comm. 2011d)

these are not isolated views. During my 15 months in France, I encountered similar cases whose fascination with Marie Antoinette had taken over the ordinary course of their lives in the same way that 'fans' of contemporary celebrities live for their idols. Indeed, research has demonstrated Marie Antoinette to be the most popular female French historical personality apparently after Joan of Arc (Binh 2010), but it is her private existence that seems to continually spark passionate fascination, more than any other character of French or universal history.

Furthermore, for some of the members of this group, the obvious fact of Marie Antoinette being dead for more than two centuries now is a mere fleeting thought, bearing no weight in comparison to the hope that she would make herself present during their visit at the Petit Trianon, through a piece of dress, a lock of hair, the scent of her powder or anything at all, bringing them closer to her. This extreme fascination (Deshayes 2016)[7] and its causes or variations, including pathological obsession (Castle 2003) and tragic stories (e.g. Ludwig II of Bavaria, see Augé 1997) cannot integrate the qualitative research, and is best suited to an exclusively ethnographic study.

The next sections focus on American and Japanese visitor discourses, which are relevant to the present research because their perceptions of Marie Antoinette and the Petit Trianon are influenced by popular culture media sources. They are also the most numerous visitors, by nationality, after the French.

American visitors at the Petit Trianon

For the American visitors, field research at the Petit Trianon distinguished two main groups, hereafter the American majority group and the American minority group (see Chapter 3). American majority-group visitor perceptions of Marie Antoinette stem from a variety of popular culture sources.[8] These respondents are generally acquainted, to a degree, with Sofia Coppola's film (if not always at first hand), although this group bases its knowledge on a series of clichés such as the ubiquitous false utterance 'Let Them Eat Cake!' which Coppola has, paradoxically, tried to dispel through her movie. It is important to note that the clichés themselves indicate the level of knowledge of the respondents; during the field survey, I noticed a tier-structured pattern of beliefs in relation to the clichés (see Figure 7.20).

American respondents manifested dichotomist views, either admiring the queen or strongly disapproving of her according to their own interpretation and reaction to the otherwise similar enculturation material they would have been exposed to. As research evidence shows, the factors responsible for the development of different attitudes lie in the level of education. A university degree shapes a different understanding, further altered in the case of respondents with art or art history degrees. A further differentiation stemmed from the geographical region of the respondents' degree or college education; for instance, respondents educated in California espoused far more open views.

Regarding the Petit Trianon and its image, the American majority-group respondents were surprised to see its simplicity, especially in comparison to the Palace of Versailles, which they ultimately preferred due to its display of luxury. Most of these respondents had expected the Petit Trianon to be not only a much more luxurious place but some even imagined it to be 'Pink' (or 'Pink-er'!). Further prompts to establish the origin of the pink colour expectation revealed that the images induced by Sofia Coppola's special effects in filming the queen's life were only partly responsible. The Ladurée macarons, indirectly introduced by Coppola's film, have been sold at the Château de Versailles since 2009. In fact, the commodified image of Marie Antoinette – as also conveyed through other Palace boutiques' merchandise – seems to have cemented the 'pink' associations.

The American minority group corresponds to visitors with art and art history knowledge drawn from their education and/or general interests. This includes art collectors and artists of all backgrounds. Also in this minority group was a small subset of history-passionate respondents. This group of respondents has the same perception of the queen and her estate as their French counterparts, film narratives being irrelevant to their perception of the site in general. In fact, these minority groups (American and French) tended to look more deeply at the site itself. It is important to stress that what seems to lead most of these respondents to a different understanding of Marie Antoinette's historical figure is mainly an artistic sensibility.

For a practical illustration of the contrast between Marie Antoinette's perception among the American majority and the American minority groups, excerpts from two visitor discourses, representative of the aforementioned minority, are provided below. (NB: these are not part of the 307-respondent sample gathered on site.) These opinions on Marie Antoinette are used also as negative evidence (through contrast) and testimony for the American majority-group visitor perceptions. Cardozie Jones and Joseph Vigliotti have been writing a musical entitled *Madame Infamy*, which reviews Marie Antoinette's destiny from a fresh rehabilitative perspective, in contrast with commonly accepted Republican clichés.[9] Their research brought them to visit the Petit Trianon and explore the space where the queen had once lived, for confirmation of their research findings. I met the respondents in July 2012, after they enquired at the Heritage Architectural Department for an unofficial guide to the Petit Trianon, as they had themselves noticed the Republican agenda's interpretation normally given by the *guide-conférenciers*, specialists in History of Art, employed by Réunion des musées nationaux (RMN). Our subsequent communication led me to discover the evolution of their own perceptions, which fully represent the marked contrast between the American majority and minority groups evidenced by the survey. Their long-term research on the subject of Marie Antoinette, together with their native (inside) knowledge of American perceptions, provide reliable support for my own findings (see Table 6.2).

Composer/lyricist Cardozie Jones' discourse is supported and complemented by the views of playwright Joseph Vigliotti, although the two differ in their approach. Whereas Jones is mostly guided by artistic sensibility, Vigliotti has remained under the influence of rational deductions. It is also

Table 6.2 Evidence and negative evidence, respectively, for American minority- and majority-group perceptions at the Petit Trianon

1 Cardozie Jones (Composer/lyricist)

'In America (and I assume in other countries as well) we don't spend much time learning about Marie Antoinette in our study of world history. In studies of cause and effect, she is simply one of many factors that exacerbated the tensions leading up to the French Revolution. What little is taught about her paints a picture of the last Queen of France: a lavish, self-indulgent and heartless woman, so hated by her people that they sent her to the guillotine. As a school-aged child, one's assumption is that she must have done something horrible to deserve such a punishment. Here, at a young age, through a cursory and extraordinarily biased glance at the life of this woman, we become assimilated into the larger social perspective of who she was and what part she played in history. When someone asks us if we know who Marie Antoinette was, we feel comfortable saying "yes".

Additionally, and what's most interesting to me is, even though we lack any true understanding (or for that matter, concern) for who she was, I would go so far as to say her name and persona are staples in American pop culture. Every year on October 31st, when Americans celebrate Halloween, "Marie Antoinette Wigs" and "Marie Antoinette Costumes" are hugely popular items, and they have been for as long as I can remember. Similar to the idea of someone like Cleopatra, the importance of the icon has far surpassed the importance of the person or the life it represents.

Any expertise I have developed on the subject of Marie Antoinette has come from an interest sparked by my best friend and now – writing partner, Joseph Vigliotti. He approached me in 2008 asking that I write the music to accompany a script he had written that parallels the lives of Marie Antoinette and an American slave. Immediately, I thought we were writing some kind of musical comedy. Based on all I knew about Marie Antoinette, the thought of comparing her to a slave seemed ludicrous. But then he sat me down and talked to me about the research he had done, and expressed to me the fervor in which he felt these two stories were kindred to one another. Any conceptions I had developed about the 'lavish, self-indulgent, and heartless' queen of France had been toppled over. Immediately, after reading his script, and diving into my own research, I realised that there was a story that had not been told. It was the story of a girl who was thrusted into circumstance and did the very best anyone could be expected to do. It was the story of a girl who felt an incredible amount of obligation to live up to the expectations of her mother. It was the story of a girl whose reputation was turned into scandal for sport. It was the story of a girl who was, ultimately, not born free.

Years have passed and we are still looking for new ways to depict her as a complete and complex person: one with wishes, fears, virtues and flaws. As artists, while we are working, above all toward integrity, we are also writing for the commercial business of American musical theatre. This means we try to find the balance between truth, and what it means to give the audience an experience that they will walk away having enjoyed (and essentially having paid for). [. . .] Specifically as a songwriter, there is something about music that I feel has the ability to enhance the potential for this story to be heard and felt. We have often been asked, "Does it have to be a musical? Why not a play?" For us, it is like asking if the sun has to rise in the morning. It is simply part of the original design and we could never imagine it existing any other way.' (Jones pers. comm. 2013)

(Continued)

Table 6.2 (Continued)

2   Joseph Vigliotti (Playwright)

'Growing up in America we often learn about different world leaders either through stories or shallow parochial text books. In retrospect, the teachings feel like headlines of a one-sided political newspaper that we find so often to be the norm these days. My personal connection to Marie Antoinette did not come until much later in life. In fact, all I knew about her was that she was beheaded for being greedy. Often times, I would get the stories of Marie Antoinette confused with stories of Imelda Marcos, the Philippine first lady known for her collection of shoes. Both were depicted for their greed and power, and both not American.

My search for the real Marie Antoinette did not come out of any interest in who she was, but rather another female in American history. Many years back I was doing research on a relatively famous American slave out of my passion for African American history. I am, by trade and passion, a theatre artist (director and writer) and always wanted to re-create this character live on stage, but always felt that there was something missing from her story, perhaps another voice or soul, but I never knew quite whose voice that was. On the back burner this story went.

Many years later, I was living in Los Angeles when Sofia Coppola directed Marie Antoinette starring Kirsten Dunst. By this time, while I had a passion for history and was very much intrigued by Coppola's fusion of punk rock and period décor, in all honesty, what I cared most about was how this queen got beheaded. Despite growing up knowing it happened, I never knew quite why or what led up to it, besides the famed line of "Let Them Eat Cake". If you have seen the movie, you know the main reason for which I attended never occurred. After two hours plus of watching a young queen be . . . just be . . . with no action . . . and no head rolling, I was greatly disappointed. [. . .] This led me to my search for who the real Marie Antoinette is. More specifically, I wanted to know what occurred from the time she left Versailles until she took her final walk onto the scaffold.

Surprisingly enough, through my research, what I discovered was that this was the missing voice, the counterpart to the American slave I was studying years earlier. I found that both these women had an uncanny number of parallels in terms of their life experiences. This fuelled my journey even more to go in deeper. What I learned to be true as a story teller and theatre artist is that every person who has ever lived is a three hundred and sixty degree person, but often history books only tell one side of that person. This is typically the side that is written down by those who have triumphed. Typically those who are silenced are those who have been, or will soon become oppressed.

In my research through film, video, biographies (both historical fiction and non) and literally walking in her foot steps through body research my opinion is that Marie Antoinette is indeed some of the things that history books say about her, but she is also many other things that books rarely write about. My job as a playwright and dramaturge is to look at the whole picture of who she was and draw conclusions. This includes not only the events of her life, but the society in which she grew up, and what the expectations of her were. [. . .] Often we put our own societal expectations on historical characters of the past without any consideration of the emotional differences that time and space play [. . .].

In my opinion, Marie Antoinette was oppressed and victimized by her circumstance. She came into power at a very young age. She was unprepared, and like all her siblings, used as a pawn to serve the needs of the empire, needs established by her mother. Though we cannot make an exact comparison to the world we live in today, we can look at young celebrities in the media today, see what growing up with power and attention does to their well-being [. . .]. Another iconic image that comes to mind when I think of what life may have been like for Marie Antoinette is Madonna. She was a young pop artist that rose to fame rather quickly, yet admits what little talent she felt she had. As she was trying to find who she was throughout her late teens and early twenties, the media would follow her around and draw opinions on who she was. There were times when she was demonized for it, and others when she was iconized for it. Later on she grew up, had children, found spirituality and purpose. Today, she is respected by many people who deem her as a legend. When asked about her youth and her choices, she notes: "It is not normal for someone to grow up and explore who they are and who they will become in front of the eyes of the world, most people get to do that exploring in private." This is exactly what happened with Marie Antoinette. All eyes were on her all of the time.' (Vigliotti pers. comm. 2013)

important to highlight the playwright's comparison between Marie Antoinette and Madonna. In fact, Madonna herself seems to have a fascination with Marie Antoinette, having associated her image with the 'decadent' queen as early as her 1990 public performances for her album *Vogue* (Figure 6.9)[10], the later *Re-Invention* tour (2004), and even her 55th birthday party celebrated through an eighteenth-century, costume-themed party on the French Riviera (2013). Through her own notoriety, Madonna perpetuates and reinforces the common American clichés surrounding the queen, an example of the continual multiplication of postmodern images.

There are clear differences between the French and American perceptions of Marie Antoinette's historical character. Whereas the perception of French nationals is dictated by elements intrinsic to the collective memory, the perception of American nationals indicates the definite influence of the social imaginary, induced not only through media sources, but also through cultural conditioning. Flooding the American stream of consciousness with media figures a few decades earlier than in Europe, technological progress has contributed to the structure of this cultural conditioning (see also Blanchard 2013). Consequently, the well-established American popular culture mostly operates within the same parameters defining postmodernity. If, for American majority group of this study, the postmodern traits of contemporary tourists (described by Urry's 'gaze') feature prominently, various cultural traditions also infiltrate these 'guiding' parameters in the case of other nationals. Furthermore, for the American majority group, research evidence indicates that the image prevails over the content. Whether their perceptions (as well as those of the Japanese) also qualify for the role of 'memories', as confirmed in the case of the French majority groups, is investigated later in the chapter.

Japanese visitors at the Petit Trianon

Discourses gathered during the survey from Japanese nationals also distinguish between a majority and a minority group, with the distinction criteria found in art history knowledge (through education or interest). The

Figure 6.9 Madonna as Marie Antoinette at the 1990 MTV awards
Courtesy Everett Collection

Japanese majority group differ from those of other nationals, most clearly because of the direct link between Japanese enculturation and the image of Marie Antoinette found in their popular culture sources. Japanese visitors belonging to the majority group showed only slight differences between women and men in their affinity towards the media sources that added to their opinion on Marie Antoinette. Women were unanimously self-declared fans (*otaku*) of Ikeda's *Rose of Versailles*, whilst the men seemed to favour Sofia Coppola's film to the famous *shōjo* manga. Although the film and manga were not the only reasons to visit, both are highly popular, and contributed to these nationals' perception prior to the visit. All Japanese visitors generally appear very attentive to details once they have arrived at the destination, invariably enhancing their historical knowledge by 'looking properly' at the site (Benoît pers. comm. 2011a) and taking it in through all their senses, as opposed to mere visual registering. Further, both the Japanese majority and minority groups spent a long time (in average 15 minutes) answering the field research survey questions, clearly reflecting in depth.

Despite being well acquainted with Coppola's film, as well as Ikeda's manga, the Japanese majority group expected the Petit Trianon to be much simpler than the Palace of Versailles, and their prior-to, and post-visit, perceptions of the site generally coincided. A direct explanation, confirmed by the survey, is provided by the appreciation and understanding on the part of respondents for eighteenth-century neoclassical and picturesque genres. The unanimously accepted fascination of the Japanese public with Marie Antoinette – the most popular historical figure in contemporary Japan (Oka 2008) – has also been confirmed by the field research. Most Japanese respondents (with the exception of four male respondents) ticked the first two boxes of Question 23, which refers to the wish to visit other places connected to the historical figure of Marie Antoinette, such as the Schönbrunn Palace in Vienna – birthplace and childhood home of Marie Antoinette – or La Conciergerie in Paris, where the queen was imprisoned before being guillotined. The latter proved slightly more popular than the former, confirming the deep empathy which Japanese respondents have for Marie Antoinette's tragic death. Within La Conciergerie stands a shrine (Figure 6.10) built for Marie Antoinette on the site of her former prison cell by the Bourbon Restoration early in the nineteenth century.[11] The contemporary institution of La Conciergerie, which is part of the Centre des monuments nationaux (CMN), within a wider interpretive discourse for this former mediaeval palace, fulfils the nostalgic needs of visitors with Royalist sympathies of a political or cultural nature, or mere admirers of Marie Antoinette, whose historical character surpasses clear political and cultural connotations. This interpretative choice seems to go beyond purely touristic commercial interests, as the institutional narrative conveyed on the site has a particularly empathic tone. This tone was also detected at the 2010 film exhibition held at La Conciergerie, with a nostalgic Marie Antoinette (represented by Norma Shearer

Figure 6.10 La Conciergerie displays a nostalgic discourse originating in the Bourbon Restoration when this shrine to Marie Antoinette was erected on the site of her former prison cell

© Bernard Acloque/courtesy Centre des monuments nationaux

in her 1938 Hollywood role) taking central place. A future exhibition on Marie Antoinette is projected to take place at this site (de Parseval pers. comm. 2017).

The wish to visit other important places linked to Marie Antoinette's life (and mostly death) highlights the pilgrimage trait which characterises the Japanese public, as does the fact that most respondents visited Versailles more than once. Indeed, one of the traits of pilgrimage is the circuit of the trail of worship (Horne 1984), which field research has confirmed to be the specific case of the Japanese public worshipping not only eighteenth-century European court culture but also Marie Antoinette. As such, the Japanese public would not only visit one particular place identified with their object of fascination or worship, but a series of places, usually in the order prescribed by those invested with authority, be they travel guides, television programmes or sometimes school education. Research evidence gained from this study suggests that the pilgrimage approach to visiting/travelling determines a far more authentic visitor experience than the usual, single-site focus of the Western approach.

David Crouch (2011:94) considers it 'strange that authenticity has spilled into tourism, often through Graburn's anthropological conduit of aligning tourism with a sacred journey. The diversity of what tourism has always been rather mocks the depth of sanctity that pilgrimage denotes'. In spite of his challenging tone, Crouch (2011) does in fact sustain this view through his own research findings on postmodern values of authenticity and their relationship with heritage and tourism, considering that the phenomenological experience provides authenticity.

Returning to our analysis and given that authenticity of the experience is accepted from a phenomenological perspective, this brings perception – emerging from fiction or reality –into question, calling for further investigation of the sources on which the fiction is based. With fiction and reality often overlapping at heritage sites, Howard (2003:80) observes that:

> The mythical heritage is very powerful, and can be taken quite seriously, though that does not excuse untruthful Interpretation. Literature provides many of these sites. The heritage of Bran Castle in Romania is more concerned with being the home of Dracula than any element of reality [Mureşan & Smith 1998]. Interpretation at such sites can be quite honest in quoting a legend, just as one can interpret an event from a work of literature [. . .]. The only problem arises when legends and literature are confused with reality.

The quote above refers to the danger of fiction overtaking reality in the case of the interpretation given to a site by its authorities. My analysis further investigates the competition between fiction and reality within visitor perceptions of a site, even when this competition is not generated by any confusion generated by an untruthful heritage interpretation. As established in Chapter 5, interpretation at the Petit Trianon is scrupulously truthful and purposely avoids linking to fiction.

The blurred boundaries between fiction and reality within Japanese visitor perceptions at the Petit Trianon first come to light through the respondents' opinions about Marie Antoinette. Of the majority group of Japanese visitors, 40 out of 44 expressed opinions that equated with those conveyed by Ikeda's manga and Coppola's film:

> A young queen who did not have the opportunity of knowing the poor living conditions of her contemporary French people, being thus a victim of the violence of the French Revolution [choice Answer 3; Question 9].

These respondents also stated that they appreciated the eighteenth-century architecture [choice Answer 13; Question 4], which may help to explain their other opinions of Marie Antoinette:

> A beautiful queen with sophisticated taste and artistic refinement [choice Answer 4; Question 9].
>
> A queen who loved the rural and far more simple and natural feel of Petit Trianon to the weighing etiquette of the Palace of Versailles [choice Answer 5; Question 9].

Yasumasa Oka (2008) confirms the general Japanese perception to have been greatly influenced by Ikeda's message, the *mangaka*'s work being the most important source of knowledge on Marie Antoinette in the absence of a detailed portrayal of the queen in Japanese schools. Furthermore, Oka (2008:23) observes that there seems to be a marked difference between the French nationals' perception of Marie Antoinette and that of the Japanese nationals. The former still tend to vilify her, as 'they' did during the eighteenth century, and the latter, by contrast, see her as a victim:

> Finally, for the Japanese, the character of Marie-Antoinette is simply the unfortunate victim of a political marriage devised to strengthen the Habsburg – Bourbon alliance: a lovely/pretty princess made queen, never having known anything other than a worry-free, luxurious life, who then becomes a tragic heroine, caught up in the turmoil of the Revolution and endless suffering. [translation mine, from the French]

An exception to this commonly held opinion was provided by two young couples who were familiar with Coppola's film but not with Ikeda's manga. They also expressed their fascination with Marie Antoinette, but they opted for Answers 1 or 2:

> An evil young queen, spoiled, capricious and spendthrift who deserved her tragic fate [choice Answer 1; Question 9].
>
> A stupid young queen, spoiled, capricious and spendthrift who nevertheless did not deserve her tragic fate [choice Answer 2; Question 9].

This exception, with its contrasting attitude of fascination and reprobation, can be explained as resulting from the identification of visitors with either the victims or the perpetrators, depending on their own psychological construct. Conversely, the Japanese minority group of nine female respondents occupies the other extreme in the range of opinions, their perception coinciding with that of other minority groups detected across French and American nationalities. For these young women from an art academic background, Marie Antoinette is:

> The Queen *par excellence* who will remain forever in collective memory for her courage and her majestic manner of facing her tragic destiny [choice Answer 7; Question 9].

For testing the degree to which fiction could be perceived as reality, Question 13 asked Japanese visitors whether they intended to also visit the house of the fictitious character Lady Oscar. Firstly, most of the respondents of the Japanese majority group failed to point out that this character was fictitious, by not ticking the choice: 'No, because it [the house] never existed, just like Lady Oscar.' Secondly, added to this general misconception, only half ticked 'Yes'. Thus, it could be concluded that despite the popularity of both characters, when it comes to built heritage, not all respondents were as interested in visiting an aristocratic mansion, as they were interested in visiting a royal residence. Naturally, the fascination with eighteenth-century court rituals (Oka 2008; Brown pers. comm. 2011) could also be the cause for the greater interest in the Petit Trianon.

This major finding of the survey, indicating the blur between fiction and reality within Japanese visitor perceptions, determined the need for a further analysis of the Japanese cultural background. This is detailed in the next section together with a comparison between the two modes of perception pertaining to the American and Japanese majority groups.

Imaginary social worlds, or authentic tourist experiences?

To understand the mechanisms behind the perceptions detailed in the previous section, and to refine research findings, we will draw next from anthropological theories which also help to establish whether these perceptions qualify as 'memories'.

The prevalence of the imaginary over reality, in the context of the public's interaction with historical and media figures, forms the subject of the work of American anthropologist John L. Caughey (1984). Reality is defined here as tangible, measurable materiality, totally distinct from the imaginary realms. Despite the Cartesian distinction between imagination and reality dominant in the West, Caughey established, through extensive ethnographic research, including schizophrenia-patient samples, that the imaginary actually plays a very important role in American culture and that it blurs with reality. Furthermore, imaginary social interaction occurs via popular culture media channels and proves to be particularly pervasive for the majority of Americans.

Although Caughey's work was published in the 1980s, and refers mainly to American society, the author has further tested his ethnographic results on various cultures, proving his hypothesis to be equally valid in other cultural contexts. My fieldwork evidence revealed that Caughey's assertions also hold true for visitor perceptions of the majority groups at the Petit Trianon. One particular thread of Caughey's research – the imaginary social relationships which contemporary individuals form with media figures – was confirmed by fieldwork at the Petit Trianon. This has helped to elucidate the origins of the particularly strong familiarity expressed in connection with Marie Antoinette, a surprisingly common denominator of visitor perceptions among the American majority group at the Petit Trianon. The prevailing image of Marie Antoinette is extremely well defined in their consciousness, although this is inspired by various external sources and, naturally, not by a personal encounter with the queen. Caughey's theory explains that by taking for granted an identity received via media channels – equally true for historical figures and contemporary celebrities – the majority of the public unquestioningly assimilates these 'media-fashioned and propagated' identities into their personal, 'imaginary social world'. Patterns of expression such as 'Marie Antoinette would have approved of that' (referring to the richly ornate *confiserie* sold by the Palace's boutiques), or 'She just didn't care about the people, she was so spoiled' (used often in discussions by respondents of the American majority group), reflects Caughey's theory. Further, internet image analysis reveals that Marie Antoinette is an American popular culture staple (see also Saint-Amand 2003; Lanser 2003) with Halloween wigs and costumes abounding and ranging from purposeful elegance to burlesque and crude grotesque. Popular culture representations suggest that Americans want to live as Marie Antoinette, court in 'her' style, entertain/play or criticise American leaders for 'decadent' lifestyles and arrogant/stupid politics (Figure 6.11; see also Maior-Barron 2015b).

Findings at the Petit Trianon suggest that popular culture media sources are responsible for creating visitors' 'imaginary social worlds', by both validating and reinforcing the social nature of the imaginary. American majority group respondents at the Petit Trianon displayed clear signs of managing the schizophrenia between the symbolic values of their 'imaginary social worlds' and tangible reality. This 'managing' is actually facilitated by the increasing lack of clear boundaries between the real and the perceived, respondents being neither in charge nor fully aware of the bases of their own beliefs. The social media of the twenty-first century also strengthen the parameters of the imaginary, while reality – understood in dualist Cartesian terms – becomes increasingly uncertain due to this inversion of values as witnessed by postmodernity.

Unlike earlier historical periods subject to the influence of media, beliefs are no longer based on clear sources but on a multitude of concurring, subliminal factors such as marketing, advertising and (in our case) heritage commodification. Whereas Anderson (1991) noticed that, starting with modernity, the members of a group would become socially engaged in interaction of an imaginary nature – for instance, by reading the same

Figure 6.11 Marie Antoinette's character in an 'imaginary social interaction' with contemporary Americans – George Bush criticised in January 2008 for lack of empathy with American people on the eve of economic crisis

Courtesy Michael McParlane/www.michaelmcparlane.com

newspaper – the pervasive nature and complexity of contemporary media makes it increasingly difficult for individuals to distinguish between different sources of information (see also Blanchard 2013).

At first glance, the Japanese perceptions of the Petit Trianon and Marie Antoinette seem to contrast with the above, as there is the added element of these visitors 'reading' into the actual encountered space and improving their historical knowledge through means other than mere factual information. Robert Brown's (2013) analysis of Japanese spatial perception, contextualised within the understanding of place and identity, revealed that phenomenological elements bear a strong influence over this perception. However, further research revealed a complex context of Japanese perception identical to the aforementioned Western 'imaginary' interaction. The main reason for the convergence of these two modes of perception lies in the collapsing of time and space attested in the contemporary Japanese travel experience, the *tabi* (travellers) searching for their own past and spatial identity in present time and far away from home (Guichard-Anguis & Moon 2009).

According to Brown (pers. comm. 2011), there is an evident Japanese fascination with European court rituals, which the Japanese perception likens to its own pre-Western past, especially the Tokugawa period. This was translated later into one of the main slogans of identity reconstruction during the Meiji period: *Bunmei Kaika* (Civilization and Enlightenment). Furthermore, the seventeenth- and in particular the eighteenth-century 'little dramas' taking place in the court of Versailles – apparently mirroring the Tokugawa political and social context – turned Versailles into the historical European court preferred by the Japanese public, as confirmed by field research evidence at the Petit Trianon.

Japanese tourism research (Guichard-Anguis & Moon 2009) strongly suggests the important role played by the imaginary in Japanese visitor perceptions of heritage sites. Firstly, when considering the source of the collapse of time and space within Japanese tourist perceptions, it must be noted that the Japanese *tabi no bunka* (culture of travel) predates its Western counterpart, through custom pilgrimages for both religious and leisure purposes, traceable to the tenth century. It is this aspect of leisure which gives it priority, since the European pilgrimage had solely religious connotations (Guichard-Anguis 2009). *Tabi* itself equates with 'walking and searching for the meaning of life' (Guichard-Anguis 2009:3), and manifests either spiritual or ludic nuances, with one of the main ingredients of *tabi* being dream and nostalgia.

The two main 'ingredients' of *tabi* are interpreted here as essential in rendering the phenomenological experience of sightseeing both powerful and valuable. The absence of the past, and space left behind, provide an acute perception of present time and its enfolding landscapes. However, it is argued here that this constant comparison of past and absence with present and presence induces the imaginary social interaction derived from Caughey's theory. Although the social interaction with media or historical figures could not be tested, the imaginary social worlds are nevertheless strongly evident in the case of the Japanese visitors at the Petit Trianon, especially when taking into account that for the majority of questionnaire respondents, there was not a clear differentiation between the real and the imaginary characters of *Rose of Versailles*. Internet image analysis also suggests that, in Japanese popular culture, from manga to anime, 'cosplay' (costume play), and Takarazuka theatre, Oscar de Jarjayes is as real as Marie Antoinette.

Nelson Graburn (1977) pioneered[12] the idea of the pilgrimage nature of tourism inducing the authenticity of experience by establishing links between authenticity and motivations for travelling and sightseeing in the context of the 'sacred journey'. The author further analysed Japanese tourism and constructions of identity (Graburn 2009) by investigating the search of the self in other times and/or far-flung destinations. Graburn (2009:21) deftly summarises this by reversing Lowenthal's (2015) famous dictum – 'the past is a foreign country' – to become: 'a foreign country is the past'.

The search for oneself through travelling is not exclusive to Japanese culture. The confluence between two of the most powerful cultural forces of postmodernity, heritage and tourism, in its role of 'social phenomenon' (Porter 2008:268) rather than industry, indicates that both heritage and tourism are responsible for the identity construction of the 'self' as well as that of the

'Memories' of Marie Antoinette   193

Figure 6.12 Artist Riyoko Ikeda – pictured in 2008 with Taiwan fans in the guise of Marie Antoinette and Lady Oscar – enjoys an ever increasing popularity as her manga, *Rose of Versailles*, continues to be discovered and cherished throughout the world

Courtesy Chiang Ying-ying/REX/Shutterstock

'other', which inherently leads to a search for identity. However, the anxieties of modern Japan, mostly translated into the fear of identity loss – from national to individual – seem to exacerbate the nature of this search. The Edo (Tokugawa) period (1603–1868) which arguably defines the Japanese modern identity before Westernisation and industrialisation, generates a permanent nostalgia and search of that past, which to many Japanese seems to be closer to their definition of the Japanese cultural essence than their uncertain and unsettling present (Creighton 2009). Yet this search is placed under the same illusions of those faced by the West, as even in Japan, traditions suffered the same process of 'invention' (Ivy 1995; Guichard-Anguis 2009) as those of the West described at length in Chapter 1.

Considering the above, are Japanese visitors different from their Western counterparts, especially Americans, whose perceptions of heritage are quintessentially postmodern?

Marilyn Ivy's reflections on the modern Japanese identity further clarify issues of Japanese tourist perception concerning this question. Ivy's analysis of the evolution of *tabi* in the context of the 1970s (the peak period of Japanese industrialisation), when emancipation occurred at many levels of society, showed not only that emancipation in *tabi* had an impact on other main developments, such as women's emancipation but also that it was facilitated by the introduction of an American model current at the time. 'Discover

Japan', the movement which crystallised the contemporary *tabi*, was in fact constructed on the bases of 'Discover America' (Ivy 1995:42). Both aimed at a national rediscovery of Japan (respectively, America), and they played upon the national, which was reinforced through an appeal to each citizen's consciousness and need of personal rediscovery.

This approach, nationalist in essence, was replaced in the course of two decades by the postmodern movement 'Exotic Japan' (Ivy 1995:48), arguably well aligned again with the international postmodern discourse of globalisation and discovery of 'other' cultures (Meethan 2001; Robinson 2001). Whereas 'Discover Japan' was an invitation for Japanese natives to rediscover themselves in a straightforward fashion, 'Exotic Japan' was a revisited version of this, seen from the construction for 'the other', through induced stereotypical images such as geisha, cherry blossoms and Fujiyama (see Ivy 1995). Yet appearances are deceptive, and an inversion of reality values becomes evident. In fact, the construction for the 'other' was targeting the younger Japanese who had become Americanised and in the course of this became separated from their own national past (foreigners in their own country). Therefore, the Japanese postmodern discourse of *tabi* is constructed on contradictions and paradoxes, claiming to portray one reality but conveying its reverse through a 'counternarrative strategy' (Ivy 1995:51), endless meanings unfolding in Derrida's (1997) deconstructive fashion of postmodernity (Berque 2002).

Contemporary Japan 'suffers' the same fate as the West, it seems. Now it must be analysed whether the uncanniness of modern Western history has also infiltrated Japan. Ivy's studies provide an affirmative answer. The uncanniness noted by Ricoeur (2004) is signalled by marginalised events of 'traditions' revived by Japanese nativist ethnology (see *Tōno Monogatari*) of the beginning of the twentieth century (Ivy 1995). The revival of these 'traditions', coinciding with their marginalisation, indicates a nostalgia for artificially sustained cultural forms (Ben-Ari 1996). This is turn suggests a denial of successful Westernisation, which in fact is embraced by contemporary Japanese society. The authenticity of traditions, marked by the elusive representation of their absence, is also questioned (Tansman 1996).

The Orientalist philosopher Augustin Berque's lifelong immersion in Japanese culture allows for a comparative analysis of Western and Japanese philosophical perceptions of space and being. Berque (2002) reveals – through the Japanese philosophy of the Kyoto School – that between the two philosophical modes there is one major difference. The Western philosophical traditions derived from Plato, the modern school of thought initiated by Descartes and more recent phenomenological theories like Heidegger's converged into a common understanding of an Absolute existence (understood either in the religious or the metaphysical sense), whose rapport with the existence of beings in space is explained through either mimetic or determinist causes but also through what Berque (2004) himself coined *médiance*. Berque (2002) shows that Nishida Kitarô (leading figure of the Kyoto School of Philosophy) considers the existence of beings in space as absolute, space and being merging into a matrix independent of other realities. This is key to understanding that Japanese culture is in essence postmodern: the interpretation of any abstract object is another object in itself.

The Japanese nationalist philosophy has become more current since the 1990s, being favoured initially by an affirmation of Japan's cultural identity 'a trend of thought known as *Nihonjinron*, which flourished especially in the seventies, though its roots can be traced at least way back to the national studies (*kokugaku*) of the Edo period, and most notably to Motoori Norinaga (1730–1801)' (Berque 2002:90). The Kyoto School philosophical thesis *Kindai no chôkoku* (overcoming modernity) together with Kitarô's concept of *basho no ronri* (logic of place), share the theme of 'absolutising the world' (Berque 2002:91), which leads to postmodern views. Since this postmodern philosophy, and its associated perception, have existed since the seventeenth century, it is consequently argued here that in Japan postmodernity preceded the modernity introduced by the West.

Are the contemporary Japanese studies such as Ivy's, or Kitarô's postmodern philosophy, further expanding the understanding of contemporary Japanese popular culture and its perceptions? As Alan Tansman (1996:202) aptly wonders while assessing the general validity of Ivy's conclusions: 'Who are these Japanese [to which the studies apply]?'

Regarding the general traits of postmodernity and whether they apply or not to the majority of Japanese, it could be argued that the attraction they have for costumes of any period – though eighteenth century is a definite favourite – suggests that within popular culture perceptions there is a clear isolation of form from an original source. Or, otherwise put, there is a separation of the image from its content, the image taking on a life of its own in typical postmodern fashion.

From the point of view of Japanese tourist perceptions, recent studies also indicate clear evidence of postmodern traits. Japanese visitors look for the familiar either in the domesticated foreignness (Graburn 2009) of the Japanese theme parks depicting European destinations (Hendry 2009) or in the international destinations which they come to know through school education and literature. Places associated with Jean-Henri Casimir Fabre in France, and Anne of Green Gables in Canada (Guichard-Anguis 2009), or Shakespeare, the Brontës and Beatrix Potter in the UK (Surman 2009) are typical examples. Moreover, not only does 'anticipation' exist in the case of Japanese visitors as much as in that of Western visitors, but their large numbers often impose demands to have this anticipation fulfilled, prompting tourism providers to construct the tourist gaze accordingly (Guichard-Anguis 2009).

Marie Antoinette at the Petit Trianon

This chapter now synthesises the interpretation of French, American and Japanese perceptions of Marie Antoinette and the Petit Trianon by drawing from relevant theories and insights gained thus far throughout the chapter.

First is Urry's construction of the gaze (Urry 1990, 1995, 2002), the main theory of tourist visual appropriation of sites which underpins the analysis in this book. The gaze is a hunt for signs in themselves (i.e. a 'typical English village'; see Culler 1981:128) and a search for distinctive elements drawn from unique objects, unfamiliarity and unusual contexts or visual environments. Of particular relevance here, Urry (1990:12) observes that the gaze collects:

> particular signs which indicate that a certain other object is indeed extraordinary, even though it does not seem to be so. [. . .] The attraction is not the object itself but the sign referring to it that marks it out as distinctive. Thus the marker becomes the distinctive sight.
> [Culler 1981:139]

In the case of the Petit Trianon, this consumption of the 'marker as the distinctive sight' has been confirmed by fieldwork research evidence, since for the French and American majority groups of visitors, the attraction to visit the site does not reside primarily in its architectural value – with most of the neoclassical or picturesque values being either ignored or secondary – but in its very connection with Marie Antoinette. For the Japanese majority group, the evidence strongly suggests this also to be the case, since despite the interest in eighteenth-century architecture, which was expressed along with the interest in Marie Antoinette, not all respondents also indicated an interest in seeing Lady Oscar's former home (a 'French château not far from Versailles', Ikeda 2002:8). The pilgrimage trait characterising the Japanese public, as earlier shown, involves consulting authorised literature on their planned routes. Naturally, being a fictional place, Lady Oscar's former home is not featured in any such literature. This further reinforces the consumption of markers, be it Marie Antoinette or Lady Oscar.

Regarding the French, American and Japanese visitor perceptions (Figure 6.13), evidence indicates that while revolutionary propaganda seems to have long-lasting effects and is still at work creating animosity, there is also an incredibly strong fascination – from admiration to obsession – with Marie Antoinette. Each attitude may be as surprising as the other. In fact, the controversy and the violence directed towards this historical figure ultimately led to her martyrdom. In parallel with the official discourse of the Republican agenda, whose portrayal attracts the aforementioned animosity, during the second half of the nineteenth century an entire romantic literary genre bloomed around the figure of the sovereign who, as inexplicably as during her life, seemed to conquer as many hearts as ever. This situation is self-propagated to the present through the cultural conditioning of contemporary visitors at the Petit Trianon, whose interest perpetuates these stories and their appeal.

For French Groups 1 and 2, regardless of the associated affects to their perceptions, the 'memories' are Republican, drawing from the French collective memory and a wider Republican official discourse. Nonetheless, there were slight differences detected between the discourses coming from these

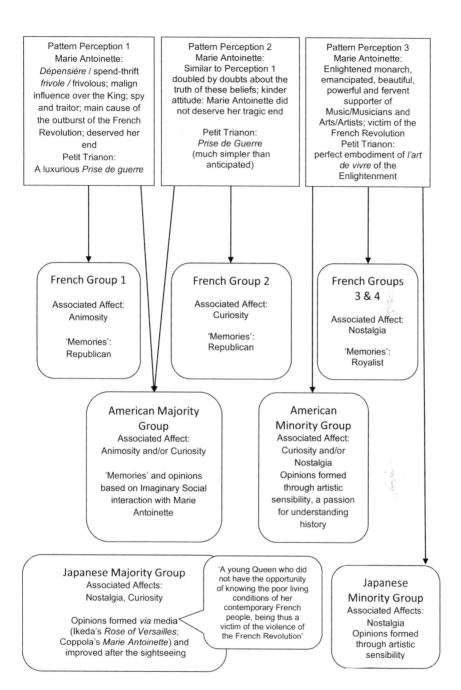

Figure 6.13 Visitor perceptions associated with emotional affects and 'memories' of Marie Antoinette and the Petit Trianon detected through fieldwork research

Author 2014

two groups, with the respondents' age group suspected to be responsible. By considering Soviet and post-Soviet individual discourses on history, James Wertsch (2002) contributes a valuable analysis of 'collective memory' and the appropriation of narratives by different generations once the nation state and its official discourse no longer identify with each other. The differences detected at the Petit Trianon suggest this crisis in the official discourse also applies to France, confirming Nora's (1984b) observations on 'places of memory', which appear in the absence of historical memory, furthermore, as a result of lack of identification between the nation and its past.

In the case of French Group 4, the 'memories' drawn from the collective memory of this minority group have a Royalist nature which is politically and culturally generated. In the case of French Group 3, the admiration (even to extreme fascination) for Marie Antoinette, coupled with nostalgia, led them to appropriate her historical character much as Royalists have done through group rituals. The French Group 3 discourses allude in fact to the presence of 'memories' of a Royalist type. However, by relating to Marie Antoinette through artistic sensibility, it is argued here that these respondents' 'memories' are culturally generated. Building upon the concept of collective memory, Jan Assmann (2012; see also Erll 2011) distinguishes between communicative and cultural memory, with the latter reuniting a set of commemorational traits and relating to mythical historical characters. According to this, the 'memories' detected at Group 3, could better fit in to this collective memory descendent, the cultural memory, not least because of the mythical dimensions which Marie Antoinette's historical character acquired. At the same time, the commemoration trait, which French Group 3 exhibited in their discourses on Marie Antoinette, links their 'memories' with Nora's (1984a) 'places of memory', although 'places of memory' themselves allude to an absence of memory on the part of a nation/group. Nora's (1984a) theory explains how 'places of memory' are capable of generating 'histories' of their own in an endless loop of identification with the object of commemoration (following a division and reconstruction of the past) under the sign of nostalgia. The nostalgia associated with Group 3 could further attest to a possible correspondence between their 'memories' and the histories imprinted in 'places of memory'. In the case of the Petit Trianon, the 'place of memory' corresponds to both the tangible (the site itself) and the intangible (Marie Antoinette), both of which reunite in a commemoration of the last Queen of France. In fact, the clear and consistent comments made by Group 3 (see Figure 6.13) could suggest that the Petit Trianon and Marie Antoinette 'places of memory' are also able to induce 'memories' (via histories) of their own. Further research on the subject is required to establish the mechanisms which would allow this connection from 'histories' to 'memories' to take place.

The perceptions of the American majority group are construed next as the equivalent of uncanny 'memories' – in line with Halbwachs (1980) and Nora (1984–1992) – as much as in the case of the French public, for whom 'memories' are drawn from the national collective memory or that of a minority, as well as perhaps from 'places of memory'. The reason for equating perceptions with 'memories' lies in the presence of an imaginary social interaction of these American respondents with Marie Antoinette. In the same fashion as the 'familiarisation' with this media figure and historical character occurs through imaginary social interaction, the perception of her image is equally recognisable and intimately felt.

Nonetheless, there seems to be a clear difference between the 'memories' of French visitors formed through the intermediary of the collective memory (and its descendent, 'cultural memory'), or even perhaps drawn from 'places of memory', and those induced for the American majority group by an imaginary social interaction, which are underlined by the collapsing of time that occurs in tourist perceptions. These are defined here as 'imaginary social memories', a type of artificial recollection. By displaying a certain cohesiveness within the group's perceptions, owed to the media and their intrinsic messages to the public, the 'imaginary social memories' are similar to those of individual 'memories' drawing from 'uncanny' types of memory. The relationship between memory and media in itself deserves a separate study, this being incidental to the wider process through which media messages feed into the 'collective memory', 'places of memory' and the contemporary social imaginary (with media ranging from the early forms of pamphlets to contemporary social media; see Anderson 1991; also Halbwachs 1992; Appadurai 1996; Erll 2011). However, if the media messages generate a certain cohesiveness, it is equally true that 'imaginary social memories' are also one-sided impressions, based on an individual's assimilation of messages (content and/or images) from media sources, tailored by each respondent's identity. Although it was not possible to test the presence of 'imaginary social memories' in the case of the Japanese majority group, the evidence indicates that these respondents also form their opinions based on media sources. For the American and the Japanese minority groups, there was not enough evidence to confirm the presence of such constructs. Based, however, on their discourses relating to the image of the Petit Trianon and their opinions on Marie Antoinette, similar to those of French Group 3, it is suspected that apart from drawing on 'collective memory turned cultural memory', these respondents could also relate to 'memories' of Marie Antoinette identified in the tangible and intangible 'place of memory' of the Petit Trianon, and respectively, of Marie Antoinette.

Notes

1 Another clear distinction was noticed between the responses of the women and men of the first two groups: within the first group, the women seem to be slightly more aggressive in their attitude towards the queen, whilst in the second group they tend to be kinder and more neutral than the men. In fact, several female respondents belonging to Group 2 expressed pity for the tragic fate of Marie Antoinette, an attitude best described by one respondent's words: 'no matter what she would have done, nobody could deserve such an end' (F; G2; 36–59;13/03/2011).
2 The film 'closest to reality' was considered Sacha Guitry's *Si Versailles m'était conté*. Group 3 members base their beliefs not so much on historical knowledge but on their own understanding of facts via art/art history background.
3 Following the result of Sunday interviews on 5/12/2010 and 6/02/2011, I chose to exclude this particular group from the interpretation of responses and to stop

200 *'Memories' of Marie Antoinette*

    further interviewing of French respondents on the first-Sunday free-entry day. Nevertheless, the five discourses gathered (5F) strongly indicated that this group does not hold a preformed opinion about Marie Antoinette.
4. A notable counter-view to the artificial, uncanny type of 'remembering', encouraged nowadays by visual culture, is found in Alison Landsberg's (1997, 2004) 'prosthetic memory'.
5. Anon. 2 (pers. comm. 2011). This respondent is not included in the ordinary course of data collection through the questionnaire.
6. The respondent and I were put in touch by the curatorial department of Château de Versailles, and communication became regular between us, which allowed me to gain a greater insight into his motivations. With his permission, I selected relevant excerpts from our conversations. This respondent is also not a part of the sample of 307 respondents.
7. Following my presentation at the ICOM-DEMHIST conference (Maior-Barron 2015a), in discussions prompted by my talk, I was made aware of another nineteenth-century case of extreme fascination with Marie Antoinette: Antonio Haghenbeck y de la Lama, former owner of what is now Museo Casa de la Bola (Mexico City).
8. For the American respondents, the media types mentioned were television and popular culture media sources on the French Revolution, such as Bud Yorkin's parody *Start the Revolution Without Me*, a 1970 film apparently aired frequently on American TV throughout the 1980s (Louis XVI and Marie Antoinette are portrayed in a typical Republican manner). Also mentioned was Mel Brooks' parody film *History of the World Part I* (although Marie Antoinette does not figure in this film). Girls' 'diary novels' were also mentioned generically. Interestingly, American respondents aged 36–59 and 60+ consistently mentioned the earlier parody productions, not always clearly distinct from each other but merged into one, whereas for the female respondents aged below 25, the 'diary' type novels were their main point of contact with Marie Antoinette's historical figure. After further investigation, I had confirmation that these 'diaries' are actually novels, written as Marie Antoinette's own mémoires. However, the respondents did not make the distinction between fiction and reality, believing in fact that these 'historical' novels would really be based on authentic mémoires of the queen. The exact source of media information for the rest of the American majority group proved difficult to identify.
9. In relation to this, following feedback via the New York Theatre Festival premiere, Cardozie Jones (pers. comm. 2014) noted: 'I think I most appreciated the women who walked away feeling empowered by a "new" Marie Antoinette story'.
10. For impersonating Marie Antoinette, Madonna wore one of Glenn Close's costumes designed for her role as the Marquise de Merteuil in *Dangerous Liaisons* (1988).
11. This was built at the same time that La Chapelle Expiatoire was erected. The Basilica of Saint Denis, which is the traditional royal crypt, also houses a memorial dedicated to the family of Louis XVI and Marie Antoinette, including their son, Louis XVII, the Child King, who died under mysterious circumstances during his incarceration. Given his young age and the treatment to which he was subjected for becoming a staunch Republican, Marie Antoinette's youngest son had perhaps the most tragic fate of all members of the royal family. Following doubts that the dead child found in the prison cell would have been the real Louis-Charles, during the nineteenth century several young men claimed his identity. However, at the turn of the twenty-first century, DNA tests were able to confirm the child had died in prison. In 2004, a Catholic and Royalist ceremonial was held for him at Saint Denis.
12. For other authors considering various links between tourism and pilgrimage, see also Turner (1969; with Turner 1978); Horne (1984) and Bauman (2003). For a valuable analysis of anthropological approaches to tourism studies, see Leite and Graburn (2009).

7 'Ange ou Démon?'

Contemporary images of the last Queen of France at the Petit Trianon

Chapter 7 is a comparative assessment of the historical, cinematic and architectural narratives of this study against the heritage narrative as it is presented today at the Petit Trianon. Through this comparison, this chapter evaluates the prevailing narrative in the context of museology and popular culture perceptions of Marie Antoinette and the Petit Trianon, thereby discovering the emerging contemporary range of images associated with her historical character at the estate. This chapter also seeks to detect the reasons behind the formation of such images and the processes that led to the unintentional strengthening of some of them, which in turn have encouraged the dissonant commodification of Marie Antoinette's historical character at the Petit Trianon.

Underpinned by its hermeneutical methodology, the analysis primarily draws from the theories of Pierre Nora, John Urry and Henri Lefebvre, all applied to the emerging images of Marie Antoinette to explain what could be defined, in a nutshell, as a 'multiplication' of postmodern images. The trait of 'places of memory', noted by Nora (1984a) for their ability to generate endless histories of their own, links with Urry's observation that the image – as object of the 'romantic gaze' – is appropriated by the visitor, overtaking the physical site and or the historical character being represented. This trait also connects with Lefebvre's idea of the signifier becoming the signified, in an uncontrolled chain of perpetuation induced by postmodern values based mainly on 'visuality'. Images perpetually generate other images, which research evidence has demonstrated to become uncontrollable, ultimately defying even the logic of their initial, intended creation. This is one of the paradoxes of postmodernity stemming from the paradox of modernity regarding the embrace/rejection of the Enlightenment's ideals.

This chapter further links the aforementioned theories with those of representation and semiotics, referring to Jean Baudrillard[1] (1994, 2001), Umberto Eco (1986); Stuart Hall (1997) and Roland Barthes (1972).[2] The circle of representation theory (Hall 1997) is considered here to be a further elaboration on the hermeneutical circle referred to in Chapters 3 and 4.

The term 'hyper-reality', which underpins the following analysis, is used in a metaphorical rather than literal sense, which would refer to visual technology. In some cases, the two merge. Therefore, hyper-reality is defined as another reality, more 'real' than the reality defined in Cartesian terms. Leaning on Baudrillard (2001), who coined the term and developed a model of four phases in the construction and workings of the hyper-real image, this chapter uses the fourth phase – the furthest from the pure representation – to explain how the media images of Marie Antoinette have become their own simulacrum, having completely replaced her historical image.

Eco (1986) further supports this idea by testing the power of hyper-real images in the context of heritage. In his quest of the 'great inauthentic' throughout the United States, the author revealed that the illusionary effects of images are not confined within popular culture milieus but are also increasingly used in art-representation practices. The fact that authenticity is a fluctuating concept is significant, especially when investigating the many strategies used in either curatorial or consumerist practices.

The cultural theorist Hall (1997) contributes another idea regarding signifying practices – the circle of representation and its reinforcement of stereotypical images – which further elucidates the process analysed in this chapter. Considering that certain images circulate within a culture, taking on particular meanings, associations and values, and that their representation and its meanings are connected to a continuous circle reinforcing them as simulacra, Hall's circle continually reinforces images over time until they come to form a closed self-perpetuating system of illusion or even a way of 'seeing the world' (Pritchard & Morgan 2010:128).

Barthes (1972) further contributes to an understanding of the processes analysed in this chapter through his theory of the myth as a semiological system as well as depoliticised speech. Barthes' representation of the value of the myth as semiological system (1972:115) resides in a spatial 'metaphor' which suggests the perpetual multiplication of images analysed here. The sign represented by the myth always divides into a signifier and a signified, with the signifier becoming another sign. By seeing image narratives as part of a language of signs, textuality and imagery are thus merged in the context of contemporary visual culture and its relationship with heritage, which are revealed here to be symbiotic.

As support for the comparative analysis of the cinematic narrative of Marie Antoinette, and the heritage narrative at the Petit Trianon, the depoliticised speech dimension, which Barthes (1972) attributes to the modern myths created by bourgeois society, explains an important trait: the content behind the images ascribed to myth has vanished. Baudrillard's (1994:43) idea – 'Myth, chased from the real by the violence of history, finds refuge in cinema' – contributes further understanding.

Based on the data collection provided in Chapters 4, 5 and 6, this chapter applies the hermeneutical paradigm principles by intersecting the messages of the 'creator', encoded by historians, cineastes, artists and heritage experts, with the decoding of these messages by visitors, all seen in the overarching context of a consumerist, visual-media oriented contemporary society (Figure 7.1). Taking into account the validity of these representations,

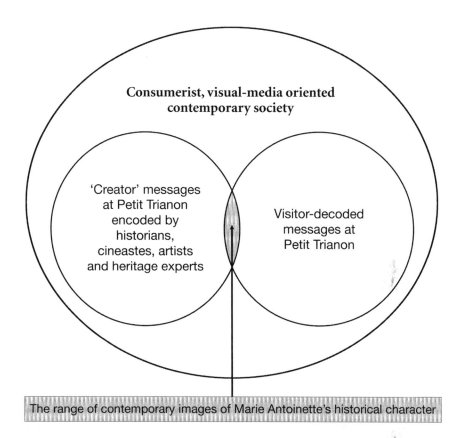

Figure 7.1 The hermeneutical paradigm applied to the study's data collection
Author 2014

interpretations and perceptions, this chapter concludes the study of the dissonant commodification of Marie Antoinette's historical character at the Petit Trianon.

Historical vs. heritage narratives of Marie Antoinette and the Petit Trianon

A comparison between the historical narrative of Marie Antoinette (Chapter 4) and today's heritage narrative of the Petit Trianon site reveals that the historical discourse and the heritage interpretation do not coincide. This is peculiar, since a heritage interpretation normally has to be based on the perceived historical truth. However, the complexity surrounding Marie Antoinette's image extends to a realm of legend, surrounding both the owner and the house, which renders historical facts secondary and makes heritage interpretation problematic. Several convergence points between the two narratives are analysed here.

The ghost image

An illustrative case for the legends woven around Marie Antoinette in relation to the Petit Trianon is that of her 'ghost' image. In 1901, two English tourists of supposed high credibility – Charlotte Anne Elizabeth Moberly and Eleanor Frances Jourdain, both dons at Oxford University – thought they had entered another dimension whilst visiting the Petit Trianon. Subsequent investigation into the phenomena of paranormal activity, and archival research, established that the two English ladies had seen the Petit Trianon as it was in the 1780s. Moreover, one of them even reported seeing the queen sketching a patch of trees near the Petit Trianon building. *An Adventure*, the book dedicated to their experience, was authored by the two Oxford dons and printed for the first time in 1911. In it, they expressed a clear feeling of a close connection between the queen and her *Domaine*. Later editions (Moberly & Jourdain 1952, 2003) include a brief review of similar nineteenth-century and early twentieth-century ghost sightings at the Petit Trianon. The Moberly-Jourdain experience was recently reinvestigated by Marc Lamont (2017).

This chapter does not enquire into the veracity of these beliefs (see also Audinot 2002), but makes use of them to illustrate how this particular image of Marie Antoinette is continually perpetuated. Although it seems that there have not been any recorded sightings of the kind since the beginning of the twentieth century, the legend of Marie Antoinette's ghost lives on. It was mentioned to me by various members of the security personnel of the Petit Trianon and also by some of the respondents interviewed, especially those living nearby, therefore in the position of visiting the site often.

One member of the Petit Trianon's security staff admitted to having seen the queen on his first day at work. As he told it, 'Her Majesty' was heading for her theatre through the internal corridor which leads towards it, turned and gave him an approving smile (Anon. 1 pers. comm. 2010).[3] Rather than characterising it as an extraordinary event, he relayed this to me saying it was an omen of good luck in his new position of guarding the royal Estate of the Petit Trianon. In fact, long-tenured security staff seemed deeply devoted to Marie Antoinette, judging by how deferential they were to her in our conversations.

It was following this field research observation made during the pilot test (November – December 2010) interviewing that I set out to investigate this adjacent dimension of Marie Antoinette's image through the first and second stage visitor discourses gathered at the Petit Trianon. After the formal end of the interview, I opened the subject of her ghostly apparitions. This led me to discover that art collectors or artistically inclined and trained respondents of any nationality either believe strongly in the queen's immortality

'*Ange ou Démon?*' 205

in a symbolic way or do not accept her end, feeling that something can still be done about it, mostly by keeping her memory alive. As for the specific belief in a ghostly dimension, this seems to be restricted to a relatively small sample of respondents.[4]

In 2010, at the first photographic exhibition organised by the Château de Versailles (McGrath 2010), the image chosen to represent the Petit Trianon was a 1953 photograph by Izis connected to the earlier noted ghostly apparition, in the context of Sacha Guitry's parody *Si Versailles m'était conté* (1954). In Izis' photograph (Figure 7.2), Marie Antoinette is seen in a white dress next to Le Temple de l'Amour [The Temple of Love]. The curatorial team criticised the choice made by Karine McGrath, head archivist of

Figure 7.2 Izis' 1953 mise en scène of the famous 1901 apparition sighting, chosen in 2010 as a representative image for the newly launched *Domaine de Marie-Antoinette*

© Paris-Match

Château de Versailles and the exhibition's main organiser. Regarding this, Ms McGrath (pers. comm. 2011) thought the choice was an obvious one because it represented a legend well known to specialists, locals and some tourists, and it implied the inseparable symbolic connection between the queen and her estate. In fact, the estate was restored in 2008 specifically to strengthen this identification. Moreover, the ghost of Marie Antoinette is allegedly seen only on the grounds of the Petit Trianon and nowhere else on the estate of the Château de Versailles.

This situation of the 'ghost' image of Marie Antoinette clearly denotes a very important aspect signalled by Nora's 'places of memory', Urry's 'romantic gaze' and Lefebvre's as well as Barthes' observations on the multiplying nature of the signifier which thus becomes the signified. In this case, the ghost apparition signalled by the two English tourists became a legend in itself, and as all legends, it does not have to have a clear origin, nor to be exact or proven true. Furthermore, this legend, although initially supported by the evidence of an actual sighting, seems to have been perpetuated by various individuals without any supporting evidence, confirming that the content behind the images ascribed to myth has vanished (Barthes 1972).

Whilst the ghost became legend, through a mythical process it further placed the historical character of Marie Antoinette in the realm of legends and fairy tales. Next are highlighted two examples of representations in popular culture, also inspired by the 1901 sighting.

Jasmine Becket-Griffith, successful American illustrator of Disney and non-Disney characters turned into faeries, was inspired to create her first range of doll figurines in 2006 by introducing faerie Antoinette. A portrayal of Marie Antoinette's ghost forms the subject of one of her Werewolves series of paintings (Figure 7.3). The artist described that inspiration struck after visiting the Petit Trianon and further confirmed to me that the subject of her painting was Marie Antoinette's ghost (Becket-Griffith pers. comm. 2017). Her proximity to the Temple of Love resembles the aforementioned 1953 mise en scène, whereas the sighting in *An Adventure* (Moberly & Jourdain 1952) locates the queen by the building of the Petit Trianon. It is likely that both artists felt as if Marie Antoinette's ghost should rather be drawn to The Temple of Love, their artistic visions connecting more easily to stories of romantic love, a fact confirmed by Jasmine Becket-Griffith (pers. comm. 2017). This is proof of the appropriation of the queen's image according to different agendas.

Rodolphe and Annie Goetzinger (2011), authors of *Marie Antoinette: La Reine fantôme*, a French *bande dessinée*, were also inspired by the aforementioned book (Moberly & Jourdain 1952) and by Jean Cocteau's preface – an artistic vision supporting the fact and further inspiring other artistic visions. The book was launched at the Librairie des Princes and in Paris through an art exhibition of limited edition prints. Although based on 'precise historical research' (Duprat 2013:217), the book's narrative takes on new dimensions, building mainly upon the 1901 sighting, though placed

'Ange ou Démon?' 207

Figure 7.3 Le Loup-Garou – Le Temple (Jasmine Becket-Griffith 2010)
Courtesy of the artist/www.strangeling.com

in the context of a different plot occurring in the 1930s. These authors do not claim authenticity but tried to give a possible explanation for the existence of Marie Antoinette's ghost on the grounds of the Petit Trianon at the beginning of the twentieth century. It is important to note, nevertheless, that their vision also connected Marie Antoinette to her beloved English Garden, with which the queen identifies in the narrative: Marie Antoinette's ghost only finds peace once the ashes of her former body are scattered on the grounds of the English Garden, her 'lost paradise' (Goetzinger & Goetzinger 2011:64).

Whilst the ghost image was linked to the aforementioned 2010 photographic exhibition at Château de Versailles through the head archivist's interpretation of the historical narrative of Marie Antoinette derived from the 1901 recorded sighting at the Petit Trianon, the ghost image has never been a part of the authorised heritage narrative at the Petit Trianon, unlike interpretations at other heritage sites which embrace connections with the paranormal (see Hanks 2015).

208 *'Ange ou Démon?'*

The Cinderella image

Whilst not directly connected to the heritage narrative of the Petit Trianon as home to Marie Antoinette, but rather to a heritage narrative of the queen's tragic death and subsequent immortality, a further illustrative example of the legendary dimensions of Marie Antoinette's image is the story of her shoe, lost on the flight of stairs leading to the guillotine. This particular image must be examined, as it constitutes one of the details that remain etched in the collective memory of her admirers. Just as Cinderella lost her glass slipper, later to be found by Prince Charming, Marie Antoinette's shoe provides a material link for the spiritual connection between the sovereign and those enamoured of her (Tapié et al. 1989). Given the aura of Romanticism which the lost shoe at the scaffold added to the perception of Marie Antoinette's historical character, this event eventually transformed into a legend. At the celebration of 200 years since the outbreak of the French Revolution, the Caen Museum of Fine Arts dedicated a special exhibition to a shoe purporting to be the very one worn by Marie Antoinette to the guillotine. The shoe, called 'à la Saint-Huberty' (Figure 7.4), was donated to their collection in the nineteenth century and exhibited for the first time in 1883. Although its authenticity is not confirmed, it is the symbol of the shoe which matters, far more than the reality, as the museography essay explains (Tapié et al. 1989).

The Cinderella image is not associated exclusively with Marie Antoinette's death, but also with her life. One of the reasons Marie Antoinette

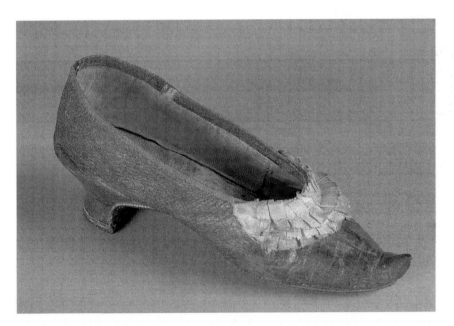

Figure 7.4 The legendary shoe purportedly worn by Marie Antoinette to the scaffold
Photo Patricia Touzard/courtesy Musée des Beaux-Arts Caen

was fiercely criticised during her reign was because of her attendance at balls given in Paris, outside the royal environment of the Court of Versailles. Without precedent, this attitude fuelled much gossip. If any guilt is to be attributed, the Age of Enlightenment is to blame for encouraging the classes to mingle more than ever during social events (Todorov 2009).

At the legendary ball on 30 January 1774, Marie Antoinette – still Dauphine de France – is said[5] to have met Count Axel von Fersen, whose historical character remains in the collective imaginary as her secret lover. This event represents another key connection to the Cinderella story, as Marie Antoinette and her entourage, attending incognito, had to limit their time at the ball due to their status and restrictions of court etiquette. The Dauphine, like Cinderella, had to disappear before midnight.

The 1774 masquerade ball is a moment particularly cherished by cineastes (Figure 7.5) and artists (see also Figures 7.18 and 7.19), strengthening the Cinderella image of Marie Antoinette, albeit with a slight inversion of the female and male roles.

While the Cinderella image was linked to the aforementioned Caen exhibition through its curatorial interpretations of the historical narrative of Marie Antoinette, the Cinderella image is not present at all in the heritage narrative of the Petit Trianon.[6]

Figure 7.5 Most recent cinematic 'Cinderella' image – Coppola's *Marie Antoinette* (2006) film dedicating important scenes to the 1774 Opera masquerade ball

© Sony Pictures/courtesy Everett Collection

The 'queen of refinement' image

Marie Antoinette's perfume, and its attendant image of refinement, is the subject of the next strand of historical research integrated by the heritage narrative of the Petit Trianon. Élisabeth de Feydeau's (2005) research on Jean-Louis Fargeon, the queen's *parfumeur*, led her to liaise with Francis Kurkdijan, currently one of the most appreciated French perfume noses, to recapture the aura of a Fargeon perfume created for Marie Antoinette. Taking inspiration from the olfactory bouquet of the Trianon gardens, the perfume, aptly named *M.A. Sillage de la Reine* [Marie Antoinette The Wake of the Queen] was meant to evoke the lingering scent of the queen's presence. Launched in 2006 (Figure 7.6), Château de Versailles sold the perfume for a limited time to help raise the necessary funds to pay for Marie Antoinette's *coffre de campagne* – an important case piece designed circa 1785 for the queen by her favourite cabinet-maker, Jean-Henri Riesener (see Salmon et al. 2008; Firmin & Rondot 2016) and acquired at auction in 2005 (Arizzoli-Clémentel 2007). Following this purchase, the piece was exhibited at the Petit Trianon (Benoît pers. comm. 2017b).

A mass-media market launch of another perfume claiming to be derived from Marie Antoinette's formula, designed by Fargeon and inherited by his apprentice Lubin in 1798, is Black Jade. Pitched to an exclusive clientele (see also Maior-Barron 2015b), this scent was launched in 2011 by Lubin House. With packaging that subtly incorporated Marie Antoinette's image, associating itself with luxury and refinement, Black Jade claimed originality through a black vial of perfume Marie Antoinette apparently kept with her in prison (Le Temple), and which she handed to the Duchesse de Tourzel before being taken to La Conciergerie. As historical authenticity is not attested by any documents, this amounts to a legend amongst the experts, based on a story transmitted through generations of the de Tourzel family (Isaac 2011). Given that historical provenance cannot be attested, the marketing campaign sourced authenticity from connoisseur expert knowledge unavailable to a public thus enticed even more to become part of this perceived exclusive circle. Building on this, a niche marketing strategy was used for the product's launch in New York.

For the owner of Lubin House, the story is 'actually less compelling than the object as a talisman, which today lies secreted away in a vault somewhere' (Isaac 2011). This attitude contrasts with that of curators such as Alain Tapié, for whom the story counts more than the object itself (see Tapié et al. 1989). Furthermore, despite publicity which seemed to convey aristocratic refinement, the date chosen to launch Black Jade in New York was 14 July 2011. Once again, there is a noticeable contrast (not to say tragic irony) between Château de Versailles' promotion of *M.A. Sillage de la Reine* to raise funds to acquire an important royal artefact associated with Marie Antoinette[7] and Lubin's celebrating the launch of their version of her perfume on a date crucial to the series of events which eventually brought

Figure 7.6 Poster advertising *M.A. Sillage de la Reine*
Courtesy Château de Versailles

her tragic end. Black Jade's story and launch fully illustrate postmodern consumerism. As the launch took place in the United States, the date's significance must have been meant as a pro-Republican statement marking solidarity between two democracies with a revolutionary past. Lubin turned what could have been a product dedicated to royalty, into a statement of cultural refinement based, however, on a dissonant appropriation of Marie Antoinette's image. This attests to the blurring of boundaries between culture and consumerism (Urry 1995) together with the evaporation of the content of the myth (Barthes 1972).

The above contrasting examples provide insights into the differences between a curatorial approach to history and a consumerist one. These insights merge into another case depicting a refined image of Marie Antoinette, that of the House of Dior, whose connections to the Petit Trianon in particular date to its beginnings. In 1950, 'Miss Dior' perfume, created in 1947, was showcased in a display stand (designed for Christian Dior by Victor Grandpierre) inspired by Le Temple de l'Amour. Furthermore, Christian Dior himself drew particular inspiration from the style of dress Marie Antoinette adopted exclusively while at the Petit Trianon. The 70th anniversary exhibition dedicated to this iconic designer features a special section devoted to his Trianon fashion creations (see Müller & Gabet 2017). In September 2013, a contract of sponsorship for restoring La Maison de la Reine at the Petit Trianon was signed between the Château de Versailles and the House of Dior. The publicity campaign for the sponsorship included the launch of the Dior Trianon makeup range in Spring 2014, whose image drew from Dior's own fashion heritage of the 1950s, however, with an updated hyper-real colouring identified in electric shades of pink along with muted pastel colours. This palette contrasts with the essential initial intent that was to be conveyed by the Queen's Norman Hamlet, which was primarily meant to represent the charm of French vernacular through natural simplicity.

Further reinforcing this disparity is the on-site imagery chosen by the contemporary House of Dior in recognition of the Maison de la Reine sponsorship. Following the signing of the contract, the company secured the most prominent advertising space possible at Château de Versailles: a publicity canvas covering nearly the entire façade of the south wing of the main Palace, which was under restoration and renovation between 2010 and 2016 to improve visitor access into the Estate of Versailles. Dior did not contribute to this particular restoration, nor did it link the advertising message specifically to their support of the Maison de la Reine at the Petit Trianon, focusing instead on its own high-fashion creations placed against the background of a different feature of the Château de Versailles, the elegant seventeenth-century Bosquet de la Colonnade, which presumably better framed the desired Dior image than the Norman vernacular of the Maison de la Reine.

Dior's sponsorship, although not unconnected, especially when considering the legacy of Christian Dior himself, proves once again the postmodern paradox which this chapter explores ontologically, through the influence of media sources, in fierce competition with heritage narratives seeking authenticity. Nevertheless, Dior's sponsorship, followed by the launch of the Dior Trianon makeup range in Japan and the United States, also embodies the marriage between curatorial and consumerist approaches in representations of heritage and the image of Marie Antoinette. Dior's product, bearing the name Trianon rather than Marie Antoinette, suggests an intended curatorial connection, Dior associating itself not only with the refined image of the queen but also appropriating the heritage space whose restoration this company supports. The commercial motives are of course also present through the choice of countries for the launch, Europe providing fewer customers than Japan or the U.S. for luxury goods associated with Marie Antoinette and her estate. Also, by giving certain nationals priority, such as Lubin did with the New York launch of Black Jade, the suggestion of a niche market flatters prospective consumers.

Finally, it must be stressed here that recently, many other perfume houses have launched their versions of Marie Antoinette's perfume, with some choosing the Trianon associations explicitly in the name (e.g. Maison Lancôme's *Lavandes Trianon*), further attesting to the postmodern uncontrolled multiplication of images connected to Marie Antoinette.

The 'queen of frivolous fashion' image

Despite the refinement with which Marie Antoinette is usually associated, there is yet another image which must be considered: that of the iconic fashion queen. This expresses frivolity, however, rather than refinement, and is thus in contradiction with the exquisite taste and elegance generally attributed to the last Queen of France. The 'Frivolous' image is most frequently encountered in popular culture, but also in some curatorial traditions such as those of fashion museums. This image is partly owed to clichéd representations, and partly an effect persisting from the mid 1770s (Figure 7.7) when Marie Antoinette attempted to gain increased legitimation at the court following the model of Louis XIV (Delpierre 1975; Weber 2006; see also Chrisman-Campbell 2015), who successfully enhanced his royal image through the use of flamboyant fashion.

The image of frivolity came to be associated indirectly with the Petit Trianon's heritage narrative following the 2011 exhibition organised by Château de Versailles with the Galliera Museum of Fashion and held at the Grand Trianon (Saillard et al. 2011). The official press release highlighted the frivolous aspects of eighteenth-century fashion, whilst stressing its free interpretations by the current fashion industry, as showcased in the exhibition. Marie Antoinette was not the sole inspiration for the exhibition's theme, but her image dominated the promotion of the event as well as the fashion creations presented. These creations were identified with her image in many ways and on many levels. For example, the exhibition poster featured Marie Antoinette appearing to wear a contemporary Vivien Westwood creation. Amongst the exhibits was also an Olivier Theyskens/ Rochas dress created for Kirsten Dunst in 2006 for the September *Vogue U.S.* special issue dedicated to Sofia Coppola's *Marie Antoinette* film release. The frivolous fashion queen was also indirectly communicated through details commonly associated with Marie Antoinette's image, such as the infamous necklace

214 *'Ange ou Démon?'*

Figure 7.7 Authentic eighteenth-century hand-coloured engraving of Marie Antoinette from *La Galerie des Modes* (Le Clere 1776)

Courtesy Mark Tramontana

of *L'Affaire du Collier* (see Figure 4.4). At the expense of historical accuracy, a replica of the necklace was used by Dior in the design of an exquisite dress featured in the exhibition catalogue (Figure 7.8). Notably, the dress was exhibited at the Grand Trianon without this representation of the infamous necklace.[8]

Figure 7.8 2007 Christian Dior Haute Couture design using a replica of the notorious necklace that contributed to the fall of the monarchy from calumnies circulated against Marie Antoinette which swayed public opinion

Photo courtesy Guy Marineau

216 *'Ange ou Démon?'*

Figure 7.9 Royalist representation of the moment etched in history as 'J'en appelle à toutes les mères!', which according to some historians was the crowning moment of eternal glory for the queen (Bouillon 1851)

Courtesy Mark Tramontana

The archetypal mother image

One of the episodes which inscribed Marie Antoinette's undisputed royal eloquence and grandeur into the great book of history was the court trial which led to her death sentence (see de Waresquiel 2016). The former queen's poignant appeal to all the mothers present ('J'en appelle à toutes les mères!'; see Figure 7.9) to imagine why, as a mother, she could not debase herself to even answer abominable questions about the alleged sexual abuse of her son, marked the moment when public opinion began to question the French Revolution's ideals. Moreover, this moment strengthened Marie Antoinette's image as the archetypal mother and woman subjected to the violent attack of a chauvinist revolution (Varaut 2006).

Marie Antoinette's role of royal mother, dutifully fulfilled and indeed doubled by devotion to her children (to whom, evidence shows, she dedicated most of her time at the Petit Trianon), is highlighted through the curatorial presentation of the 2008 restoration by exhibiting, for example, the Dauphin's 'goat-drawn carriage' at the entrance of the historic

Figure 7.10 At Petit Trianon, the goat-drawn carriage of the first Dauphin, who died in 1789, having suffered from a degenerative spinal condition

Author collection/2008 photo courtesy Philippe Baudin

house museum (Figure 7.10). Further items specifically related to the mother role are displayed in the upper storeys of the building. The heritage narrative intentionally chose to highlight this important role played by the queen, albeit indirectly conveyed through the striking presence of the carriage placed at the beginning of the ordinary visit route. The layout and particularly the display of the other two floors accessible with guided visits reinforce this image, in contrast to the cinematic narrative images detailed next.

In conclusion, the heritage narrative of the Petit Trianon does not resonate with the clichés of Republican history, due to a largely rehabilitative curatorial tradition at the site. As demonstrated above, through the queen's image of refinement, as well as that of the archetypal mother, both detected in the heritage narrative of the Petit Trianon, an affinity exists with what could be considered a Royalist historiography. The other images detailed in this chapter (the ghost, Cinderella and the frivolous fashion queen) originate in either local lore, history and/or popular culture, and integrate with the heritage narrative in an indirect and unintentional way, as previously analysed.

Cinematic vs. heritage narratives of Marie Antoinette at the Petit Trianon

In this section, the cinematic narrative originating in Sofia Coppola's film *Marie Antoinette* (2006) is assessed against the heritage narrative of the Petit Trianon. Coppola's film was identified by the fieldwork research as the only cinematic/media production bearing influence on the perception of the site among the American and Japanese majority groups. These nationals' perception of the heritage site of the Petit Trianon, as well as the historical character of Marie Antoinette, was explored in Chapter 6. This section establishes the process through which the film narrative came to prevail over the heritage narrative of the site, inducing as a result a certain image of Marie Antoinette.

This section is divided into two parts: the first examines the direct media influence of the film over the perception of the site, and certain film elements used by Château de Versailles management in the construction of the site's image. The second part provides an overview of the film's influence on wider off-site perceptions of Marie Antoinette, with the film considered to be solely a media source rather than a cinematic narrative. In doing so, this section provides a clearer insight into the subliminal influence of the media, testing John Caughey's theory of 'imaginary social worlds', and basing the analysis on the prevalence of the imaginary over reality. Chapter 6 concluded that this prevalence in the context of 'imaginary social worlds' applied to the American and Japanese majority-group visitors at the Petit Trianon.

Coppola's Marie Antoinette *and* Château de Versailles *marketing strategies*

Tom Selwyn (2010) considers that there are two strands of media influences to be considered in the case of tourist attractions; both are analysed in the following two sections. The first is generated by the tourist attraction itself through its own publicity, marketing and other media designed to influence the perception of its visitors. The second is generated independent of the tourist attraction, through media channels which contribute nevertheless to a certain perception of the tourist attraction.

Studies concerning the role of tourist sites (such as museums) in creating media messages (Hooper-Greenhill 1995) reveal that the influence of this type of media is as important as that of popular culture mass media. In the case of the Petit Trianon, however, the media do not play a central role in conveying its curatorial interpretation. Nevertheless, where the Petit Trianon's visitor perceptions are concerned, fieldwork research detected an association of the site with the colour pink. This could be attributed to Coppola's film *Marie Antoinette* (2006).

First and foremost, the process leading to the uncontrolled commodification of Marie Antoinette's historical character, as well as the reinforcement of the image of the sovereign as portrayed in Sofia Coppola's film trailer and advertising campaign (Figure 7.11), were accidental. Merchandise connected

Figure 7.11 *Marie Antoinette* (2006) – film-set images with elaborate confectionery reinforced the cliché 'Let Them Eat Cake!' which in fact Coppola had purposely tried to dispel

© Sony Pictures/courtesy Everett Collection

(even if indirectly) to this image is sold at the Château de Versailles boutiques. Fieldwork research suggested that it was the general merchandising (the presentation of merchandise) which unintentionally sealed a certain commodified image of Marie Antoinette in the perception of the majority groups. It must be stressed that this merchandising was not meant to associate the cultural heritage of the site with the film, but merely to address revenue needs.

In May 2006, two Hollywood films connected to the most visited museums in France (DGE 2016) were launched at the Cannes Film Festival: *The Da Vinci Code* and *Marie Antoinette*. The former, benefitting from having Tom Hanks in the leading male role, and being based on Dan Brown's bestseller novel, relates to the Louvre Museum. This recent popular culture connection between Hollywood and the Louvre seems to have attracted a significant number of visitors to the site (Long & Robinson 2009), and the museum has fully embraced the association, offering the visitor trail 'The Da Vinci Code: Between Fiction and Fact',[9] whilst private tour operators organise 'Da Vinci Code' tours starting from the Pyramid outside the museum. Unlike the Louvre, Château de Versailles does not explicitly associate itself with Sofia Coppola's film production.

Having become an Établissement Public in 1995 (it was previously a national museum, financed by the French State), Château de Versailles has had greater management freedom since, but also considerably increased financial pressures. Considering the revenue needed by Château de Versailles to remain open and function properly, this cannot be taken lightly. It was the need for increased revenue that stimulated, in part, the 2008 Petit Trianon restoration, which was anticipated to increase popularity and visitor numbers at the site. However, the promotion of the Petit Trianon was also seen as part of the solution to the overcrowding of the main Palace by diverting the visitor flow (Baudin pers. comm. 2010).

It must be reiterated that the management of the UNESCO heritage site Château de Versailles is an entirely separate entity from its curatorial department. This analysis focuses on Château de Versailles management actions and their repercussions on the perception of the Petit Trianon site, and not on the heritage interpretation formulated by its curators. Led by contrasting agendas, the two perspectives clash: whilst management actions are meant to increase revenue, the curatorial team is concerned with preserving the site's heritage authenticity values. It is not the aim here, however, to argue against commercial associations of heritage sites with film productions. The dominating postmodern visual culture creates not only the perfect context for such associations but also a demand which needs to be fulfilled (see Beeton 2016; also Agarwal & Shaw 2018). This enables the provision of increased revenue for the sustenance of heritage sites. What is argued against here is the process of commodification based on heritage inauthenticity and historical inaccuracies, which can occur when such associations are not controlled by those in charge of managing the heritage sites. This is supported by the research findings at the Petit Trianon, which conclude the present analysis by demonstrating how the elimination of a single element, the macaron, might have avoided the uncontrolled heritage commodification of the historical character of Marie Antoinette.

Fieldwork research has shown that, for the French, Japanese and American majority groups, the prevailing image of Marie Antoinette is generated by media through nation-specific cultural conditioning,[10] supported to a certain degree by the management's 'Place Making' (Tunbridge & Ashworth 1996; Morgan 2004; Misiura 2006; Huertas Roig et al. 2010; see also Govers & Go 2009). Also, for these groups, the fieldwork research confirmed the prevailing images of Marie Antoinette and the Petit Trianon to be associated with the colour pink.[11] This finding could not be tested on the survey sample of Japanese visitors, so the limitation was compensated for by an internet analysis focused on the image of Marie Antoinette (Maior-Barron 2015b). The results suggest that the colour pink – moreover pink macarons – association applies to Japanese popular culture sources. The Japanese lifestyle magazine *Best Flower Arrangement* (2012) dedicated an article to the Marie Antoinette style, in fact, a faithful copy of Coppola's set prop style with macarons taking centre stage. More importantly, *Vogue Japan* October 2012 featured a special fashion piece inspired by Marie Antoinette. Alongside an exquisite and refined image of a beautiful Marie Antoinette with big, (and mostly pink!) hair, pink Ladurée macarons also took centre stage (Figure 7.12).

Having established that the prevailing images of Marie Antoinette are associated with the colour pink and with pink macarons, the question is, 'Why?'. Sofia Coppola's film was not known first-hand by a majority of respondents,[12] yet their images of both the Petit Trianon and Marie Antoinette were those induced by the film. This major finding of the field research determined that further exploration into a transfer of values occurred within the uncontrolled heritage commodification of the historical character of Marie Antoinette.

In their retail merchandising, Château de Versailles adopted, from Sofia Coppola's *Marie Antoinette*, not only the hyper-reality of the colour pink, running as a theme throughout its boutiques, but also, and more specifically, the Ladurée brand of macarons featured in the film.[13] The connection with Ladurée, whose shop opened in 2009 at the Château de Versailles (Figure 7.13), sealed the bubble-gum pink image of both Marie Antoinette and the Petit Trianon through the 'Marie Antoinette' macarons sold in pink boxes at the Ladurée boutique, located at the exit of the main Palace tour.[14] Since the usual visit route led from this point of exit to the Petit Trianon (based on field observations on how tourists consume the estate and on casual discussions, following the interviewing), the majority groups participating in my 2010–2012 survey had visited the boutique before setting off to the Petit Trianon.[15]

Whilst true that there are other products within the Marie Antoinette 'pink' theme (Figure 7.14) throughout the Château de Versailles boutiques – from pink crayons souvenirs and pink tins of tea[16] to pink luxury merchandise[17] – it is the connection between the macaron and the Republican cliché 'Let Them Eat Cake!' (see Figure 7.15) which has enough impact to commodify Marie Antoinette's image through dissonance and to threaten heritage authenticity.

Figure 7.12 Original photo featured in 'All the Riches a Girl Can Have' – Ymre as Marie Antoinette in *Vogue Japan*, October 2012

Photo Giampaolo Sgura/courtesy *Vogue Japan* with permission of the model

Figure 7.13 Ladurée retail shop at Château de Versailles, opened in 2009
Author photo 2014/courtesy Château de Versailles

Figure 7.14 A pink theme runs throughout the boutique displays related to Marie Antoinette at Château de Versailles
Author photo 2014/courtesy Château de Versailles

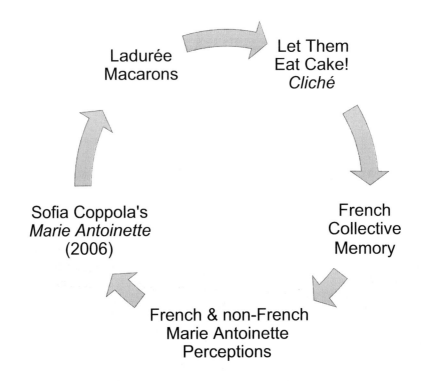

Figure 7.15 The uncontrolled dissonant commodification of Marie Antoinette's historical character based on Hall's (1997) circle of representation theory

Author 2014

In this instance, the dissonance incorporated into heritage commodification builds on John Tunbridge and Gregory Ashworth (1996), whilst authenticity refers to the history criteria by Ashworth and Howard (1999). Ladurée was founded in 1862, having patented the double-deck macarons much later in the 1930s. The macarons featured in Coppola's trailer are thus an anachronism now adopted by the Palace's boutiques. The Ladurée macaron is not only an imported image, reinforcing inauthenticity and historical inaccuracies, but is also responsible for the dissonant commodification of Marie Antoinette's historical character at the Petit Trianon. In regards to dissonant commodification, Tunbridge and Ashworth (1996:22) observe that:

> Much tourism in particular requires the reduction of a rich and complex past to a set of easily recognisable characteristics: the heritage product must be rapidly assimilated into the existing experience, expectations and historical understanding of a visitor with limited local knowledge and quite definite expectations of what this heritage product should contain.
> [Cohen 1979]

'Ange ou Démon?' 225

Given the dissonant heritage of Marie Antoinette, which characteristics should be referred to, and how could these be conveyed? Reality became fiction, and fiction became reality again – a constant, long-established process, clearly translated today into the vast literature written about the last Queen of France. Imagination is the reason fiction prevails over reality at the Petit Trianon. But 'Imagination inspires Imagination' (Augé 1997:98), which equates with an uncontrolled perpetuation of images, further and further distanced from the initial content. Moreover, the blurred boundaries between postmodern culture and consumerism (Urry 2002) complicate the picture even further. When considering that images are at the core of the commodification process and heritage products (from abstract representation to actual mass-made souvenirs), it is easier to understand this uncontrolled perpetuation in the context of dissonant heritage. However, as noted in Chapter 5, the dissonant heritage associated with Marie Antoinette has an 'alchemical' nature which, as this study establishes, renders its correspondent heritage commodification a highly lucrative commercial proposition. By having acquired the status of symbol, Marie Antoinette's historical character can be appropriated comfortably across a wide range of products and by a wide range of consumers, through selectivity and identity negotiation. Moreover, the fashion of 'pink', and of macarons, which Coppola's film instilled in popular culture perceptions of Marie Antoinette, has become an image unto itself, desired and indiscriminately appropriated widely, from the United States to Japan, as shown next.

Returning to the Petit Trianon, the 'pink' expectation which visitors now have, also illustrates Urry's anticipation theory as noted in Chapter 2: media-preformed images play an important role in conditioning the visitors' perception of a site. Moreover, this is a case of Eco's (1986) 'hyper-reality' prevalence over the real in the context of heritage sites perceptions, as the exaggerated visual effects induced initially by Coppola's film launch, and perpetuated by the commodified image based thereon, ultimately determine the visual quality of the real site. The hyper-reality used by Coppola was confirmed by the film director herself (Poirson 2009:238):

> I immediately wanted to bring my vision to the film: offset, colourful, and certainly not historical. I wanted the public to feel right at home in the 18th century, as they had felt in the Japan portrayed in *Lost in Translation*. To achieve this, we had to create an energy and modernity breaking with the cold tone of period drama and historical films. I used pop-rock music to express Marie-Antoinette's distress, flashier colours than in real life, and close-ups of Kirsten Dunst's face, so that viewers could connect with her. Marie-Antoinette had to be a young girl alive. [translation mine]
> [*Le Journal du Dimanche*, 21 May 2006]

Interestingly, the majority of respondents display symptoms of a total inversion of media and reality values – that is to say, media messages are unquestioningly accepted as reality. Only on my prompting did they wonder, though briefly, whether the focus of truth rather lies in the immediate reality presented to

226 'Ange ou Démon?'

them on their visit. A comment by one of the respondents illustrates the above: she was 'not quite sure' but had a 'feeling that during Marie Antoinette's time they didn't yet have sneakers' (F; U.S./MjG; -25; 10/04/2011). This refers to a shot from Coppola's film showing Marie Antoinette's shoe collection, which intentionally included a pair of bubble-gum pink Converse sneakers.

The uncontrolled self-multiplication of images leads to unforeseen effects to be dealt with by the creators of the initial images (Barthes 1972; Baudrillard 1994). In the case of the Petit Trianon and its recent restoration, the clashing agendas of the various authorities in charge of the management and heritage interpretation of the estate led to increased commodification of the image of Marie Antoinette in a completely unplanned direction.[18] As such, despite the aim of the curatorial restoration team to objectively portray this historical character, the commodification incited by Sofia Coppola's film actually strengthened the clichés to which her historical character is commonly associated. The process fully illustrates the circle of representation defined by Hall (1997). Moreover, it is the cliché that actually makes the connection between the French national collective memory representation of Marie Antoinette and the perceptions other nations have (Figure 7.15).

Coppola's Marie Antoinette *as an external media source*

So far, the juxtaposition between the cinematic and the heritage narratives analysed in this study has been examined from the point of view of media images generated by Coppola's film. Although indirectly, these images have had an impact on the perception of the Petit Trianon through the marketing strategies of Château de Versailles.

As noted earlier, external channels which shape tourist perceptions independently from the tourist attractions themselves provide the second thread of investigation for subliminal media influence. Analysing the visual culture of tourism, David Crouch (2010a, 2010b) emphasises that this does not act on a *tabula rasa*, the encounter between the space and the tourist being constructed a priori on a series of components (Crouch & Lübbren 2003).

To discover how this *tabula* is encoded by the media, this section considers Coppola's film to be an external media source rather than a cinematic narrative linked to the Petit Trianon. With media channels working independently in an endless number of ways, this strand of media influence poses complex questions. Given the notoriety of Marie Antoinette, and the conflicting perceptions which her historical character inspires, assessing such independent influence in the case of the Petit Trianon would make the subject of another study.

First, it is helpful to consider a few examples indicative of what the media generally conveys – independently of the site of Château de Versailles – about the image of Marie Antoinette. Hermeneutical analysis (see Data Sets 12 and 15 in Chapter 3; see also Chapter 4) regarding how Marie Antoinette is perceived by various groups (from Republicans to Royalists), revealed that these perceptions correspond with her images in history, ranging from taboo to iconic. It became apparent, for example, that the French press perpetuates

Republican clichés by default when criticising contemporary political figures. Moreover, political inclinations of a publication cannot always predict the manner in which Marie Antoinette's image is portrayed. A relevant example comes from a 2009 *Point de Vue* article (see Figure 7.16) which derogatorily

Figure 7.16 Point de Vue (2009) article negatively likens Carla Bruni, wife of French President Nicolas Sarkozy, to Marie Antoinette

Courtesy Point de Vue

likened Carla Bruni, wife of the French President Nicolas Sarkozy, to Marie Antoinette (see also Allen 2009a, 2009b). Similar comparisons were made in relation to the next First Lady, Valérie Trierweiler (Samuel 2013).

Besides such clichés, internet image analysis focused on individual blogs and sites (see Maior-Barron 2015b) revealed niche perceptions which align with those of the minority groups detected at the Petit Trianon. Naturally, further variations exist. For instance, contemporary gothic artists are fascinated by Marie Antoinette and drawn to the tragedy of her story. Others cherish her Enlightenment artistic contribution to the eighteenth century. In short, individual, as well as group affinities and agendas, draw producers and consumers of images towards various aspects of her history, legends and image.

Returning to our assessment of Coppola's film as an external media source, a first observation is that since the film's release, the media seems to associate Marie Antoinette with the colour pink, and with pink macarons! In support of the postmodern paradox analysed here, the pink colour and pink macarons usually associated with Republican clichés surrounding the queen are assimilated into recent representations of Marie Antoinette in popular culture, although not always consciously or in an intentionally derogatory manner, and at times quite the opposite (Figure 7.17). Representations of

Figure 7.17 Fairy-tale photographer and fantasy costume designer Viona Ielegems (www.viona-ielegems.com) chose the authentic eighteenth-century setting of Castle D'Ursel incorporating the colour pink and macarons for a representation of Marie Antoinette

Photo circa 2011/courtesy the artist

and advertisements associated with Marie Antoinette's character became ever pinker after her visual reinvention by Coppola.

Did Coppola's film have such a considerable impact in the noticeable revival of interest in Marie Antoinette's character? It seems so. After the film's launch in 2006, Marie Antoinette's historical figure was used in advertisements more than ever (see Maior-Barron 2015b). It is also true that Marie Antoinette as an advertising figure is nothing new. In fact, during her reign (Weber 2006; Haru Crowston 2013), she reportedly encouraged her *marchands de modes*, *coiffeur* and *parfumeur* to use her name to entice the custom of the aristocracy and bourgeoisie alike (see Sapori 2010; Autié et al. 2007; de Feydeau 2005, 2011). This attitude – unprecedented for a queen – earned her constant criticism (Sheriff 2003; see also Chrisman-Campbell 2015). Antoine Lilti (2017) also counts Marie Antoinette amongst the first modern celebrities.

In contemporary representations of Marie Antoinette, fashion has also changed, becoming ever more flamboyant and candy-pink in order to fulfil consumer expectations. Through her hyper-real representations, Coppola offered a visual trend for those wishing to associate themselves with this image by emphasising their emancipation from the old-fashioned perceptions of both Marie Antoinette and the eighteenth century.

Marie Antoinette's historical character also seems to have inspired pop stars to reinvent themselves in her image. Such is the case, in their popular culture endeavours, of Katy Perry (*Killer Queen* perfume launch 2012) and Beyoncé (*The Mrs. Carter Show* 2013). Internet analysis of the images of these two pop artists who do not explicitly associate themselves with Marie Antoinette, revealed that the connections are created by internet assimilation of their images by users. In some instances, this assimilation occurs via Madonna's impersonation of the queen, which has become a style in its own right. The circle of representation (Hall 1997) is once more in operation. This also exemplifies the self-perpetuation of images and resulting distortions, the image becoming the content in an endless chain of representations further and further away from their initial object (Barthes 1972) and ultimately, copies without an original (Baudrillard 1994). Fully reflecting the latter, more recently, the pop artist Rihanna was selected as the most illustrative contemporary celebrity to pose as Marie Antoinette in a *CR Fashion Book* (09/2016) whose editor wanted to draw attention to the timeless symbol of controversial womanhood which Marie Antoinette represents. Interestingly, a year later, Rihanna herself chose to launch the 'Fenty x Puma workout range Marie Antoinette 2017', in fact her own style incorporating certain elements from the updated visual reinvention of Marie Antoinette, such as the 'millennial' pink.[19]

Finally, another pop artist well-known for the visually striking performances and ever changing representational identities, Lady Gaga also chose Marie Antoinette as inspiration for one of her albums, which won the 2010 Brit Awards (Figure 7.18). Lady Gaga has a different approach to

230 *'Ange ou Démon?'*

Figure 7.18 Lady Gaga's 'Marie Antoinette' at the Brit Awards 2010
Photoshot/courtesy Everett Collection

representing the queen, she nevertheless bases her representations on stereotypical images, merging and assimilating them with other popular myths. Thus, Lady Gaga merged the Cinderella and ghost images of Marie Antoinette into one. Lady Gaga is aware that the message is what counts (Van Meter 2012). Confirming the uncontrolled perpetuation of images further distanced from their initial message, the artist mixed and merged a tailored image of Marie Antoinette for an ever-fascinated audience. Lady Gaga, in her minimal white-lace body piece, which was revealed from under her 'ghost' cloak when she was handed her Brit Awards trophy, soon became an exhibition piece herself at Madam Tussaud's in Hollywood – the copy becoming an original in popular culture consumption.

Coppola's film seems to have influenced the fashion industry which, despite having consistently cherished Marie Antoinette, has now (post film launch) embraced representations of the queen's style in the vein of Coppola's vision. It must be stressed here that, on Coppola's part, this effect was intended (and worked towards), as she is part of a new generation of film directors whose work spans several areas of popular culture – amongst which fashion and music, along with film – and whose success is not measured any longer exclusively through box-office figures (for details on Coppola's own endeavours to commodify her artistic work, see Cook 2014). Coppola's leading actress in the role of Marie Antoinette, Kirsten Dunst, has also had her own impact on the image of Marie Antoinette in the fashion industry. Recently, leading fashion houses have copied her style – again, it was not Marie Antoinette's, but Coppola's, designed for Dunst. This further illustrates the theories referenced above. In fact, Marie Antoinette is the subject of frequent fashion shoots, still inspired by Annie Leibovitz's film-launch *Vogue U.S.* September 2006 issue.[20] In the same way the publicity trailer of the film conveyed a message contrasting with the film's actual narrative, as previously noted, the costumes used for the publicity fashion shots were not the same as those featured in the film.[21] Instead, these are updated versions meant to bring Marie Antoinette's image into contemporaneity. The situation signals the effects of the collapse of time, further suggesting that postmodernity fantasises not only about what the past *would have been like* but also imagines what the past *would look like today*. Artist Christine Comyn, best captures this updated Marie Antoinette through a large scale triptych (Figure 7.19), described by Comyn (pers. comm. 2017) as: 'the most flamboyant Marie-Antoinette of my series [. . .] representing the cliché image we all have of this young queen.'

Figure 7.19 Marie Antoinette and her contemporary cliché image in art, from the series *La douceur de l'Ignorance* (2010) by Christine Comyn (courtesy the artist); an exhibition catalogue for this series (Comyn 2010) was sold at the Petit Trianon boutique

232 'Ange ou Démon?'

Private individual or independent shops (Etsy) and blogs (see Data Set 15; Chapter 3) have also embraced Coppola's new Marie Antoinette style, from fashion and body art to wedding venues, cakes and catering suggestions. Many choose to link into the 'cake' film image at the Petit Trianon (Figure 4.10), moreover the bubble-gum pink is the visual common denominator for Marie Antoinette's image in these instances, as well as for internet art and photography in general. The shots range, however, from abstract to borderline pornographic, different identities assimilating differently the same material. Arjun Appadurai's (1996) apt observations theoretically underpin how contemporary media (and the globalisation to which media sources contribute) can create new consumption patterns of images. Furthermore, Appadurai shows how images are borrowed today through contemporary media in ways often surprising to their originators.

It also seems that Coppola's film, by bringing Marie Antoinette's character to the fore in the media, inadvertently generated an invitation or a challenge to other cineastes, actors and performers to further explore Marie Antoinette's historical character. Amongst a series of television programs and documentaries on Marie Antoinette in 2011, the first European Marie Antoinette ballet premiered in France at the Royal Opera of Château de Versailles (see Maior-Barron 2015b).

Possibly meant as a cinematic reply to Coppola's *'rose bonbon'* film (Charbon 2012), another production centred on Marie Antoinette was released in France in 2012 under the direction of Benoît Jacquot and starring top model and Hollywood actress Diane Kruger (Figure 4.6), the first film embodiment of a Sapphic Marie Antoinette. The fictional plot does not claim historical authenticity. Based on Chantal Thomas' novel *Les Adieux à la Reine*, Jacquot's film came to be in a conflict of interests with its literary source: whilst Thomas tried to rehabilitate the queen through her fictitious plot, Jacquot reinforced calumnies of infidelity, this time by attributing to Marie Antoinette a female lover, Duchesse de Polignac, rather than the usual favourite of the cineastes, Count von Fersen. This particular example brings two insights. Firstly, artistic license can work against messages intended for the public, as Jacquot only wanted to add psychological depth to the plot which he treated in an anthropological manner in order to analyse eighteenth-century life at the Court of Versailles. Secondly, Kruger felt a personal resonance and identification with Marie Antoinette, whose role she was convinced she had to play because of similarities of age, nationality and her mother's name, Maria Theresa (see Charbon 2012). Thus, the actress became the perfect candidate for a faithful copy. Diane Kruger, however, discerned these similarities on a personal, rather than an acting-skills level. This is further proof of the blurred boundaries between fiction and reality, and of the image prevailing over the content. In this instance, the psychological character of Marie Antoinette was ignored not only by the film director but also by his star actress, both overly focused on personal, identity-driven quests.

While examples such as the above abound, this study does not include an exhaustive analysis of the identities which have appropriated, or have been influenced by, Coppola's Marie Antoinette. Instead, this section focuses on finding a pattern to better understand visitor perceptions of Marie Antoinette at the Petit Trianon. At first glance, the above findings could suggest an impossibility of finding patterns of perception, as postmodern culture is 'increasingly centred around visual experience in which subjects become lost in a blizzard of signs' (Edensor 2005:105). However, Selwyn (2010) believes that the hallucinating media images connected to sites of visit are in fact juggled by tourists through their own 'self' images. Cultural identity plays an important role in representation (Hall & du Gay 2003) which it helps construct, as demonstrated by the examples above. Equally, the process of interpellation through which images address the viewer as 'you' (Sturken & Cartwright 2009) ensures a homogenisation of the viewers' perception of certain messages intended by various agencies (including advertising agencies). Moreover, the collapse of time, coupled with enhanced technology – both particular traits of postmodernity – favour the fulfilment of individual or group fantasies, fulfilment based on the imaginary social interaction noted by Caughey (1984). Long and Robinson (2009) also contribute a valuable review of the complex relationship between tourism, popular culture and the media which highlights the role played by imagination.

What brings together all the above examples, issues and most of the array of different appropriations of the same original is the evaporation of the content of the myth (Barthes 1972) and the refuge of this myth in cinema (Baudrillard 1994), a milieu in which it found its content. Needless to note, such content is a copy and not the original. Richard Voase (2010), studying the cinema and the eroding of historicity, provides an even more unsettling suggestion: not only that Baudrillard's theory is tested and proved to be valid, but moreover the copy comes to be preferred even when the original is not absent. The author gives the example of a Gwyneth Paltrow lookalike, praised for being more Gwyneth than Gwyneth herself.

Considering that media and the tourist imagination are converging cultures (Crouch et al. 2005), images are given absolute primacy in these circumstances and become the source of negotiable identities, accelerated in heritage by the nature of the concept itself, constantly under the manipulation by different agencies (Howard 2003). This analysis concludes by associating the majority of the emerging images of Marie Antoinette with clichés (which provided data for the coding and theming of the research; see Chapter 3). During the field survey, it became clear that the clichés themselves indicated the respondent's level of knowledge related to the historical character of Marie Antoinette. This enabled the construction of a tier-structured pattern of beliefs directly associated with different clichés (Figure 7.20). It was art history knowledge, however, which dispelled clichés, not historical knowledge. Art history knowledge is defined here through criteria gained from the fieldwork research at the Petit Trianon and the characteristics of

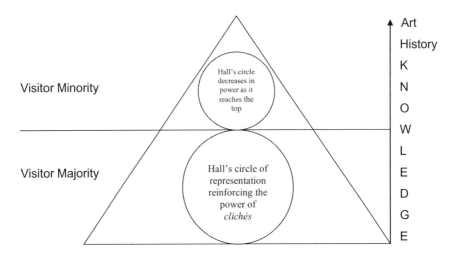

Figure 7.20 A tiered model of cliché reproduction through Hall's (1997) circle of representation amongst the majority and the minority groups of the survey at Petit Trianon, 2010–2012

Author 2014

the minority groups (see Chapter 3 and 6). The minority groups which differentiated themselves from the majority through various criteria also proved to favour particular stereotypical images, although these were not as consistently present within the consciousness of the group. Consequently, the more common the cliché and its image, the less knowledge of Marie Antoinette's historical character, along with a wider spread (or greater prevalence) among the public to accept the cliché as unquestionable truth. Hall's circle of representation illustrates the reinforcement of clichés and/or stereotypes within each group, also influencing group perception.

The majority of the public visiting the Petit Trianon since 2006, after the release of Sofia Coppola's film, form the base of the tier structure, represented by an isosceles triangle. This group proved difficult to interview, as its members were interested in the site mainly at a visual level and visited mostly out of curiosity (as revealed through interviews). Moreover, the respondents were disappointed by the difference between media portrayal and the reality experienced during their visit.

Clichés such as 'lavish', 'luxurious' and 'decadent' clearly show the direct influence of the Republican historical portrayal of Marie Antoinette, perhaps via Sofia Coppola's narrative or through the influence of other types of media (see French majority groups). The colour pink, so often mentioned due to the director's special effects, and unintentionally strengthened by the Château de Versailles' commodification process, proved the strong influence that cinematic images can subliminally induce. In this case, the transmission occurred through the commodification of this image by the managerial team of the site itself, as explained earlier. With the base tier representing the majority of visitors, and the top tier bringing together the other minority groups of the survey, could it be concluded that for most visitors at the Petit Trianon the cinematic narrative prevails over the heritage narrative? The answer to this question takes shape through two statements gathered by field research at the Petit Trianon. Firstly, a reply illustrative of the general disregard for historical truth among majority-group visitors when asked to grade the closeness of Sofia Coppola's film narrative to historic reality:

> *I don't know and I don't care, even if it wasn't true is much better than reality, we need to dream on, otherwise what have we got left?*
> (F; G2; 36–59; 17/04/2011)

Secondly, the Petit Trianon head curator Jérémie Benoît (pers. comm. 2010a) explained the reason for which the curatorial team withholds more specific information about the true character of Marie Antoinette from the heritage interpretation given at the Petit Trianon:

> *What can we do? We have to let the public perceive what it wants, scandal, immorality, etc., as that is what interests them; if we were to tell them the truth outright, they would ask for their money back!*

Architectural vs. heritage narratives of the Petit Trianon

When juxtaposing the eighteenth-century architectural narrative of the Petit Trianon with its contemporary heritage narrative, two aspects come to the fore: the representational and the non-representational traits intrinsic to any landscape (Crouch 2010b). In this instance, the architectural narrative is examined in the light of an eighteenth-century neoclassic and picturesque landscape. Despite controversy on the relationship between representational and non-representational attributes associated to art and cultural landscapes– some theorists completely separate them, whereas others consider them fluid and merging into one another (see Crouch 2010b) – here these are identified separately so as to better structure the analysis of the juxtaposition between the two narratives. Consequently, the representational attributes are further associated with cultural resonance (Crouch 2010b), and the non-representational attributes – regarding functionality of the landscape's elements – with cultural feelings (Schorch 2014). Whereas the cultural resonance applies in the case of the minority groups interviewed, which base their perception mainly on art-history knowledge, the cultural feelings evoked by the Petit Trianon refer to members of the majority groups, some of whose opinions of Marie Antoinette improved after their visit. This was a key finding of the field research.[22]

The representational qualities of the architectural narrative, embodied by the initial messages encrypted in Marie Antoinette's creation at the Petit Trianon, translate today into a symbolic interpretation of the site. The symbology of the Petit Trianon would relate to art and architecture experts in particular, including the curatorial and heritage architectural teams who worked on its restoration. The heritage narrative (as constructed by the specialist team) and the architectural narrative, are in a nearly perfect alignment with each other. Those familiar with this symbology are in the minority, and these representational details bear little relevance to the majority of visitors. Yet something must be 'speaking' to those who, despite their lack of expert knowledge, register an improvement of their opinion on Marie Antoinette. The answer lies in the non-representational aspects of the landscape of the Petit Trianon, providing a physical encounter for its visitors. This analysis does not use the phenomenological approach of tourist perception (Cohen 1979) since this tends to counteract rather than to complement the appropriation of heritage places through the mediated gaze (Urry 1995; Malpas 2008). Furthermore, the analysis is not based on the concept of 'senses of place and senses of time' (see Ashworth & Graham 2005), which relates to heritage sites and their staged, manipulated making.

Instead, in order to analyse the proposed juxtaposition and to detect the reasons some non-expert visitors change their opinion of Marie Antoinette once they experienced at first hand the Petit Trianon, as home to Marie Antoinette – a 'place of memory' (see Nora 1984a) – this section employs Bourdieu's (1977) theory of 'cultural anthropology'. In Bourdieu's definition, the human habitat as *habitus* is essential in defining cultures in general, and peoples' existences in particular. The details of habitat construction are able to tell a full story about the particularities and traits of the humans inhabiting it. This is the principle taken into consideration when referring to the symbolic dimension of the Petit Trianon. Furthermore, the following analysis selectively draws on the anthropological manner of interpreting, through symbology, certain material features and museographic objects, connecting both with transcendental archetypes (Bernea et al. 1999; Bodenstein 2007) and daily practices (de Certeau 1984; Christensen 2011).

The underlying link between these theories is the suggestion that nostalgia is the key factor in the alteration of visitor perceptions of a site or museum (Gregory & Witcomb 2007; for other recent contributions and discussions on the subject of nostalgia, see also Chapter 6), whether present prior to the visit or unexpectedly flaring up during it, as was the case with some of the majority-group visitors. Consequently, this section abides by the anthropological principle that a place can speak in many ways if one could only understand the symbology behind appearances or emotionally connect with the place. To this end, I will sketch an itinerary of the Petit Trianon and briefly record the 'voices' of the house, the garden, their many features, Le Petit Théâtre and, finally, the Queen's Hamlet.

As a building, the Petit Trianon is striking for its neoclassical proportions, symmetry, and simplicity (Figure 7.21). Upon entering, the few personal belongings of the queen invite nostalgic reflection, despite a nostalgic atmosphere not being a deliberate feature of the heritage narrative of the Petit Trianon (Benoît pers. comm. 2014). Amongst these belongings are her childhood paintings by Weikert depicting her in a theatre play with her siblings. The queen's upbringing at the Austrian Court of her mother Maria Theresa must have contrasted strongly with the rigid etiquette she was suddenly plunged into as a young bride, arriving at Versailles aged 14.

The little carriage belonging to her eldest son, also contributes to a nostalgic first impression, as one is reminded that Marie Antoinette was also a mother, and that this place was shared with her family. In fact, when one takes the guided visit of the upper floors, the idea of the place as a family home becomes clearer, in stark contrast to the den of iniquity from Republican clichés. The main bedrooms upstairs belonged to the king (the most sumptuous bedroom in the house, although Louis XVI had never spent the night there), his sister Madame Élisabeth (Figure 7.22) who became Marie Antoinette's closest friend, the royal children and their nannies. In fact, the

Figure 7.21 Petit Trianon, the cube that inspired countless copies because of its beguiling simplicity

Author photo 2011/courtesy Château de Versailles

Figure 7.22 Madame Élisabeth's room at Petit Trianon – the King's sister became the usual companion of Marie Antoinette and the royal children at Petit Trianon, and she later shared their life in prison and even death by guillotine, being executed shortly after Marie Antoinette

Author photo 2011/courtesy Château de Versailles

place was known to host female company and generally the life was focused around the royal children's daily activities.

The *champêtre* (countryside) feel of the entire estate, is enforced through the extensive constructed views from each window. Documents relating to the building works confirm what is suggested by these views: that the queen must have been a keen gardener and that she loved nature. It was in fact this garden that preoccupied her the most, the work of transformation starting the moment she entered into possession of the Petit Trianon in 1774 (Baulez 1977). Whilst the improvements to the house were merely done at the level of furnishings (Figure 7.23) and a few aesthetic and functional architectural details (Lablaude 2006a, 2006b), the garden underwent a complete make-over, becoming one of the most accomplished examples of the eighteenth-century French Jardin Anglais (see de Lille 1782; Carmontelle 1779; Le Rouge 1776–1779; de Ligne 1781/1922; Lablaude 2010).

The design of the garden embellished by its *fabriques*, such as the Temple of Love (Figure 7.24), the Belvedere (Figure 7.25), the Grotto, and the

Figure 7.23 In the queen's bedroom at Petit Trianon, until funds could be allocated for refurbishment in 1787–1788 (Hans 2007), the previous occupants' furniture was kept; the bed exhibited today is a period substitute

Author photo 2011/courtesy Château de Versailles

Figure 7.24 Le Temple de L'Amour (1781) at Petit Trianon, designed by Richard Mique, features a replica of Bouchardon's statue – L'Amour making a bow for himself out of Hercule's club

Author photo 2011/ courtesy Château de Versailles

Figure 7.25 Le Belvédère (1781) at Petit Trianon, the music garden kiosk
Author collection/2013 photo courtesy Philippe Baudin

Hamlet (Figure 7.26), has been considered the most refined expression of the new art of gardening, in tune with nature's feel rather than against it. The publications of the time praised the exquisite manner in which the context of the Petit Trianon had been accomplished. In one of his famous poems, L'Abbé de Lille (1782:15) regarded the garden and its owner as one:

> Alike her auguste and young deity,
> Trianon joins grace and majesty
> For her it is adorned, and it is adorned through her.
>   [translation mine]

Today, despite the loss of most of the trees planted at the time (Lablaude 2010), the garden retains its charm and air of a peaceful retreat. Contrary to the common beliefs about the Petit Trianon being mainly a retreat for the selfish pleasure of its owner, the estate had a protocol (Arizzoli-Clémentel 2008b) and educational function. Diplomatic receptions for European royalty and aristocracy were held at the Petit Trianon and Marie Antoinette was in charge of organising these protocol events, which were known for the exquisite attention to detail and highly welcoming attitude of the queen.

Figure 7.26 Le Hameau de la Reine (1783–1786), designed by Richard Mique on the Norman rural architecture model, was Marie Antoinette's choice over the Roman classical or exotic themes more typical to the eighteenth-century English Garden. Le Moulin, pictured here, like other buildings of the Hamlet, was a functional mill in Marie Antoinette's time

Author photo 2012/courtesy Château de Versailles

Marie Antoinette insisted on serving her guests along with her servants, an unprecedented attitude for a queen of France. Furthermore, apart from being used by Marie Antoinette for her own children, who spent most of their time with the queen when at the Petit Trianon, the farm of Le Hameau (Figure 7.27) was part of a greater project undertaken by Louis XVI primarily at his experimental farm at Rambouillet, in order to improve the ovine and cattle stock of the country (Saule & Arminjon 2010). Also, de Nolhac's (1906:383) curatorial expertise reveals that 'the Hamlet was occupied by several rustic households, who lived on the spot and carried on real farming operations. The queen established there the families of a farmer, a gardener, and a keeper.'

The Queen's Theatre (Bellessort 1933; Lablaude 2002) is a clear reminder of Marie Antoinette's artistic nature (Du Bled 1891), thus perfectly completing her anthropological portrait. Taking a guided tour, one would be astounded to learn that this delightful mini copy of the Versailles Opera

Figure 7.27 The picturesque La Ferme is enhanced by its functional role as an educational farm since 1993, with livestock looked after by Fondation Assistance aux Animaux, an inspired interpretive and managerial decision

Author photo 2011/courtesy Château de Versailles

was not built in gilded marble but far cheaper materials, such as pressed cardboard. The effect was nevertheless exquisite, at only a fraction of the cost. The theatre performances were accessible to a close circle of friends, as normally the queen would not be allowed to act in public: another example of Marie Antoinette's emancipation of the role of the queen of France by aligning it with female liberation, favoured by Enlightenment ideals (Mauzi 1960, 2008). Unfortunately, as Thomas (2011a) aptly observes, due to other members of the court such as Madame de Pompadour previously known to perform in theatre plays, Marie Antoinette came to be blamed for acting as a royal mistress rather than a queen. Furthermore, the queen's affinity for roles of servants and peasants, with whom she tried to identify within the limits of her imposed noble status, led to even further criticism, as well as the unfounded however ubiquitous 'shepherdess' image. Partly attributed to Marie Antoinette on the basis of the existence of the Farm at the Petit Trianon, the shepherdess image is clarified by curator de Nolhac (1906:384):

> No credence must be given to the numerous legends that are rife on the subject of the Hamlet, such as that which shows us the royal family

'*Ange ou Démon?*' 243

playing at shepherds and shepherdesses, and assuming various rustic characters in order to live in the Hamlet. This is a ridiculous fable. Marie Antoinette never played at keeping farm, and the king never disguised himself as a miller; but it is a sufficiently piquant sight to see them interesting themselves so intimately in agricultural labour, and seeking recreation and rest amid these rustic surroundings.

In 1785 Marie Antoinette's last performance at Le Petit Théâtre (Figure 7.28) was in the role of Rosine in Beaumarchais' play *Le Barbier de Séville* (Desjardins 1885). Despite fierce criticism for imprudence on the part of the queen for playing such an anti-Royalist theatre role, the event confirms the participation which the aristocracy and royalty manifested towards the Enlightened ideas of the time, which they did not regard as a threat but, on the contrary, worthy of support.

Lastly, the Queen's Hamlet shows very clearly that the eighteenth-century ideals of a return to nature and its associated values are not as pressing for contemporary society. In fact, a closer look reveals that the idyllic Norman village has lost its charm ever since the queen left it. None of the later inhabitants gave it the same care and importance. Consulted archive documents attest to the March 1809 demolition of one of the most important buildings

Figure 7.28 Le Petit Théâtre de la Reine (1780) at Petit Trianon and its rustic scene décor today

Author photo 2014/courtesy Château de Versailles

Figure 7.29 Foundations of the former La Laiterie de Préparation, highlighting a nostalgic absence at Petit Trianon

Author photo 2011/courtesy Château de Versailles

of Le Hameau, a structure reserved for dairy production (Figure 7.29). Since Napoléon's sister (Pauline de Borghese), and second wife (Marie Louise), to whom he successively offered the Petit Trianon, were not interested in farming activities, it was demolished rather than repaired after the 1809 hurricane. By contrast, the non-rustic parts were repaired. Even the restorations undertaken since the Petit Trianon became a museum in 1867 have always focused on other parts of the estate, prioritised over the vernacular-inspired architecture which became secondary to the royal dimension that defines the Petit Trianon today. Nevertheless, Le Hameau underwent extensive archaeological research (Heitzmann 2000, 2001, 2002, 2003, 2005, 2006), as did other parts of the estate (Heitzmann 2009; see also 1988, 2004, 2007a, 2007b).

Finally, the anthropological tour would not be complete without moving closer to La Maison de la Reine (Figure 7.30), the most important vernacular structure of the Queen's Hamlet. Its derelict interiors are not opened to the public, yet once one approaches it, despite the beautifully tended surrounding gardens, there is a sense of abandonment and even mystery. Whilst some visitors linger, trying to peer through the clouded glass, others pass by

Figure 7.30 Moving closer to La Maison de la Reine at Petit Trianon transforms the picture from idyllic to nostalgic
Author photo 2011/courtesy Château de Versailles

hurriedly. A bench underneath the porch provides a perfect place for resting and admiring the lake and the Tour of Marlborough, if one wishes to do so. All this will change, once the restoration of La Maison de la Reine, sponsored by the House of Dior, is completed. Due to a lack of documents and a focus on authenticity of the material and of the concept, the expert team had to decide that the period which will be interpreted here is that of Empress Marie Louise (which by contrast benefits of ample documentation and even visible traces of material furnishings; Baudin pers. comm. 2014). It remains to be seen how visitors will respond to a restoration focusing on a period other than that of Marie Antoinette.

'Ange ou Démon?'

This chapter investigated the emerging images of Marie Antoinette, following the juxtaposition of the historical, cinematic and architectural narratives against the heritage narrative of the site of the Petit Trianon. The application of theories relevant to the analysis of this chapter revealed that the origins

Figure 7.31 All in a shop window! The entire conflated repertoire of Marie Antoinette images, Bergdorf Goodman Christmas 2008

Photo/courtesy Anne Corrons

and development of these images in time is often difficult to disentangle. The collective imaginary has mixed and merged their initial contents, thus creating an alchemy from which resulted the crystallised images reviewed throughout the chapter.

A particular trait noticeable in the contemporary augmentation of this alchemical process is the time-space compression which David Harvey (1989 cited in Urry 1995:177) sees as defining postmodernity. Furthermore, through Harvey's theory, Urry (1995) explains the perpetuation and reinforcement of signs (Chapter 2), on which this chapter draws in order to formulate a conclusion. These signs, understood as the ever-renewed signifiers according to Barthes' (1972) theory and fieldwork research at the Petit Trianon, are shown to prevail among the majority groups of visitors. When further combining these insights with Hall's circle of representation, it becomes evident why Marie Antoinette's images came to replace the content ever since her reign. It is also evident that, should Marie Antoinette somehow make herself present today, the army of her copies would overcome the real person in the opinions of the public, who take these images as truth. Not only would they be disappointed but, as Voase (2010) has discovered, the copies would definitely be 'more like' Marie Antoinette than Marie Antoinette herself.

Consequently, the analysis of the present chapter affords insights into the reasons behind the contemporary appropriation, by most visitors at the Petit Trianon, of the (post)modern myth 'Marie Antoinette' through the commodification of this historical character. Thus is generated an endless chain of representations increasingly distanced from the absent reality that inspired them in the first place, or an endless series of copies without an original (Baudrillard 1994). With culture and commerciality merging, it becomes irrelevant whether Marie Antoinette is an *'Ange ou Démon'*, as the chapter set out to discover. Marie Antoinette is what every visitor/consumer wants her to be. Furthermore, contradictory images of Marie Antoinette, held to be authentic by various parties (see Figure 7.31) and once freely appropriated according to different agendas, allow postmodernity to revel in the entire conflated-image repertoire, once upon a time divided between two extremes: the martyr queen (*Ange*) and the frivolous queen (*Démon*).

Notes

1 The theory of Baudrillard is used extensively in this chapter to explain the process of postmodern images whose meanings escaped the authority of their creators. In the investigation of the postmodern social and ideological production of meaning, Linda Hutcheon (2002:6–7) considers that from 'this perspective what we call "culture" is seen as the *effect* of representations, not their source.' Hutcheon sees Baudrillard as one of the main theorists whose work aids in understanding the postmodern production and reproduction of signs.

2 It is acknowledged that visual culture analyses need to be detached from language analyses, given that they operate within different parameters (Balm & Holcomb 2003; Heywood et al. 2012). Schirato and Webb (2010) provide a

248   'Ange ou Démon?'

counterargument for these views by successfully linking visual analyses of art spaces to their intrinsic narratives. In this chapter, a mixture of the two types of analysis is used in order to bring together the messages of the four major narratives of the book and the images they generate.

3   My personal communication with various other security staff detected three others who believed in the existence of Marie Antoinette's ghost, despite the absence of personal sightings. They all preferred to remain anonymous.
4   Twelve respondents alluded to a belief in the possible existence of Marie Antoinette's ghost. The respondents (10F; 2M) were part of French Group 2 (5F); residents of the Yvelines; Group 3 (4F; 2M); American Minority Group (1F).
5   In fact, Count von Fersen was already introduced at Court a few months previously. He also attended several of Marie Antoinette's balls given at Versailles (see Fersen 1902). It is true, however, that at the ball in Paris, quasi-incognito in a mask, Marie Antoinette was able to address Fersen in an unofficial status. Once her identity was discovered, she was obliged to leave.
6   Nevertheless, the shoe, called 'à la Saint-Huberty', was part of the recent exhibition on Marie Antoinette organised in Japan by the Château de Versailles (see Firmin & Rondot 2016).
7   Hasquenoph (2008) criticised Château de Versailles for consumerist motives, despite the limited edition sale of the product and the charitable nature of the campaign.
8   See the exhibition leaflet, www.chateauversailles.fr/resources/pdf/en/actualites/leaflet_18.pdf.
9   See www.louvre.fr/en/routes/da-vinci-code.
10 Contemporary media did not prove to influence the French majority-group visitors, but the collective memory which is at the source of their perceptions of Marie Antoinette is textually mediated by official historical narratives (see Wertsch 2002; also Nora 2013) which, as this study has proven, primarily draw on eighteenth-century revolutionary media sources on Marie Antoinette.
11 When answering Question VII (see Appendix A.2) American respondents belonging to the majority group made an unprompted association with the colour pink for the Petit Trianon and Marie Antoinette. Therefore, after the first week of interviewing, I tested this association on all the subsequent respondents by prompting an answer on a colour association of the site and also Marie Antoinette, when asking Question IX. The French Groups 1 and 2, when asked the aforementioned questions (see Appendix A.1), associated the site and the owner, first and foremost, with a luxurious and frivolous note, which when prompted to associate with a colour, resulted in the *rose bonbon* (candy pink) analysed by Chapter 7. The French and American minority groups, by contrast, associated it with muted pastel colours, especially green and/or blue/blue-grey.
12 With the exception of the Japanese majority group for whom this was confirmed.
13 The pink theme coupled with macarons in relation to merchandise associated with Marie Antoinette seems to have been appropriated also by other places connected to Marie Antoinette, directly and indirectly. This is based on observation at other French heritage sites – Palais de Compiègne and Château de Fontainebleau as of October 2014 – but also at the Huntington Library boutique in California as of October 2017. The latter draws a connection with Marie Antoinette through the former owner, Arabella Huntington, and her admiration for Marie Antoinette and the royal family. The Petit Trianon was a source of inspiration for the building of the Huntington Mansion and its gardens.
14 In March 2013, Ladurée also launched a limited edition range of blue Marie Antoinette macarons. During my last field research trip to Versailles in August 2014, I learnt that Ladurée's original pink macaron Marie Antoinette had become a special edition item released only for Christmas, Valentine's Day and Easter (see

'Ange ou Démon?' 249

Data Set 14; Chapter 3). Pink Ladurée Marie Antoinette hampers were available for delivery in the Paris area, through the internet, as of September 2017.

15 It must be noted that a counterpoint to the 'pink' commodification is found in a recent heritage-authenticity driven range, focusing on refinement, including reproductions of Marie Antoinette's porcelain ware, which she used at the Petit Trianon (the Sèvres design of *'perles et barbeaux'*, see Figure 3.2). Furthermore, in an attempt to control the intangible heritage of the site, as of 2012 Château de Versailles legally trademarked the Château de Versailles brand including 'Marie-Antoinette' (see *Perspective* 2014).
16 In August 2014, pink boxes of Ladurée tea, bearing the name *Thé Marie Antoinette* were sold in the Château de Versailles Ladurée shop and other Paris branches, including Charles de Gaulle Airport where they are best sellers in comparison with other flavours (Anon. 3,4,5; pers. comm. 2014).
17 There is an updated version of Marie Antoinette-style gloves (see 'gloves Prestige', priced at 3900 euros as of August 2014), also incorporating in the design a contemporary candy-pink colour.
18 However, this is not an isolated case with theory (Cameron & Mengler 2013) acknowledging the fluidity of imagery and materiality connected to heritage sites; see Conclusion.
19 See www.cosmopolitan.com/style-beauty/fashion/g9213210/rihanna-fenty-puma-shop/
20 Annie Leibovitz revisited the 2006 fashion shoots (see *Vogue U.S.* May 2014), replacing the actors from Coppola's film with top models, another example of postmodern multiplication of images. Her 2006 *Vogue* September cover was selected to be amongst the 16 iconic covers from the past 125 years of *Vogue* magazine (see *Vogue U.S.* September 2017).
21 Milena Canonero's designs for the film's costumes were awarded an Oscar for 'Best Historical Drama Costumes'.
22 The visit to the Petit Trianon further improved (already positive) opinions of Marie Antoinette in the case of the majority of Japanese respondents, and unexplainably improved opinions (although the improvement was incremental) in the case of approximately a third of the members of French Group 2 and of the American majority group.

Conclusion

Through its analyses, this book contributes to dispelling some of modernity's most persistent founding myths, myths which continue to distort the destinies of historical figures – lives long ago sacrificed at the altar of political illusions and power. While the key findings of this study relate to the field of heritage and tourist consumption studies and support the idea of a visual prevalence within tourist consumption forms, individually and collectively they also reflect the manipulation of the past during the modern nationalist era. Further, the findings demonstrate the importance of art history education in forming a more objective grasp of history. Finally, they attest to the powerful postmodern influence of images in creating prejudice and distorted understandings of knowledge that many heritage-tourism consumers unknowingly carry with them.

Within this study, the historical figure in question is Marie Antoinette. Pivotal to the analysis in detecting the distortions of her character were visitor perceptions detected at the Petit Trianon, perceptions analysed against the contemporary heritage interpretation of the site. Specifically, the following findings from the study explain the 'alchemical dissonant heritage' commodification (termed coined here) of Marie Antoinette's historical character at the Petit Trianon, and moreover reveal an ongoing process through which distorted images of this controversial monarch persist in contemporary visitor perceptions at the Petit Trianon.

The analysis contained in this book was specially designed as a formula suitable to the unique combination of extreme animosity and fascination which the historical character of Marie Antoinette exerts, even more so within political and cultural contexts where a reversal of fiction and reality became the norm. Fabricated 'truths' that suddenly gain popularity, featuring dubious pedigrees that remain unquestioned by the majority, completely reflect how easily collective perceptions can be manipulated when there is not a clear record of the past kept by an established authority. (This fact is more relevant than ever in today's political and cultural context.) The conveyors as well as the receivers seem to have been successfully deceived, by the nationalist nineteenth century, into believing that they belong to a clear historical past, whilst postmodernity ensures this illusion to be as successfully perpetuated by consumer culture and its unethical commodification of the past. This formula is a reflective model for a far wider context than the commodification of Marie Antoinette's historical figure at the Petit Trianon, as it applies universally to complex postmodern visitor perceptions of historical figures that bear legendary connotations and whose true character cannot be readily grasped.

Research implications for the heritage field

This study highlighted the prevalence today of visual culture defined by complex modes of interaction with the contemporary (and sometimes palpable) reality. Harnessing these modes becomes imperative when conveying past messages of realities from long ago. In this sense, Affleck and Kvan (2008) propose a paradigm which links heritage institutions to the virtual communities of potential and actual visitors. From the perspective of heritage interpretation specifically, the present study revealed the complexity of multiple and often clashing narratives connected to heritage sites, a complexity which has particular relevance to the aim of 'Translation' upheld by New Museology. This complexity indicates a clear need for museum professionals to take into consideration all of these narratives, which eventually could bring reconciliation. In this respect, when considering the interpretation in museums of the dissonant heritage represented by the Highland Clearances, Laurence Gouriévidis (2010:97–98) remarks that empathy and identification are 'forceful rhetorical tools often relying on sensory aspects which cannot fail to induce a strong emotional response in the viewer, not least when dramatic scenes are reconstructed with [. . .] elaborate stage-management.' When such scenographic and rhetorical devices are not the chosen paradigm of interpretation, such as in the case of the Petit Trianon (see Chapter 5), recent research (Savenije & de Bruijn 2017) suggests that emotional engagement could enhance historical understanding of museum and heritage interpretations through historical empathy, which can be created by confronting the viewer with multiple narratives placed in their historical context. Based on a test involving school children, this psychology and cultural heritage research brings evidence for the possibility of creating historical empathy even in the case of sensitive case studies (e.g. slavery, the Holocaust). Similarly, research on emotion networking in heritage making (Rana et al. 2017) proposes that conflicting feelings emerged from dissonant heritage could be overcome through group discussions on the meaning of various objects belonging to former adversaries in past conflicts. Yet it remains to be seen whether historical understanding and/or reconciliation could truly be gained in any such ways by visitors of all ages and of different cultural, and particularly political, backgrounds when the multiple narratives to be presented pertain to actors and agencies involved in opposing sides of such highly controversial historical events such as the French Revolution.

From the perspective of visitor perceptions, the present study revealed the paramount importance which popular culture plays in contemporaneity, with cinematic narratives taking central stage. The study's key findings (see below) highlight a cautionary tale against traps set for heritage authenticity through these narratives. Research highlighting the fluidity of imagery and materiality connected to heritage sites (Cameron & Mengler 2013) proposes a potential remedial paradigm: 'authorising the unauthorised' discourses, with the unauthorised originating in visitor comments on social media in this case. Indeed, systematic detection and control over the sources generating inauthenticity and misconceptions at heritage sites could be the answer. However, when considering the collapsed barriers between imagery and materiality, as Jean Baudrillard (1994) observes, postmodern perceptions have become uncontrollable, as the distinction between reality and images vanished due to the signifier and signified having imploded upon each other, unhinging the original meaning. Recent research (Favero 2014b) revisited Baudrillard's theory on simulacra and simulation together with other visual culture theories, notably that of Gilles Deleuze (1994), which conversely to Baudrillard and akin to deconstructivist views, claims that reality and images should not be considered as a dichotomy and that, moreover, the original should not hold ascendency over the copy. The noted anthropological study (Favero 2014b) contributes insights into the 'liquid visions' generated by digital images (considered in their life cycle from producers to consumers), suggesting, albeit based on a restricted sample, that despite the blurred boundaries between images and reality today, there is no confusion to speak of, as the users are in control of the images which they consume. Furthermore, instead of avoiding the intensive use of visual devices in the context of contemporary art and popular culture, for instance, a new way of conveying and receiving messages – and meanings – could be developed (Favero 2014a) by 'learning to look beyond the frame'. In line with this, recent research (Jones et al. 2017) even suggests that heritage authenticity could be gaining from the use of images and replicas found in 3-D reconstructions of artefacts, as the importance and the aura of the original are, in fact, reinforced. Whilst it is undeniable that understanding the nature and relationships of digital images with reality and materiality would contribute to an eventual harnessing of these images and of their meanings, returning to the research at the Petit Trianon and its implications to the heritage field, from the perspective of visual predominance and its traps to heritage authenticity, this study reconfirms Baudrillard's views that the original has been overshadowed by its copies and the original meaning is (at least temporarily) lost.

Limitations and future research

The research included the design of an Authenticity model in Chapter 2 when examining the range of sites spanning heritage authenticity aimed at tourist consumption (see Table 2.1). Found on a self-generating cycle between authenticity and commodification of heritage, the classification employed as distinction criteria a heritage authenticity definition found in Ashworth and Howard (1999). This was done in conjunction with a literature review concerning the heritage industry, supported by fieldwork evidence and observations concerning the perception of authenticity by the majority of the visitors at the Petit Trianon. However, these observations took into account the perspective of Urry's 'tourist romantic gaze' as one of the main factors responsible for the commodification of contemporary heritage sites. Throughout the book, this model offered the sole perspective on authenticity and was validated by research analysis. Other forms of authenticity were only incidentally reviewed by Chapter 2 and Chapter 6 (when analysing the Japanese visitor perceptions of heritage sites), which could be construed as a possible limitation of this study. Furthermore, the comparison of the architectural and heritage narratives in Chapter 7 deliberately excluded phenomenological perceptions of tourist spaces (Cohen 1972, 1979), as these would have been at odds with the visual appropriation of space on the basis of which the research was conceived. Given, however, that research evidence suggests nostalgia to be a possible reason for the improvement of opinions on Marie Antoinette occurring whilst visiting the Petit Trianon, further research on this understudied factor of heritage perception could benefit from testing visitor authenticity forms.

A prime candidate would be existential authenticity because of its intimate connection with nostalgia, established through emotional links. Furthermore, this type of authenticity has been highlighted by heritage studies (Steiner & Reisinger 2006:300) as potentially useful 'as a framework for practical market research and for planning activities based on tourists' aspirations to existential authenticity.' Such further research could provide alternatives for practitioners in what concerns the Petit Trianon's heritage interpretation. Chapter 5 explained the limitations which curators currently face in the interpretation of the Petit Trianon. Whilst the nature of the dissonant heritage would continue to be an obstacle to this interpretation, elements that appeal to existential authenticity could enhance the intrinsic nostalgic feel of the Petit Trianon without clashing with either the curatorial authenticity principles or the dominant Republican discourse. Elements of a successful heritage interpretation in connection to existential authenticity, related incidentally to the eighteenth-century and Marie Antoinette, are put together by the International Perfume Museum in Grasse.[1] Personal objects related to olfactory senses are found in Marie Antoinette's *nécessaire de voyage* for the Varennes flight (see Chapters 4 and 6), currently on display at this museum. Such elements appealing to the existential authenticity of a visit could perhaps be employed at the Petit Trianon through an evocation of period scents (even in the absence of the actual objects).

Elements appealing to existential authenticity by engaging senses other than the visual – olfactory, auditory and tactile sensations – have been successfully employed in alternative heritage interpretations of heritage sites.

Historic Royal Palaces (a charity looking after royal residences in the United Kingdom, amongst which are Hampton Court and the Tower of London), are continually testing various techniques for evoking the past, thereby avoiding reliance on single methods and favouring instead 'multiple triggers for the visitor's experience' (Barnes pers. comm. 2014).

Consequently, a planned comparative future research on the heritage interpretation and visitor perceptions of the royal sites at Versailles and Hampton Court will expand the findings of the present study through analyses facilitated by theories pertaining to visual culture and emotional culture in connection to phenomenology. Starting from the premise that landscape allows for a greater scope in 'authenticity' of visitor perceptions than built heritage, and is able to reflect more accurately the initial message of the creators (Lefebvre 1991; Berque 2013), this future project looks at the garden landscapes of the two royal heritage sites. In line with the aforementioned heritage and tourist sources, different types of authenticity will be tested: heritage authenticity sourced in the intrinsic qualities of the viewed object versus tourist authenticity sourced in the phenomenological experience of the viewer. An important indicator for this part of the analysis will be identified in the difference between the initial functions of the two garden landscapes. Whereas the representational qualities of the seventeenth-century garden landscape aimed to impress through monumentality, by contrast, eighteenth-century gardens were designed to lead to an intimate interaction between the viewer and the viewed. In fact, the 'unformed' characteristics of the picturesque landscapes were meant to invite a phenomenological interaction (see Macarthur 2007).

The future project will give equal importance to tourist anticipation mediated by visual culture and tourist motivations analysed through emotional culture theories that emphasise the importance of the place in visit fulfilment. Tourist anticipation will be measured through the effect of media and other forms of visual imagery contributing to the blur of boundaries between art history periods and genres in contemporary popular culture. Tourist anticipation and motivations in relation to authenticity and modes of experiencing heritage sites are central to these sites' interpretation and management, making this future research relevant to a major aim of New Museology: translating art history and history for wider audiences.

Key findings

Returning to the present study, the Conclusion is completed by a review of the research key findings. Historical and cinematic narratives, relevant to contemporary visitor perceptions of Marie Antoinette at the Petit Trianon, contributed important insights. By cross-referencing Republican and Royalist sources detected in both academia and popular culture media channels, the study defined the encoding of Marie Antoinette's image imprinted into the French collective memory and its perception by other nationals. Essential findings converged into the following insight: all of the authors contributing to the encoding of Marie Antoinette's contemporary perception are conditioned by their own cultural and political background (with the hermeneutical circle as well as the principle of prejudice fully explaining these limitations) to the extent that reality becomes fiction becomes reality. Moreover, all of the aforementioned analyses evidenced that there are as many 'Marie Antoinettes' as there are academic or popular culture authors on the subject. The important finding of this part of the analysis relates to dissonant heritage, since the cultural heritage of the French Revolution and Marie Antoinette are in antithetical positions. Best described through the zero-sum trait of heritages, the dissonance between these two exponents of French cultural heritage is at the root of the persisting negative perception of Marie Antoinette for the majority, especially because the French Revolution is the founding myth of contemporary French society as well as the perceived birthplace of modernity's human rights.

By contrast, the analysis of the architectural and heritage narratives revealed a generally consistent positive perception of Marie Antoinette among a minority of art and art history experts, including that of the curatorial and architect expert team in charge of interpreting the Petit Trianon. The different understanding that art education essentially generates extends to the perceptions held by the survey's minority groups at the Petit Trianon. Research evidence suggests that the most effective antidote to distortion, and the greatest aid in achieving an objective portrayal of this controversial historical character, lies in art history knowledge. When supported by literary and artistic sensibility, it was a degree of knowledge of art history which proved the common thread among respondents who were consistently able to dismantle the many myths surrounding Marie Antoinette, bringing instead to the fore her contribution to art history as well as to the history of the queens of France. This contribution lies in a feminine emancipation of the political and cultural roles assigned to her, which she challenged until the end: first by fulfilling and surpassing her duties as an Imperial daughter and gage for one of the most important European peace treaties of the eighteenth century; then in her roles as a royal spouse and mother, an Enlightenment monarch and a fervent supporter of the arts and artists; and last though not least, as an eighteenth-century symbol of the Christian monarchic tradition. Regarding her Catholic faith, I want to stress that this offers far greater insight into the religious and moral conditioning that Marie Antoinette received than most historians are willing to consider seriously. Moreover, it is this particular difference of faith, between historical characters of the past and contemporary secularised society, which favours the perpetuation of many historical misinterpretations. Nevertheless, even within the Catholic milieu, opinions on Marie Antoinette are strongly divided.

Interpreted according to the hermeneutical paradigm, the aforementioned narratives, in conjunction with fieldwork research findings of the survey conducted at the Petit Trianon over 15 months, revealed the predominance of Republican perceptions of Marie Antoinette, generated either directly by a political agenda or indirectly, through clichés circulated by historical, literary or popular media channels. Accordingly, the perception of the French majority groups was conditioned by the national collective memory, whilst within the perception of the American and the Japanese majority groups, the cinematic narrative prevailed over others. However, not only do French visitor perceptions equate artificial personal memories derived from the national collective memory, but other, non-French, contemporary visitor perceptions could also take on the value of such 'memories', a concept coined here as 'imaginary social memories'. The process was explained in light of Caughey's (1984) 'imaginary social worlds' theory. It was also revealed that, as opposed to the survey's French and American majority groups at the Petit Trianon, with few exceptions, the Japanese majority group has a positive image of Marie Antoinette. This is because the cinematic narratives which influenced their perceptions have underlining positive tones due to their authors' agendas (female emancipation in the case of Riyoko Ikeda, and troubled young womanhood in the case of Sofia Coppola).

However, the research also detected that Coppola's *Marie Antoinette* was the cause for the uncontrolled commodification of Marie Antoinette's historical character, mainly through the candy-pink, hyper-reality of the film, and the featured abundance of Ladurée macarons. Ladurée opened its boutique at Château de Versailles in 2009. Unexpectedly, the influence of these elements over visitor perceptions was not directly generated by the film's narrative but by its promotional trailer – benefitting, as a rule, from a far wider audience than the film itself – which played on the powerful effect of various images to increase viewing rates. Further, for commercial reasons, the message conveyed by the promotional trailer was developed in stark contrast to that of the film director's overall vision. In the light of evidence provided by the visitor perceptions survey at the Petit Trianon, the commodification of Marie Antoinette's historical character through Ladurée macarons revealed a psychological and subliminal 'appropriation' of the Petit Trianon and Marie Antoinette, through media images. The colour 'pink', and the indirect associations that visitors at the Petit Trianon made with Coppola's image of the Petit Trianon and Marie Antoinette (generated and 'franchised' in popular culture by the visual narrative of her film, as even visitors unfamiliar with Coppola's film 'bought into' this association), was reinforced through the macarons available at the Château de Versailles.

Yet in the case of the Marie Antoinette, another important finding sheds further light on the perception and appropriation of her historical character by different identities. The very nature of the dissonant heritage associated with Marie Antoinette, which this study coined as 'alchemical', explains how Marie Antoinette, by having acquired the status of symbol, can be comfortably appropriated through selectivity and identity negotiation. What to some signals sophistication, to others shouts 'frivolity', such connotative meanings allowing for the 'alchemical dissonant heritage' commodification of Marie Antoinette to establish a highly lucrative commercial proposition.

Conclusion 257

The last key finding signalled by the research, lies in evidence that a visit to the Petit Trianon further improved (already positive) opinions of Marie Antoinette in the case of the majority of Japanese respondents and unexplainably improved opinions (although the improvement was incremental) in the case of approximately a third of the members of French Group 2 and of the American majority group. The consistently positive opinion of the minority groups was further reinforced by the visit. This study suggests nostalgia to be the reason. Moreover, the 'place of memory' (Nora 1984a) which is the Petit Trianon as home to Marie Antoinette, could be a generator not only of 'histories', as theory suggests, but also of 'memories' which themselves are generators of a different understanding of the historical character of Marie Antoinette, a subject for future study. Furthermore, Art, and the feelings that it evokes, could perhaps be a better conveyor of past truths, when authentic history sources have been compromised. After all, 'We are all descendants of Parsifal and Walt Disney' (Augé 1997:100), prone to evading reality in favour of the imaginary, but also essentially on a quest towards the truth, even if occasional detours from it suggest the contrary.

In conclusion, the gained insights through this study attest to Marie Antoinette having transcended her political, social and cultural dimensions, and

Figure 8.1 Nostalgic 'Places of Memory' for that which is lost – Marie Antoinette at Petit Trianon

Author photo 2010/courtesy Château de Versailles

having acquired the status of symbol, whether fiercely criticised or highly admired. The extreme variations found in the perception of her historical character reinforce the polyvalent value of the symbol thus comfortably appropriated by a wide variety of identities. Yet between the hate/animosity of the majority and the love/adulation of a minority, the last Queen of France remains deeply misunderstood. The Petit Trianon, recently restored, assists in the more objective assessment of clichés and myths, 'speaking' for its former owner's true identity, and, in its uncontested nostalgic appeal, it seems certain that it will continue to do so.

Note

1   The very nature of a perfume museum appeals to the olfactory senses, therefore relating to existential authenticity. The next-door villa acquired by the museum for its 2008 expansion has become host to a vintage dress collection, boasting among its exhibits a genuine eighteenth-century unused roll of fabric. Under the dim light meant to protect the fabrics from fading, already enveloped by the seductive scents of the tour of the museum, one experiences a perception completely different from the usual visual consumption (observations made during my visit to the International Perfume Museum in Grasse, 26 January 2009).

Appendices
Questionnaires

Appendix A.1
Semi-structured questionnaire for French nationals completed by the interviewer – French-language version also applied to other nationals

English translation

[For questions I-XVIII, see A.2]

XIX. Are you proud to have amongst the French cultural heritage, Domaine de Versailles?

    ☐ Yes, please specify: . . .
    ☐ No, please specify: . . .
    ☐ Indifferent

XX. What is your nationality?

    ☐ French
    ☐ Other (please specify): . . .

XXI. With what other cultures have you got affinities? (Please specify all that apply):

XXII. Do you speak a foreign language (different than your native language)?

    ☐ Yes, please specify:
    ☐ No

XXIII. Do you often socialise with people of different nationalities than your own?

    ☐ Yes, please specify:
        ☐ Professional setting
        ☐ Leisure, hobbies
        ☐ Travel
        ☐ Other(s), please specify: . . .
    ☐ No

XXIV. When you are travelling, do you usually visit the cultural heritage sites of the city, region, or country you are visiting?

- ☐ Yes
- ☐ No

XXV. Age

- ☐ under 25 years old   ☐ 26 to 35 years old
- ☐ 36 to 59 years old   ☐ over 60 years old

XXVI. Occupation

- ☐ Student (please specify if your subject is connected to art history or history): . . .
- ☐ Employee (please specify if your activity is connected to art history or history): . . .
- ☐ Civil servant/State employee (please specify if your activity is connected to art history or history): . . .
- ☐ Retired (please specify if your activity was connected to art history or history): . . .
- ☐ Other (please specify): . . .

Thank you for your participation in this survey, which is part of a doctoral study on Marie Antoinette and the Petit Trianon.

Denise Maior-Barron,
Plymouth University, UK

Appendix A.2

Semi-structured questionnaire for American nationals completed by the interviewer – English-language version also applied to other nationals

I. Have you visited or intend to visit the Palace of Versailles?

- ☐ Yes:
  - ☐ Yes, I visited it already, before coming here
  - ☐ Yes, I will visit it later in the day
- ☐ No, why?
  - ☐ No, I came specially for visiting the Petit Trianon
  - ☐ No, . . .

II. Is this your first visit at Petit Trianon?

- ☐ Yes
- ☐ No, when:
  - ☐ I visited before the 2008 restoration
  - ☐ I visited after the 2008
- ☐ What do you think of the refurbishment?
- ☐ What do you think of the museum interpretation?

III. What parts of the Petit Trianon have you visited?

- ☐ The main House
- ☐ The Gardens
- ☐ The Queen's Hamlet
- ☐ The Queen's Theatre

IV. What is the reason of your visit to the Petit Trianon?

- ☐ It is part of the Estate of Versailles
- ☐ As I have never visited it before
- ☐ I love the Petit Trianon
- ☐ I am an admirer of Marie Antoinette
- ☐ I wanted to see if the place lived up to its reputation/out of curiosity
- ☐ I saw it in a film, cartoon, internet, etc. and wanted to visit it (specify please). . .
- ☐ I am interested in the architecture of the place
- ☐ I am interested in the design of the Gardens
- ☐ I am interested in the vernacular architecture of the Queen's Hamlet
- ☐ Other: . . .

V. How did you hear about Marie Antoinette for the first time?

- ☐ At school
- ☐ From history books/publications
- ☐ From novels
- ☐ Through Media, please specify:
  - ☐ Internet
  - ☐ Cinema
  - ☐ TV
  - ☐ Radio
  - ☐ Journals
  - ☐ Other: . . .

VI. Did you know, prior to your visit, that the place was linked to Marie Antoinette?

- ☐ Yes
- ☐ No

VII. What was your image of the place before visiting?

VIII. What is your impression now, after visiting?

IX. What was your opinion about Marie Antoinette before visiting?

X. What is your opinion about her now, after the visit?

XI. Do you feel that you found out anything new by visiting?

- ☐ Yes, please specify . . . .
- ☐ No

XII. Did you know that there were other famous women who inhabited the Petit Trianon?

- ☐ Yes, please specify . . .
- ☐ No

XIII. Which is your favourite part of Marie Antoinette's Estate?

- ☐ The main House
- ☐ The Gardens
- ☐ The Queen's Hamlet
- ☐ The Queen's Theatre

XIV. Have you visited or intend to visit the Grand Trianon?

- ☐ Yes:
  - ☐ Yes, I visited it already, before coming here.
  - ☐ Yes, I will visit it later in the day.
- ☐ No, why?
  - ☐ No, I came specially for visiting the Petit Trianon.
  - ☐ No, . . .

XV. Which is your favourite part of the Palace of Versailles' Estate?

- ☐ Versailles Palace
- ☐ The Park of Versailles Palace

- ☐ *The Estate of Marie-Antoinette* (Petit Trianon)
- ☐ The Grand Trianon

XVI. How long did it take to visit Petit Trianon?
XVII. Have you watched the documentaries presented on the ground floor?
XVIII. Did you know there are another two floors (the entresol/mezzanine and the attic) that could be visited by booking a guided tour?
XIX. What is your nationality?
XX. Are you on holiday in France?

- ☐ Yes
- ☐ No
- ☐ Other

XXI. What other historical sites have you visited/do you intend to visit during your stay?
XXII. Your age group:

- ☐ – 25
- ☐ 26–35
- ☐ 36–59
- ☐ 60 +

XXIII. What is your occupation?

- ☐ Student (please specify if your subject is related to art history or history)
- ☐ Employed (please specify if your profession is related to art history or history)
- ☐ Retired (please specify if your past profession was related to art history or history)
- ☐ Other

Thank you for your participation in this survey, which is part of a doctoral study on Marie Antoinette and the Petit Trianon.

Denise Maior-Barron,
Plymouth University, UK

Appendix A.3
Multiple-choice questionnaire for Japanese nationals – designed in French, translated into Japanese for on-site self-completion by Japanese participants

English translation

1. Have you already visited, or do you intend to visit the Palace of Versailles?

    ☐ Yes:
    - ☐ Yes, I have already visited it prior to this visit
    - ☐ Yes, I will visit it next

    ☐ No, why?
    - ☐ No, I have only come to visit Petit Trianon
    - ☐ No, I have only come to visit Petit Trianon and Grand Trianon
    - ☐ No, I have only come to visit Petit Trianon and the Park of Versailles Palace
    - ☐ No, I have come to visit Petit Trianon, Grand Trianon and the Park of Versailles Palace

2. Have you visited Petit Trianon prior to today?

    ☐ Yes
    - ☐ I have visited it before the 2008 restoration.
    - ☐ I have visited it after the 2008 restoration.

    ☐ No

3. Which areas of the Petit Trianon Estate have you visited?

    - ☐ Petit Trianon (The main House)
    - ☐ The Gardens
    - ☐ The Queen's Hamlet
    - ☐ The Queen's Theatre

4. What is the reason which enticed you to visit Petit Trianon?
   (please tick all options applicable to your case)

    - ☐ Because it is part of the Palace of Versailles' Estate
    - ☐ Because I hadn't visited it before

Appendices 267

- ☐ Because I love the Petit Trianon
- ☐ Because I am passionate about Marie Antoinette
- ☐ Because I have read the manga *Rose of Versailles*
- ☐ Because I have seen the anime *Lady Oscar*
- ☐ Because I have seen the film *Lady Oscar* by Jacques Demy (1979)
- ☐ Because I have seen the film *Marie Antoinette* by W. S. Van Dyke (1938)
- ☐ Because I have seen the film *Marie Antoinette* by Jean Delannoy (1956)
- ☐ Because I have seen the film *Marie Antoinette* by Sofia Coppola (2006)
- ☐ To see if the reality of it matched the image I had in my mind
- ☐ Out of curiosity
- ☐ For the 18th century architecture
- ☐ For the English Garden
- ☐ For the Queen's Hamlet
- ☐ Other: . . .

5. **When did you first hear about Marie Antoinette?**

   - ☐ Through the media, specify:
     - ☐ TV
     - ☐ *Lady Oscar* anime (TMS 1979–1980)
     - ☐ Other: . . .
     - ☐ Internet
     - ☐ Cinema
     - ☐ the film *Marie Antoinette* by Sofia Coppola (2006)
     - ☐ Other: . . .
     - ☐ Radio
     - ☐ Periodicals
     - ☐ the manga *Rose of Versailles* (1972)
     - ☐ Other: . . .
     - ☐ Other: . . .
   - ☐ At school
   - ☐ From history books
   - ☐ From novels

6. **Did you know before your arrival on site that Petit Trianon was connected to Marie Antoinette?**

   - ☐ Yes
   - ☐ No

7. **What image did you have of the site before the visit?**

   - ☐ A place of beauty and grandeur, like Versailles Palace
   - ☐ A beautiful place, but much more modest than Versailles Palace

268 *Appendices*

8. **What is your current impression?**
   (please tick all applicable options)

   ☐ It is just as I had imagined
   ☐ It is much smaller than I had imagined
   ☐ It is much more modest than I had imagined
   ☐ It does not correspond with the image that I had

9. **What was your impression of Marie Antoinette before visiting Petit Trianon?**
   (please tick all applicable options)

   ☐ An evil young queen, spoiled, capricious and spendthrift, who deserved her tragic fate
   ☐ A stupid young queen, spoiled, capricious and spendthrift, who nevertheless did not deserve her tragic fate
   ☐ A young queen who did not have the opportunity of knowing the poor living conditions of her contemporary French people, being thus a victim of the violence of the French Revolution
   ☐ A beautiful queen with sophisticated taste and artistic refinement
   ☐ A queen who loved the rural and far more simple and natural feel of Petit Trianon to the weighing etiquette of the Palace of Versailles
   ☐ A good queen with a generous character, who loved nature, children, simplicity and genuineness in people as well as things
   ☐ The Queen par excellence, who shall remain forever in collective memory for her courage and the majestic way she stood up to her tragic fate

10. **What is your current opinion of her?**

    ☐ The same as the one I had before the visit
    ☐ Opposite to the one I had before the visit
    ☐ Better than the one I had before visiting Petit Trianon
    ☐ Worse than the one I had before visiting Petit Trianon

11. **Do you have the impression that you have discovered something new during your visit to Petit Trianon?**

    ☐ Yes (please tick all applicable options):
      ☐ The collections of art objects and furniture
      ☐ The history of the place
      ☐ More information about the life of the queen
      ☐ The existence of other famous women who resided at Petit Trianon
      ☐ The architecture of the place and other parts of the Estate
      ☐ The gardens, with their variety of architectural structures

☐ The Queen's Hamlet
☐ Other: . . .
☐ No

12. **Did you know that other famous women resided at Petit Trianon?**

    ☐ Yes, specify (you can tick several options):
       ☐ Mme de Pompadour
       ☐ Mme du Barry
       ☐ Pauline de Borghese
       ☐ Marie Louise
       ☐ The Duchess of Orléans
       ☐ Empress Eugénie
    ☐ No

13. **Do you also intend to visit the house of Lady Oscar?**

    ☐ Yes
    ☐ No, why?
       ☐ No, I have come to visit only the Petit Trianon
       ☐ No, because it no longer exists
       ☐ No, because it has never existed, just like Lady Oscar

14. **Which is your favourite area of the *Estate of Marie-Antoinette*?**

    ☐ Petit Trianon
    ☐ The gardens
    ☐ The Queen's Hamlet
    ☐ The Queen's Theatre

15. **Do you intend to visit the Grand Trianon?**

    ☐ **Yes:**
       ☐ Yes, I have already visited it before coming here.
       ☐ Yes, I will visit it next.
    ☐ **No, why?**
       ☐ No, I have come to visit only Petit Trianon
       ☐ No, I have come to visit Petit Trianon and the Versailles Palace
       ☐ No, I have come to visit Petit Trianon and the Park of Versailles Palace
       ☐ No, I have come to visit Petit Trianon, the Versailles Palace and the Park of Versailles Palace

16. **Which is your favourite part of the Palace of Versailles' Estate?**

    ☐ Versailles Palace
    ☐ The Park of Versailles Palace
    ☐ *The Estate of Marie-Antoinette* (The Petit Trianon)
    ☐ The Grand Trianon

17. How long did it take to visit Petit Trianon?

    ☐ Less than 30 minutes
    ☐ Approximately 45 minutes
    ☐ Approximately 1 hour
    ☐ Approximately 1 hour and a half
    ☐ Approximately 2 hours
    ☐ More than 2 hours

18. Did you watch the documentaries presented on the ground floor?

    ☐ Yes
    ☐ No

19. Did you know there are another two floors (the entresol/mezzanine and the attic) that could be visited by booking a guided tour? (you may ask for booking details at the reception)

    ☐ Yes
    ☐ No

20. What is your nationality?

    ☐ Japanese
    ☐ Other (please specify): . . .

21. Are you on holiday in France?

    ☐ Yes:
        ☐ for 2 days
        ☐ for 3 days
        ☐ for 4 days
        ☐ for 5 days
        ☐ for 6 days
        ☐ for 7 days
        ☐ for more than a week
    ☐ No

22. Did you visit or do you intend to visit other tourist attractions during your holiday in France?

    ☐ Yes:
        ☐ The Louvre
        ☐ Other art museums
        ☐ Other history museums
        ☐ Other historical palaces/castles in the vicinity of Paris
        ☐ Paris and its tourist attractions
        ☐ Other tourist destinations in France
    ☐ No

23. Have you ever visited or do you intend to visit in the future other places connected to Marie Antoinette?

    ☐ Yes:
        ☐ The Schönbrunn Palace in Austria
        ☐ The Conciergerie in Paris
        ☐ Others
    ☐ No

24. Age

    ☐ under 25 years old   ☐ 26 to 35 years old
    ☐ 36 to 59 years old   ☐ over 60 years old

25. Occupation

    ☐ Student (please specify if your subject is connected to art history or history):

        ☐ Yes   ☐ No

    ☐ Employee (please specify if your activity is connected to art history or history):

        ☐ Yes   ☐ No

    ☐ Civil servant/State employee (please specify if your activity is connected to art history or history):

        ☐ Yes   ☐ No

    ☐ Retired (please specify if your activity was connected to art history or history):

        ☐ Yes   ☐ No

    ☐ Other (please specify): . . .

Thank you for your participation in this survey, which is part of a doctoral study on Marie Antoinette and the Petit Trianon.

Denise Maior-Barron,
Plymouth University, UK

Appendix A.4
Semi-structured anonymous questionnaire for the Petit Trianon security personnel (self-completed)

English translation

I. *For how long have you been working at Petit Trianon?*

II. *Is this your first position at Petit Trianon? If not, could you please specify what other positions you have previously held?*

III. *In what capacity are you employed?*

- ☐ Full-time (tenure) contract state employee
- ☐ Temporary employee
- ☐ Replacement/part-time employee

IV. *What are the reasons which enticed you to seek work at Petit Trianon?*

V. *Where did you first hear about Marie Antoinette?*

- ☐ At school
- ☐ In books, or history books (please specify):
- ☐ Through the media (please specify):
  - ☐ TV
  - ☐ Internet
  - ☐ Cinema
  - ☐ Radio
  - ☐ Periodicals
  - ☐ Other: . . .

Note: On the last page of the questionnaire you can find a list of films on either the French Revolution, or the life of Marie Antoinette. Please tick which films you have seen, and your opinion on their historical accuracy, on a scale of 1 to 5 (1 being the closest to historical truth, and 5 the furthest).

VI. *Did you know, before taking employment here, that Petit Trianon was connected to Marie Antoinette?*

- ☐ Yes
- ☐ No

VII. *What was your impression of the place before becoming acquainted with it through your work?*
VIII. *What is your current impression of the place?*
IX. *What was your impression of Marie Antoinette before coming to work at Petit Trianon?*
X. *What is your current impression of her?*
XI. *Have you discovered anything new or special during your employment at Petit Trianon?*
XII. *Do you have anything out of the ordinary to recount regarding Petit Trianon?*
XIII. *Please recount the most striking anecdote/s that you know, involving tourists at Petit Trianon.*
XIV. *What are the most interesting questions asked by the tourists?*
XV. *What are the most frequent questions asked by the tourists?*
XVI. *If you have worked at Petit Trianon before the 2008 restoration, have you noticed a change in the number, origin and interest manifested by tourists after this event? (Please specify)*
XVII. *According to your direct observations, which are the main nationalities visiting Petit Trianon? Could you rank them in decreasing order, starting with the one you estimate to be most numerous?*

   1. . . .
   2. . . . .
   3. . . . .
   4. . . . .
   5. . . . .
   6. . . . .
   7. . . . .

XVIII. *In your opinion, is there a connection between the increasing numbers of visitors at Petit Trianon since 2006, and Sofia Coppola's film Marie Antoinette?*

   ☐ Yes
   ☐ No
   ☐ Other, please specify: . . .

XIX. *What do you think of the restoration? Do you find the place more appealing in its new presentation?*
XX. *Do you have the impression that Petit Trianon is:*

   ☐ The home of Marie Antoinette
   ☐ A museum dedicated to her
   ☐ Both
   ☐ Other, please specify: . . .

274 *Appendices*

XXI. *In your opinion, is the contemporary Petit Trianon similar to what it was during the time of Marie Antoinette?*

- Yes
- No
- Other, please specify: . . .

XXII. *Are you aware of other famous women who may have resided at Petit Trianon?*

- Yes, please specify: . . .
- No

XXIII. *Which is your favourite part of the Estate of Marie-Antoinette?*

- Petit Trianon
- The Gardens
- The Queen's Hamlet
- The Queen's Theatre

XXIV. *Which is your favourite part of the Palace of Versailles' Estate?*

- Versailles Palace
- The Park of Versailles Palace
- *The Estate of Marie-Antoinette* (The Petit Trianon)
- The Grand Trianon

XXV. *Are you pleased to be working on a historical site of international renown?*

XXVI. *Are you proud to count the Palace of Versailles Estate among the French cultural heritage?*

- Yes, please specify:
- No, please specify:
- Indifferent

XXVII. *What is your nationality?*

- French
- Other, please specify:

XXVIII. *What other culture/s do you feel you have an affinity with?*

XXIX. *Do you speak a foreign language (different than your native language)?*

- Yes, please specify:
  - English
  - Italian
  - German
  - Spanish
  - French
  - Other/s: . . .
- No

XXX. Do you often socialise with people of different nationalities than your own?

- ☐ Yes, please specify:
  - ☐ Professional setting
  - ☐ Leisure, hobbies
  - ☐ Travel
  - ☐ Other(s), please specify: . . .
- ☐ No

XXXI. When you are travelling, do you usually visit the cultural heritage sites of the city, region, or country you are visiting?

- ☐ Yes
- ☐ No

XXXII. Age

- ☐ under 25 years old   ☐ 26 to 35 years old
- ☐ 36 to 59 years old   ☐ over 60 years old

XXXIII. Sex

☐ F ☐ M

XXXIV. Level of education

- ☐ Collège (secondary school, up to 16 years old)
- ☐ Lycée (sixth form, 16 to 18 years old)
  - ☐ Baccalaureate
  - ☐ Baccalaureate PLUS
- ☐ University (please specify your subject)
  - ☐ DEUG (university degree awarded after 2 years of undergraduate study)
  - ☐ Bachelor's degree
  - ☐ Master's degree
- ☐ PhD
- ☐ Other

Thank you for your participation in this survey, which is part of a doctoral study on Marie Antoinette and the Petit Trianon.

Denise Maior-Barron,
Plymouth University, UK

Appendix A.5
Film list used for the survey (* denotes official English film titles, according to IMDb)

1. *Lady Oscar* by Jacques Demy (1979)
2. *Si Versailles m'était conté [Royal Affairs in Versailles*]* by Sacha Guitry (1954)
3. *Madame Du Barry* by Christian-Jaque (1954)
4. *L'Affaire du collier de la reine [Queen's Necklace*]* by Marcel L'Herbier (1946)
5. *La Révolution Française [The French Revolution*]* by Robert Enrico (1989)
6. *La Marseillaise* by Jean Renoir (1938)
7. *Danton* by Andrzej Wajda (1983)
8. *Liberté, égalité, choucroute [Freedom, equality, sauerkraut]* by Jean Yanne (1985)
9. *Jefferson à Paris [Jefferson in Paris*]* by James Ivory (1995)
10. *Marie Antoinette* by W.S. Van Dyke (1938)
11. *L'Enfant-Roi [Louis XVII] [The child King]* by Jean Kemm (1923)
12. *La Fayette* by Jean Dréville (1961)
13. *L'Autrichienne [That Austrian woman]* by Pierre Granier-Deferre (1989)
14. *Madame du Barry* by William Dieterle (1934)
15. *Ridicule* by Patrice Leconte (1996)
16. *Chouans!* by Philippe de Broca (1988)
17. *Marie Antoinette* by Sofia Coppola (2006)
18. *Lady Oscar* (TMS 1979–1980), anime of the manga *Rose of Versailles* by Riyoko Ikeda (1972)
19. *Marie Antoinette, Reine de France [Shadow of the Guillotine*]* by Jean Delannoy (1956)
20. Others: . . .

References

Adam, É. et al. (2013) *Versailles: L'Ombre de Marie-Antoinette [bande dessinée]*. Grenoble et Versailles: Glénat & Château de Versailles.
Affleck, J. & Kvan, T. (2008) A Virtual Community as the Context for Discursive Interpretation: A Role in Cultural Heritage Engagement, *International Journal of Heritage Studies*, 14(3), 268–280.
Agarwal, S. & Shaw, G. (2018) *Heritage, Screen and Literary Tourism*. Bristol: Channel View.
Ageron, C.-R. (1984) L'Exposition coloniale de 1931: Mythe républicain ou mythe imperial?, in P. Nora (Ed.) *Les lieux de mémoire: La République*. Paris: Gallimard, 561–591.
Agulhon, M. (1984) La Mairie: Liberté. Égalité. Fraternité, in P. Nora (Ed.) *Les lieux de mémoire: La République*. Paris: Gallimard, 167–193.
Alcouffe, D. (1999) Un aspect du goût de Marie-Antoinette: Les vases en pierres dures, *Versalia*, 2, 6–15.
Alderman, D.H. (2008) Place, Naming and the Interpretation of Cultural Landscapes, in B. Graham & P. Howard (Eds.) *The Ashgate Research Companion to Heritage & Identity*. Aldershot: Ashgate, 195–213.
Allen, P. (2009a) Carla Bruni 'is a Modern-Day Marie Antoinette: French Magazine Slams First Lady as Self-Obsessed', *The Mail*, 29 October.
Allen, P. (2009b) Carla Bruni Attacked as New Marie Antoinette of France by Magazine, *The Telegraph*, 29 October.
de Alméras, H. (1907) *Marie-Antoinette et les pamphlets royalistes et révolutionnaires*. Paris: Librairie Mondiale.
de Alméras, H. (1935) *Marie-Antoinette – Les Amoureux de la Reine d'après les pamphlets*. Paris: Albin Michel.
de Andia, B. (Ed.) (1978) *De Bagatelle à Monceau 1778–1978: les folies du XVIIIème siècle à Paris* [exhibition catalogue]. Paris: Délégation à l'Action Artistique de la Ville de Paris.
de Azeredo Grünewald, R. (2006) Pataxó Tourist Arts and Cultural Authenticity, in M.K. Smith & M. Robinson (Eds.) *Cultural Tourism in a Changing World: Politics, Participation and (Re)Presentation*. Clevedon: Channel View, 203–214.
AlSayyad, N. (2001a) Global Norms and Urban Forms in the Age of Tourism: Manufacturing Heritage, Consuming Tradition, in N. AlSayyad (Ed.) *Consuming Tradition, Manufacturing Heritage: Global Norms and Urban Forms in the Age of Tourism*. Abingdon: Routledge, 1–33.

AlSayyad, N. (Ed.) (2001b) *Consuming Tradition, Manufacturing Heritage: Global Norms and Urban Forms in the Age of Tourism*. Abingdon: Routledge.

AlSayyad, N. (Ed.) (2004) *The End of Tradition?* Abingdon: Routledge.

Amalvi, C. (1984) Le 14 Juillet: Du Dies irae à Jour de fête, in P. Nora (Ed.) *Les lieux de mémoire: La République*. Paris: Gallimard, 421–472.

Anderson, B. (1991) *Imagined Communities: Reflections on the Origins and Spread of Nationalism* [1st ed. 1983]. London: Verso.

Andrieux, J.-Y. (2011) *Patrimoine: Sources et Paradoxes de l'identité*. Rennes: Presses Universitaires de Rennes.

Anholt, S. (2010) *Places: Identity, Image and Reputation*. Basingstoke: Palgrave Macmillan.

Anonymous Respondent 1 (2010) [*Security Staff Member*]; [conversation Petit Trianon] Personal Communication, 18 December.

Anonymous Respondent 2 (2011) [*Artist/Marie Antoinette aficionado*]; [conversation Petit Trianon] Personal Communication, 22 January.

Anonymous Respondent 3 (2014) [*Ladurée shop assistant – Château de Versailles boutique*]; [conversation on site] Personal Communication, 21 August.

Anonymous Respondent 4 (2014) [*Ladurée shop assistant – Paris boutique*]; [conversation on site] Personal Communication, 27 August.

Anonymous Respondent 5 (2014) [*Ladurée shop assistant – Charles de Gaulle Airport boutique*]; [conversation on site] Personal Communication, 27 August.

Appadurai, A. (Ed.) (1986) *The Social Life of Things: Commodities in Cultural Perspective*. Cambridge: Cambridge University Press.

Appadurai, A. (1996) *Modernity at Large: Cultural Dimensions of Globalization*. Minneapolis: University of Minnesota Press.

Appleby, J. et al. (1994) *Telling the Truth about History*. New York: W.W. Norton.

Appleton, J. (2006) UK Museum Policy and Interpretation: Implications for Cultural Tourism, in M.K. Smith & M. Robinson (Eds.) *Cultural Tourism in a Changing World: Politics, Participation and (Re)Presentation*. Clevedon: Channel View, 257–270.

Arizzoli-Clémentel, P. & Ducamp, E. (Eds.) (1998) *Vues et plans du Petit Trianon à Versailles [par Châtelet] – Recueil du Petit Trianon conservé à la Biblioteca Estense de Modène, Italie*. Paris: Alain de Gourcuff.

Arizzoli-Clémentel, P. (2007) Enrichissements et acquisitions de l'année 2005, *Versalia*, 10, 15–16.

Arizzoli-Clémentel, P. (2008a) Réouverture, après restauration, du Petit Trianon, *La Revue des Musées de France – Revue du Louvre*, 5, 16–17.

Arizzoli-Clémentel, P. (2008b) *L'Album de Marie-Antoinette: Vues et Plans du Petit Trianon à Versailles*. Montreuil: Gourcuff Gradenigo.

Arizzoli-Clémentel, P. & Gorguet-Ballesteros, P. (Eds.) (2009) *Fastes de cour et cérémonies royales: Le costume de cour en Europe (1650–1800)* [exhibition catalogue]. Paris: Réunion des musées nationaux.

Armenteros, C. et al. (Eds.) (2008) *Historicising the French Revolution*. Newcastle upon Tyne: Cambridge Scholars.

Arnold, S.J. & Fischer, E. (1994) Hermeneutics and Consumer Research, *Journal of Consumer Research*, 21(1), 55–70.

Ashworth, G.J. & Larkham, P.J. (1994) *Building a New Heritage: Tourism, Culture and Identity in the New Europe*. Abingdon: Routledge.

Ashworth, G.J. & Howard, P. (1999) *European Heritage: Planning and Management*. Exeter: Intellect.
Ashworth, G.J. & Graham, B. (Eds.) (2005) *Senses of Place: Senses of Time*. Aldershot: Ashgate.
Ashworth, G.J. (2008) The Memorialization of Violence and Tragedy: Human Trauma as Heritage, in B. Graham & P. Howard (Eds.) *The Ashgate Research Companion to Heritage & Identity*. Aldershot: Ashgate, 231–244.
Assmann, J. (2012) *Cultural Memory and Early Civilization: Writing, Remembrance and Political Imagination* [1st German ed. 1992]. Cambridge: Cambridge University Press.
Audinot, D. (2002) *Les mystères du Trianon. Voyages vers l'au-delà*. Agnières (Somme): JMG.
Auerbach, C.F. & Silverstein, L.B. (2003) *Qualitative Data: An Introduction to Coding and Analysis*. New York: New York University Press.
Augé, M. (1997) *L'Impossible Voyage: Le Tourisme et ses images*. Paris: Payot & Rivages.
Autié, L. et al. (2007) *Journal de Léonard coiffeur de Marie-Antoinette*. Paris: Les Éditeurs Libres.
Backman Rogers, A. (2012) The Historical Threshold: Crisis, Ritual and Liminality in Sofia Coppola's Marie-Antoinette (2006), *RELIEF*, 6(1), 80–97.
Baczko, B. (1984) Le Calendrier Républicain: Décréter l'éternité, in P. Nora (Ed.) *Les lieux de mémoire: La République*. Paris: Gallimard, 37–83.
de Baecque, A. (1988) *La Caricature révolutionnaire*. Paris: Presses du CNRS.
de Baecque, A. (1997) *The Body Politic: Corporeal Metaphor in Revolutionary France 1770–1800* [1st French ed. 1993]. Stanford: Stanford University Press.
de Baecque, A. (2012) Marie-Antoinette démaquillée, *Le Monde des Livres*, 22 March.
Baker, K.M. (Ed.) (1987a) *The Old Regime and the French Revolution; Vol. 7, University of Chicago Readings in Western Civilization*. Chicago: University of Chicago Press.
Baker, K.M. (Ed.) (1987b) *The French Revolution and the Creation of Modern Political Culture; Vol. 1, the Political Culture of the Old Regime*. Oxford: Pergamon Press.
Baker, K.M. (1990) *Inventing the French Revolution: Essays on French Political Culture in the Eighteenth Century*. Cambridge: Cambridge University Press.
Baker, K.M. & Kaplan, S.L. (1991) Introduction, in R. Chartier *The Cultural Origins of the French Revolution* [transl. L.G. Cochrane]. Durham: Duke University Press.
Baker, K.M. (1992) The Maupeou Revolution: The Transformation of French Politics at the End of the Old Regime, *Historical Reflections*, 18(2), 1–16.
Baker, K.M. (1993) *Au tribunal de l'opinion. Essais sur l'imaginaire politique au XVIIIe siècle*. Paris: Payot.
Baker, K.M. (Ed.) (1994) *The French Revolution and the Creation of Modern Political Culture; Vol. 4, the Terror*. Oxford: Pergamon Press.
Baker, K.M. & Reill, P.H. (Eds.) (2001) *What's Left of Enlightenment? A Postmodern Question*. Stanford, CA: Stanford University Press.
Ball, L. (2011) Prosper Mérimée et l'invention des Monuments historiques dans la France du XIXe siècle, in C. Mansfield & S. Seligman (Eds.) *Narrative and the*

Built Heritage: Papers in Tourism Research. Saarbrücken: VDM Verlag, 141–162.

Balm, R. & Holcomb, B. (2003) Unlosing Lost Places: Image Making, Tourism and the Return to Terra Cognita, in D. Crouch & N. Lübbren (Eds.) *Visual Culture and Tourism*. Oxford: Berg, 157–174.

Bandiera, J.D. (1985) Le recueil des plans du Petit Trianon de Richard Mique, *Actes du colloque 'Versailles'*, 5, [pages unknown].

Barker, E. (Ed.) (1999) *Contemporary Cultures of Display*. New Haven: Yale University Press & The Open University.

Barnes, J. (2014) [*Chief Executive of Historic Royal Palaces since 2017; Previously Conservation & Learning Director*]; [conversation at Palace of Compiègne – ICOM DEMHIST Conference] Personal Communication, 8 October.

Barthes, R. (1966) *Introduction to the Structural Analysis of the Narrative*, Stencilled Occasional Paper, 8. Birmingham: University of Birmingham, Centre for Contemporary Cultural Studies.

Barthes, R. (1972) *Mythologies* [transl. Jonathan Cape Ltd] [1st French ed. 1957]. London: Random House Vintage Classics.

Barthes, R. (1977) *Image-Music-Text*. Glasgow: Fontana.

Barton, H.A. (1967) The Origins of the Brunswick Manifesto, *French Historical Studies*, 5(2), 146–169.

Bascou, M. et al. (Eds.) (2008) *Louvre: Musée du Louvre, Fastes de la Cour de France au XVIIIe siècle* [exhibition catalogue]. Japon: The Asahi Shimbun.

Baudin, P. (2010) [*Architecte D.P.L.G et Architecte du Patrimoine; 1991–2014 collaborateur de P.-A. Lablaude, Architecte en Chef des Monuments Historiques*]; [conversation Versailles] Personal Communication, 13 December.

Baudin, P. (2011a) [conversation Petit Trianon] Personal Communication, 22 April.

Baudin, P. (2011b) [email] Personal Communication, 18 May.

Baudin, P. (2011c) [conversation Petit Trianon] Personal Communication, 2 December.

Baudin, P. (2012) [conversation Versailles] Personal Communication, 4 June.

Baudin, P. (2013) [telephone conversation] Personal Communication, 9 May.

Baudin, P. (2014) [conversation Versailles] Personal Communication, 21 August.

Baudrillard, J. (1994) *Simulacra and Simulation* [transl. S.F. Glaser] [1st French ed. 1981]. Ann Arbor: University of Michigan.

Baudrillard, J. (2001) *Selected Writings* [ed. M. Poster]. Palo Alto, CA: Stanford University Press.

Baulez, C. (1977) Le domaine de Trianon, *Connaissance de Paris et de la France*, 35, 20–27.

Baulez, C. (1978) Notes sur quelques meubles et objets d'art des appartements de Louis XVI et Marie-Antoinette, *Revue du Louvres et des musées de France*, 5/6, 359–373.

Baulez, C. (1989) Versailles à l'encan, *Connaissance des Arts*, hors-série *Les Arts sous la Révolution*, 34–42.

Baulez, C. (1999) Huit chaises pour la salle à manger de Marie-Antoinette au Hameau de Trianon, *Versalia*, 2, 30–31.

Baulez, C. (2001) Deux terrines de la Manufacture de la Reine, *Versalia*, 4, 16–17.

Baulez, C. (2007) *Deux siècles d'histoire de l'art: Études et chroniques de Christian Baulez*. Versailles: Société des Amis de Versailles.

Bauman, Z. (2003) From Pilgrim to Tourist – or a Short History of Identity, in S. Hall & P. du Gay (Eds.) *Questions of Cultural Identity*. London: SAGE, 18–36.

Becket-Griffith, J. (2017) [*Fairy Artist*]; [email] Personal Communication, 17 August.

Beckman, J. (2014) *How to Ruin a Queen: Marie Antoinette, the Stolen Diamonds and the Scandal That Shook the French Throne*. London: John Murray.

Beeton, S. (2016) *Film-Induced Tourism* [1st ed. 2005]. Clevedon: Channel View.

Bellessort, A. (1933) Le théâtre de Marie-Antoinette, *Revue des Deux Mondes*, 16, 624–645.

Ben-Amos, A. (1984) Les Funérailles de Victor Hugo: Apothéose de l'événement spectacle, in P. Nora (Ed.) *Les lieux de mémoire: La République*. Paris: Gallimard, 473–522.

Ben-Ari, E. (1996) Review: *Discourses of the Vanishing: Modernity, Phantasm, Japan* by Marilyn Ivy, *Monumenta Nipponica*, 51(2), 273–275.

Bendix, R. (1997) *In Search of Authenticity: The Formation of Folklore Studies*. Madison: University of Wisconsin Press.

Benjamin, W. (1973) *Illuminations*. London: Fontana.

Bennett, T. (1995) *The Birth of the Museum: History, Theory, Politics*. Abingdon: Routledge.

Benoît, J. (2010a) [*Conservateur en chef chargé des Trianons*]; [conversation Versailles] Personal Communication, 28 October.

Benoît, J. (2010b) [email] Personal Communication, 30 November.

Benoît, J. (2010c) [email] Personal Communication, 20 December.

Benoît, J. (2011a) [conversation Versailles/Petit Trianon] Personal Communication, 30 March.

Benoît, J. (2011b) [email] Personal Communication, 28 April.

Benoît, J. (2014) [conversation Versailles] Personal Communication, 19 August.

Benoît, J. (2016) *Le Petit Trianon: Château de Marie-Antoinette*. Versailles: Château de Versailles; Paris: Artlys.

Benoît, J. (2017a) [email] Personal Communication, 22 August.

Benoît, J. (2017b) [email] Personal Communication, 6 October.

Berly, C. (2003) Marie-Antoinette sur le Net: de l'usage de la reine ou des usages d'une mémoire royale et féminine, *Annales historiques de la Révolution française*, 333, 85–101.

Berly, C. (2006) *Marie-Antoinette et ses biographes: Histoire d'une écriture de la Révolution française*. Paris: L'Harmattan.

Berly, C. & Martin, J.-C. (2010) *Marie-Antoinette*. Paris: Citadelles & Mazenod.

Berly, C. (2011) *Cycle Marie-Antoinette au-delà d'un livre* [Talk on Marie Antoinette at Château de Versailles] Personal attendance, 16 March.

Berly, C. (2012) *La Reine scandaleuse: Idées reçues sur Marie-Antoinette*. Paris: Le Cavalier Bleu.

Berly, C. (2013) *Le Versailles de Marie-Antoinette: Le Château et le Domaine de Trianon*. Paris & Versailles: Artlys & Établissement public du château, du musée et du domaine national de Versailles.

Berly, C. (2015a) Le Versailles de Stefan Zweig, *Château de Versailles*, 16, 74–80.

Berly, C. (2015b) *Louise Élisabeth Vigée Le Brun: Peindre et écrire Marie-Antoinette et son temps*. Paris: Artlys.

Bernea, H. et al. (Eds.) (1999) *Martor: Revue d'Anthropologie du Musée du Paysan Roumain*, 4.

Berque, A. (2002) Overcoming Modernity, Yesterday and Today, *European Journal of East Asian Studies*, 1(1), 89–102.

Berque, A. (2004) Millieu et identité humaine/Milieu and Human Identity, *Annales de Géographie*, 113(638), 385–399.

Berque, A. (2013) *Thinking through Landscape*. Abingdon: Routledge.

Bertière, S. (2002) *Marie-Antoinette l'insoumise; T. 4, Les Reines de France au temps des Bourbons*. Paris: du Fallois.

Bertière, S. (2006) Louis XVI et Marie-Antoinette: Un couple disjoint, in Institut de la Maison de Bourbon (Ed.) *Marie-Antoinette face à l'histoire* [Sorbonne Colloquium]. Paris: François-Xavier de Guibert, 67–78.

Bertière, S. (2011) [*Marie Antoinette Biographer*]; [conversation Versailles] Personal Communication, 20 November.

Bertière, S. (2014) [email] Personal Communication, 11 September.

Besson, R. (2014) Dominique Briand, Le cinéma peut-il nous apprendre l'histoire de France?, *Lectures: Les comptes rendus* [online]; Available at: http://lectures.revues.org/13751 [Accessed: 26 February 2014].

Beurdeley, M. (1981) *La France à l'encan 1789–1799: Exode des objets d'art sous la Révolution*. Paris: J. Tallandier.

Bhabha, H.K. (1994) *The Location of Culture*. Abingdon: Routledge.

Biard, M. (2006) De la 'Toinettomania' au retour des écrits contre-révolutionnaires dans nos librairies, *La Quinzaine Littéraire*, 934, 21–22.

Biard, M. & Leuwers, H. (2007) Regards croisés. L'an deux mille six, ou la 'toinettomania', rêve étrange s'il en fût jamais, *Annales historiques de la Révolution française*, 347, 157–158.

Biard, M. (2009) Des 'bons avis' aux critiques assassines, *Annales historiques de la Révolution française*, 357, 47–66.

Bigorne, R. (Ed.) (1998) *Mémoires du XVIIIe siècle* [exhibition catalogue]. Bordeaux: Musée Goupil.

Binh, N.T. (Ed.) (2010) *Monuments Stars du 7ème Art* [exhibition catalogue]. Paris: Éditions du patrimoine/Centre des monuments nationaux.

Blakemore, S. & Hembree, F. (2001) Edmund Burke, Marie Antoinette, and the Procedure Criminelle, *The Historian*, 63(3), 505–520.

Blanchard, M.A. (Ed.) (2013) *History of the Mass Media in the United States: An Encyclopedia*. Abingdon: Routledge.

Blanning, T.C.W. (1986) *The Origins of the French Revolutionary Wars*. New York: Longman Group.

Blanning, T.C.W. (1987) *The French Revolution: Aristocrats versus Bourgeois?* Basingstoke: Macmillan Education.

Du Bled, V. (1891) Les Comédiennes de la Cour: La Duchesse du Maine, Madame de Pompadour et la Reine Marie-Antoinette, *Revue Des Deux Mondes*, juillet–août, 823–863.Bloch, M. (1997) *Apologie pour l'histoire ou Métier d'historien*. Paris: Armand Colin.

Bloom, P. (2016) *Against Empathy: The Case of Rational Compassion*. London: Penguin Books.

Blunt, A. (2003) Collective Memory and Productive Nostalgia: Anglo-Indian Home-Making at McCluskieganj, *Environment and Planning D: Society and Space*, 21, 717–738.

Bodenstein, F. (2007) The Emotional Museum: Thoughts on the 'Secular Relics' of Nineteenth-Century History Museums in Paris and Their Posterity, *Conserveries*

mémorielles: Revue transdisciplinaire de jeunes chercheurs, 9| 2011 [online]; Available at: http://cm.revues.org/834 [Accessed: 19 April 2011].
Bossard, R. (2001) La famille royale réunie autour du dauphin en 1782, *Versalia*, 4, 20–22.
Boswell, D. & Evans, J. (Eds.) (1999) *Representing the Nation: A Reader: Histories, Heritage and Museums*. Abingdon: Routledge.
Bouchenot-Déchin, P. (2004) *L'Absente*. Paris: Plon.
Bouchenot-Déchin, P. (2006) *Au nom de la Reine* [1st ed. 1998]. Paris: Plon.
Bouchenot-Déchin, P. (2010) [*Château de Versailles researcher/historian*]; [conversation Versailles] Personal Communication, 21 November.
Bouchenot-Déchin, P. (2011) [email] Personal Communication, 11 January.
Bourdieu, P. & de Saint-Martin, M. (1976) Anatomie du goût, *Actes de la recherche en sciences sociales*, 2–81.
Bourdieu, P. (1977) *Outline of a Theory of Practice*. Cambridge: Cambridge University Press.
Bourdieu, P. (1984) *Distinction: A Social Critique of the Judgement of Taste* [transl. R. Nice] [1st French ed. 1979]. London: Routledge & Kegan Paul.
Boyatzis, R.E. (1998) *Transforming Qualitative Information: Thematic Analysis and Code Development*. Thousand Oaks: SAGE.
Boyer, M.-F. & Halard, F. (1995) *Les Lieux de la Reine*. Paris: Thames & Hudson.
Boym, S. (2001) *The Future of Nostalgia*. New York: Basic Books.
Boysson, B. et al. (Eds.) (2005) *Marie-Antoinette: Le gout d'une reine* [exhibition catalogue]. Paris: Somogy; Bordeaux: Musée des Arts Décoratifs.
Bradshaw, P. (2006) Marie Antoinette, *The Guardian*, 20 October.
de Brancion, L.C. (2003) *Carmontelle au jardin des illusions*. Château de Saint-Rémy-en-l'Eau: Monelle Hayot.
Braun, V. & Clarke, V. (2006) Using Thematic Analysis in Psychology, *Qualitative Research in Psychology*, 3, 77–101.
Brethes, R. (2011) Manga-Antoinette: Elle sera la star du Festival d'Angoulême. Riyoko Ikeda a fait découvrir Versailles à des millions de Japonais, *Le Point/Culture*, janvier, [no pages].
Brewer, J.D. (2000) *Ethnography*. Buckingham: Open University Press.
Briand, D. (2013) *Le cinéma peut-il nous apprendre l'histoire de France?* Caen: CRDP de Basse-Normandie.
Brocklehurst, H. & Phillips, R. (Eds.) (2004) *History, Nationhood and the Question of Britain*. Basingstoke: Palgrave Macmillan.
Brown, H. (2006) *Ending the French Revolution: Violence, Justice and Repression from the Terror to Napoleon*. Charlottesville: University of Virginia Press.
Brown, R. (2011) [*Head of School of Architecture, Plymouth University; PhD Supervisor 2010–2013*]; [MARE500 feedback; email] Personal Communication, 21 February.
Brown, R. (2013) Emplacement, Embodiment and Ritual: Some Considerations from *Shikii wo matagu* for Our Understanding of Place and Identity, in S. Bandyopadhyay & G. Garma Montiel (Eds.) *The Territories of Identity: Architecture in the Age of Evolving Globalisation*. Abingdon: Routledge, 31–41.
Brunt, P. (1997) *Market Research in Travel and Tourism*. Oxford: Butterworth-Heinemann.
Burke, E. (1790) *Reflections on the Revolution in France and on the Proceedings in Certain Societies in London Relative to that Event*. London: J. Dodsley.

Burrows, S. (2006) *Blackmail, Scandal, and Revolution: London's French Libellistes, 1758–92.* Manchester: Manchester University Press.

Busby, G. & Klug, J. (2001) Measuring Movie-Induced Tourism: Challenges and Problems, *Journal of Vacation Marketing*, 7(4), 316–332.

Busby, G. & Laviolette, P. (2006) Narratives in the Net: Fiction and Cornish Tourism, in P. Payton (Ed.) *Cornish Studies* [Vol. 14]. Exeter: University of Exeter Press, 142–163.

Busby, G. & Meethan, K. (2008) Cultural Capital in Cornwall: Heritage and the Visitor, in P. Payton (Ed.) *Cornish Studies* [Vol. 16]. Exeter: University of Exeter Press, 146–166.

Busby, G. et al. (2011) Madrid: Literary Fiction and the Imaginary Urban Destination, *Journal of Tourism Consumption and Practice*, 3(2), 20–37.

Busby, G. & Haines, C. (2013) Doc Martin and Film Tourism: The Creation of Destination Image, *Tourism*, 61(2), 105–120.

Butler-Kisber, L. (2010) *Qualitative Inquiry: Thematic, Narrative and Arts-Informed Perspectives.* Los Angeles: SAGE.

Byrne, E. & McQuillan, M. (1999) *Deconstructing Disney.* London: Pluto Press.

Cameron, F. & Mengler, S. (2013) Authorising the Unauthorised: Liquidity, Complexity and the Heritage-Tourist in the Era of Social Media, in R. Staiff et al. (Eds.) *Heritage and Tourism: Place, Encounter, Engagement.* Abingdon: Routledge, 45–62.

Campan, J.L.H. [Madame] (1823) *Mémoires sur la vie privée de Marie-Antoinette.* Paris: Baudouin.

Campan, J.L.H. [Madame] (1988) *Mémoires de Madame Campan, Première Femme de Chambre de Marie-Antoinette* [ed. J. Chalon]. Paris: Mercure de France.

Campbell, C. (1987) *The Romantic Ethic and Spirit of Modern Consumerism.* Oxford: Basil Blackwell.

Campbell, G. et al. (2017) Nostalgia and Heritage: Potentials, Mobilisations and Effects, *International Journal of Heritage Studies*, 23(7), 609–611.

Campbell, P.R. (2006) *The Origins of the French Revolution: Problems in Focus.* Basingstoke: Palgrave Macmillan.

Campion-Vincent, V. & Shojaei Kawan, C. (2002) Marie-Antoinette et son célèbre dire: deux scénographies et deux siècles de désordres, trois niveaux de communication et trois modes accusatoires, *Annales historiques de la Révolution française*, 327, 29–56.

Carbonell, B.M. (Ed.) (2004) *Museum Studies: An Anthology of Contexts.* Malden, MA: Blackwell.

Carlier, Y. (2006) L'exceptionnel mobilier de Riesener pour le boudoir de Marie-Antoinette à Fontainebleau, *L'Estampille – L'Objet d'art*, 410, 62–69.

Carlier, Y. (2016) Le boudoir de Marie-Antoinette à Trianon, *Château de Versailles*, 22, 56–61.

Carman, J. (2005) *Against Cultural Property: Archaeology, Heritage and Ownership.* London: Duckworth.

Carmontelle (1779) *Jardin de Monceau près de Paris.* Paris: Delafosse.

Carrott, R.G. (1989) The Hameau de Trianon: Mique, Rousseau and Marie-Antoinette, *Gazette Des Beaux-Arts*, janvier, 19–28.

Castelot, A. (1950) *Madame Royale.* Paris: Perrin.

Castelot, A. (1953) *Marie-Antoinette.* Paris: Perrin.

Castelot, A. (1968) *Louis XVII: L'énigme résolue* [1st Belgian ed. 1947]. Paris: Perrin.
Castelot, A. (1971) *Le Rendez-vous de Varennes ou les occasions manquées*. Paris: Perrin.
Castelot, A. (1989) *Marie-Antoinette*. Paris: Perrin.
Castle, T. (2003) Marie-Antoinette Obsession, in D. Goodman (Ed.) *Marie-Antoinette: Writings on the Body of a Queen*. Abingdon: Routledge, 199–238.
Caughey, J.L. (1984) *Imaginary Social Worlds: A Cultural Approach*. Lincoln: University of Nebraska Press.
de Certeau, M. (1984) *The Practice of Everyday Life* [transl. S. Rendall] [1st French ed. 1980]. Berkeley: University of California Press.
Chalon, J. (1988) *Chère Marie-Antoinette*. Paris: Perrin.
Chapman, M. (2007a) *Preciousness, Elegance, and Femininity: The Personal Taste of Queen Marie-Antointte*, San Francisco: Fine Arts Museum; Versailles: Château de Versailles.
Chapman, M. (2007b) Revival: The Cult of Marie-Antoinette, in M. Chapman et al. (Eds.) *Marie-Antoinette and the Petit Trianon at Versailles* [exhibition catalogue]. San Francisco: Fine Arts Museum; Versailles: Château de Versailles, 25–35; 76–85.
Chapman, M. et al. (Eds.) (2007) *Marie-Antoinette and the Petit Trianon at Versailles* [exhibition catalogue]. San Francisco: Fine Arts Museum; Versailles: Château de Versailles.
Charbon, R. (2012) Dans *Les Adieux à la reine*, de Benoît Jacquot, l'actrice franco-allemande [Diane Kruger] est une époustouflante Marie Antoinette – la mère de toutes les drag-queens. Rencontre royale, *Têtu*, 24–27.
Chartier, R. (1991) *The Cultural Origins of the French Revolution* [transl. L.G. Cochrane] [1st French ed. 1989]. Durham: Duke University Press.
Chazal, G. et al. (Eds.) (2001) *Trois nobles dames: Madame de Pompadour, Marie-Antoinette et Joséphine* [exhibition catalogue]. Tokyo: TBS.
Chazan, D. (2014) Former Call-Girl Zahia Dehar Depicted as Marie-Antoinette Sparks Row in France, *The Telegraph*, 13 April.
Chelcea, S. et al. (1998) *Cercetarea Sociologică: Metode şi Tehnici* [Sociological Research: Methodology and Methods]. Deva: Destin.
Chéry, A. (2011) Histoire d'un non-objet historiographique: Le cas Louis XVI, *L'Atelier du Centre de recherches historiques*, 07 | 2011 [online]; Available at: http://acrh.revues.org/3677 [Accessed: 16 March 2014].
Chéry, A. (2015) *L'image de Louis XV et Louis XVI entre tradition et création: Stratégies figuratives et inscription dans l'espace public, 1715–1793*. Ph.D. Dissertation, Université Jean Moulin, Lyon 3.
Chhabra, D. et al. (2003) Staged Authenticity and Heritage Tourism, *Annals of Tourism Research*, 30(3), 702–719.
Choffé, L. (2004) Le jardin champêtre de Trianon: L'alliance du pittoresque à la botanique, *Versalia*, 7, 56–69.
Chrisman-Campbell, K. (2015) *Fashion Victims: Dress at the Court of Louis XVI and Marie-Antoinette*. New Haven: Yale University Press.
Christensen, K. (2011) Ideas versus Things: The Balancing Act of Interpreting Historic House Museums, *International Journal of Heritage Studies*, 17(2), 153–168.

Citton, Y. (2009) Du bon usage de l'anachronisme (*Marie-Antoinette*, Sofia Coppola et Gang of Four), *Studies on Voltaire and the Eighteenth Century*, 7, 231–247.

Clark, T.J. (1999) *Farewell to an Idea: Episodes from a History of Modernism*. New Haven: Yale University Press.

Clegg, M. (2010) *The Secret Diary of a Princess* [Historical Fiction] [Kindle Edition]. Madame Guillotine.

Clohesy, A.M. (2013) *Politics of Empathy: Ethics, Solidarity, Recognition*. Abingdon: Routledge.

Cobban, A. (1999) *The Social Interpretation of the French Revolution* [1st ed. 1964]. Cambridge: Cambridge University Press.

Coffey, A. (1999) *The Ethnographic Self: Fieldwork and the Representation of Identity*. London: SAGE.

Cohen, E. (1972) Towards a Sociology of International Tourism, *Social Research*, 39, 164–182.

Cohen, E. (1979) A Phenomenology of Tourist Types, *Sociology*, 13(2), 179–201.

Cohen, E. (1988a) Traditions in the Qualitative Sociology of Tourism, *Annals of Tourism Research*, 1(15), 29–46.

Cohen, E. (1988b) Authenticity and Commoditization in Tourism, *Annals of Tourism Research*, 1(15), 371–386.

Cohn, D. (2001) *Le Propre de la fiction* [1st English ed. 1999]. Paris: Seuil.

Coles, T. (2004) Tourism, Shopping, and Retailing: An Axiomatic Relationship? in A.A. Lew et al. (Eds.) *A Companion to Tourism*. Malden, MA: Blackwell, 360–371.

Collins, J. (2011) Melted Gold and National Bodies: The Hermeneutics of Depth and the Value of History in Brazilian Racial Politics, *American Ethnologist*, 38(4), 683–700.

Colwill, E. (1989) Just Another *Citoyenne*? Marie-Antoinette on Trial, 1790–1793, *History Workshop Journal*, 28(1), 63–87.

Colwill, E. (2003) Pass as a Woman, Act Like a Man: Marie-Antoinette as Tribade in the Pornography of the French Revolution, in D. Goodman (Ed.) *Marie-Antoinette: Writings on the Body of a Queen*. Abingdon: Routledge, 139–169.

Cook, P. (2006) Portrait of a Lady: Sofia Coppola, *Sight and Sound*, 16(11), 36–40.

Cook, P. (2014) History in the Making: Sofia Coppola's Marie Antoinette and the New Auteurism, in T. Brown & B. Vidal (Eds.) *The Biopic in Contemporary Film Culture*. Abingdon: Routledge, 212–226.

Comyn, C. (2010) *Marie-Antoinette & La Douceur de L'Ignorance* [essay K. Hemmerechts]. Tielt: Lanoo.

Comyn, C. (2017) [*Contemporary Artist*]; [email] Personal Communication, 31 August.

Corsane, G. (Ed.) (2005) *Heritage, Museums and Galleries: An Introductory Reader*. Abingdon: Routledge.

Cosandey, F. (2000) *La Reine de France. Symbole et pouvoir, XVe–XVIIIe siècle*. Paris: Gallimard.

Cottret, M. (Ed.) (1994) *Madame de Staël / Réflexions sur le procès de la Reine, par une Femme*. Montpellier: Presses du Languedoc.

Cowell, B. (2008) *The Heritage Obsession: A Battle for England's Past*. Stroud: Tempus Publishing.

Crang, M. (1997) Picturing Practices: Research through the Tourist Gaze, *Progress in Human Geography*, 21(3), 359–373.
Craveri, B. (2008) *Marie-Antoinette et le scandale du collier* [transl. É. Deschamps-Pria] [1st Italian ed. 2006]. Paris: Gallimard.
Crawford, M. (1992) The World in a Shopping Mall, in M. Sorkin (Ed.) *Variations on a Theme Park: The New American City and the End of Public Space*. New York: Hill & Wang, 3–30.
Crawshaw, C. & Urry, J. (1997) Tourism and the Photographic Eye, in C. Rojek & J. Urry (Eds.) *Touring Cultures: Transformations of Travel and Theory*. Abingdon: Routledge, 176–195.
Creighton, M. (2009) The Heroic Edo-Ic: Travelling the History Highway in Today's Tokugawa Japan, in S. Guichard-Anguis & O. Moon (Eds.) *Japanese Tourism and Travel Culture*. Abingdon: Routledge, 37–75.
Crooke, E. (2000) *Politics, Archaeology and the Creation of a National Museum of Ireland*. Dublin: Irish Academic Press.
Crooke, E. (2001) Confronting a Troubled History: Which Past in Northern Ireland's Museums?, *International Journal of Heritage Studies*, 7(2), 119–136.
Crooke, E. (2007) *Museums and Community: Ideas, Issues and Challenges*. Abingdon: Routledge.
Cross, E. (2011) The Myth of the Foreign Enemy? The Brunswick Manifesto and the Radicalization of the French Revolution, *French History*, 25(2), 188–213.
Crouch, D. (Ed.) (1999) *Leisure/Tourism Geographies: Practices and Geographical Knowledge*. Abingdon: Routledge.
Crouch, D. & Lübbren, N. (Eds.) (2003) *Visual Culture and Tourism*. Oxford: Berg.
Crouch, D. (2004) Tourist Practices and Performances, in A.A. Lew et al. (Eds.) *A Companion to Tourism*. Malden, MA: Blackwell, 85–95.
Crouch, D. et al. (Eds.) (2005) *The Media and the Tourist Imagination: Converging Cultures*. Abingdon: Routledge.
Crouch, D. (2009) The Diverse Dynamics of Cultural Studies and Tourism, in T. Jamal & M. Robinson (Eds.) *The SAGE Handbook of Tourism Studies*. London: SAGE, 82–97.
Crouch, D. (2010a) The Perpetual Performance and Emergence of Heritage, in E. Waterton & S. Watson (Eds.) *Culture, Heritage and Representation: Perspectives on Visuality and the Past*. Farnham: Ashgate, 57–71.
Crouch, D. (2010b) Flirting with Space: Thinking Landscape Relationally, *Cultural Geographies*, 17(1), 5–18.
Crouch, D. (2011) Re-Investing Authenticity: Tourism, Place and Emotions, *International Journal of Heritage Studies*, 17(1), 94–95.
Crouch, D. (2012) Meaning, Encounter and Performativity: Threads and Moments of Space-Times in Doing Tourism, in L. Smith et al. (Eds.) *The Cultural Moment in Tourism*. Abingdon: Routledge, 19–37.
Crouch, D. (2015) Affect, Heritage, Feeling, in E. Waterton & S. Watson (Eds.) *The Palgrave Handbook of Contemporary Heritage Research*. Basingstoke: Palgrave Macmillan, 177–190.
de Croÿ d'Havré, L.-E. [Duchesse de Tourzel] (1883) *Mémoires de Madame la duchesse de Tourzel, gouvernante des enfants de France pendant les années 1789, 1790, 1791, 1792, 1793, 1795* [2 vols.]. Paris: E. Plon.
de Croÿ-Solre, E. [Duc] (1906–1921) *Journal inédit du duc de Croÿ (1718–1784)* [4 vols.]. Paris: Flammarion.

Cullen, L. & Young, A. (2006) *Moi & Marie Antoinette*. Bloomsbury Children's [5–9 years].
Culler, J. (1981) Semiotics of Tourism, *American Journal of Semiotics*, 1, 127–140.
Cuno, J. (Ed.) (2004) *Whose Muse: Art Museums and the Public Trust*. Princeton: Princeton University Press.
Cuno, J. (Ed.) (2009) *Whose Culture? The Promise of Museums and the Debate over Antiquities*. Princeton: Princeton University Press.
d'Abbes, P. (1908) Trianon, *Le Magasin pittoresque*, 3(9), 86–88.
Dalberg-Acton, J.E.E. (2000) *Lectures on the French Revolution*. Indianapolis: Liberty Fund.
Dallet, S. (2007) Faire ou subir les révolutions, in M. Biard & H. Leuwers, Regards croisés. L'an deux mille six, ou la 'toinettomania', rêve étrange s'il en fût jamais, *Annales historiques de la Révolution française*, 347, 168–175.
Dams, B.H. & Zega, A. (1995) *La folie de Bâtir: Pavillons d'agrément et folies sous l'Ancien Régime*. Paris: Flammarion.
Dann, G.M.S. (1981) Tourism Motivation: An Appraisal, *Annals of Tourism Research*, 8(2), 187–219.
Dann, G.M.S. (2005) Children of the Dark, in G.J. Ashworth & R. Hartmann (Eds.) *Horror and Human Tragedy Revisited: The Management of Sites of Atrocities for Tourism*. New York: Cognizant, 233–252.
Darnton, R. (1979) *The Business of Enlightenment: A Publishing History of the 'Encyclopédie' 1775–1800*. Cambridge, MA: Harvard University Press.
Darnton, R. (1982) *The Literary Underground of the Old Regime*. Cambridge, MA: Harvard University Press.
Darnton, R. (1995) *The Forbidden Best-Sellers of Pre-Revolutionary France*. New York: W.W. Norton.
Darnton, R. & Roches, D. (Eds.) (1989) *Revolution in Print: The Press in France*. Berkeley: University of California Press.
Darnton, R. (2010) *The Devil in the Holy Water or the Art of Slander from Louis XIV to Napoleon*. Philadelphia, PA: University of Pennsylvania Press.
Dassas, F. (2006) Entre cour et jardin: Marie-Antoinette et les arts, in Institut de la Maison de Bourbon (Ed.) *Marie-Antoinette face à l'histoire* [Sorbonne Colloquium]. Paris: François-Xavier de Guibert, 121–128.
Dassas, F. (2008) De la rocaille au néoclassicisme, in M. Bascou et al. (Eds.) *Louvre: Musée du Louvre, Fastes de la Cour de France au XVIIIe siècle* [exhibition catalogue]. Japan: The Asahi Shimbun, 6–9.
Davey, N. (2012) Hermeneutical Aesthetics and an Ontogeny of the Visual, in I. Heywood et al. (Eds.) *The Handbook of Visual Culture*. Oxford: Berg, 131–151.
Davies, P. (2006) *The Debate on the French Revolution*. Manchester: Manchester University Press.
Davies, C. (2011a) [*Architectural Historian/Marie Antoinette aficionado*]; [email] Personal Communication, 3 November.
Davies, C. (2011b) [email] Personal Communication, 4 November.
Davies, C. (2011c) [email] Personal Communication, 9 November.
Davies, C. (2011d) [email] Personal Communication, 15 November.
Davis, S.G. (1996) The Theme Park: Global Industry and Cultural Form, *Media, Culture and Society*, 18, 399–422.
Debord, G. (1994) *Society of the Spectacle* [transl. D. Nicholson-Smith] [1st French ed. 1967]. New York: Zone Books.

Debord, G. (1998) *Comments on the Society of the Spectacle* [transl. M. Imrie] [1st French ed. 1988]. London: Verso.

Delahaye, O. (2015) [*Chargé du récolement des dépôts/Informatisation des collections*; Château de Versailles]; [email] Personal Communication, 11 February.

Delalex, H. et al. (2013) *Marie-Antoinette, la vie à Versailles*. Versailles: Château de Versailles; Paris: du Chêne.

Delalex, H. (2015) *Un jour avec Marie-Antoinette*. Paris: Flammarion.

Deleuze, G. (1994) *Difference and Repetition* [transl. P. Patton] [1st French ed. 1968]. New York: Columbia University Press.

Delpierre, M. (1975) Marie-Antoinette, reine de la mode, *Versailles*, 59, 37–46.

Denning, S. (2000) *The Springboard: How Storytelling Ignites Action in Knowledge-Era Organizations*. Boston, MA: Butterworth-Heinemann.

Denzin, N.K. (1997) *Interpretive Ethnography: Ethnographic Practices for the 21st Century*. Thousand Oaks: SAGE.

Denzin, N.K. & Lincoln, Y.S. (Eds.) (2013) *Collecting and Interpreting Qualitative Materials* [1st ed. 1998]. Thousand Oaks: SAGE.

Département de Seine et Oise, *Petit Trianon et Hameau: Dossier des scellés, états des lieux, projets d'utilisation et de vente, 1793–1796*. Archives Départamentales de Seine et Oise; Serie Q.

Derrida, J. (1997) *Of Gramatollogy* [transl. G.C. Spivak] [1st French ed. 1967]. Baltimore: Johns Hopkins University Press.

Deshayes, T. (2016) Léopold Double (1812–1881): 'L'amoureux de Marie-Antoinette', *Versalia*, 19, 133–143.

Desjardins, G. (1885) *Le Petit Trianon – Histoire et description*. Versailles: L. Bernard.

Desjardins, G. (1894) Supplément à l'histoire du Petit Trianon, *Mémoires de la Société des Sciences Morales, des Lettres et des Arts de Seine-et-Oise*, 18, 129–141; 238–265.

DGE [La Direction Générale des Entreprises] (2016) *Les Sites Touristiques en France: Mémento du Tourisme*. Available at: www.entreprises.gouv.fr/etudes-et-statistiques/statistiques-du-tourisme/accueil [Accessed: 6 October 2017].

d'Hézecques, F. de France (1873) *Souvenirs d'un page à la cour de Louis XVI*. Paris: Didier.

Dicks, B. (2000) *Heritage, Place and Community*. Cardiff: University of Wales Press.

Dicks, B. (2004) *Culture on Display: The Production of Contemporary Visibility*. Buckingham: Open University Press.

Dobbins, A. (2013) In Defense of Sofia Coppola's Marie Antoinette, 18 June [online]; Available at: www.vulture.com/2013/06/defense-of-sofia-coppolas-marie-antoinette.html [Accessed: 19 April 2014].

Doyle, W. (1980) *Origins of the French Revolution*. Oxford: Oxford University Press.

Doyle, W. (2002) *The Oxford History of the French Revolution*. Oxford: Oxford University Press.

Doyle, W. (2009) *Aristocracy and Its Enemies in the Age of Revolution*. Oxford: Oxford University Press.

Dudley, S. (Ed.) (2010) *Museum Materialities: Objects, Engagements, Interpretations*. Abingdon: Routledge.

Dumas, A. (2002) *Le Collier de la reine* [1849–1850]. Paris: Gallimard.

Dumas, A. (2004a) *Ange Pitou* [1851]. Paris: Fabbri.

Dumas, A. (2004b) *La Comtesse de Charny* [1852–1855]. Paris: Fabbri.

Dumas, A. (2005) *Le Chevalier de Maison-Rouge: Épisode de 93* [1845]. Paris: Gallimard.
Dumas, A. (2012) *Joseph Balsamo: Mémoires d'un médecin* [1846–1848]. Paris: Gallimard.
Duprat, A. (2006) *Marie-Antoinette. Une reine brisée*. Paris: Perrin.
Duprat, A. (2007) Les éclats d'une reine, in M. Biard & H. Leuwers, Regards croisés. L'an deux mille six, ou la 'toinettomania', rêve étrange s'il en fût jamais, *Annales historiques de la Révolution française*, 347, 162–167.
Duprat, A. (2011) Marie-Antoinette, une icône française?, in A. Bellavitis & N. Edelman (Eds.) *Genre, femmes, histoire en Europe*. Nanterre: Presses Universitaires de Paris Ouest, 71–93.
Duprat, A. (2012) [*Marie Antoinette Author*]; [conversation at La Sorbonne] Personal Communication, 14 March.
Duprat, A. (2013) *Marie-Antoinette 1755–1793: Images et visages d'une reine*. Paris: Autrement.
Dupuy, P. (2007) Une Reine Au Cinéma, in M. Biard & H. Leuwers, Regards croisés. L'an deux mille six, ou la 'toinettomania', rêve étrange s'il en fût jamais, Annales historiques de la Révolution française, 347, 159–162.
Durand, R. (2001) *La Politique de l'enseignement au XIXe siècle: L'exemple de Versailles*. Paris: Les Belles Lettres.
Duvernois, C. (2008) *Trianon: Le domaine privé de Marie-Antoinette*. Arles: Actes Sud.
Eco, U. (1986) *Travels in Hyper-Reality*. London: Picador.
Edelstein, D. (2009) *The Terror of Natural Right: Republicanism, the Cult of Nature & the French Revolution*. Chicago: The University of Chicago Press.
Edensor, T. (2001) Performing Tourism, Staging Tourism: (Re)producing Tourist Space and Practice, *Tourist Studies*, 1(1), 59–82.
Edensor, T. (2002) *National Identity, Popular Culture and Everyday Life*. Oxford: Berg.
Edensor, T. (2005) Mediating William Wallace: Audio-Visual Technologies in Tourism, in D. Crouch et al. (Eds.) *The Media and the Tourist Imagination: Converging Cultures*. Abingdon: Routledge, 105–118.
Edensor, T. (2009) Tourism and Performance, in T. Jamal & M. Robinson (Eds.) *The SAGE Handbook of Tourism Studies*. London: SAGE, 543–557.
Edson, G. (2004) Heritage: Pride or Passion, Product or Service?, *International Journal of Heritage Studies*, 10(4), 333–348.
Ehrenreich, B. (2005) *Bait and Switch: The (Futile) Pursuit of the American Dream*. New York: Metropolitan Books.
Ephrussi, C. (1879) Inventaire de la collection de la reine Marie-Antoinette, *Gazette Des Beaux-Arts*, novembre, 389–408.
Erickson, C. (2005) *The Hidden Diary of Marie Antoinette: A Novel* [Historical Fiction]. New York: St. Martin's.
Erll, A. (2011) *Memory in Culture* [transl. S.B. Young]. Basingstoke: Palgrave Macmillan.
Fairclough, G. et al. (Eds.) (2008) *The Heritage Reader*. Abingdon: Routledge.
Farge, A. (1994) *Subversive Words: Public Opinion in Eighteenth-Century France* [transl. R. Morris]. University Park, PA: Pennsylvania State University Press.
Farr, E. (2013) *Marie-Antoinette and Count Fersen: The Untold Love Story* [1st ed. 1995]. London: Peter Owen.

Farr, E. (2016) *Marie-Antoinette et le comte de Fersen: La correspondance secrète*. Paris: L'Archipel.

Fauth, J. & Dermansky, M. (n.d.) Top 7 Alternatives to Marie Antoinette, *About.com Hollywood Movies* [online]; Available at: http://worldfilm.about.com/od/titlesaz/tp/marieantoinette.htm [Accessed: 18 April 2014].

Favero, P. (2014a) Learning to Look Beyond the Frame: Reflections on the Changing Meaning of Images in the Age of Digital Media Practices, *Visual Studies*, 29(2), 166–179.

Favero, P. (2014b) Liquid Visions. Digital Images between Anthropology, Consumer Technologies and Contemporary Art, *Archivio Antropologico Mediterraneo*, 16(2), 33–48 [online]; DOI: 10.7432/AAM160203; XVII.

Fawcett, C. & Cormack, P. (2001) Guarding Authenticity at Literary Tourism Sites, *Annals of Tourism Research*, 28(3), 686–704.

Featherstone, M. (1991) *Consumer Culture & Postmodernism*. London: SAGE.

Félix, J. (2006) *Louis XVI et Marie-Antoinette: Un couple en politique*. Paris: Payot & Rivages.

Fersen, A. [Count von] (1902) *Diary and Correspondence of Count Axel Fersen Grand-Marshal of Sweden relating to the Court of France* [transl. K. Prescott Wormeley] [1st French ed. 1878]. Boston: Hardy, Pratt & Co.

de Feydeau, É. (2005) *Jean-Louis Fargeon, parfumeur de Marie-Antoinette*. Paris: Perrin & Château de Versailles.

de Feydeau, É. (2011) *Les parfums: histoire, anthologie, dictionnaire*. Paris: R. Laffont.

de Feydeau, É. (2012) *L'herbier de Marie-Antoinette*. Paris: Flammarion.

Le Figaro (2006) Marie Antoinette: La princesse, L'icône, L'insoumise, *Le Figaro*, hors-série.

Fiquet, J. (2015) *Le mariage forcé ou Marie-Antoinette humiliée*. Paris: J. Tallandier.

Firmin, G. (2014) [*Conservateur Château de Versailles*]; [conversation Versailles] Personal Communication, 13 August.

Firmin, G. & Rondot, B. (2016) *Marie-Antoinette, une reine à Versailles* [exhibition catalogue]. Tokyo: Nippon Television Network Corporation.

Firmin, G. (2017a) 27. Jean-Baptiste André Gautier-Dagoty (1740–1786) Marie-Antoinette devant le temple de l'Amour, Enrichissement des collections de l'année 2015, *Versalia*, 20, 27–28.

Firmin, G. (2017b) [email] Personal Communication, 10 August.

Fjellman, S.M. (1992) *Vinyl Leaves: Walt Disney World and America*. Boulder, CO: Westview Press.

Fladmark, J.M. (Ed.) (2000) *Heritage and Museums: Shaping National Identity*. Shaftesbury: Donhead.

Fleischmann, H. (1908) *Les pamphlets libertins contre Marie-Antoinette: D'après des documents nouveaux et les* pamphlets *tirés de l'enfer de la Bibliothèque nationale*. Paris: Les Publications Modernes.

Flores, P. (2013) Fashion and Otherness: The Passionate Journey of Coppola's Marie Antoinette from a Semiotic Perspective, *Fashion Theory*, 17(5), 605–622.

Forbes, N. et al. (Eds.) (2009) *Europe's Deadly Century: Perspectives on 20th Century Conflict Heritage*. English Heritage & EU Culture 2000 Programme: Landscapes of War, English Heritage.

Fort, B. (1991) *Fictions of the French Revolution*. Evanston, IL: Northwestern University Press.

Foucart, B. (1986) Viollet-le-Duc et la restauration, in P. Nora (Ed.) *Les lieux de mémoire: La Nation II*. Paris: Gallimard, 612–649.

Fraisse, G. (1989) *Muse de la raison: La démocratie exclusive et la différence des sexes*. Aix-en-Provence: Alinéa.

Franck, E. (1993) Requiem pour l'Autrichienne, *L'Express*, 14 October.

Frank, S. (2016) *Wall Memorials and Heritage: The Heritage Industry of Berlin's Checkpoint Charlie*. Abingdon: Routledge.

Fraser, A. (2001) *Marie Antoinette: The Journey*. London: Weidenfeld & Nicolson.

Fraser, A. (2006) *Marie-Antoinette: Biographie*. Paris: Flammarion.

French, P. (2006) Marie-Antoinette Review, *The Observer*, 22 October.

Freud, S. (1919) Das Unheimliche, in *Gesammelte Werke XII*. Frankfurt: S. Fischer, 227–268.

Funk-Brentano, F. (1901) *L'Affaire du Collier*. Paris: Hachette.

Fureix, E. (2005) Le deuil de la Révolution dans le Paris de la Restauration, in J.-Y. Mollier et al. (Eds.) *Repenser la Restauration*. Paris: Nouveau Monde, 17–29.

Furet, F. & Richet, D. (1973) *La Révolution française* [1st ed. 1965]. Paris: Fayard.

Furet, F. (1978) *Interpreting the French Revolution*. Cambridge: Cambridge University Press.

Furet, F. & Ozouf, M. (1989) *A Critical Dictionary of the French Revolution* [transl. A. Goldhammer]. Cambridge, MA: Harvard University Press.

Gabet, O. (2008) Marie-Antoinette, d'Eugénie aux Vanderbilt, in X. Salmon et al. (Eds.) *Marie-Antoinette* [exhibition catalogue]. Paris: Réunion des musées nationaux, 378–379.

Gadamer, H.G. (2004) *Truth and Method*. London: Bloomsbury Academic.

Gaehtgens, T.W. (1984) *Versailles, de la résidence royale au musée historique*. Anvers: Mercator.

Galletti, S. (2012) Female Agency and Early Modern Urbanism: The Paris of Maria de' Medici, *Journal of the Society of Architectural Historians*, 71(2), 186–203.

Garric, J.-P. (2014) *Vers une agriteture: architecture des constructions agricoles (1789–1850)*. Wavre: Mardaga.

Gedi, N. & Elam, Y. (1996) Collective Memory – What Is It?, *History & Memory: Studies in Representation of the Past*, 8(1), 30–50.

Geffroy, A. (1866) La reine Marie-Antoinette d'après les documens [sic] authentiques de Vienne, *Revue Des Deux Mondes*, 63, 642–686.

Gellner, E. (1993a) *Nations and Nationalism*. Oxford: Blackwell.

Gellner, E. (1993b) *Culture, Identity and Politics*. Cambridge: Cambridge University Press.

Gérard, A. (1970) *La Révolution Française: Mythes et Interprétations, 1789–1970*. Paris: Flammarion.

Gervereau, L. & Constans, C. (Eds.) (2005) *Le musée révélé: L'histoire de France au château de Versailles*. Paris: R. Laffont; Versailles: Château de Versailles.

Gill, D.W.J. (2015) Context Matters: Malibu Memoirs: Marion True Breaks Silence, *Journal of Art Crime*, 14, 65–71.

Gillman, D. (2010) *The Idea of Cultural Heritage*. Cambridge: Cambridge University Press.

Giorgi, A. & Giorgi, B. (2008) Phenomenology, in J.A. Smith (Ed.) *Qualitative Psychology: A Practical Guide to Research Methods* [1st ed. 2003]. London: SAGE, 26–52.

Girardet, R. (1984) Les trois couleurs: Ni blanc, ni Rouge, in P. Nora (Ed.) *Les lieux de mémoire: La République*. Paris: Gallimard, 5–35.

Girault de Coursac, P.P. (1962) *Marie-Antoinette et le scandale de Guines*. Paris: Gallimard.

Girault de Coursac, P.P. (1990) *Louis XVI et Marie-Antoinette: Vie conjugale – vie politique*. Paris: O.E.I.L.

Glentzer, M. (2009) Houston Ballet Presents Marie, *The Houston Chronicle*, 12 February.

Godfroy, M.F. (2013) *Marie-Antoinette pour les nuls*. Paris: First-Gründ.

Goetz, A. (2006) À Propos de L'Invention du Mythe de Marie-Antoinette, une Lecture des Goncourt de Dumas et de Zweig, in Institut de la Maison de Bourbon (Ed.) *Marie-Antoinette face à l'histoire* [Sorbonne Colloquium]. Paris: François-Xavier de Guibert, 130–143.

Goetzinger, R. & Goetzinger, A. (2011) *Marie Antoinette: La Reine fantôme*. Paris: Dargaud.

de Goncourt, J.E. (1858) *Histoire de Marie-Antoinette*. Paris: Didot.

Goodman, D. (2003a) Introduction: Not Another Biography of Marie-Antoinette!, in D. Goodman (Ed.) *Marie-Antoinette: Writings on the Body of a Queen*. Abingdon: Routledge, 1–15.

Goodman, D. (Ed.) (2003b) *Marie-Antoinette: Writings on the Body of a Queen*. Abingdon: Routledge.

Goss, J. (2004) The Souvenir: Conceptualizing the Object(s) of Tourist Consumption, in A.A. Lew et al. (Eds.) *A Companion to Tourism*. Malden, MA: Blackwell, 327–336.

Gottdiener, M. (2001) *The Theming of America: American Dreams, Media Fantasies, and Themed Environments*. Boulder, CO: Westview Press.

Gottlieb, A. (1982) Americans' Vacations, *Annals of Tourism Research*, 9, 165–187.

de Gouges, O. (1979) Declaration of the Rights of Woman and Female Citizen [1791], in D. Gav Levy et al. (Eds.) *Women in Revolutionary Paris, 1785–1795*. Urbana, IL: University of Illinois Press, 92–96.

Goulemot, J.-M. & Walter, É. (1984) Les Centenaires de Voltaire et de Rousseau: Les deux lampions des Lumières, in P. Nora (Ed.) *Les lieux de mémoire: La République*. Paris: Gallimard, 381–420.

Gouriévidis, L. (2010) *The Dynamics of Heritage: History, Memory and the Highland Clearances*. Abingdon: Routledge.

Govers, R. & Go, F. (2009) *Place Branding: Glocal, Virtual and Physical Identities, Constructed, Imagined and Experienced*. Basingstoke: Palgrave Macmillan.

Graburn, N. (1977) Tourism: The Sacred Journey, in V.L. Smith (Ed.) *Hosts and Guests: The Anthropology of Tourism*. Philadelphia, PA: University of Pennsylvania Press, 17–32.

Graburn, N. (2009) The Past and the Other in the Present: Kokunai Kokusaika Kanko – Domestic International Tourism, in S. Guichard-Anguis & O. Moon (Eds.) *Japanese Tourism and Travel Culture*. Abingdon: Routledge, 21–36.

Graham, B. et al. (2000) *A Geography of Heritage: Power, Culture & Economy*. London: Arnold.

Graham, B. & Howard, P. (2008a) Introduction: Heritage and Identity, in B. Graham & P. Howard (Eds.) *The Ashgate Research Companion to Heritage & Identity*. Aldershot: Ashgate, 1–15.

Graham, B. & Howard, P. (Eds.) (2008b) *The Ashgate Research Companion to Heritage & Identity*. Aldershot: Ashgate.

Graham, B. & Cook, S. (2010) *Rethinking Curating: Art after New Media*. Cambridge, MA: The MIT Press.

Granger, C. (2005) *L'empereur et les arts: La liste civile de Napoléon III*. Paris: École des Chartes.

Greenfield, J. (2007) *The Return of Cultural Treasures* [1st ed. 1989]. Cambridge: Cambridge University Press.

Gregory, K. & Witcomb, A. (2007) Beyond Nostalgia: The Role of Affect in Generating Historical Understanding at Heritage Sites, in S. Knell et al. (Eds.) *Museum Revolutions: How Museums Change and Are Changed*. Abingdon: Routledge, 263–275.

Gretzel, U. & Fesenmaier, D.R. (2009) Information Technology: Shaping the Past, Present, and Future of Tourism, in T. Jamal & M. Robinson (Eds.) *The SAGE Handbook of Tourism Studies*. London: SAGE, 558–580.

Gromort, G. (1928) *Le Hameau de Petit Trianon: Histoire et description*. Paris: Vincent, Fréal.

de Groot, J. (2010) Historiography and Virtuality, in E. Waterton & S. Watson (Eds.) *Culture, Heritage and Representation: Perspectives on Visuality and the Past*. Farnham: Ashgate, 91–103.

Groote, P. & Haartsen, T. (2008) The Communication of Heritage: Creating Place Identities, in B. Graham & P. Howard (Eds.) *The Ashgate Research Companion to Heritage & Identity*. Aldershot: Ashgate, 181–194.

Grouvel, F. (1964) Derniers visages d'enfants royaux, *La Revue française de l'élite européenne*, octobre, 169, 23–28.

Gruder, V.R. (2002) The Question of Marie-Antoinette: The Queen and the Public Opinion before the Revolution, *French History*, 16(3), 269–298.

Guichard-Anguis, S. (2009) Introduction: The Culture of Travel (*Tabi no Bunka*) and Japanese Tourism, in S. Guichard-Anguis & O. Moon (Eds.) *Japanese Tourism and Travel Culture*. Abingdon: Routledge, 1–17.

Guichard-Anguis, S. & Moon, O. (Eds.) (2009) *Japanese Tourism and Travel Culture*. Abingdon: Routledge.

Habermas, J. (1989) *The Structural Transformation of the Public Sphere: An Inquiry into a Category of Bourgeois Society* [transl. T. Burger & F. Lawrence]. Cambridge, MA: MIT Press.

Halbwachs, M. (1980) *The Collective Memory* [transl. ed. F.J. Ditter & V. Yazdi Ditter] [1st French ed. 1950]. New York: Harper & Row.

Halbwachs, M. (1992) *On Collective Memory* [transl. L. Coser]. Chicago: Chicago University Press.

Hall, J.A. (Ed.) (1998) *The State of the Nation: Ernest Gellner and the Theory of Nationalism*. Cambridge: Cambridge University Press.

Hall, S. (1995) New Cultures for Old, in D. Massey & P. Jess (Eds.) *A Place in the World? Places, Cultures and Globalization*. Oxford: Oxford University Press, 175–214.

Hall, S. (1997) The Work of Representation, in S. Hall (Ed.) *Representation: Cultural Representations and Signifying Practices*. London: SAGE, 13–64.

Hall, S. & du Gay, P. (Eds.) (2003) *Questions of Cultural Identity* [1st ed. 1996]. London: SAGE.

Hallam, E. & Hockey, J.L. (2001) *Death, Memory and Material Culture*. Oxford: Berg.

Hanks, M. (2015) *Haunted Heritage: The Cultural Politics of Ghost Tourism, Populism, and the Past*. Abingdon: Routledge.

Hans, P.-X. (2007) The History of the Petit Trianon; (2007b) the Queen's Bedroom, or Chambre à coucher de treillage (Trellis Bedroom), in M. Chapman et al. (Eds.) *Marie-Antoinette and the Petit Trianon at Versailles* [exhibition catalogue]. San Francisco: Fine Arts Museum; Versailles: Château de Versailles, 15–23; 135–136.

Hans, P.-X. (2010) [*Conservateur en chef au musée national des châteaux de Versailles et de Trianon, en charge du mobilier et des objets d'art*]; [conversation Versailles] Personal Communication, 9 December.

Hardman, J. (2016) *The Life of Louis XVI*. New Haven: Yale University Press.

Harris, C. (2016) *Queenship and Revolution in Early Modern Europe: Henrietta Maria and Marie Antoinette*. New York: Palgrave Macmillan.

Harrison, R. et al. (2008) Heritage, Memory and Modernity: An Introduction, in G. Fairclough et al. (Eds.) *The Heritage Reader*. Abingdon: Routledge, 1–12.

Harrison, R. (2012) *Heritage: Critical Approaches*. Abingdon: Routledge.

Harrison, R. (2013) Forgetting to Remember, Remembering to Forget: Late Modern Heritage Practices, Sustainability and the 'Crisis' of Accumulation of the Past, *International Journal of Heritage Studies*, 19(6), 579–595.

Haru Crowston, C. (2013) *Credit, Fashion, Sex: Economies of Regard in Old Regime France*. Durham: Duke University Press.

Harvey, D.C. (1989) *The Condition of Postmodernity*. Oxford: Blackwell.

Harvey, D.C. (2001) Heritage Pasts and Heritage Presents: Temporality, Meaning and the Scope of Heritage Studies, *International Journal of Heritage Studies*, 7(4), 319–338.

Harvey, D.C. (2008) The History of Heritage, in B. Graham & P. Howard (Eds.) *The Ashgate Research Companion to Heritage & Identity*. Aldershot: Ashgate, 19–36.

Hasquenoph, B. (2008) Les dessous fric d'un parfum de charme, *Louvre Pour Tous* [online]; Available at: www.louvrepourtous.fr/Les-dessous-fric-d-un-parfum-de,042.html [Accessed: 12 October 2017].

Hayek, N.G. (préf. de) & (avant-propos de) Aillagon, J.-J. (2009) *Le Petit Trianon: Domaine de Marie-Antoinette*. Paris: Beaux Arts.

Hazard, P. (1946) *La Pensée européenne au XVIIIe siècle*. Paris: Fayard.

Heidegger, M. (1971) *On the Way to Language* [transl. P.D. Hertz]. New York: Harper & Row.

Hein, G. (1998) *Learning in the Museum*. Abingdon: Routledge.

Heitzmann, A. (1988) Un jeu de bague sous l'Empire à Trianon, *Gazette des Beaux-Arts*, Mars, 203–312.

Heitzmann, A. (2000) Une cuisine pour Marie-Antoinette à Trianon: Le réchauffoir du Hameau, *Versalia*, 3, 76–85.

Heitzmann, A. (2001) Hameau de Trianon: La laiterie de préparation, *Versalia*, 4, 72–79.

Heitzmann, A. (2002) Restauration au Hameau de Trianon: La tour de Marlborough et la laiterie de propreté, *Versalia*, 5, 32–43.

Heitzmann, A. (2003) Hameau de Trianon: Une salle de bal dans la grange, *Versalia*, 6, 36–44.

Heitzmann, A. (2004) Le domaine de Trianon sous le Premier Empire, *Versalia*, 7, 112–127.

Heitzmann, A. (2005) Hameau de Trianon: Le moulin, *Versalia*, 8, 46–58.
Heitzmann, A. (2006) Trianon: La ferme du Hameau, *Versalia*, 9, 114–129.
Heitzmann, A. (2007a) Le Pavillon frais en son jardin, *Versalia*, 10, 58–77.
Heitzmann, A. (2007b) Fouilles archéologiques dans le jardin du Pavillon frais, *Versalia*, 10, 78–79.
Heitzmann, A. (2009) Les jeux de bague de Trianon, *Versalia*, 12, 77–96.
Hemmings, F.W.J. (1979) *Alexandre Dumas, the King of Romance*. New York: Charles Scribner's Sons.
Hems, A. & Blockley, M. (Eds.) (2005) *Heritage Interpretation: Theory and Practice*. Abingdon: Routledge.
Hendry, J. (2009) Fantasy Travel in Time and Space: A New Japanese Phenomenon?, in S. Guichard-Anguis & O. Moon (Eds.) *Japanese Tourism and Travel Culture*. Abingdon: Routledge, 129–144.
Hennebelle, D. (2017) Une reine musicomane, *Château de Versailles*, 25, 26–31.
Henning, M. (2006) *Museums, Media and Cultural Theory*. Berkshire: Open University Press.
Herbert, D.T. (2001) Literary Places, Tourism and the Heritage Experience, *Annals of Tourism Research*, 28(2), 312–333.
Hernández Martínez, A. (2008) Conservation and Restoration in Built Heritage: A Western European Perspective, in B. Graham & P. Howard (Eds.) *The Ashgate Research Companion to Heritage & Identity*. Aldershot: Ashgate, 245–266.
Hertz, R. (Ed.) (1997) *Reflexivity & Voice*. Thousand Oaks: SAGE.
Hetherington, K. (2014) Museums and the 'Death of Experience': Singularity, Interiority and the Outside, *International Journal of Heritage Studies*, 20(1), 72–85.
Heuer, J. (1998) *Foreigners, Families, and Citizens: Contradictions of National Citizenship in France, 1789–1830*. Ph.D. Dissertation, University of Chicago.
Hewison, R. (1987) *The Heritage Industry: Britain in a Climate of Decline*. London: Methuen.
Heywood, I. et al. (Eds.) (2012) *The Handbook of Visual Culture*. Oxford: Berg.
Hill, H. (2003) *Architecture and the Politics of Gender in Early Modern Europe*. Aldershot: Ashgate.
Himelfarb, H. (1986) Versailles, fonctions et légendes, in P. Nora (Ed.) *Les lieux de mémoire: La Nation II*. Paris: Gallimard, 235–292.
Hobsbawm, E.J. & Ranger, T. (Eds.) (1983) *The Invention of Tradition*. Cambridge: Cambridge University Press.
Hobsbawm, E.J. (1983) Mass-Producing Traditions: Europe, 1870–1914, in E.J. Hobsbawm & T. Ranger (Eds.) *The Invention of Tradition*. Cambridge: Cambridge University Press, 263–307.
Hobsbawm, E.J. (1992) *Nations and Nationalism since 1780: Programme, Myth, Reality* [1st ed. 1990]. Cambridge: Cambridge University Press.
Hodge, C.J. (2011) A New Model for Memory Work: Nostalgic Discourse at a Historic Home, *International Journal of Heritage Studies*, 17(2), 116–135.
Hohenadel, K. (2006) French Royalty as seen by Hollywood Royalty, *The New York Times*, 10 September.
Hollinshead, K. (2009) Theme Parks and the Representation of Culture and Nature: The Consumer Aesthetics of Presentation and Performance, in T. Jamal & M. Robinson (Eds.) *The SAGE Handbook of Tourism Studies*. London: SAGE, 269–289.

Hollis, E. (2009) *The Secret Lives of Buildings: From the Parthenon to the Vegas Strip*. London: Portobello Books.
Hooper-Greenhill, E. (1992) *Museums and the Shaping of Knowledge*. Abingdon: Routledge.
Hooper-Greenhill, E. (Ed.) (1994) *Museums and Their Visitors*. Abingdon: Routledge.
Hooper-Greenhill, E. (Ed.) (1995) *Museum, Media, Message*. Abingdon: Routledge.
Hooper-Greenhill, E. (2000) *Museums and the Interpretation of Visual Culture*. Abingdon: Routledge.
Hooper-Greenhill, E. (2004) Changing Values in the Art Museum: Rethinking Communication and Learning, in B.M. Carbonell (Ed.) *Museum Studies: An Anthology of Contexts*. Oxford: Blackwell, 556–575.
Hooper-Greenhill, E. (2007) *Museums and Education: Purpose, Pedagogy, Performance*. Abingdon: Routledge.
Hoppe, S. & Breitling, S. (Eds.) (2016) *Virtual Palaces, Part II: Lost Palaces and Their Afterlife Virtual Reconstruction between Science and Media* [online publication]. München: Palatium. Available at: www.courtresidences.eu/uploads/publications/virtual-palaces-II.pdf [Accessed: 15 September 2017].
Horne, D. (1984) *The Great Museum*. London: Pluto.
Horvat, M.T. (n.d.) Book-Review on the work *Trianon, A Novel of Royal France* by Elena Maria Vidal [online]; Available at: http://traditioninaction.org/bkreviews/A_007br_Trianon.htm [Accessed: 23 July 2014].
Howard, P. (2001) *MA European Heritage: Planning and Management*, Seminar Course, Plymouth University, Faculty of Arts, 4 October, Personal Attendance.
Howard, P. (2003) *Heritage: Management, Interpretation, Identity*. London: Continuum.
Howard, P. (2013) A Geographer in Heritage: Responding to 'Decennial Reflections', *International Journal of Heritage Studies*, 19(4), 373–376.
Huertas Roig, A. et al. (2010) Place-Making or Place Branding? Case Studies of Catalonia and Wales, in G.J. Ashworth & M. Kavaratzis (Eds.) *Towards Effective Place Brand Management: Branding European Cities and Regions*. Cheltenham: Edward Elgar, 116–134.
Hughes, G. (1995) Authenticity in Tourism, *Annals of Tourism Research*, 22(4), 781–803.
Hunt, L. (Ed.) (1989) *The New Cultural History*. Berkeley: University of California Press.
Hunt, L. (1991) The Many Bodies of Marie-Antoinette: Political Pornography and the Problem of the Feminine in the French Revolution, in L. Hunt (Ed.) *Eroticism and the Body Politic*. Baltimore: Johns Hopkins University Press, 108–131.
Hunt, L. (1992) *The Family Romance of the French Revolution*. Abingdon: Routledge.
Hunt, L. (Ed.) (1993) *The Invention of Pornography: Obscenity and the Origins of Modernity*. New York: Zone Books.
Hunt, L. (2003) The Many Bodies of Marie-Antoinette: Political Pornography and the Problem of the Feminine in the French Revolution, in D. Goodman (Ed.) *Marie-Antoinette: Writings on the Body of a Queen*. Abingdon: Routledge, 117–138.
Hunt, L. (2004) *Politics, Culture and Class in the French Revolution* [1st ed. 1984]. Berkeley: University of California Press.

Hunt, D. (2004) *The Picturesque Garden in Europe* [1st ed. 2002]. London: Thames & Hudson.

Hutcheon, L. (1986–1987) The Politics of Postmodernism: Parody and History, *Cultural Critique*, 5, 179–297.

Hutcheon, L. (2002) *The Politics of Postmodernism* [1st ed. 1989]. Abingdon: Routledge.

Hyde, M. (2017) Watching Her Step: Marie-Antoinette and the Art of Walking, in S. Caviglia (Ed.) *Body Narratives: Motion and Emotion in the French Enlightenment*. Turnhout: Brepols, 119–155.

Hyounggon, K. & Jamal, T. (2007) Touristic Quest for Existential Authenticity, *Annals of Tourism Research*, 34(1), 181–201.

Ibrahim, N. et al. (2011) Cultural Learning in Virtual Heritage: An Overview, in H. Badioze Zaman et al. (Eds.) *IVIC 2011, Part II, LNCS 7067*. Berlin: Springer, 273–283.

Ikeda, R. (1978) *Claudine . . .!* [*shōjo manga* publ. in *Margaret Comics*]. Tokyo: Shueisha.

Ikeda, R. (2002) *La Rose de Versailles* [*shōjo manga*]. Bruxelles: Kana.

Ikeda, R. (2011) Talk, *La Maison de la Culture du Japon*, 2 February, Personal Attendance.

IMDb (2006) *Marie Antoinette* by Sofia Coppola – Box Office Mojo [online]; Available at: www.boxofficemojo.com/movies/?page=intl&id=marieantoinette.htm [Last Accessed: 25 March 2018].

Inglis, F. (2000) *The Delicious History of the Holiday*. Abingdon: Routledge.

Irazábal, C. (2004) Architecture and the Production of Postcard Images: Invocations of Tradition vs. Critical Transnationalism in Curitiba, in N. AlSayyad (Ed.) *The End of Tradition?* Abingdon: Routledge, 144–170.

Isaac, T. (2011) Black Jade: On the Trail of Marie Antoinette's Last Scent, *Vanity Fair*, 21 October.

Ivy, M. (1995) *Discourses of the Vanishing: Modernity, Phantasm, Japan*. Chicago: University of Chicago Press.

Jallut, M. (Ed.) (1955) *Marie-Antoinette, archiduchesse, dauphine et reine* [exhibition catalogue]. Paris: Réunion des musées nationaux.

Jallut, M. (1969) Les collections de Marie-Antoinette, *Arts asiatiques*, 20, 209–220.

Jamal, T. & Robinson, M. (Eds.) (2009) *The SAGE Handbook of Tourism Studies*. London: SAGE.

Jencks, C. & Neves, T. (2000) A Walk on the Wild Side: Urban Ethnography Meets the *Flâneur*, *Cultural Values*, 4(1), 1–17.

Jokilehto, J. (1999) *A History of Architectural Conservation*. Oxford: Butterworth-Heinemann.

Jokilehto, J. (2005) *Definition of Cultural Heritage*, References to Documents in History [1st version 1990], in *ICCROM Working Group 'Heritage and Society'*.

Jokinen, E. & Veijola, S. (1997) The Disoriented Tourist: The Figuration of the Tourist in Contemporary Cultural Critique, in C. Rojek & J. Urry (Eds.) *Touring Cultures: Transformations of Travel and Theory*. Abingdon: Routledge, 23–51.

Jones, C. (2013) [*Composer/Lyricist*]; [email] Personal Communication, 1 May.

Jones, C. (2014) [email] Personal Communication, 3 September.

Jones, S. et al. (2017) 3D Heritage Visualisation and the Negotiation of Authenticity: The ACCORD Project, *International Journal of Heritage Studies*, 1–22, [online]; DOI:10.1080/13527258.2017.1378905.

Jourdan, A. (1997) *Les Monuments de la Révolution 1770–1804: Une histoire de représentation.* Paris: Honoré Champion.

Kafker, F.A. & Laux, J.M. (Eds.) (1989) *The French Revolution: Conflicting Interpretations* [1st ed. 1968]. Malabar, FL: R.E. Krieger.

Kaiser, T.E. (2000) Who's Afraid of Marie-Antoinette? Diplomacy, Austrophobia and the Queen, *French History*, 14(3), 241–271.

Kaiser, T.E. (2003a) Ambiguous Identities: Marie-Antoinette and the House of Lorraine from the Affair of the Minuet to Lambesc's Charge, in D. Goodman (Ed.) *Marie-Antoinette: Writings on the Body of a Queen.* Abingdon: Routledge, 171–198.

Kaiser, T.E. (2003b) From the Austrian Committee to the Foreign Plot: Marie-Antoinette, Austrophobia, and the Terror, *French Historical Studies*, 26(4), 579–617.

Kalay, Y.E. et al. (Eds.) (2008) *New Heritage: New Media and Cultural Heritage.* Abingdon: Routledge.

Kant, I. (1999) *The Critique of Pure Reason* [transl. P. Guyer & A. Wood] [1st ed. 1781]. Cambridge: Cambridge University Press.

Kapferer, J.-N. (1990) *Rumeurs. Le plus vieux média du monde* [1st ed. 1987]. Paris: Seuil.

Kaplan, F.E.S. (Ed.) (1994) *Museums and the Making of 'Ourselves': The Role of Objects in National Identity.* London: Leicester University Press.

Kaplan, S.L. (1995) *Farewell, Revolution: Disputed Legacies, France 1789/1989.* Ithaca: Cornell University Press.

Karamzine, N.M. (1867) *Lettres d'un voyageur russe en France, en Allemagne et en Suisse (1789–1790).* Paris: Meillier.

Karamzine, N.M. (1885) *Voyage en France, 1789–1790* [transl. A. Legrelle]. Paris: Hachette.

Karp, I. & Lavine, S.D. (Eds.) (1991) *Exhibiting Cultures: The Poetics and Politics of Museum Display.* Washington, DC: Smithsonian Institution Press.

Karp, I. et al. (Eds.) (1992) *Museums & Communities: The Politics of Public Culture.* Washington, DC: Smithsonian Institution Press.

Kates, G. (Ed.) (1997) *The French Revolution: Recent Debates and New Controversies.* Abingdon: Routledge.

Kavanagh, G. (2000) *Dream Spaces: Memory and the Museum.* London: Leicester University Press.

Kayser, C. et al. (Eds.) (2003) *L'enfant chéri au siècle des Lumières: Après l'Émile* [exhibition catalogue]. Paris: L'Inventaire.

Kenji Tierney, R. (2007) Beauty Up: Exploring Contemporary Japanese Body Aesthetics, *American Anthropologist*, 109(4), 773–774.

Kim, S. et al. (2009) Small Screen, Big Tourism: The Role of Popular Korean Television Dramas in South Korean Tourism, *Tourism Geographies*, 11(3), 308–333.

Kirshenblatt-Gimblett, B. (1998) *Destination Culture: Tourism, Museums, and Heritage.* Berkeley: University of California Press.

Knell, S. et al. (Eds.) (2007) *Museum Revolutions: How Museums Change and Are Changed.* Abingdon: Routledge.

Knudsen, B.T. & Waade, A.M. (Eds.) (2010) *Re-investing Authenticity: Tourism, Place and Emotions.* Bristol: Channel View.

Korstanje, M.E. & George, B.P. (2014) Consuming Tourism as Its Media Representations: The Widening Gap between Being and Media Mediated Knowing, *TURyDES*, 7(17), 1–19.

Koselleck, R. (2004) *Futures Past: On the Semantics of Historical Time* [transl. K. Tribe] [1st German ed. 1979]. New York: Columbia University Press.

Kozinets, R.V. (2010) *Netnography: Doing Ethnographic Research Online*. Los Angeles: SAGE.

Kreps, C.F. (2003) *Liberating Culture: Cross-Cultural Perspectives on Museums, Curation and Heritage Preservation*. Abingdon: Routledge.

Krippendorff, K. (2013) *Content Analysis: An Introduction to Its Methodology* [1st ed. 1980]. London: SAGE.

Kuisel, R.F. (1993) *Seducing the French: The Dilemma of Americanization*. Berkeley: University of California Press.

Kurzweil, A. (2001) *The Grand Complication*. New York: Hyperion.

L'Abbé de Lille (1782) *Les Jardins Ou L'Art D'Embellir les Paysages: Poème*. Paris: Philippe-Denys Pierres.

Lablaude, P.-A. (2002) La restauration du théâtre de la reine au Petit Trianon, *Monumental*, 162–165.

Lablaude, P.-A. (Baudin, P. et al.) (2006a) *Étude préalable à la restauration des intérieurs, premier volet: rez-de-chussée*. Établissement public du musée et du domaine national de Versailles, Direction du patrimoine, Juin.

Lablaude, P.-A. (Baudin, P. et al.) (2006b) *Étude préalable à la restauration des intérieurs, second volet: entresol et attique*. Établissement public du musée et du domaine national de Versailles, Direction du patrimoine, Octobre.

Lablaude, P.-A. (Bahba, S. et al.) (2007) *Étude préalable de restauration des façades*. Établissement public du musée et du domaine national de Versailles, Direction du patrimoine, Août.

Lablaude, P.-A. (2010) *Les Jardins de Versailles*. Tours: Scala.

de Laborde, A. (1808) *Description des nouveaux jardins de la France et de ses anciens châteaux*. Paris: Delance.

de La Borde, J.B. et al. (1781–1784) *Description générale et particulière de la France*. Paris: Pierres.

de La Borde, J.B. et al. (1784–1797) *Voyage pittoresque de la France*. Paris: Lamy.

L.A. Mayer Museum for Islamic Art (2009) *The Art of Time: The Sir David Salomons Collections of Watches and Clocks*. Jerusalem: L.A. Mayer Museum for Islamic Art.

Lamont, M. (2017) *The Mysterious Paths of Versailles: An Investigation of a Psychical Journey Back in Time*. Ishpeming, MI: Book Venture.

Lamy, G. (2005) L'éducation d'un jardinier royal au Petit Trianon: Antoine Richard (1734–1807), *Polia, revue de l'art des jardins*, 4, 57–73.

Lamy, G. (2010) Le Jardin d'Éden, le paradis terrestre renouvellé dans le Jardin de la Reine à Trianon de Pierre-Joseph Buc'hoz, Bulletin du Centre de recherche du château de Versailles [online]; Available at: http://crcv.revues.org/10300 [Accessed: 16 March 2014].

Landes, J.B. (1988) *Women and the Public Sphere in the Age of the French Revolution*. Ithaca: Cornell University Press.

Landsberg, A. (1997) America, the Holocaust, and the Mass Culture of Memory: Toward a Radical Politics of Empathy, *New German Critique*, 71, 63–86.

Landsberg, A. (2004) *Prosthetic Memory: The Transformation of American Remembrance in the Age of Mass Culture*. New York: Columbia University Press.

Lanoë, C. et al. (Eds.) (2011) *Cultures de Cour, Cultures du Corps XIVe-XVIIIe siècle*. Versailles: Centre de recherche du château de Versailles.

Lanser, S.S. (2003) Afterword – Eating Cake: The (Ab)uses of Marie-Antoinette, in D. Goodman (Ed.) *Marie-Antoinette: Writings on the Body of a Queen*. Abingdon: Routledge, 273–289.

Largardère, G. et al. (Eds.) (2008) *Les Quatre Saisons de Carmontelle: Divertissement et illusions au siècle des Lumières* [exhibition catalogue]. Sceaux: Musée de l'Ile de France; Paris: Somogy.

Lash, S. (1990) *Sociology of Postmodernism*. Abingdon: Routledge.

Lash, S. & Urry, J. (1994) *Economies of Signs & Space*. London: SAGE.

Lasky, K. (2013) *Marie-Antoinette: Princess of Versailles, Austria – France, 1769* [Historical Fiction]. Scholastic.

de La Tour du Pin, L. [Marquise] (1920) *Journal d'une femme de cinquante ans; T.1 1778–1815*. Paris: R. Chapelot.

Lau, R.W.K. (2010) Revisiting Authenticity: A Social Realist Approach, *Annals of Tourism Research*, 37(2), 478–498.

Laugier, M.-A. (1753) *Essai sur l'architecture*. Paris: Duchesne.

Laval, A. (2017) Marie-Antoinette et la passion du théâtre, *Château de Versailles*, 25, 16–25.

Lavedan, P. (1944) Richard Mique, architecte de Marie-Antoinette, *Bulletin de la Société de l'Histoire de l'Art Français*, 25.

Lecoq, A.-M. (1986) La Symbolique de l'État: Les images de la monarchie des premiers Valois à Louis XIV, in P. Nora (Ed.) *Les lieux de mémoire: La Nation II*. Paris: Gallimard, 145–192.

Ledoux-Lebard, D. (1989) *Versailles, Le Petit Trianon: Le mobilier des inventaires de 1807, 1810 et 1839*. Paris: Éd. de l'Amateur.

Lee, L. (2017) Wonderland Recursion: Versailles as Japan's Imaginary Playground, *Contemporary French and Francophone Studies*, 21(1), 100–108.

Lee, R. (2013) Historical Fiction: Warts and All, *The Historian*, 117, 16–21.

Lefebvre, G. (1939) *Quatre-Vingt-Neuf: L'année de la Révolution*. Paris: Maison du Livre Français.

Lefebvre, H. (1991) *The Production of Space* [transl. D. Nicholson-Smith] [1st French ed. 1983]. Oxford: Blackwell.

Le Goff, J. & Nora, P. (Eds.) (2011) *Faire de l'histoire. Nouveaux problèmes, nouvelles approches, nouveaux objets* [1st ed. 1974]. Paris: Gallimard.

Le Goff, J. (2014) *Faut-il vraiment découper l'histoire en tranches?* Paris: Seuil.

Leite, N. & Graburn, N. (2009) Anthropological Interventions in Tourism Studies, in T. Jamal & M. Robinson (Eds.) *The SAGE Handbook of Tourism Studies*. London: SAGE, 35–64.

Leith, J.A. (1965) *The Idea of Art as Propaganda in France 1750–1799: A Study in the History of Ideas*. Toronto: University of Toronto Press.

Le Loarer, B. & Bouvarel, C. (2014) *Rois et reines de France*. Toulouse: Milan.

Lenman, R. (2003) British Photographers and Tourism in the Nineteenth Century: Three Case Studies, in D. Crouch & N. Lübbren (Eds.) *Visual Culture and Tourism*. Oxford: Berg, 91–108.

Léonard [Léonard-Alexis Autié] (1905) *Souvenirs de Léonard [Autié], coiffeur de la reine Marie-Antoinette*. Paris: Fayard.

Le Rouge, G.-L. (1776–1779) *Détails des nouveaux jardins à la mode – Jardins anglo-chinois*. Paris: Le Rouge.

de Lescure, M. (1866) *Correspondance secrète inédite sur Louis XVI, Marie-Antoinette, la cour et la ville de 1777 à 1792* [2 vols.]. Paris: Henri Plon.

de Lescure, M. (1867a) *Le Palais de Trianon – Histoire – Description catalogue des objets exposés sous les auspices de La Majesté L'Impératrice*. Paris: Henri Plon.
de Lescure, M. (1867b) *La vraie Marie-Antoinette*. Paris: Henri Plon.
Lever, É. (1991) *Marie-Antoinette* [1st ed. 1985]. Paris: Fayard.
Lever, É. (2000a) *Marie-Antoinette: The Last Queen of France* [transl. C. Temerson]. New York: Farrar, Straus & Giroux.
Lever, É. (2000b) *Marie-Antoinette: La dernière reine*. Paris: Gallimard.
Lever, É. (2002) *Marie-Antoinette, journal d'une reine*. Paris: R. Laffont.
Lever, É. (2004) *L'Affaire du Collier*. Paris: Fayard.
Lever, É. (2005a) *Marie-Antoinette: Correspondance (1770–1793)*. Paris: J. Tallandier.
Lever, É. (2005b) *Les dernières noces de la monarchie: Louis XVI, Marie-Antoinette*. Paris: Fayard.
Lever, É. (2006a) *C'était Marie-Antoinette*. Paris: Fayard.
Lever, É. (2006b) La Correspondance de la dauphine et de la reine, in Institut de la Maison de Bourbon (Ed.) *Marie-Antoinette face à l'histoire* [Sorbonne Colloquium]. Paris: François-Xavier de Guibert, 29–49.
Lever, É. (2006c) *Marie-Antoinette: Un destin brisée*. Paris: Réunion des musées nationaux.
Lever, É. & Garcia, J. (2008) *Marie-Antoinette: Le triomphe de l'élégance et du luxe*. Boulogne-Billancourt: Beaux-Arts.
Lichfield, J. (2006) New Portrait of a Princess: A Revolution in French Thinking, *The Independent*, 30 January.
Light, D. (2011) Culture, Heritage and Representation: Perspectives on Visuality and the Past, *International Journal of Heritage Studies*, 17(1), 89–91.
Light, D. (2015) Heritage and Tourism, in E. Waterton & S. Watson (Eds.) *The Palgrave Handbook of Contemporary Heritage Research*. Basingstoke: Palgrave Macmillan, 144–158.
de Ligne, C.-J. [Prince] (1814) *Mémoires*. Paris: Champion.
de Ligne, C.-J. [Prince] (1922) *Coup d'oeil sur Beloeil et sur une une grande partie des jardins d'Europe (1781)*. Paris: Ernest de Ganay, Bossard.
Lilti, A. (2017) *The Invention of Celebrity* [transl. L. Jeffress] [1st French ed. 2015]. Cambridge: Polity Press.
Littler, J. & Naidoo, R. (Eds.) (2005) *The Politics of Heritage: The Legacies of 'Race'*. Abingdon: Routledge.
Llobera, J.R. (1996) *The God of Modernity: The Development of Nationalism in Western Europe*. Oxford: Berg.
Logan, W. & Reeves, K. (Eds.) (2009) *Places of Pain and Shame: Dealing with 'Difficult' Heritage*. Abingdon: Routledge.
Long, P. & Palmer, N.J. (Eds.) (2007) *Royal Tourism: Excursions around Monarchy*. Clevedon: Channel View.
Long, P. & Robinson, M. (2009) Tourism, Popular Culture and the Media, in T. Jamal & M. Robinson (Eds.) *The SAGE Handbook of Tourism Studies*. London: SAGE, 98–114.
Lorin, M. (2014a) [*Association Marie-Antoinette Secretary and Co-Founder*]; [email] Personal Communication, 8 August.
Lorin, M. (2014b) [conversation Malesherbes] Personal Communication, 17 August.
De Lorme, E. (2006) *Pavillons et fêtes sous l'Ancien Régime*. Saint-Rémy-en-L'Eau: Monelle Hayot.

Delorme, P. (2011) *Marie-Antoinette: Épouse de Louis XVI, mère de Louis XVII*. Paris: Pygmalion.

Lowenthal, D. (1989) Nostalgia Tells It Like It Wasn't, in M. Chase & C. Shaw (Eds.) *The Imagined Past: History and Nostalgia*. Manchester, NH: Manchester University Press, 18–32.

Lowenthal, D. (1996) *Possessed by the Past: The Heritage Crusade and the Spoils of History*. New York: Free Press.

Lowenthal, D. (2006) 'Reparition, Restitution, Reparations', Lecture given at the British Academy, 8 December.

Lowenthal, D. (2009) Patrons, Populists, Apologists: Crises in Museum Stewardship, in L. Gibson & J. Pendlebury (Eds.) *Valuing Historic Environments*. Farnham: Ashgate, 19–31.

Lowenthal, D. (2015) *The Past Is a Foreign Country* [1st ed. 1985]. Cambridge: Cambridge University Press.

Lyons, M. (1994) *Napoleon Bonaparte and the Legacy of the French Revolution*. New York: St Martin's Press.

Van Maanen, J. (Ed.) (1995) *Representation in Ethnography*. Thousand Oaks: SAGE.

Van Maanen, J. (2011) *Tales of the Field: On Writing Ethnography* [1st ed. 1988]. Chicago: The University of Chicago Press.

Macarthur, J. (2007) *The Picturesque: Architecture, Disgust and Other Irregularities*. Abingdon: Routledge.

Macaulay, A. (2009) Off with Her Head? Sure, but Let Her Dance to Shostakovich First, *The New York Times*, 3 March.

MacCannell, D. (1973) Staged Authenticity: Arrangements of Social Space in Tourist Settings, *American Journal of Sociology*, 79, 589–603.

MacCannell, D. (1999) *The Tourist: A New Theory of the Leisure Class* [1st ed. 1976]. Berkeley: University of California Press.

Macdonald, S. & Fyfe, G. (Eds.) (1996) *Theorizing Museums: Representing Identity and Diversity in a Changing World*. Oxford: Blackwell.

Macdonald, S. (Ed.) (1998) *The Politics of Display: Museums, Science, Culture*. Abingdon: Routledge.

Macdonald, S. (2003) Museums, National, Postnational and Transcultural Identities, *Museum and Society*, 1(1), 1–16.

Macdonald, S. (Ed.) (2006) *A Companion to Museum Studies*. Malden, MA: Wiley-Blackwell.

Macdonald, S. (2009) *Difficult Heritage: Negotiating the Nazi Past in Nuremberg and Beyond*. Abingdon: Routledge.

Macleod, E.V. (1998) *A War of Ideas: British Attitudes to the Wars against Revolutionary France, 1792–1802*. Aldershot: Ashgate.

Macleod, N. (2006) Cultural Tourism: Aspects of Authenticity and Commodification, in M.K. Smith & M. Robinson (Eds.) *Cultural Tourism in a Changing World: Politics, Participation and (Re)Presentation*. Clevedon: Channel View, 177–190.

Mahler, C. (1887) Le Petit Trianon, d'après un livre récent de M.G. Desjardins, *Mémoires de la Société des sciences morales, des lettres et des arts de Seine-et-Oise*, 15, 175–214.

Maior-Barron, D. (2011) Petit Trianon, Home to Marie Antoinette, in C. Mansfield & S. Seligman (Eds.) *Narrative and the Built Heritage: Papers in Tourism Research*. Saarbrücken: VDM Verlag, 40–62.

Maior-Barron, D. (2014) Palace of Versailles, UNESCO Heritage Site: Survivor of the French Revolution, in International Association of World Heritage Professionals e.V. (Ed.) *The Right to [World] Heritage*, IAWHP e.V. – DAAD Conference. BTU Cottbus-Senftenberg, Germany, 23–25 October.

Maior-Barron, D. (2015a) Conflicting Legacies at the *Estate of Marie-Antoinette*: Petit Trianon, a Theoretical Case of Dissonant Heritage, in *The Legacy of House Museums Promoting Dialogue among Generations*, ICOM DEMHIST Conference, Mexico City/Mexico, 19–21 October.

Maior-Barron, D. (2015b) *Petit Trianon and Marie Antoinette: Representation, Interpretation, Perception*. Ph.D. Dissertation, Plymouth University, UK in collaboration with Château de Versailles, France.

Maisonnier, É. et al. (Eds.) (2006) *Marie-Antoinette, femme réelle, femme mythique* [exhibition catalogue]. Paris: Magellan & Cie.

Malpas, J. (2008) New Media, Cultural Heritage and the Sense of Place: Mapping the Conceptual Ground, *International Journal of Heritage Studies*, 14(3), 197–209.

Mansfield, C. & Seligman, S. (Eds.) (2011) *Narrative and the Built Heritage: Papers in Tourism Research*. Saarbrücken: VDM Verlag.

Mansfield, C. (2015) *Researching Literary Tourism*. Plymouth: TKT.

Maral, A. (2012) *Marie-Antoinette – Un destin tragique*. Rennes: Ouest-France.

Maral, A. (2016) *Les Femmes de Versailles*. Paris: Perrin; Versailles: Château de Versailles.

Marie, P. (1984) La Bibliothèque des Amis de l'Instruction du IIIe Arrondissement: Un temple, quartier du Temple, in P. Nora (Ed.) *Les lieux de mémoire: La République*. Paris: Gallimard, 323–351.

Marling, K.A. (Ed.) (1997) *Designing Disney's Theme Parks: The Architecture of Reassurance*. Paris: Flammarion.

Marrand-Fouquet, C. (1989) *La Femme au temps de la Révolution*. Paris: Stock-Laurence Pernoud.

Marshall, C. & Rossman, G.B. (2011) *Designing Qualitative Research* [1st ed. 1989]. London: SAGE.

Martens, P. (Ed.) (2016) *Virtual Palaces, Part I: Digitizing and Modelling Palaces* [online publication]. Leuven: Palatium. Available at: www.courtresidences.eu/uploads/publications/virtual-palaces-I.pdf [Accessed: 15 September].

Martin, J.-C. (1984) La Vendée, région-mémoire: Bleus et blancs, in P. Nora (Ed.) *Les lieux de mémoire: La République*. Paris: Gallimard, 595–617.

Martin, J.-C. (2006) *Violence et Révolution. Essai sur la naissance d'un mythe national*. Paris: Seuil.

Martin, J.-C. (2007) *Vendée et Révolution. Accepter la mémoire pour écrire l'histoire*. Paris: Perrin, Tempus.

Martin, J.-C. (2010) *La Terreur. Part maudite de la Révolution*. Paris: Gallimard.

Martin, J.-C. (2011) Massacres, tueries, exécutions et meurtres de masse pendant la Révolution, quelles grilles d'analyse? – Les massacres aux temps des Révolutions, La Révolution française [online]; Available at: http://lrf.revues.org/201 [Accessed: 15 March 2014].

Martin, M. (2011) *Dairy Queens: The Politics of Pastoral Architecture from Catherine De' Medici to Marie-Antoinette*. Cambridge, MA: Harvard University Press.

Mason, H.T. (Ed.) (1998) *The Darnton Debate: Books and Revolution in the Eighteenth Century*. Oxford: Voltaire Foundation.

Mason, J. (2002) *Qualitative Researching* [1st ed. 1996]. London: SAGE.
Mason, L. & Rizzo, T. (1999) *The French Revolution: A Document Collection*. Boston, MA: Houghton Mifflin Company.
Mason, L. (2003) 'We're Just Little People, Louis': Marie-Antoinette on Film, in D. Goodman (Ed.) *Marie-Antoinette: Writings on the Body of a Queen*. Abingdon: Routledge, 239–251.
Masson, R. (2013) Marie-Antoinette dans l'intimité d'une reine [Album], *Château de Versailles de l'Ancien Régime à nos jours*, hors-série, 1, 4–98.
Maudlin, D. (2015) *The Idea of the Cottage in English Architecture 1760–1860*. Abingdon: Routledge.
Mauger, B. (2011) Marie-Antoinette, héroïne insoumise d'un manga, *Le Monde*, 28 January.
Mauricheau-Beaupré, C. (1934) Deux commodes de la chambre du roi; présentation nouvelle de la chambre de la reine au Petit Trianon, *Bulletin des musées de France*, 2, 49–53.
Mauzi, R. (1960) *L'Idée du bonheur au XVIIIe siècle*. Paris: Armand Colin.
Mauzi, R. (2008) *L'art de vivre d'une femme au XVIIIe siècle; Suivi du 'Discours sur le bonheur' de Madame du Châtelet*. Paris: Desjonquères.
Maza, S. (2003) The Diamond Necklace Affair Revisited (1785–1786): The Case of the Missing Queen, in D. Goodman (Ed.) *Marie-Antoinette: Writings on the Body of a Queen*. Abingdon: Routledge, 73–97.
Mazeau, G. (2008) Bling-bling à Versailles, *Annales historiques de la Révolution française*, 352, 263–266.
McDowell, S. (2008) Heritage, Memory and Identity, in B. Graham & P. Howard (Eds.) *The Ashgate Research Companion to Heritage & Identity*. Aldershot: Ashgate, 37–54.
McGrath, K. (Ed.) (2010) *Versailles photographié, 1850–2010* [exhibition catalogue]. Paris: Artlys & Versailles: Château de Versailles.
McGrath, K. (2011) [*Chef du service des archives de l'Établissement public du musée et du domaine national de Versailles*]; [conversation Versailles] Personal Communication, 10 January.
McIntosh, A.J. & Prentice, R.C. (1999) Affirming Authenticity: Consuming Cultural Heritage, *Annals of Tourism Research*, 26(3), 589–612.
McIntyre, D. & Wehner, K. (Eds.) (2001) *National Museums: Negotiating Histories*. Canberra: National Museum of Australia.
McLean, F. & Cooke, S. (2003a) Constructing the Identity of a Nation: The Tourist Gaze at the Museum of Scotland, *Tourism, Culture and Communication*, 4, 153–162.
McLean, F. & Cooke, S. (2003b) The National Museum of Scotland: A Symbol for a New Scotland?, *Scottish Affairs*, 45, 111–127.
McLean, F. (2008) Museums and the Representation of Identity, in B. Graham & P. Howard (Eds.) *The Ashgate Research Companion to Heritage & Identity*. Aldershot: Ashgate, 283–297.
McLelland, M. (2000) *Male Homosexuality in Modern Japan: Cultural Myths and Social Realities*. Richmond: Curzon Press.
McMahon, D.M. (2001) *Enemies of the Enlightenment: The French Counter-Enlightenment and the Making of Modernity*. Oxford: Oxford University Press.
Meethan, K. (2001) *Tourism in Global Society: Place, Culture, Consumption*. Basingstoke: Palgrave Macmillan.

Meethan, K. et al. (Eds.) (2006) *Tourism Consumption and Representation: Narratives of Place and Self.* Wallingford: CAB International.

Meethan, K. (2011) Narrating and Performing Tourist Space: Notes towards Some Conceptual and Methodological Issues, in C. Mansfield & S. Seligman (Eds.) *Narrative and the Built Heritage: Papers in Tourism Research.* Saarbrücken: VDM Verlag, 129–140.

Mendelsohn, D. (2009) *How Beautiful It Is and How Easily It Can Be Broken: Essays.* New York: Harper Perennial.

Van Meter, J. (2012), Dream Girl, *Vogue U.S.*, April, 803–809.

Meyer, D. (1974) Meubles et objets d'art des collections royales à Versailles. I – À propos du mobilier de Marie-Antoinette au Petit-Trianon. II – Une pendule et deux candelabres du comte d'Artois au Temple, *Revue du Louvre et des musées de France*, 4/5, 279–286.

Meyer, D. (1976) Les antichambres et les salons du Petit Trianon, *Revue du Louvre et des musées de France*, 3, 208–212.

Michelet, J. (1847–1853) *Histoire de la Révolution Française* [7 vols.]. Paris: Chamerot.

Michelet, J. (1867) *Histoire de France au dix-huitième siècle* [Vol. 17]. Paris: Chamerot.

Minsky, M. (1980) Telepresence, *OMNI Magazine*, June, 45–51.

Mique, R. (1998) *Recueil des plans du Petit Trianon* [Facsimile of the Original Plans of the Architect of Le Hameau Dating Back to the 1780s]. Paris: A. de Gourcouff.

Misiura, S. (2006) *Heritage Marketing.* Oxford: Butterworth-Heinemann.

Moberly, C.A.E. & Jourdain, E.F. (1952) *An Adventure* [1st ed. 1911]. London: Faber and Faber.

Moberly, C.A.E. & Jourdain, E.F. (2003) *Les Fantômes de Trianon: Une aventure.* Monaco: du Rocher.

de Montety, E. (2006) Evelyne Lever: 'L'émouvante reine n'émeut pas', *Le Figaro*, 25 May.

de Montjoie, G. (1814) *Eloge historique et funèbre de Louis XVI, roi de France et de Navarre: précédé des fastes des Bourbons: suivi de la déclaration de S.M., adressée à tous les Français à sa sortie de Paris, le 20 juin 1791.* Paris: Lebégue.

Montupet, P. (2006) Marie-Antoinette par Pierre de Nolhac (1859–1936), in É. Maisonnier et al. (Eds.) *Marie-Antoinette, femme réelle, femme mythique* [exhibition catalogue]. Paris: Magellan & Cie, 85–93.

Morel, J.-M. (1776) *Theorie des Jardins.* Paris: Pissot.

Morgan, N. & Pritchard, A. (1998) *Tourism Promotion and Power: Creating Images, Creating Identities.* Chichester: John Wiley & Sons.

Morgan, N. (2004) Problematizing Place Promotion, in A.A. Lew et al. (Eds.) *A Companion to Tourism.* Malden, MA: Blackwell, 173–183.

Morishita, M. (2010) *The Empty Museum: Western Cultures and the Artistic Field in Modern Japan.* Farnham: Ashgate.

Mornet, D. (1933) *Les origines intellectuelles de la Révolution française (1715–1787).* Paris: Armand Colin.

Mossiker, F. (1961) *The Queen's Necklace.* New York: Simon & Schuster.

Moulin, J.-M. (1975) Deux commodes de l'appartement intérieur de Marie-Antoinette à Compiègne, *Revue du Louvre et des musées de France*, 3, 173–181.

Mugerauer, R. (1995) *Interpreting Environments: Tradition, Deconstruction, Hermeneutics.* Austin: University of Texas Press.

Mugerauer, R. (2001) Openings to Each Other in the Technological Age, in N. AlSayyad (Ed.) *Consuming Tradition, Manufacturing Heritage: Global Norms and Urban Forms in the Age of Tourism*. Abingdon: Routledge, 90–110.

Müller, F. & Gabet, O. (2017) *Christian Dior, Couturier du Rêve* [exhibition catalogue]. Paris: Musée des Arts Décoratifs.

Mureşan, A. & Smith, K.A. (1998) Dracula's Castle in Transylvania: Conflicting Heritage Marketing Strategies, *International Journal of Heritage Studies*, 4(2), 73–85.

Murray, R. (2006a) Writer/Director Sofia Coppola Talks about 'Marie Antoinette', *About.com Hollywood Movies* [online]; Available at: http://movies.about.com/od/marieantoinette/a/mariesc101006.htm [Accessed: 18 April 2011].

Murray, R. (2006b) Marie Antoinette Movie Review, *About.com Hollywood Movies* [online]; Available at: http://movies.about.com/od/marieantoinette/gr/marie101906.htm [Accessed: 18 April 2011].

Napier, S.J. (1998) Vampires, Psychic Girls, Flying Women and Sailor Scouts, in D.P. Martinez (Ed.) *The Worlds of Japanese Popular Culture: Gender, Shifting Boundaries and Global Culture*. Cambridge: Cambridge University Press, 91–109.

National Museum of Women in the Arts (2012) *Royalists to Romantics: Women Artists from Versailles, the Louvre and Other French National Collections* [exhibition catalogue]. London: Scala; Washington DC: National Museum of Women in the Arts.

Necker, G. & de Staël, B. (1818) *Considérations sur les principaux evénémens* [sic] *de la Révolution françoise* [sic]. Paris: Delaunay.

de Nolhac, P. (1898a) *Marie-Antoinette Dauphine*. Paris: Calmann-Levy.

de Nolhac, P. (1898b) Marie-Antoinette & Vigée-Lebrun, *Revue de l'art ancien et moderne*, décembre, 523–528.

de Nolhac, P. (1899a) *La Reine Marie-Antoinette*. Paris: Calmann-Levy.

de Nolhac, P. (1899b) Les consignes de Marie-Antoinette au Petit-Trianon, *Revue de l'histoire de Versailles et de Seine-et-Oise*, 1, 74–80.

de Nolhac, P. (1906) *Versailles and the Trianons*. New York: Dodd, Mead & Co.

de Nolhac, P. (1925) *Études sur la Cour de France. Le Trianon de Marie-Antoinette*. Paris: Calmann-Levy.

de Nolhac, P. (1927) *Trianon*. Paris: Louis Conard.

de Nolhac, P. (préf. de) & Hirschauer, C. (avant-propos de) (1927) *Marie-Antoinette et sa cour* [exhibition catalogue]. Versailles: Bibliothèque de Versailles [impr. La Gutenberg].

Nora, P. (1984a) *Entre Mémoire et Histoire – La problématique des lieux*, in P. Nora (Ed.) *Les lieux de mémoire: La République*. Paris: Gallimard, XV–XLII.

Nora, P. (1984b) De la République à la Nation, in P. Nora (Ed.) *Les lieux de mémoire: La République*. Paris: Gallimard, 651–659.

Nora, P. (1984c) Lavisse, Instituteur national: Le 'Petit Lavisse', évangile de la République, in P. Nora (Ed.) *Les lieux de mémoire: La République*. Paris: Gallimard, 247–289.

Nora, P. (1984d) Le Dictionnaire de pédagogie de Ferdinand Buisson: Cathédrale de l'école primaire, in P. Nora (Ed.) *Les lieux de mémoire: La République*. Paris: Gallimard, 353–378.

Nora, P. (1992) La Génération, in P. Nora (Ed.) *Les lieux de mémoire: Les France III*. Paris: Gallimard, 931–971.

Nora, P. (Ed.) (1984–1992) *Les lieux de mémoire: La République* 1984 [1 vol.], *La Nation* 1986 [3 vols.], *Les France* 1992 [3 vols.]. Paris: Gallimard.

Nora, P. (Ed.) (1996–1998) *Realms of Memory: The Construction of the French Past Conflicts and Divisions* [Vol.1], *Traditions* [Vol. 2], *Symbols* [Vol. 3] [transl. A. Goldhammer]. New York: Columbia University Press.

Nora, P. et al. (2002) *Discours de réception de Pierre Nora à l'Académie française et réponse de René Rémond suivis des allocutions prononcées à l'occasion de la remise de l'épée*. Paris: Gallimard.

Nora, P. (2011a) *Historien Public*. Paris: Gallimard.

Nora, P. (Ed.) (2011b) *Présent, nation, mémoire*. Paris: Gallimard.

Nora, P. (2013) *Recherches de la France*. Paris: Gallimard.

O'Brien, C.C. (Ed.) (1986) *Edmund Burke: Reflections on the Revolution in France and on the Proceedings in Certain Societies in London Relative to That Event*. London: Penguin Books.

O'Connell, L.M. (1989) *Architecture and the French Revolution: Change and Continuity under the Conseil des Bâtiments Civils (1795–1799)*. Ph.D. Dissertation, UMI Dissertation Services.

O'Hagan, S. (2006) Sofia Coppola Interview, *The Observer*, 8 October.

Oka, Y. (2008) Marie-Antoinette et le Japon, in M. Bascou et al. (Eds.) *Louvre: Musée du Louvre, Fastes de la Cour de France au XVIIIe siècle* [exhibition catalogue]. Japon: The Asahi Shimbun, 22–31.

Olick, J.K. et al. (Eds.) (2011) *The Collective Memory Reader*. Oxford: Oxford University Press.

Orba li, A. & Woodward, S. (2009) Tourism and Heritage Conservation, in T. Jamal & M. Robinson (Eds.) *The SAGE Handbook of Tourism Studies*. London: SAGE, 314–332.

d'Orléans-Bragance, I. (1993) *Moi, Marie Antoinette*. Paris: R. Laffont.

Ory, P. (1984a) Le Grand Dictionnaire de Pierre Larousse: Alphabet de la République, in P. Nora (Ed.) *Les lieux de mémoire: La République*. Paris: Gallimard, 229–246.

Ory, P. (1984b) Le Centenaire de la Révolution Française: La preuve par 89, in P. Nora (Ed.) *Les lieux de mémoire: La République*. Paris: Gallimard, 523–560.

Osamu, T. (1995) *Sengo manga gojūnenshi* [A Fifty-Year History of Postwar Comics]. Tokyo: Chikuma.

Osborne, P.D. (2000) *Travelling Light: Photography, Travel and Visual Culture*. Manchester: Manchester University Press.

Outram, D. (1989) *The Body and the French Revolution: Sex, Class and Political Culture*. New Haven: Yale University Press.

Ozouf, J. & Ozouf, M. (1984) Le Tour de la France par deux enfants: Le petit livre rouge de la République, in P. Nora (Ed.) *Les lieux de mémoire: La République*. Paris: Gallimard, 291–321.

Ozouf, M. (1984) Le Panthéon: L'École normale des morts, in P. Nora (Ed.) *Les lieux de mémoire: La République*. Paris: Gallimard, 139–166.

Ozouf, M. (1988) *Festivals and the French Revolution* [transl. A. Sheridan]. Cambridge, MA: Harvard University Press.

Ozouf, M. (2011) *La cause des livres*. Paris: Gallimard.

Paradis, T. (2004) Theming, Tourism, and Fantasy City, in A.A. Lew et al. (Eds.) *A Companion to Tourism*. Malden, MA: Blackwell, 195–209.

De Parseval, B. (2017) [*Chargée d'offre culturelle/Centre des monuments nationaux*]; [email] Personal Communication, 4 August.

Pastorello, T. (2010) La sodomie masculine dans les pamphlets révolutionnaires, *Annales historiques de la Révolution française*, 361, 91–130.

Pateman, C. (1988) *The Sexual Contract*. Stanford: Stanford University Press.
Pearce, P.L. (1993) Fundamentals of Tourist Motivation, in D.G. Pearce & R.W. Buttler (Eds.) *Tourism Research: Critiques and Challenges*. Abingdon: Routledge, 113–134.
Pearce, S.M. (Ed.) (1989) *Museum Studies in Material Culture*. London: Leicester University Press; Washington, DC: Smithsonian Institution Press.
Pearce, S.M. (Ed.) (1994) *Interpreting Objects and Collections*. Abingdon: Routledge.
Pearce, S.M. (1995) *On Collecting: An Investigation into Collecting in the European Tradition*. Abingdon: Routledge.
Pearce, S.M. (1998) The Construction and Analysis of the Cultural Heritage: Some Thoughts, *International Journal of Heritage Studies*, 4(1), 1–9.
Perspective (2014) Développement: Le Château défend sa marque, *Perspective*, 124, 11.
Pestel, F. (2017) Memory That Governs by Itself? Appropriations of Versailles Memory, *European Review of History/Revue européenne d'histoire*, 24(4), 527–551.
Peters, R.A. (2012) Reading Royalty in Dumas, Le Collier de la reine, *Textual Practice*, 26(2), 181–217.
Petitfils, J.-C. (2006) Marie-Antoinette et la politique, in Institut de la Maison de Bourbon (Ed.) *Marie-Antoinette face à l'histoire* [Sorbonne Colloquium]. Paris: François-Xavier de Guibert, 51–66.
Petitfils, J.-C. (2011) L'Affaire du Collier de la Reine, *Château de Versailles de l'Ancien Régime à nos jours*, juillet-septembre, 2, 14–22.
Phillips, D. (1997) *Exhibiting Authenticity*. Manchester: Manchester University Press.
Pincemaille, C. (2003) L'impératrice Eugénie et Marie-Antoinette: Autour de l'exposition rétrospective des souvenirs de la reine au Petit Trianon en 1867, *Versalia*, 6, 124–134.
Poirier, A. (2006a) An Empty Hall of Mirrors, *The Guardian*, 27 May.
Poirier, A. (2006b) A Queen-Sized Sensation, *The Guardian*, 3 October.
Poirson, M. (2007) Le grand théâtre d'un tout petit monde: *Marie-Antoinette* de Sofia Coppola, *Théâtres*, printemps, 128–138.
Poirson, M. (2009) Marie-Antoinette, héroïne paradoxale d'une fiction patrimoniale contrariée, in L. Schifano & M. Poirson (Eds.) *Filmer le 18e siècle*. Paris: Desjonquères, 229–252.
Polkinghorne, D.E. (1988) *Narrative Knowing and the Human Sciences*. Albany, NY: State University of New York Press.
Pommier, É. (1986) Versailles, l'image du souverain, in P. Nora (Ed.) *Les lieux de mémoire: La Nation II*. Paris: Gallimard, 193–234.
Poria, Y. et al. (2003) The Core of Heritage Tourism, *Annals of Tourism Research*, 30(1), 238–254.
Porter, B.W. (2008) Heritage Tourism: Conflicting Identities in the Modern World, in B. Graham & P. Howard (Eds.) *The Ashgate Research Companion to Heritage & Identity*. Aldershot: Ashgate, 267–282.
Poulot, D. (1997) *Musée, nation, patrimoine, 1789–1815*. Paris: Gallimard.
Poulot, D. (1998a) *Patrimoine et modernité*. Paris: L'Harmattan.
Poulot, D. (1998b) Versailles, lieu de mémoire, *Les Collections de l'Histoire*, hors-série, 2, 40–41.

Prentice, R. (2004) Tourism Motivation and Typologies, in A.A. Lew et al. (Eds.) *A Companion to Tourism*. Malden, MA: Blackwell, 261–279.

Price, L. (1992) Vies privées et scandaleuses: Marie-Antoinette and the Public Eye, *The Eighteenth Century*, 33(2), 176–192.

Price, M. (2002) *The Fall of the French Monarchy: Louis XVI, Marie Antoinette and the Baron de Breteuil*. London: Macmillan.

Priestland, D. (2010) *The Red Flag: Communism and the Making of the Modern World* [1st ed. 2009]. London: Penguin Books.

Pritchard, A. & Morgan, N. (2010) 'Wild On' the Beach: Discourses of Desire, Sexuality and Liminality, in E. Waterton & S. Watson (Eds.) *Culture, Heritage and Representation: Perspectives on Visuality and the Past*. Farnham: Ashgate, 127–143.

Proshansky, H.M. et al. (1983) Place-Identity: Physical World Socialization of the Self, *Journal of Environmental Psychology*, 3, 57–83.

Prost, A. (1984) Les Monuments aux Morts: Culte républicain? Culte civique? Culte patriotique?, in P. Nora (Ed.) *Les lieux de mémoire: La République*. Paris: Gallimard, 195–225.

Pujol, L. & Champion, E. (2012) Evaluating Presence in Cultural Heritage Projects, *International Journal of Heritage Studies*, 18(1), 83–102.

de Raïssac, M. (2011) *Richard Mique: Architecte du roi de Pologne Stanislas Ier, de Mesdames et de Marie-Antoinette*. Paris: Honoré Champion.

Rana, J. et al. (2017) Moved by the Tears of Others: Emotion Networking in the Heritage Sphere, *International Journal of Heritage Studies*, 23(10), 977–988.

Rátz, T. (2006) Interpretation in the House of Terror, Budapest, in M. Smith & M. Robinson (Eds.) *Cultural Tourism in a Changing World: Politics, Participation and (Re)Presentation*. Clevedon: Channel View, 244–256.

Reijnders, S. (2010) Places of the Imagination: An Ethnography of the TV Detective Tour, *Cultural Geographies*, 17(1), 37–52.

Reisinger, Y. & Steiner, C.J. (2006) Reconceptualising Object Authenticity, *Annals of Tourism Research*, 33(1), 65–86.

Renard, J.-B. (2010) La construction de l'image des hommes politiques par le folklore narratif. Anecdotes, rumeurs, légendes, histoires drôles, Mots. Les langages du politique [online], 92 | 2010; Available at: http://mots.revues.org/19418 [Accessed: 16 March 2014].

Rendall, J. (1984) *The Origins of Modern Feminism: Women in Britain, France and the United States, 1780–1860*. New York: Schoken Books.

Revel, J. (1991) Marie Antoinette and Her Fictions: The Staging of Hatred, in B. Fort (Ed.) *Fictions of the French Revolution*. Evanston, IL: Northwestern University Press, 111–129.

Revel, J. & Hunt, L. (Eds.) (1995) *Histories: French Constructions of the Past* [transl. A. Goldhammer]. New York: The New Press.

Rheims, G. (1925) Le bureau de Marie-Antoinette au Petit Trianon, *La Revue de L'Art*, 47, 262–268.

Richards, L. (2009) *Handling Qualitative Data: A Practical Guide*. London: SAGE.

Ricoeur, P. (2004) *History, Memory, Forgetting* [transl. K. Blamey & D. Pellauer] [1st French ed. 2000]. Chicago: University of Chicago Press.

Roberts, L.C. (1997) *From Knowledge to Narrative: Educators and the Changing Museum*. Washington, DC: Smithsonian Institution Press.

Robinson, M. (2001) Tourism Encounters: Inter and Intra-Cultural Conflicts and the World's Largest Industry, in N. AlSayyad (Ed.) *Consuming Tradition,*

Manufacturing Heritage: Global Norms and Urban Forms in the Age of Tourism. Abingdon: Routledge, 34–67.

Robinson, M. & Andersen, H.-C. (Eds.) (2002) *Literature and Tourism: Essays in the Reading and Writing of Tourism.* London: Thomson.

Robinson, M. & Picard, D. (2009a) Moments, Magic and Memories: Photographing Tourists, Tourist Photographs and Making Worlds, in M. Robinson & D. Picard (Eds.) *The Framed World: Tourism, Tourists and Photography.* Aldershot: Ashgate, 1–38.

Robinson, M. & Picard, D. (Eds.) (2009b) *The Framed World: Tourism, Tourists and Photography.* Aldershot: Ashgate.

Robson, C. (2002) *Real World Research: A Resource for Social Scientists and Practitioners-Researchers* [1st ed. 1993]. Malden, MA: Blackwell.

Rofe, M.W. (2006) New Landscapes of Gated Communities: Australia's Sovereign Islands, *Landscape Research*, 31(3), 309–317.

Rofe, M.W. & Szili, G. (2009) Name Game 1: Place Names as Rhetorical Devices, *Landscape Research*, 34(3), 361–370.

Rofe, M.W. (2013) Considering the Limits of Rural Place Making Opportunities: Rural Dystopias and Dark Tourism, *Landscape Research*, 38(2), 262–272.

Rofe, M.W. (2016) The City of Corpses? Contested Urban Identity and the Stigma of Crime in Adelaide, South Australia, *Landscape Research*, 41(8), 966–979.

Rojek, C. (1997) Indexing, Dragging and the Social Construction of Tourist Sights, in C. Rojek & J. Urry (Eds.) *Touring Cultures: Transformations of Travel and Theory.* Abingdon: Routledge, 52–74.

Rondot, B. (2008) Répondre aux désirs de la reine, in X. Salmon et al. (Eds.) *Marie-Antoinette* [exhibition catalogue]. Paris: Réunion des musées nationaux, 242–253.

Roy, A. (2004) Nostalgias of the Modern, in N. AlSayyad (Ed.) *The End of Tradition?* Abingdon: Routledge, 63–86.

Rucca-Lusikka (2007) Japanese blog on *Marie Antoinette* (2006), 2 February [online]; Available at: https://rucca-lusikka.com/blog/archives/378 [Last Accessed: 24 March 2018].

Russell, N. (2006) Collective Memory before and after Halbwachs, *The French Review*, 79(4), 792–804.

Rykner, D. (2010a) Un projet de statuts pour Versailles: une nouvelle défaite de l'histoire de l'art, *La Tribune de l'Art*, 10 Avril [online]; Available at: www.latribunedelart.com/un-projet-de-statuts-pour-versailles-une-nouvelle-defaite-de-l-histoire-de-l-art [Accessed: 10 June 2014].

Rykner, D. (2010b) Les nouveaux statuts de Versailles publiés au Journal Officiel, *La Tribune de l'Art*, 14 Novembre [online]; Available at: www.latribunedelart.com/les-nouveaux-statuts-de-versailles-publies-au-journal-officiel [Accessed: 10 June 2014].

Saillard, O. et al. (Eds.) (2011) *Le XVIIIe au goût du jour: Couturiers et créateurs de mode au Grand Trianon/the 18th Century Back in Fashion: Couturiers and Fashion Designers in the Grand Trianon* [exhibition catalogue]. Versailles: Château de Versailles; Paris: Artlys & Musée Galliera.

Saint-Amand, P. (2003) Terrorizing Marie-Antoinette, in D. Goodman (Ed.) *Marie-Antoinette: Writings on the Body of a Queen.* Abingdon: Routledge, 253–272.

Saldaña, J. (2013) *The Coding Manual for Qualitative Researchers* [1st ed. 2009]. Los Angeles: SAGE.

Salmon, X. (2005) *Marie-Antoinette: Images d'un destin*. Paris: M. Lafon.
Salmon, X. (2008) Le Petit Trianon: Lieu des abus ou des idées nouvelles, *Dossier de l'art*, 150, 52–63.
Salmon, X. et al. (Eds.) (2008) *Marie-Antoinette* [exhibition catalogue]. Paris: Réunion des musées nationaux.
Samuel, H. (2013) Valérie Trierweiler 'Succumbs to Marie-Antoinette Syndrome of Life of Luxury', *The Telegraph*, 7 February.
Samuel, R. (1994) *Theatres of Memory: Past and Present in Contemporary Culture* [3 vols.]. London: Verso.
Sapori, M. (2010) *Rose Bertin: Couturière de Marie-Antoinette*. Paris: Perrin.
Sather-Wagstaff, J. (2015) Heritage and Memory, in E. Waterton & S. Watson (Eds.) *The Palgrave Handbook of Contemporary Heritage Research*. Basingstoke: Palgrave Macmillan, 191–204.
Saudan, M. & Saudan-Skira, S. (1987) *De folie en folies: La découverte du monde des jardins*. Genève: Le septième Fou.
Saule, B. & Arminjon, C. (2010) *Sciences et curiosités à la cour de Versailles*. Paris: Réunion des musées nationaux.
Savenije, G.M. & de Bruijn, P. (2017) Historical Empathy in a Museum: Uniting Contextualisation and Emotional Engagement, *International Journal of Heritage Studies*, 23(9), 832–845.
Schama, S. (1989) *Citizens: A Chronicle of the French Revolution*. London: Penguin Books.
Schifano, L. (2009) Rêver le XVIIIe siècle: Entretien avec Chantal Thomas, in L. Schifano & M. Poirson (Eds.) *Filmer le 18e siècle*. Paris: Desjonquères, 43–54.
Schirato, T. & Webb, J. (2010) Inside/Outside: Ways of Seeing the World, in E. Waterton & S. Watson (Eds.) *Culture, Heritage and Representation: Perspectives on Visuality and the Past*. Farnham: Ashgate, 19–37.
Schlehe, J. et al. (2010) *Staging the Past: Themed Environments in Transcultural Perspectives*. New York: Columbia University Press.
Schofield, J. (2008) Heritage Management, Theory and Practice, in G. Fairclough et al. (Eds.) *The Heritage Reader*. Abingdon: Routledge, 15–30.
Schorch, P. (2014) Cultural Feelings and the Making of Meaning, *International Journal of Heritage Studies*, 20(1), 22–35.
Schouten, F. (2006) The Process of Authenticating Souvenirs, in M.K. Smith & M. Robinson (Eds.) *Cultural Tourism in a Changing World: Politics, Participation and (Re)Presentation*. Clevedon: Channel View, 191–202.
Scott, J. (1990) *A Matter of Record: Documentary Sources in Social Research*. Cambridge and Oxford: Polity Press & Basil Blackwell.
Seignobos, C. (1891) *Scènes et épisodes de l'histoire nationale*. Paris: Armand Colin & Cie.
Selby, M. (2010) People-Place-Past: The Visitor Experience of Cultural Heritage, in E. Waterton & S. Watson (Eds.) *Culture, Heritage and Representation: Perspectives on Visuality and the Past*. Farnham: Ashgate, 39–55.
Selwyn, T. (Ed.) (1996) *The Tourist Image: Myth and Myth Making in Tourism*. Chichester: John Wiley & Sons.
Selwyn, T. (2010) The Tourist as Jugler in a Hall of Mirrors: Looking through Images at the Self, in E. Waterton & S. Watson (Eds.) *Culture, Heritage and Representation: Perspectives on Visuality and the Past*. Farnham: Ashgate, 195–214.
Seth, C. (2006) *Marie Antoinette: Anthologie et dictionnaire*. Paris: R. Laffont.

Sévillia, J. (2006) L'Amère Patrie, *Le Figaro*, hors-série, 98–99.
Sévillia, J. (2010) *Historiquement Correct: Pour en finir avec le passé unique* [1st ed. 2003]. Paris: Perrin.
Sévillia, J. (2011) [*Le Figaro Associate Senior Editor and Rehabilitative History Author*]; [conversation at Versailles] Personal Communication, 20 November.
Sévillia, J. (2017) [email] Personal Communication, 4 September.
Shamoon, D. (2007) Revolutionary Romance: The Rose of Versailles and the Transformation of Shōjo Manga, in F. Lunning (Ed.) *Networks of Desire* [Vol. 2]. Minneapolis: University of Minnesota Press, 3–17.
Sheriff, M.D. (2003) The Portrait of the Queen, in D. Goodman (Ed.) *Marie-Antoinette: Writings on the Body of a Queen*. Abingdon: Routledge, 45–71.
Silverman, D. (2007) *A Very Short, Fairly Interesting, and Reasonably Cheap Book about Qualitative Research*. London: SAGE.
Silverman, H. (2015) Heritage and Authenticity, in E. Waterton & S. Watson (Eds.) *The Palgrave Handbook of Contemporary Heritage Research*. Basingstoke: Palgrave Macmillan, 69–88.
Simpson, M.G. (2001) *Making Representations: Museums in the Post-Colonial Era* [1st ed. 1996]. Abingdon: Routledge.
Smith, D. (2012) *Devenir historien*. Paris: Publications de la Sorbonne.
Smith, J.A. & Osborn, M. (2008) Interpretative Phenomenological Analysis, in J.A. Smith (Ed.) *Qualitative Psychology: A Practical Guide to Research Methods* [1st ed. 2003]. London: SAGE, 53–80.
Smith, L. (2006) *The Uses of Heritage*. Abingdon: Routledge.
Smith, L. (2008) Heritage, Gender and Identity, in B. Graham & P. Howard (Eds.) *The Ashgate Research Companion to Heritage & Identity*. Aldershot: Ashgate, 159–178.
Smith, L. et al. (Eds.) (2012) *The Cultural Moment in Tourism*. Abingdon: Routledge.
Smith, L. (2012) The cultural 'work' of tourism, in L. Smith et al. (Eds.) *The Cultural Moment in Tourism*. Abingdon: Routledge, 210–234.
Smith, L. (2013) Editorial, *International Journal of Heritage Studies*, 19(4), 325–326.
Smith, L. (2016) Changing Views? Emotional Intelligence, Registers of Engagement and the Museum Visit, in V. Gosselin & P. Livingstone (Eds.) *Museums as Sites of Historical Consciousness: Perspectives on Museum Theory and Practice in Canada*. Vancouver: UBC Press, 101–121.
Smith, L. & Campbell, G. (2016) The Elephant in the Room: Heritage, Affect and Emotion, in W. Logan et al. (Eds.) *A Companion to Heritage Studies*. Chichester: Wiley-Blackwell, 443–460.
Smith, L. & Campbell, G. (2017) 'Nostalgia for the Future': Memory, Nostalgia and the Politics of Class, *International Journal of Heritage Studies*, 23(7), 612–627.
Smith, M.K. & Robinson, M. (Eds.) (2006) *Cultural Tourism in a Changing World: Politics, Participation and (Re)Presentation*. Clevedon: Channel View.
Smith, P. (2012) [*Ethnographic Research Seminar Course, Plymouth University, Faculty of Arts*]; [conversation Plymouth] Personal Communication, 8 November.
Söderhjelm, A. (1930) *Fersen et Marie-Antoinette. Correspondance et journal intime inédits du comte Axel de Fersen*. Paris: Kra.
Sorkin, M. (Ed.) (1992) *Variations on a Theme Park: The New American City and the End of Public Space*. New York: Hill & Wang.

Soryo, F. (2016) *Marie-Antoinette: La jeunesse d'une reine* [shōjo manga]. Versailles et Grenoble: Château de Versailles & Glénat.

Soulavie, J.-L. [L'Abbé] (1801) *Mémoires historiques et politiques du règne de Louis XVI, depuis son mariage jusqu'à sa mort* [6 vols.]. Paris: Treuttle et Würtz.

de Staël, G. [Madame La Baronne] [Anon.] (1793) *Réflexions sur le procès de la Reine, par une Femme*. Aoust [s.l.].

de Staël, G. [Madame La Baronne] (1818) *Considérations sur les principaux evénémens* [sic] *de la Révolution françoise* [sic] [publ. by Duc de Broglie and Baron A. de Staël] [3 vols.]. Paris: Delaunay.

Staiff, R. et al. (2013) *Heritage and Tourism: Place, Encounter, Engagement*. Abingdon: Routledge.

Stalnaker, J. (2010) *The Unfinished Enlightenment: Description in the Age of the Encyclopedia*. New York: Cornell University Press.

Steiner, C.J. & Reisinger, Y. (2006) Understanding Existential Authenticity, *Annals of Tourism Research*, 33(2), 299–318.

Stone, B. (2002) *Reinterpreting the French Revolution: A Global-Historical Perspective*. Cambridge: Cambridge University Press.

Sturken, M. & Cartwright, L. (2009) *Practices of Looking: An Introduction to Visual Culture* [1st ed. 2001]. Oxford: Oxford University Press.

Surman, B. (2009) The Search for the Real Thing: Japanese Tourism to Britain, in S. Guichard-Anguis & O. Moon (Eds.) *Japanese Tourism and Travel Culture*. Abingdon: Routledge, 193–202.

Suzuki, K. (1998) Pornography or Therapy? Japanese Girls Creating the Yaoi Phenomenon, in S.A. Inness (Ed.) *Millennium Girls: Today's Girls around the World*. Lanham, MD: Rowman & Littlefield, 243–267.

Tackett, T. (2003) *When the King Took Flight*. Cambridge, MA: Harvard University Press.

Tannock, S. (1995) Nostalgia Critique, *Cultural Studies*, 9(3), 453–464.

Tansman, A. (1996) Review: Discourses of the Vanishing: Modernity, Phantasm, Japan by Marilyn Ivy, *Journal of Japanese Studies*, 22(1), 197–202.

Tapié, A. et al. (Eds.) (1989) *Le Soulier de Marie Antoinette: Essai muséographique*. Caen: Musée des Beaux-Arts, Château de Caen.

Taylor, J. (1994) *A Dream of England: Landscape, Photography and the Tourist's Imagination*. Manchester: Manchester University Press.

Taylor, J.P. (2001) Authenticity and Sincerity in Tourism, *Annals of Tourism Research*, 28(1), 7–26.

Tester, K. (Ed.) (1994) *The Flâneur*. Abingdon: Routledge.

Thomas, C. (1989a) *La Reine scélérate: Marie-Antoinette dans les pamphlets*. Paris: Seuil.

Thomas, C. (1989b) Marie-Antoinette ou les malheurs de la séduction, in A. Tapié et al. (Eds.) *Le Soulier de Marie Antoinette: Essai muséographique*. Caen: Musée des Beaux-Arts, Château de Caen, 29–40.

Thomas, C. (1999) *The Wicked Queen: The Origins of the Myth of Marie-Antoinette* [transl. J. Rose]. New York: Zone Books.

Thomas, C. (2002) *Les Adieux à la Reine*. Paris: Seuil.

Thomas, C. (2003) The Heroine of the Crime: Marie-Antoinette in Pamphlets, in D. Goodman (Ed.) *Marie-Antoinette: Writings on the Body of a Queen*. Abingdon: Routledge, 99–116.

Thomas, C. (2004) *Farewell, My Queen: A Novel* [1st Touchstone ed.]. New York: Simon & Schuster.
Thomas, C. (2011a) [*Cycle 'Marie-Antoinette au-delà d'un livre'*]; [talk on Marie Antoinette at Petit Trianon] Personal attendance, 22 January.
Thomas, C. (2011b) [*Marie Antoinette Author*]; [conversation Petit Trianon] Personal Communication, 22 January.
Thompson, C.J. et al. (1994) The Spoken and the Unspoken: A Hermeneutic Approach to Understanding Consumers' Expressed Meanings, *Journal of Consumer Research*, 21, 432–453.
Tilden, F. (1970) *Interpreting Our Heritage* [1st ed. 1957]. Chapel Hill: University of South Carolina Press.
de Tilly, A. [Comte] (1828) *Mémoires du comte Alexandre de Tilly, pour servir à l'histoire des mœurs de la fin du XVIIIe siècle* [3 vols.]. Paris: Chez les Marchands de Nouveautés.
Todorov, T. (1995) *Les abus de la mémoire*. Paris: Arléa.
Todorov, T. (2009) *In Defence of the Enlightenment*. London: Atlantic Books.
Toku, M. (2007) Shōjo Manga! Girls' Comics! A Mirror of Girls' Dreams, in F. Lunning (Ed.) *Networks of Desire* [Vol. 2]. Minneapolis: University of Minnesota Press, 19–32.
Tolia-Kelly, D.P. et al. (2017) *Heritage, Affect and Emotion: Politics, Practices and Infrastructures*. Abingdon: Routledge.
Tollfree, E.L. (2006) Le mobilier de Marie-Antoinette à la Wallace Collection, *Versalia*, 9, 156–177.
Tuetey, A. (1914) Inventaire de plaques anciennes et objets de curiosités de Marie-Antoinette confiées à Daguerre et Lignereux, marchands bijoutiers le 10 octobre 1789, *Archives de l'art français*, T.VIII, 286–319.
Tunbridge, J.E. & Ashworth, G.J. (1996) *Dissonant Heritage: The Management of the Past as a Resource in Conflict*. Chichester: John Wiley & Sons.
Tunbridge, J.E. et al. (2013) Decennial Reflections on a Geography of Heritage (2000), *International Journal of Heritage Studies*, 19(4), 365–372.
Turner, V.W. (1969) *The Ritual Process: Structure and Anti-Structure*. London: Routledge & Kegan Paul.
Turner, V.W. & Turner, E. (1978) *Image and Pilgrimage in Christian Culture*. New York: Columbia University Press.
Tythacott, L. (2012) The Empty Museum: Western Cultures and the Artistic Field in Modern Japan, *International Journal of Heritage Studies*, 18(1), 105–106.
Upton, D. (2001) 'Authentic' Anxieties, in N. AlSayyad (Ed.) *Consuming Tradition, Manufacturing Heritage: Global Norms and Urban Forms in the Age of Tourism*. Abingdon: Routledge, 298–306.
Urry, J. (1990) *The Tourist Gaze: Leisure and Travel in Contemporary Societies* [1st ed.]. London: SAGE.
Urry, J. (1992) The Tourist Gaze 'Revisited', *American Behavioral Scientist*, 36, 172–186.
Urry, J. (1995) *Consuming Places*. Abingdon: Routledge.
Urry, J. (1999) Sensing Leisure Spaces, in D. Crouch (Ed.) *Leisure/Tourism Geographies: Practices and Geographical Knowledge*. Abingdon: Routledge, 34–45.
Urry, J. (2002) *The Tourist Gaze: Leisure and Travel in Contemporary Societies* [2nd ed.]. London: SAGE.

Urry, J. & Larsen, J. (2011) *The Tourist Gaze 3.0* [3rd ed.]. London: SAGE.

Uzzell, D.L. (1989a) The Hot Interpretation of War and Conflict, in D.L. Uzzell (Ed.) *Heritage Interpretation: The Natural & Built Environment* [Vol. 1]. London: Belhaven, 33–47.

Uzzell, D.L. (Ed.) (1989b) *Heritage Interpretation* [2 vols.]. London: Belhaven.

Uzzell, D.L. (1996) Creating Place Identity through Heritage Interpretation, *International Journal of Heritage Studies*, 1(4), 219–228.

Uzzell, D.L. & Ballantyne, R. (2008) Heritage That Hurts: Interpretation in a Postmodern World, in G. Fairclough et al. (Eds.) *The Heritage Reader*. Abingdon: Routledge, 502–513.

Varaut, A. (2006) Le procès de Marie-Antoinette, in Institut de la Maison de Bourbon (Ed.) *Marie-Antoinette face à l'histoire* [Sorbonne Colloquium]. Paris: François-Xavier de Guibert, 145–161.

Veal, A.J. (2006) *Research Methods for Leisure and Tourism: A Practical Guide* [1st ed. 1992]. London: Prentice Hall.

Vergo, P. (Ed.) (1989) *The New Museology*. London: Reaktion Books.

Verlet, P. (1949) La table à ouvrage de Marie-Antoinette, *Revue des Musées de France*, juillet–août, 162–163.

Verlet, P. (1961) Le boudoir de Marie-Antoinette à Fontainebleau: Mobilier et décoration, *Art de France*, 1, 159–168.

Vidal, E.M. (2010) *Trianon, a Novel of Royal France* [1st ed. 1997]. Long Prairie, MN: Neumann.

Vidal, E.M. (2014a) [*Pseudonym for Russell, M.-E.; Author of Marie Antoinette Historical Fiction*]; [email] Personal Communication, 6 September.

Vidal, E.M. (2014b) [email] Personal Communication, 7 September.

Vigée Le Brun, L.-É. (1835–1837) *Souvenirs de Madame Louise-Élisabeth Vigée-Lebrun* [3 vols.]. Paris: H. Fournier.

Vigée Le Brun, L.-É. (2009) *Les femmes régnaient alors, la Révolution les a détrônées; Souvenirs* (ed. D. Masseau). Paris: Tallandier.

Vigliotti, J. (2013) [*Playwright*]; [email] Personal Communication, 2 May.

Voase, R. (2010) Visualizing the Past: Baudrillard, Intensities of the Hyper-Real and the Erosion of Historicity, in E. Waterton & S. Watson (Eds.) *Culture, Heritage and Representation: Perspectives on Visuality and the Past*. Farnham: Ashgate, 105–123.

Vottero, M. (2011a) Le goût Marie-Antoinette sous le Second Empire, in Conférence de Michael Vottero, conservateur du Patrimoine, organisée par la Bibliothèque de Marmottan, 6 Avril.

Vottero, M. (2011b) [*Conservateur du patrimoine aux Monuments historiques et Inventaire*]; [email] Personal Communication, 15 April.

Vovelle, M. (1984) La Marseillaise: La guerre ou la paix, in P. Nora (Ed.) *Les lieux de mémoire: La République*. Paris: Gallimard, 85–136.

Vovelle, M. (2012) Cachez ces nippons . . . Ou Marie-Antoinette au pays des mangas, *Annales historiques de la Révolution française*, 368, 129–136.

Waitt, G. (2000) Consuming Heritage: Perceived Historical Authenticity, *Annals of Tourism Research*, 27(4), 835–862.

de Waldner de Freundstein, H.-L. [Baronne d'Oberkirch] (1853) *Mémoires de la baronne d'Oberkirch* [2 vols.]. Paris: Charpentier.

Walpole, H. (1823) *Mémoires des dix dernières années du règne de George II, d'après les manuscrits originaux d'Horace Walpole, comte d'Oxford*. Paris: J.-G. Dentu.

Walsh, K. (1992) *The Representation of the Past: Museums and Heritage in the Post-Modern World*. Abingdon: Routledge.

Wang, N. (1999) Rethinking Authenticity in Tourism Experience, *Annals of Tourism Research*, 26(2), 349–370.

de Waresquiel, E. (2016) *Juger la Reine: 14, 15, 16 octobre 1793*. Paris: Tallandier.

Wasserstrom, J.N. et al. (Eds.) (2000) *Human Rights and Revolutions*. Lanham, MD: Rowman & Littlefield.

Watelet, C.-H. (1774) *Essai sur les jardins*. Paris: Prault.

Watelet, C.-H. (1777) La Maison de campagne ou la comédie d'après nature, in C.-H. Watelet (Ed.) (1784) *Recueil de quelques ouvrages de M. Watelet*. Paris: Prault.

Waterton, E. (2010) Branding the Past: The Visual Imagery of England's Heritage, in E. Waterton & S. Watson (Eds.) *Culture, Heritage and Representation: Perspectives on Visuality and the Past*. Farnham: Ashgate, 155–172.

Waterton, E. & Watson, S. (Eds.) (2010) *Culture, Heritage and Representation: Perspectives on Visuality and the Past*. Farnham: Ashgate.

Waterton, E. (2013) Heritage, Tourism and Its Representations, in R. Staiff et al. (Eds.) *Heritage and Tourism: Place, Encounter, Engagement*. Abingdon: Routledge, 64–84.

Waterton, E. & Watson, S. (2013) Framing Theory: Towards a Critical Imagination in Heritage Studies, *International Journal of Heritage Studies*, 19(6), 546–561.

Watson, J. & Hill, A. (2006) *Dictionary of Media and Communication Studies*. London: Hodder Arnold.

Watson, N. (2007) Shakespeare on the Tourist Trail, in R. Shaughnessy (Ed.) *The Cambridge Companion to Shakespeare and Popular Culture*. Cambridge: Cambridge University Press.

Watson, S. (Ed.) (2007) *Museums and Their Communities*. Abingdon: Routledge.

Watson, S. (2010) Constructing Rhodes: Heritage Tourism and Visuality, in E. Waterton & S. Watson (Eds.) *Culture, Heritage and Representation: Perspectives on Visuality and the Past*. Farnham: Ashgate, 249–270.

Watson, S. & Waterton, E. (2010) Reading the Visual: Representation and Narrative in the Construction of Heritage, *Material Culture Review*, 71, 84–97.

Weber, C. (2006) *Queen of Fashion: What Marie Antoinette Wore to the Revolution*. New York: H. Holt & Co.

Weber, M. (2001) *The Protestant Ethic and the Spirit of Capitalism* [transl. T. Parsons] [1st German ed. 1920]. Abingdon: Routledge.

Webster, N.H. (1936) *Louis XVI and Marie-Antoinette before the Revolution*. London: Constable & Co.

Webster, N.H. (2010) *Bourdieu for Architects*. Abingdon: Routledge.

Wertsch, J.V. (2002) *Voices of Collective Remembering*. Cambridge: Cambridge University Press.

Wetherell, M. (2012) *Affect and Emotion: A New Social Science Understanding*. London: SAGE.

Willis, D. (2010) Let them eat free macarons, *Examiner.com*, 19 March [online]; Available at: www.examiner.com/article/let-them-eat-free-macarons [Accessed: 4 September 2014].

Winter, T. (2013) Going Places: Challenging Directions for the Future of Heritage Studies, *International Journal of Heritage Studies*, 19(4), 395–398.

Winter, T. (2014a) Beyond Eurocentrism? Heritage Conservation and the Politics of Difference, *International Journal of Heritage Studies*, 20(2), 123–137.

Winter, T. (2014b) Heritage Studies and the Privileging of Theory, *International Journal of Heritage Studies*, 20(5), 556–572.

Winter, T. (2015) Heritage and Nationalism: An Unbreachable Couple?, in E. Waterton & S. Watson (Eds.) *The Palgrave Handbook of Contemporary Heritage Research*. Basingstoke: Palgrave Macmillan, 331–345.

Witcomb, A. (2003) *Re-Imaging the Museum: Beyond the Mausoleum*. Abingdon: Routledge.

Wood, A.F. (2005) 'What Happens [in Vegas]': Performing the Post-Tourist Flâneur in 'New York' and 'Paris', *Text and Performance Quarterly*, 25(4), 315–333.

Young, L. (2017) *Historic House Museums in the United States and the United Kingdom: A History*. Lanham, MD: Rowman & Littlefield.

Zeck, J. (1990) La garniture de cheminée de Marie-Antoinette en ivoire tourné conservée à l'Ermitage, *Bulletin de la Société de l'histoire de l'art français*, 145–148.

Zéro de conduite (2012) Les Adieux à la reine vus par l'historienne Cécile Berly, *Zéro de conduite*, 24 March [online]; Available at: www.zerodeconduite.net/blog/18904-les-adieux-a-la-reine-vus-par-l-historienne-cecile-berly.html#.U8QFJrHb7R8 [Accessed: 2 May 2012].

Zukin, S. (1993) *Landscapes of Power: From Detroit to Disney World*. Berkeley, CA: University of California Press.

Zweig, S. (1932) *Marie-Antoinette: Bildnis eines mittleren Charakters*. Wien: Insel-Verlag.

Zweig, S. (1933a) *Marie-Antoinette* [transl. A. Hella]. Paris: B. Grasset.

Zweig, S. (1933b) *Marie Antoinette: The Portrait of an Average Woman* [transl. E. & C. Paul]. Garden City, NY: Garden City.

Index

Note: page numbers in **bold** refer to tables; page numbers in *italics* refer to figures.

Académie des Sciences Morales, des Lettres et des Arts de Versailles et d'Ile-de-France (Académie de Versailles) 108
Affair of the Diamond Necklace 88, 99; film *The Affair of the Necklace* (2001) 95; novel *Le Collier de la reine* (1849–1850) 94 (*see also* Dumas *père*, Alexandre; French Monarchy, fall of the); a replica of the necklace at Versailles *95*; *see also* Collier, *L'Affaire du*
Albanel, Christine 129, 133, 137
'alchemical dissonant heritage' 3–4, 6–7, 7n1, 155–157, 250, 256
AlSayyad, Nezar 34, 43, 46–47
Ancien Régime 1, 75, 77, 99, 108, 155; and Bourbon dynasty 19; as a conglomerate of clichés 117; and David, Jacques-Louis 146; failing 96; French public opinion of 67; and Marie Antoinette 114; misconceptions about 26; negative image of 4, 87, 151; and the Petit Trianon 85, 147; *see also* French Monarchy
Anderson, Benedict 5, 8n6, 45, 76–77, 174, 190; modern monuments 30; nationalism and print capitalism 13–15, 17, 23, 199; the role of imagination in creating national identities and solidarity 10–11, 28n2
Arizzoli-Clémentel, Pierre 133, 138, 143, 210, 240
Ashworth, Gregory 3, 5, 12, 26–27, 30, 36, 41–43, **41, 42,** *43*, 47, 131–133, *133*, 137, 147, 155–157, 160, 174, 221, 224, 236, 253
Assmann, Jan 173, 198

Association Marie-Antoinette 66, 90, 108
Austrophobia / French phobia of Austrians 4, 78; *see also* Marie Antoinette, animosity

Barry, Madame du 141
Barthes, Roland 33, 100; denotative meaning of photographs 66; the multiplying nature of the signifier 206, 226, 229, 247 (*see also* post-structuralism); myth 202, 212, 233; semiotics and structuralism 7, 8n8, 82, 201
Basilique (Royale) de Saint-Denis 80n8, **178,** 200n10; *see also* Centre des monuments nationaux
Baudin, Philippe 55, 59, 64, 66, 131, 133–135, 154, 161n11, 162n18, 220, 245
Baudrillard, Jean: copies without an original 229, 247 (*see also* Lady Gaga; Madonna); postmodern production and reproduction of signs 247n1; the refuge of myth in cinema 202, 233; simulacra and simulation 7, 33, 36, 201–202, 226, 252
Baulez, Christian 133–135, 161n5, 238
Benoît, Jérémie 55, 59, 65–67, 80n12, 128, 131, 135, 138, 141, 149, 154, 161n11, 175, 185, 210, 235, 237
Bhabha, Homi **41,** 131, 160
biopic 97–99, *98*, 110, 114–115, 117–118, 121
Bourbon Restoration 185, *186*; *see also* Basilique (Royale) de Saint-Denis; La Chapelle Expiatoire; Charles X / Comte d'Artois; La Conciergerie; Louis XVIII / Comte de Provence

320 Index

Bourdieu, Pierre 5, 10, 40, 236; 'cultural capital' 17–18, 76, 157, 159
Bran Castle 42, 187; *see also* Dracula
Bunmei Kaika 192

Catholic(s) 155; ceremonial 200n11; faith 127n18 (*see also* Marie Antoinette, Catholic faith); groups 65; milieu 107, 255; scholars 107; tradition 96
Caughey, John L. 7, 33, 41, 84, 163, 189–192, 218, 233, 256
Centre de recherche du château de Versailles 108
Centre des monuments nationaux 185, *186*
Centre national de la recherche scientifique 85, 126n2
champêtre: feel 238; Jardin *141*
La Chapelle Expiatoire 64, 80n8, 171, *171*, 200n10; *see also* Centre des monuments nationaux; counter-memory
Charles X / Comte d'Artois 80n8
Château de Fontainebleau 248n13
Château de Versailles: as Établissement Public 138, 149, 220; management 61, 82, 134, 149, 156–157, 218, 220, 226; *see also* Petit Trianon (restoration), sponsorships
Château de Versailles Spectacles 79n7, 149
Chinese Communist Revolution 20; *see also* Communism
Les Chouans 80n8, *171*
Christian Dior SE 130, 141, 212–215, *215*, 245
cliché: in Coppola's film 117, *219*; 'Let Them Eat Cake!' 1, **56**, 86, 179, 221, *224*; representations and image 213, 231, *231*, 233; reproduction and circulation 84, 94, 104, 108, 183, 226, 233–234, *234*, 256 (*see also* Madonna; Republican, clichés; slander); thematic analysis 163, 233
Collier, L'Affaire du 214
Communism 20, 24
La Conciergerie 60, **90**, 185, *186*, 210; *see also* Centre des monuments nationaux
Coppola, Sofia 6, 26, 52, 61, 80n9, 82, 84–86, 96, 99, 101, 103, 108, 110–121, 127n16, 129, 149, 156, 166, 176, *176*, 179–180, **182**, 185, 187–188, *209*, 213, 218–226, *219*, *224*, 228–235, 249n20, 256

counter-memory 6, 12, 26, 155, 171, *171*
'cultural capital' 10, 17, 76, 157–160; destination-based 159; personal 135; Royal *158*, 159, 172, *172*; *see also* Bourdieu, Pierre; heritage(s)

David, Jacques-Louis 146
Da Vinci Code, The: film 110, 220; visitor trail 220; *see also* Louvre
Debord, Guy 36
Diderot, Denis 18, 144, 146
discourse(s): 'authorised heritage'/ dominant 26–27, 253 (*see also* Smith, Laurajane); collective memory in French literary and intellectual 173; French Enlightenment 77, 144, 146 (*see also philosophes*); heritage 132–134; historical (incl. Republican and/or Royalist) 10, 14, 19–22, 26, 53–54, 85–86, **89**, 94, 100, 105–108, 116–118, 126n4, 155, 203; internet/social media/ unauthorised 105, 252; language 33; museum/interpretive 47, 185; official/political 15–16, 18, 20–21, 26–27, 45, 58, 95, 106, 155, 196, 198; popular 133; professional 133; rehabilitative 96, 106 (*see also* narrative); Soviet and Post-Soviet individual 198 (*see also* Wertsch, James); travel 34, 194; urban 162n19; visitor 6–7, 49, 58, 64–65, 67, 71–75, **71**, *75*, 92, 109, 115, 163–164, 174–189, 196–200, 200n3, 204; *see also* Marie Antoinette (conflicting) discourse(s)
Disney **43**, 206; Walt 257; *see also* Disneyland
Disneyland 36, **43**, 206; *see also* Eco, Umberto
Dracula 42, 187
Dumas *père*, Alexandre 8n1, 94–95, 126n5
Dunst, Kirsten *111*, *112*, *113*, 115, 116, 118, *176*, **182**, *209*, 213, *219*, 225, 231

Eco, Umberto 7, 36, **43**, 47, 161n4, 201–202, 225
École de Chaillot 60
Edo period 193, 195; *see also* Tokugawa period
Élisabeth, Madame 237, *238*

Index   321

English Garden 34, 139, 146, 207, *241*; *see also* Jardin Anglais
Enlightenment: Civilization and 192 (*see also Bunmei Kaika*; Meiji); French 3–4, 18, 20, 24, 34, 76–77, 144, 147–148, 166, 209; German 24; ideals 24, *75*, 77, 146–147, 201, 242; ideas 11, 18, 144, 147, 157; key figures 100, 144, 146, 161n8 (*see also philosophes*); and the last monarchic couple of the Ancien Régime 147; and Marie Antoinette 228; monarch 2, 166, 255; principles 18, 144, 146–147; values 15, 147
ethnography 5, 7, 39, 49, 55–57, 65, 72, 179, 189
etiquette 4, **87**, 110, 143, 146, 151, 188, 209, 237
Eugénie, Empress 77, 128–129, 135, 148, 150, *150*, 157

Fargeon, Jean-Louis **83**, 210
Fersen, Hans Axel, (Count von) 87, **89**, 97, 103, 108, 109, *109*, 112, 116, 119–121, *120*, *121*, *122*, 125, 164, 209, 232, 248n5
film 6, 8n6, 32, 38, **42**, **43**, 60, 74–75, 78, 84, 95, 100, 110, 112, 117–118, 133, 166, 176, 180, **182**, 185, 200n8, 220, 225, 230–232; filmography 110, 115; French 65, 101, *102*, 170, 199n2, 232; Hollywood 95, 97, *98*, 114, 117–118, 186, 220; *see also* biopic; Coppola, Sofia
flâneur 38–39; *see also* 'romantic gaze'
French Academy [Académie Française] 11; *see also* Nora, Pierre
French Monarchy 14, 80n8, **88**, **89**, 108, 151, 165; fall of the 86, **89**, *95*; negative image of the 4, **87**; symbol of the 1, 4, 103
French Revolution 2–3, 10–16, 18–27, 34, 53, 64–65, 73, 75, 77, 84, **88**, 90, *90*, 94–97, 99, 103–104, 107, 115–116, 119, 123–126, 135, 139, 143, 146, 161n5, 164–166, *169*, 171, *171*, 176, **181**, 188, 200n8, 208, 216, 251, 255

Gabriel, Ange-Jacques 141
Gadamer, Hans-Georg 24, 50–51, 57
Gellner, Ernest 8n4, 10, 13, 22–24, 76, 146
globalisation 40, 45–46, 194, 232; *see also* media; 'romantic gaze'
Gouges, Olympe de 96

Gouriévidis, Laurence 27, **42**, 173, 251
Gustav III, King of Sweden (alias 'Comte de Haga') 143, *144*; *see also* Petit Trianon (historic and heritage), eighteenth century protocol receptions

Halbwachs, Maurice 6–7, 11, 27, 49–50, 52–54, 78–79, 79n4, 84, 156, 163, 171–174, 198–199
Hall, Stuart 7, 33, 66, 117, 132, 157, 201–202, *224*, 226, 229, 233–234, *234*, 247
Heidegger, Martin 44, 50–52, 57, 194
heritage(s): authenticity 2, 5–6, 10, 30, 34–36, 41–48, **41**, **42**, **43**, *43*, 128, 131–139, 155, 187–195, 202–213, 220–221, 244, 248n15, 252–254 (*see also* hyper-reality); commodification 2, 5, 10, 27, 37, 41–46, **43**, 131–133, *133*, 190, 225, 251, 253 (*see also* Marie Antoinette commodification); cultural 1–3, 8n5, 10–12, 19–20, 25–28, 30, **41**, **42**, **43**, 45–46, 49, 54, 64, 75–77, *75*, 79n3, 103, 139–140, 155, 157, 219, 251, 255; as cultural capital 3, 10, 157–160, *158*, 171–172, *172*; dissonant 2–3, 6, 12, 21, 25–27, 86, 128, 155–157, 162n19, 224–225, 251, 253, 255–256 (*see also* 'alchemical dissonant heritage'; Ashworth, Gregory; counter-memory; Tunbridge, John); French 25, 60, 248n13; industry 5–6, 37, 41, 128, 157, 162n19, 253; intangible 8n5, 249n15; interpretation 1, 6, 26–27, **42**, 46, 49, 128, 131–139, *133*, 148–149, 155–157, 162n21, 163, 174–175, 187, 203, 220, 226, 235, 250–254; management 148, 159, 161n17, 220, 254 (*see also* Château de Versailles, management); manipulation of 10, 12, 19, 25–28, **41**, 45, 157, 233, 250; media and cultural *75*; national identity and cultural *75*; tangible 8n5, 30; tourism and cultural *75*; zero-sum trait of 27, 103–105, 123, 125–126, 157, 255
'heritigisation' 44; *see also* Hewison, Robert
hermeneutics 2, 5–7, 11, 49–59, 79n3, 82, 86, 107, 117, 125, 128, 138, 172, 201–203, *203*, 226, 255; *see also* Gadamer, Hans-Georg; Hall, Stuart; Heidegger, Martin; Mugerauer, Robert; Ricoeur, Paul

Hewison, Robert 30; heritage industry 37; 'heritigisation' 44–45
Hobsbawm, Eric 5, 10–13, 15–17, 23, 25, 28n2, 54, 76–77, 174
Hossein, Robert 92, 93, 164; see also Marie Antoinette, death-bicentenary show
Howard, Peter J. 5, 11, 27, 30, 41–47, **41, 42,** 43, 49, 73, 131–133, 137, 147, 157, 160, 163, 175, 187, 224, 233
Huntington Library: boutique 248n13; see also Marie Antoinette commodification
hyper-reality 36, **41, 43,** 46–47, 117, 201, 221, 225, 256; see also Eco, Umberto; 'society of the spectacle'

Ikeda, Riyoko 6, 52, 59–61, 79n7, 80n12, 82, 84, 97, 110, 114, 118–127, 127n18, 185, 187–188, 193, 196, 256
'imaginary social memories' 7, 163, 175, 199, 256; see also Caughey, John L.
imagination: imaginary enemy (see Hobsbawm, Eric; Nazi Germany; 'production of space'); 'imaginary social worlds' (see Caughey, John L.; 'imaginary social memories'); 'imagined communities' (see Anderson, Benedict); tourist 233 (see also 'romantic gaze')
Institut d'histoire de la Révolution française 64
International Council on Monuments and Sites 8n7

Japanese: fascination with Marie Antoinette 185, 187; fascination with the eighteenth-century and court ritual 118, 139, 185, 187, 192 (see also Tokugawa period); manga 104, 121, 123 (see also Rose of Versailles); mangaka (see Ikeda, Riyoko); otaku 185 (see also visitors, Japanese)
Jardin Anglais 8n2, 87, 143–144, 177, 238; see also champêtre; Petit Trianon (estate)
Joseph II, Emperor of the Austro-Hungarian Empire 143; see also Petit Trianon (historic and heritage), eighteenth century protocol receptions

Kant, Immanuel 18, 23, 37
king(s): access to the 26; 'the bad and the good' 165 (see also Michelet, Jules); the beheading of Charles I 13; 'for a day' 36 (see also peasant(s), 'for a day'; tourists); the mistress/*favorite* 87, 141, 143; 'of Romance' 94 (see also Dumas *père*, Alexandre); see also Louis XVII, the Child King; Sun King

Ladurée 66, 117, 149, 180, 221–224, 222, 223, 224, 248n14, 249n16, 256; see also Coppola, Sofia; *Marie Antoinette* (2006)
Lady Gaga 229, 230, 230
Lady Oscar 74, 118–119, 123, 169, 189, 193, 196; see also Rose of Versailles
Lamballe, Princesse de 161n9
Landsberg, Alison 200n4
Lefebvre, Henri 5, 17, 29, 31–33, 35, 47–48, 54, 76, 171, 201, 206, 254
Léonard [Autié] 96, 229
lieux de mémoire 10, 25, 54; see also Nora, Pierre
Llobera, Josep R. 8n4, 14, 22–24
Louis XIV 1, 143, 213
Louis XV 87, 141, 143
Louis XVI 20, 86–90, 87, 88, 89, 90, 95, 119, 141, 164, 200n9, 200n11, 237, 241; commemoration 64, 80n8, 171, 171; historical rehabilitation 21, 90, 103, 105–106, 126n12
Louis XVII, the Child King (Dauphin Louis-Charles, previously Duc de Normandie) / *Chou d'Amour* 88, 90, 154, 200n11
Louis XVIII / Comte de Provence 80n8
Louvre: Carrousel du 60; collection of 145; museum 1, 134, 139, 154, 161n13, 220, 248n8, 270

macarons 66, 180, 221–225, 222, 223, 224, 228, 228, 248n13, 248n14, 256; see also cliché, 'Let Them Eat Cake!'; Ladurée
Madame Royale (Princesse Marie-Thérèse-Charlotte of France) / *Mousseline* 88, 154
Madonna 183, 183, 184, 229
Marie Antoinette: animosity 151, 174, 196, 197, 250, 258 (see also Austrophobia / French phobia of Austrians; Revolutionary, pamphlets;

slander); Catholic faith 52, 106–108, 255; death-bicentenary show 92–94, *93*; (extreme) fascination 72, 77, 90, 94, 97, 117, 150, 160n4, 176–179, 183, 196, 198, 200n8, 250 (*see also* Japanese, fascination with Marie Antoinette); identity negotiation and appropriation (*see* 'alchemical dissonant heritage'; Marie Antoinette commodification); and martyrdom 4, 106, 178, 196; on screen (*see* film)

Marie Antoinette (film, 2006) 6, 80n9, 82, 110–118, *111*, *112*, *113*, *116*, *176*, *209*, 218–219, *219*; *see also* Coppola, Sofia; Marie Antoinette, on screen

Marie Antoinette (and Ancien Régime): challenging the Court etiquette 4, 143, 146, 151; emancipation/history of the role of the queens of France 4, 97, 143, 151, 153–155, 157, 242; *see also* Enlightenment, monarch

Marie Antoinette (conflicting) discourse(s): Catholic defamatory historical 90 (*see also* slander; Soulavie, L'Abbé); Catholic rehabilitative historical/historical fiction 106–108 (*see also* Louis XVI, historical rehabilitation); historical-fiction 105; internet 105; Librairie des Princes 104; nostalgic *186* (*see also* La Conciergerie)

Marie Antoinette (and French Revolution): paper (queen) 14, 22, 100–103 (*see also* Revolutionary, pamphlets); reciprocally impinging cultural heritage 3, 19, 27, 103, 255 (*see also* heritage(s), zero-sum trait of); trial and death-sentence 90, 92, *93*, 216, *216*

Marie Antoinette (and French Third Republic): Republican portrayal of, antithesis with French Revolution 103–104; *see also* heritage(s), zero-sum trait of; Republican, (history/political) agenda

Marie Antoinette (and modernity/postmodernity): celebrity 229 (*see also* Fargeon, Jean-Louis; Léonard [Autié]); legend(s) 90, 138, 203–206, 208, *208*, 209, 210, 228, 242 (*see also* Marie Antoinette image (at contemporary Petit Trianon); Marie Antoinette image (nineteenth-century Republican history); Marie Antoinette image (postmodernity))

Marie Antoinette commodification 1–8, 7n1, 8n9, 10, 14, 25, 28–29, 33–34, 48–50, 53, 58, 66, 73, 76, 78–79, 110, 133, 149, 155–156, 201, 203, 218–226, *225*, 234–235, 247, 248n15, 250, 256; *see also* 'alchemical dissonant heritage'

Marie Antoinette exhibitions 59, 138–139, 161n6, 248n5

Marie Antoinette image (at contemporary Petit Trianon): archetypal mother 216–217; Cinderella 208–209, *209*, 217, 230 (*see also* shoe 'à la Saint-Huberty'); ghost 204–207, 217, 230; 'queen of frivolous fashion' 213–214, 217 (*see also* museums, fashion); 'queen of refinement' 115, 119, 210–213, 217 (*see also* 'alchemical dissonant heritage'; Marie Antoinette commodification

Marie Antoinette image (eighteenth-century official representations): adulated queen *91*

Marie Antoinette image (eighteenth-century public opinion, and to this day): hated queen 92, *181*; *see also* Republican, clichés; Revolutionary

Marie Antoinette image (nineteenth-century Republican history, and to this day): 'shepherdess' *167*, *168*, 242–243; *see also* Republican, clichés

Marie Antoinette image (painting history) 8n1, *136*, *140*, 151–154, *152*, *153*, *154*, 161n7, 161n12, 161n13, 237

Marie Antoinette image (postmodernity): in bubble-gum/candy/millennial pink 61, 66, *111*, *112*, 115, *176*, 180, 212, *215*, *219*, 221, *222*, *223*, *225*–229, *228*, *231*, 232, 234, 248n11, 248n13, 248n14, 248n15, 249n16, 249n17, 256; *see also* hyper-reality; Marie Antoinette commodification

Marie Antoinette image (Royalist and art-history generated): brave *169*; charitable *168*; 'Enlightened monarch, emancipated, beautiful, charitable, powerful and a fervent supporter of Music/Musicians and Arts/Artists' *166*; *see also* film; Marie Antoinette; Marie Antoinette image (painting history); Morgan, Michèle; Royalist(s), 'memories'

Marie Louise, Empress 141, 244–245
Maria Theresa, Empress 87, 88, 161n12, 232, 237
media *see* heritage(s); Revolutionary, clichés; Revolutionary, media; Revolutionary, pamphlets
Meiji: culture 121; period 192
memory: 'collective memory' (*see* Halbwachs, Maurice); and commemoration (*see* counter-memory; Nora, Pierre); 'cultural memory' 173, 198–199 (*see also* Assmann, Jan); and group identity (*see* Republican, 'memories'; Royalist(s), 'memories'); and history dialectic (*see* 'imaginary social memories'; 'places of memory'; Ricoeur, Paul); 'prosthetic' (*see* Landsberg, Alison); transmission through generations (*see* Halbwachs, Maurice; Nora, Pierre)
Michelet, Jules 94, 165
Mique, Richard 32, 139, *141*, 143, *239*, *241*
Montmédy flight 89, *165*
Montres Breguet 131, 138
Morgan, Michèle *170*
Mugerauer, Robert 6, 45, 49–52, 79n3, 128
museums: fashion 213; French national 149; and 'heritigisation' 45 (*see also* Hewison, Robert); historic house **41**, 128–129, 135, 156, 160n1 (*see also* Petit Trianon (estate); Young, Linda); and identity 160 (*see also* Petit Trianon (historic and heritage)); and in/authenticity 36, **41**, **42**, 48n2 (*see also* New Museology); and interpretation of dissonant heritage 6, 128, 155, 251 (*see also* Gouriévidis, Laurence); and new media **41**, 47; as 'places of memory' 30; in postmodernity 37; and tourism 35, 218; 'Tradition' and nineteenth-century 134, 160; 'Translation' and contemporary **41**, 160 (*see also* Bhabha, Homi)

Napoléon I (Bonaparte) 20, 96, 141, 146, 244
Napoléon III 157
narrative: architectural (*see* Petit Trianon (art and architecture)); cinematic (*see* film; Japanese, manga); heritage (*see* museums; Petit Trianon (historic and heritage)); historical (*see* Marie Antoinette; Petit Trianon (historic and heritage)); 'meaning' 83; rehabilitative history 5, 10, 22–28, 58, 60, 96
nationalism 12, 22, 28, 31, 54, 77; modernist theory of (*see* Anderson, Benedict; Gellner, Ernest); nineteenth-century 5, 8n4, 13–16, 19, 22, 45; primordialist theory of (*see* Llobera, Josep R.); theories 10
Nazi Germany 28n2; Fascism 20, 24; Nazism 24, 97
neoclassicism 39, 140, 144, 146–147, 185, 196, 237; *see also* Gabriel, Ange-Jacques
New Museology **41**, **42**, 134–135, 251, 254; *see also* Vergo, Peter
de Nohlac, Pierre 4, 129, 138, 144, 150–151, 154–155, 161n10, **178**, 241–242
Nora, Pierre 5–7, 10–13, 20, 23, 25–31, 28n1, 37, 41, 44–45, 47, 49–51, 53–54, 76–77, 84, 86, 131, 163, 165–166, 173–174, 198, 201, 206, 236, 248n10, 257

Palais de Compiègne 248n13 (*see also* Marie Antoinette commodification); Russian Tsar alias 'Comte du Nord' 143 (*see also* Petit Trianon (historic and heritage), eighteenth century protocol receptions)
patrimonialisation 44–45, 54, 131; *see also* 'heritigisation'; Nora, Pierre
patterns: consumption 46; expressions and illustration in manga 121; French politicised milieu 85; Japanese visitor 59; language expression 190; old, defining the role of the queen of France 153; (visitor) perception 72, 197, 233; profession-specific 103; social 119; and thematic analysis 55 (*see also* ethnography)
peasant(s): 'for a day' 36 (*see also* tourists); 242; *see also* Petit Trianon, Marie Antoinette theatre acting
Petit Trianon (art and architecture): eighteenth-century art landscape 32; neoclassical style/proportions and value 39, 140, 144, 196, 237; *see also* English Garden; neoclassicism

Petit Trianon (estate): Le Belvédère *121*, *240*; Le Boudoir *142*; Cabinet des Glaces Mouvantes *112*, *113*; Cour d'Honneur 2, 80n13; l'étage noble 63, 238, 239; *fabriques* 8n2, *121*, 139, 144, 177, 238; La Ferme 8n2, *121*, *170*, 242, *242*; Le Hameau de la Reine 8n2, 63, *121*, 127n14, 140–142, *140*, *142*, *158*, 169, 241, *241*, 244; Jardin Anglais 87, *121*, 143–144, 177, 238; Jardin Français *141*, *237*; La Maison de la Reine 130, 141–142, *142*, 212, 244–245, *245*; Le Moulin *121*, *158*, *241*; Le Pavillon Français *154*; Le Petit Théâtre de la Reine 8n2, 79n7, 177, 236, 241–243, *243*; réchauffoir and domestiques quarters 135; La Salle de Billiard 161n13; La Salle des Gardes 129; Le Temple de L'Amour *121*, 139, *144*, 153, *168*, 205, *205*, *207*, 212, *239*; Tour of Marlborough 245

Petit Trianon (historic and heritage): dissonant heritage 6, 128, 155–157, 253 (*see also* heritage(s), dissonant); educative role for the royal offspring 144–145, *145*, 240–241; eighteenth century protocol receptions 143–144, *144*, 240–241; eighteenth-century estate 2, *2*, 8n2, 51, 78, 87, 119, 139–148, 204, 235–236; Eugénie, Empress and Nolhac, Pierre de; as historical/heritage site 32, 35, 37, 60, 118, 135, 159, 203; as (historic house) museum 34, 52, 128, 134–135, 148–150, 159–160, 244 (*see also* museums, historic house); as home to Marie Antoinette (and her royal family) 31–32, 49–51, 67, 74, 129, 135–137, 139, 147, 161n13, 163, 236, 257; and identity (*see* Eugénie, Empress; Marie Antoinette; de Nohlac, Pierre; visitors); image 4, 8n9, 14, 49, 77, 84–85, 110, *121*, 164, 166, 177, 180, 185, *197*, 199, 221, 248n11, 256 (*see also* Marie Antoinette image (postmodernity); visitor perceptions); and Marie Antoinette stewardship 64, 238, 240; Marie Antoinette theatre acting 242; as 'place of memory' 5, 10, 29, 31, 44, 198–199, 236, 257;

Queen Victoria and Prince Albert visit 157, 159; as royal cultural capital 157–160, *158*, 172, *172*; as royal residence 32, 35, 47, 143; and tourist anticipation 38, 225 (*see also* 'romantic gaze'); and tourist consumption 63, 128, 155–160, 196 (*see also* visitors)

Petit Trianon (restoration) 5, 30, 34, 44, 46, 74, 82, 110, 128–132, *132*, 138–140, 216, 220; expert team 30, 46, 59, 128, 133–135, 139–140, 148–155, 236, 253, 255; heritage interpretation 1–2, 4–6, 27, 30, 46, 61, 74, 128, 135–137, *136*, 139, 148–151, *150*, 153–160, *153*, *154*, 174–175, 187, 207, 218, 226, 235, 251, 253 (*see also* Petit Trianon (historic and heritage), dissonant heritage); promotion and renaming 6, 48n1, 129, 137–138, *137*, 159 (*see also* Château de Versailles, management; Marie Antoinette exhibitions); sponsorships (incl. 2018 restoration) (*see* Christian Dior SE; Montres Breguet)

philosophes 144, 146; *see also* Diderot, Denis

picturesque 40, 77, 147–148, 185, 196, 235, *242*, 254; *see also* English Garden

'places of memory' 5–7, 11–12, 26–27, 29–31, 41, 44, 47, 49–51, 53–54, 76, 163, 173–174, 198–199, 201, 206, 257; *see also* Nora, Pierre

Polignac, Duchesse de 126n8, 232

Pompadour, Madame de 141, 242

Popular Memory Group 27

post-structuralism 7

Priestland, David 24, 146

'production of space' 31–33; *see also* Lefebvre, Henri

Queen(s) of France: access to the 26; 'the bad and the good' 165 (*see also* Michelet, Jules); 'for a day' 36 (*see also* king(s), 'for a day'; peasant(s), 'for a day'; tourism); history of the 97; role of the 4, 143, 151; Salic Law 143 (*see also* Marie Antoinette (and Ancien Régime), emancipation/history of the role of the queens of France

Republican: agency 94; (history/political) agenda 3, 25–26, 58, 94–96, 110, 116, 151, 164–166, 180, 196 (see also discourse(s), historical; Dumas père, Alexandre); alchemy 12; clichés 58, 74–75, 78, 86, 97, 99, 104–108, 110, 116–117, 120, *121*, 126n4, 138, 151, 166, *167*, *168*, 180, 217, 221, *224*, 227–228, 237; dominant discourse 253 (see also discourse(s), 'authorised heritage'/dominant); historians/history 96, 118–119, 138, 165, 234 (see also Michelet, Jules); ideology 155; legitimacy 19; 'memories' 164–172, 196, *197*; memory 12; milieu 155; official discourse 196 (see also discourse(s), official/political); principles/content and connotations in education 13, 15–18, 25, 84, 166, *167* (see also Anderson, Benedict; Hobsbawm, Eric; Nora, Pierre); research sources 254; school curriculum and Coppola's film unsuitability 115–116, *116*; sympathies 86, 90, 94 (see also Dumas père, Alexandre)

Réunion des musées nationaux 126n1, 148–149, 180

Revolutionary: agents 4; alchemy 12; calendar 25; clichés 78; Committee 89, 90; contra- 117; figures 56, 96 (see also Gouges, Olympe de; Robespierre, Maximilien); history 103; legacy 20; media 248n10; pamphlets 6, 8n6, 13–15, 22, 28n2, 58, 77–78, 82, 83, 87, 88, 100–101, 117, 123, 199; past 25, 211; political agenda 58, 146; principles/content and education (see Republican, principles/content and connotations in education); propaganda 4, 13–16, 21–22, 77, 85, 94, 100, 110, 144, 146, 151, 164–166, 196

Ricoeur, Paul 1, 6, 11, 24, 27, 49–54, 79n1, 172–173, 194

Robert, Hubert 32, 139, 143

Robespierre, Maximilien 16, 21

'romantic gaze' 29–30, 33–35, 40–44, 46, 76, 201, 206, 253; see also Urry, John

Rose of Versailles 6, 59–60, 74, 79n6, 82, 84, 110, 114, 118–127, *120*, *121*, *122*, *124*, *125*, 127n17, 127n19, 127n21, 169, 185, 192, *193*

Rousseau, Jean-Jacques 14, 144, 146

Royalist(s) 90, 155, 226; biographies of Marie Antoinette 95, 106; circles 66; ceremonials 80n8, 200n11 (see also Louis XVI; Louis XVII, the Child King (Dauphin Louis-Charles, previously Duc de Normandie) / *Chou d'Amour*); groups 65, 80n8 (see also *Les Chouans*); historiography 83, 217; 'memories' 164–172, *197*, 198; representations of Marie Antoinette *168*, *169*, *216*; research sources 254; supporters/loyalties 89, *109* (see also Fersen, Hans Axel, (Count von)); sympathies 86, 90, 157, 185; writers 90

Russian Communist Revolution 20; see also Priestland, David

Schönbrunn Palace 87, 185

Shearer, Norma 97, 98, 185–186

shoe 'à la Saint-Huberty' 248n5

simulacra see Baudrillard, Jean

slander: French court 58, 102–103; see also revolutionary, pamphlets

Smith, Laurajane 26, 45–46, 157, 160, 162n20, 175

'society of the spectacle' 36; see also Debord, Guy

Soulavie, L'Abbé 90

Sun King 1, 143, 165; see also Louis XIV

tabi no bunka 192–194

Tivoli 146

Todorov, Tzvetan 2, 4, 27, 209

Tokugawa period 192–193

tourism: cultural 8n7, 35; heritage 46, 250 (see also heritage(s), tourism and cultural); Japanese 192 (see also *tabi no bunka*); mass 34, 40, 44, 162n20 (see also 'romantic gaze')

tourists 29, 32–40, *63*, 65, 74, 80n13, 159, 174, 183, 204, 206, 221, 233, 253; see also visitors

Tourzel, Duchesse de 210

tradition: the invention of (see Hobsbawm, Eric; Nora, Pierre); manufacturing (see AlSayyad, Nezar; museums)

Tuileries 88, 89, *122*

Tunbridge, John 3, 12, 26–27, 36, 45, *133*, 155, 157, 221, 224

United Nations Educational, Scientific and Cultural Organisation 1, 8n5, 156, 161n17, 220
Urry, John 5, 29, 33–44, **41**, **42**, **43**, 47, 52, 76, 133, 159, 183, 196, 201, 206, 212, 225, 236, 247, 253

Varennes: flight to **89**, *109*, 164, *165*, *169*, 253; *see also* Montmédy flight
Vergo, Peter **42**, 134–135
Vigée Le Brun, Madame [Marie Louise Élisabeth] 95–96, *136*, *140*, 150
visitor groups: American majority **71**, *75*, 78, 84, 86, 109–110, 138, 179–180, 183, 189–190, 196, 198–199, 200n8, 218, 221, 225–226, 248n11, 249n22, 256–257; American minority **71**, 115, 179–180, 189, 199, 248n4, 248n11, 257; French majority **71**, *75*, 78, 84, 86, 109, 138, 164–166, *165*, 169, 196, 199n1, 221, 234, 248n4, 248n10, 248n11, 249n22, 256–257; French minority **71**, 78, 115, 119, 126n1, 164, 166, 169–174, 180, 189, 198–199, 199n2, 257; Italian **71**; Japanese majority 48n1, **71**, *75*, 78, 84, 110, 114, 118, 120, 138, 185, 189, 192, 218, 221, 248n12, 249n22, 256–257; Japanese minority **71**, 185, 188, 199, 257; majority and minority 234–235, *235*; Middle East **71**, 176, *176*; Spanish **71**, 73, 175–176
visitor perceptions 67, 73; American 7, 78, 175, 179–180, *181*, 183, 195–199; French 7, 50, 55, 183, 195–199, 256; Japanese 6–7, 59–60, 74–75, 78, 118–120, 123, 175–176, 183, 187–189, 191–197, 199, 253; Republican 255
visitors 67, **68**, **69**, 73–74, 79, 156, 176–179, **178**; American 6, 65, 67–71, **68**, **69**, 70, 72–76, 82, 84, 105, 179, 199, 200n8; French 7, 67–71, **68**, **69**, 70, 73, 75, 78–79, 95, 118, 126n1, 164, 174, 199, 200n3; Italian **68**, **69**, 95, 119, 175–176; Japanese 6, 59, 65, 67–75, **68**, **69**, 70, 80n10, 80n12, 82, 118, 183–189, 192–193, 221; Spanish **68**, **69**, 175

Wertsch, James 198

Young, Linda **41**, 128, 156–157, 160n1